The Sociology of Health and Medicine

WITHDRAWN FROM
THE LIBRARY

UNIVERSITY OF
WINCHESTER

D1333682

KA 0388560 7

The Sociology of Health and Medicine

A Critical Introduction

Second Edition

Ellen Annandale

polity

UNIVERSITY OF WINCHESTER
LIBRARY

Copyright © Ellen Annandale 2014

The right of Ellen Annandale to be identified as Author of this Work has been asserted in accordance with the UK Copyright, Designs and Patents Act 1988.

First edition published in 1998 by Polity Press
This second edition first published in 2014 by Polity Press

Polity Press
65 Bridge Street
Cambridge CB2 1UR, UK

Polity Press
350 Main Street
Malden, MA 02148, USA

All rights reserved. Except for the quotation of short passages for the purpose of criticism and review, no part of this publication may be reproduced, stored in a retrieval system, or transmitted, in any form or by any means, electronic, mechanical, photocopying, recording or otherwise, without the prior permission of the publisher.

ISBN-13: 978-0-7456-3461-6
ISBN-13: 978-0-7456-3462-3 (pb)

A catalogue record for this book is available from the British Library..

Typeset in 10 on 11.5pt Palatino by
Servis Filmsetting Ltd, Stockport, Cheshire
Printed and bound in Great Britain by T.J. International Ltd, Padstow, Cornwall

The publisher has used its best endeavours to ensure that the URLs for external websites referred to in this book are correct and active at the time of going to press. However, the publisher has no responsibility for the websites and can make no guarantee that a site will remain live or that the content is or will remain appropriate.

Every effort has been made to trace all copyright holders, but if any have been inadvertently overlooked the publisher will be pleased to include any necessary credits in any subsequent reprint or edition.

For further information on Polity, visit our website: www.politybooks.com

UNIVERSITY OF WINCHESTER

306. 461
ANN

03885607

Contents

Figures and tables

Figures

Tables

Preface to the second edition

Fifteen years have passed since the first edition of *The Sociology of Health and Medicine* was published. It has taken a long time to prepare the second edition, and very little of the content of the original edition remains. The book has not been updated, but almost totally rewritten. This reflects the fast-paced change in the parent discipline of sociology over the intervening years, but also the continued growth of research on health, illness and healthcare. The same basic structure remains, but a glance at the content or the References list will give a sense of the extent of the new material. As with the first edition, the intention is to draw attention to the ways issues of health and healthcare are fundamental to our wider understanding of society, past and present. In the second edition, this has been extended globally. While the book cannot in any sense claim to cover health, illness and healthcare in all parts of the world, it does aim as much as is possible in the limited space available to situate the issues raised in a global context, even where the predominant focus is on research generated in the UK and the US. Like the original edition, the book has been written for advanced undergraduates and postgraduate students with an existing knowledge of sociology or the wider social sciences.

Acknowledgements

It has taken me far too many years to prepare this second edition. I owe special thanks to my editor at Polity, Jonathan Skerrett, for his endless patience and for sticking with me. I am also grateful to Polity's readers for helpful suggestions on early drafts of chapters and for feedback from the reviewers of the final manuscript. Special thanks also go to David Field for comments and editorial checking.

1

Enduring theoretical legacies

Theory is important because it connects the subfield of the sociology of health and illness to the larger sociological landscape. Historically, this connection has been quite weak, chiefly because matters of health and illness were of limited interest within the wider discipline. This changed quite markedly in the mid-to-late 1990s when cracks started to appear in the terrain of wider social theory as it began to shift under the weight of new and then poorly understood matters such as embodiment, risk and the global biopolitics of health, all matters of longstanding interest within the subfield. The relationship between theory and research is reciprocal: extant theories gradually fall out of fit with societies as they change and new approaches are called for. For example, theories with a time-honoured reliance on a distinction between the social and the biological and upon fixed categories of gender, class and ethnicity now struggle to assist in the analysis of new diseases, new medical practices, and the meaning of health in today's complex global economy. Consequently, the sociology of health and illness has also changed its foci over the years. In the process it has secured an ever-firmer theoretical footing within the wider discipline.

This chapter covers the origins and early development of the discipline but it is intended to have much more than historical value. While different theoretical perspectives have arisen and held sway during different decades and therefore are to an extent 'of their time', this does not mean they are no longer relevant. Indeed, the applicability of the political economy and symbolic interactionist perspectives which we will consider here will be clear when we revisit them in the chapters which follow. Even Parsonsian structural functionalism, which many might dub the most antiquated of theories, has been reappraised and found more valuable than once assumed.

Medicine and sociology: critical connections

There is now a substantial body of reflective writing on the origins and development of medical sociology. Much of this is told from the vantage of the West, particularly the US and the UK, where the disciplinary roots are found in the two decades following World War II. The effect of this is that other countries tend to be positioned as 'coming late' to the field and as unintentionally authorizing *Western* history as *the* history. That said, accounts of how medical sociology took shape around the world often refer to three things: (i) to a shared desire to understand the social patterning of health in unequal societies and the implications for society of health-profiles shifting from acute to chronic illnesses; (ii) to a need to grapple with the dominant medico-centric approach to health and healthcare in the society concerned; and (iii) with some exceptions – such as Russia where early research was guided by Marxist–Leninist theory (Dmitrieva 2001) – to being stimulated by, but nonetheless remaining somewhat critical of, the structural functionalist concern with illness as social deviance (see e.g. Bloom 2002; Figlio 1987; Johnson 1975; Nuñes 2001).

These origins were distinctly double-edged. On the one hand, 'medicine nurtured, funded, and sponsored medical sociology early in its development' and structural functionalism made it academically respectable (Cockerham and Scambler 2010: 4). Yet, as commentators have been quick to point out, on the other hand, this led sociology into the arms of medicine, stunting its academic growth in the process. Back in 1957, in his analysis of US medical sociology, Robert Straus drew a heuristic distinction between the 'sociology *of* medicine' and 'sociology *in* medicine'. As he put it, in the former 'the sociologist stands apart and studies medicine as an institution or behaviour system', while in the latter, he – and the majority were indeed men, though Straus may not have intended to signal this – 'is collaborating with the medical specialist in trying to help him in the performance of his educational or therapeutic functions' (Straus 1957: 203). Straus depicted medical sociologists as chameleon-like as they traversed this divide in their research. He particularly cautioned against pressures from health practitioners for sociologists to recast their research findings in terms understandable to them, remarking that it is a small step from adopting medical language to eventually *acting like* and even coming to *think like* a physician (Straus 1957).

This warning was not necessarily heeded in the 1960s and 1970s. Writing twenty years on from Straus, Murcott looked back critically upon a period of 'medico-centrism' in which sociologists adopted the value-judgements of medicine, such as the belief that failure to recover from illness is a result of non-compliance with physicians' instructions. She explains that topics chosen for investigation were often defined against an implicit medical template – 'fringe medicine, lay definitions of illness, marginal professions, self medicine', and so on (Murcott 1977: 157). Yet, as Straus also remarked, if the sociologist 'sticks resolutely to pure sociology', typically this will be 'misunderstood, ignored or rejected' (1957: 104). Some years later, Horobin depicted this tenuous experience as inhabiting 'the interstices between the citadel of medicine and the suburb of sociology' (1985: 95). Many writers of the 1970s and beyond have felt that medical sociology should divorce itself from – or at least be sceptical of – medicine and develop an alternative social approach (see, e.g., Gold 1977). An agenda was therefore set: to turn away from the problematic 'biomedical perspective' to a 'social model' of health and healthcare. To consider how this occurred, we first need to look a little more closely at sociology's wider debate with biomedicine, both then and now.

The debate with biomedicine

In his (largely US-focused) history of the discipline, Bloom remarks that medical sociology has persistently 'developed in a trajectory that follows its parent discipline but with reference always to the changing institutional dynamics of medicine' (2002: 273). In other words, as the fabric of biomedicine changes, so too do the kind of critical analyses that sociologists weave, but the broad running threads remain consistent. Social scientists have argued that the conventional depiction of medical science as a progressive march forward in the conquest of illness fails to appreciate that medical knowledge is never disinterested. Rather, as we will see in the course of this chapter, it reflects and reproduces the dominant ideas of the society of its time.

Jewson (1976) charts this early process through the emergence of three distinctive medical cosmologies, or frameworks, within which practitioners make sense of the signs and symptoms of illness and formulate treatment plans, over the formative period between 1770 and 1870. He reveals that medical cosmologies are modes of social interaction embedded in the social relations of the production of medical knowledge. In the early period, which he characterizes as 'bedside medicine', medical practitioners worked within a person-oriented cosmology where judgements were made in terms of the personal attributes of the individual sick person. In order to survive in what was a competitive environment, at a time when medical practice was controlled by a coterie of rich fee-paying patients who had access to a wealth of practitioners of various kinds (Pelling and Webster 1979), the physician 'sought to discover the particularistic requirements of his patient in order to satisfy them to the exclusion of his ubiquitous rivals' (Jewson 1976: 233). The personal rapport that was necessary in order to secure business depended on the physician recognizing the patient as an integrated psychosomatic entity in which physical and emotional disturbance were indivisible.

This person-oriented cosmology was eclipsed with development of 'hospital medicine' in the early nineteenth century. With the development of hospitals, medical elites were no longer reliant on patronage; instead, they had a ready mass of indigent patients at their disposal. The control of medical knowledge passed from the patient, who was now expected to 'endure and wait', to the clinician. A new disease cosmology emerged within which any 'interest in the unique qualities of the whole person evaporated to be replaced by studies of specific organic lesions and malfunctions' (Jewson 1976: 235). This was consolidated in the mid nineteenth century with the development of 'laboratory medicine'. During this period, the patient as a sentient being moved out of the frame altogether to become a material thing to be analysed, and disease became 'a physio-chemical process to be explained according to the blind inexorable laws of natural science' (Jewson 1976: 238).

The modern form of biomedicine that eventually emerged has been typified in a variety of ways, but three characteristics are usually central. First, it is *reductivist*, assuming that disease is a problem of the individual body, rather than a result of the interaction of the individual and the social world. For example, recalling a grand-rounds presentation in a US teaching hospital, Scheper-Hughes and Lock recount the case of a woman suffering from chronic headaches:

> In halting sentences the patient explained before the class of two hundred that her husband was an alcoholic who occasionally beat her, that she had been virtually housebound for the past five years looking after her senile and incontinent mother-in-law, and that she worried constantly about her teenage son who is flunking out of high school. Although the woman's story elicited considerable sympathy from the students, many grew restless with the line of clinical questioning, and one finally interrupted the professor to demand: 'But what is the *real* cause of the headaches?'
>
> (Scheper-Hughes and Lock 1987: 8)

The second, associated, characteristic of the biomedical model is the *doctrine of specific aetiology*. According to René Dubos (1960), with the shift from disease as lack of harmony between the sick person and the environment towards the pathophysiology of treatment of individual illnesses, medical training was directed towards the recognition of specific causes. But this provides a complete account of disease causation in very few cases. Moreover, a simple cause–effect model inadequately represents the diagnostic process. Clinical signs, such as elevated blood pressure, do not simply present themselves to the medical practitioner, they are filtered through the interpretations of symptoms and experiences by both the physician and the patient (and in many cases those close to the patient) (Mishler 1989). As Mol relates in her study of atherosclerosis of the leg (vascular disease), 'a doctor cannot diagnose intermittent claudication alone' – rather, 'when doctor and patient act together in the consultation room they jointly give shape to the reality of the patient's hurting legs' (2007: 24, 27).

The final characteristic of biomedicine is the claim to *scientific neutrality* – in other words, that medicine can be rational, objective and value-free, treating each individual according to their, need irrespective of imputed moral worth. While this may be the intention, numerous studies have revealed that decision-making is often framed normatively. For example, Nurok and Henckes (2009) researched the influence of social values on pre-hospital resuscitation in Paris and New York. The following is an extract from their field-notes:

> Waiting with a New York paramedic team, we receive a call for a patient living in a housing project known by the team to have many patients with HIV/AIDs. The team complains about being given another lousy case and starts driving to the call without much conviction. On arrival we find a patient almost unconscious with a very low respiratory rate. Upon seeing this, the paramedics pick up their pace and according to protocol, rapidly provide supplemental oxygen, place an IV catheter, and administer Naloxone [a drug that reverses the effects of narcotic overdose]. The patient regains consciousness and starts breathing normally. The team recognises that the patient has probably overdosed on drugs and she is placed in the ambulance and transferred to the hospital without any display of empathy.
>
> (Nurok and Henckes 2009: 506)

The authors argue that this illustrates the competing values of a case. First, the paramedics make a judgement that the patient has low social value and show little interest in the case. But when they arrive they find that she is in a severe state and establish that they can do something to treat her. Yet when she has been treated, they refocus on her as a drug overdose, which devalues her and they fail to show any obvious compassion.

The 'biomedical model' is a theoretical construct initially formed by social scientists, to critique the medical practices of the 1960s and 1970s. Judged by how often it is still used today, it has proven to be highly valuable as an analytic tool. Of course, medical science and medical practice have changed enormously since then. Clarke and colleagues argue that medicine is being 'transformed from the inside out through old and new social arrangements that implement biomedical, computer, and information sciences and technologies to intervene in health, illness, healing, the organisation of medical care, and how we think about and live "life itself"' (Clarke et al. 2010a: 2). This is part of the 'epistemic shift from the clinical gaze initiated in the eighteenth century ... to the emergent molecular gaze of today' (Clarke et al. 2010a: 4). This is not to say that the original defining features of the 'biomedical model' are obsolete, more that the object to which they are applied has changed, as we will see as this chapter unfolds.

Using the example of AIDS, Waldby (1996: 32) argues that 'biomedical knowledge is always a discourse about social order, worked out in bodily terms'. Her interest is in how medicine deploys sexual identity as an 'explanation' for HIV transmission by drawing upon conceptions of the female and the feminized body (e.g. that of the gay man) as pathological points of contrast to the normative heterosexual male body. Specifically, within medical texts, the heterosexual male body is presented as self-enclosed and impermeable, as being able to maintain the necessary rigid boundary between the inside of the body and the outside world to avoid the transmission of the HIV virus. In contrast, the female body and that of gay men is seen as permeable (for example, in pregnancy and birth for women, in anal sex for gay men) and therefore as unstable and vulnerable to, as well as responsible for, viral transmission. The male body, which 'penetrates but which is never penetrated, is protected from this association', as heterosexual men secure an image as stable, self-enclosed and untroubled, while women and gay men are seen as 'fluid' and unstable (Waldby 1996: 77). This has particular significance for the discipline of epidemiology (the study of patterns of disease) and for preventative public health measures which involve the identification of risk groups, largely in order to protect the 'general population'. Waldby argues that, in this context, the 'general population' is virtually synonymous with heterosexual males. A threat to heterosexual men, then, is perceived as a threat to all and efforts are directed at the identification of risks associated with deviant others such as (some) women and gay men.

Waldby's (1996) criticism of biomedicine through the example of AIDS illustrates how medicine reflects and reproduces the dominant ideas of the society of its time. Intrinsic to this evaluation is the proposition that medicine cannot simply be understood on its *own* terms as an objective science. To do so would taint sociological research with a medico-centric bias, in the manner already outlined some years ago by Straus (1957). It was partly in response to these concerns that early medical sociologists consciously turned their attention away from *biological* towards *social* processes. This was consolidated in Eliot Freidson's ground-breaking book, *Profession of Medicine*. Freidson declared that medicine and sociology had different remits: medical sociologists, he wrote, should not be interested in the doctor's job, which is 'to test and refine medical concepts of illness and its treatment'; rather, their focus should be the social reality of human life which 'while never wholly independent of other levels of reality, can be treated usefully as a reality in itself' (1988 [1970]: 211). By taking on this distinction, medical sociologists were carving out an intellectual domain all of their own (Strong 1979). This is crystallized in shifts in terminology over time from 'medical sociology', to the 'sociology of health and illness', to the 'sociology of health' (though all these terms are in use today and for this reason are used more or less interchangeably in this book). The social imperialism and disembodied approach that was to characterize much of the field until the early 1990s was an expansion of the belief held by sociology's nineteenth-century 'founding fathers' that social interaction – the principal object of enquiry – could never be reduced to biology or physiology. The work of Talcott Parsons, the originator of structural functionalism and, according to some, the inventor of medical sociology (Mol 2007), made a strong contribution to this distinctly sociological approach to the study of health, illness and healthcare.

Parsons and structural functionalism

Parsons was critical of conceptualizations of health which appeal to general human welfare and well-being, such as the World Health Organisation definition of health as 'a state of complete physical, mental, and social well-being and not merely the absence of disease or infirmity' (WHO 1948[1]). Rather, he conceived of health as a valued social commodity, an essential resource for individual achievement and the smooth running of society. In his influential book *The Social System*, he wrote, 'too low a general level of health, too high an incidence of illness, is dysfunctional: this is in the first instance because illness incapacitates the effective performance of social roles' (1951: 430).

For Parsons, health was the capacity of the 'individual living system' (or organism) to maintain the 'favourable self-regulated state' essential to the 'effective performance of an indefinitely wide range of functions', in relation both to the body itself and to its social environments (1978: 69). Conversely, illness was the individual's inability to realize this capacity. He drew a distinction between 'real' illness and malingering. It was the former which concerned him most because he felt that, with 'real' illness, the individual 'cannot be expected simply to "pull himself [sic] together" and proceed to get well' (Parsons 1978: 70).

Parsons coined the concept of the 'sick role' to refer to the niche provided for the individual to recuperate from illness free from the stresses of everyday life in order eventually to return to normal social functioning (as an employee, parent and so on). Viewed as a pure type rather than a literal empirical description, the sick role has four defining features, two of which can be described as 'rights' and two as 'obligations'. The two 'rights' consist of exemption from normal social responsibilities and from blame for ill-health, and the two 'obligations' are to want to get well (and not to use illness as a way of avoiding the stresses and strains of life) and to seek competent professional help and to trust and cooperate with the physician or other healthcare provider. Parsons felt that acting in a consumerist fashion and 'shopping around' for care should be strongly discouraged. The rights and obligations of the patient's 'sick role' are mirrored in the 'physician role' which applies universalistic standards to the care of patients. This role, as Parsons depicts it, is 'functionally specific' – that is, concerned with 'problems of the patient's health rather than with other sorts of personal problems'; is 'performance oriented' – in other words, intervenes and helps rather than passively sits by; is 'predominantly affectively neutral', or not biased towards certain patients; and is 'oriented towards professional values' rather than towards self-interest (such as financial gain) (Parsons 1978: 75).

A range of critical comments have been levied against Parsons' work over the years, notably in regard to the sick role. The most frequently made are:

(1) Entry to the sick role is not as straightforward as Parsons implied; seriousness, the legitimacy of the illness, and the varying cultural expectations of how one should behave when ill (related, e.g., to class, race, gender, age) all play a crucial role.
(2) Illness is not morally neutral in the way that Parsons implied. The patient is not exempted from responsibilities: they are still vital. Furthermore, many health conditions are stigmatized.
(3) The sick role pertains to acute conditions and cannot relate to chronic illness.
(4) Parsons assumed that the patient would willingly comply with the physician when, in actuality, patients are not passive and the doctor–patient relationship is often imbued with conflict.
(5) Parsons replicated the gendered division of labour of the early 1950s, assuming the male role of producer in the public sphere of employment and the female role of reproducer in the domestic sphere of the home. Since it was the health of the former he sought to restore, Parsons' sick role was inherently male.

Parsons, who died in 1979, responded to some of these criticisms, rebutting some and re-stating his original position in response to others. In relation to chronic illness, he explained that he was not necessarily referring to full recovery but rather to accepting the medical management that would facilitate return to functioning whenever possible (Parsons 1975, 1978). Yet, it might be argued that the hard work of normalizing chronic illness – managing the condition and trying to be as 'well' as possible – *in itself* contributes to the erosion of medical authority. In other words, the *patient* often becomes the expert, not the physician. While Parsons got the point that patients are not always passive and often take an active part in their own treatment, he still insisted that, in the last instance, 'there must be a built-in institution-alised superiority of the professional roles, grounded in responsibility, competence, and occupational concern' (Parsons 1975: 271; see also Parsons 1978).

In the 1970s and 1980s much of the commentary was wholly critical of Parsons. This remains largely the case today. Indeed, for Thomas (2010: 39) he is the wearer of the 'medico-centric crown' *par excellence*. However, others have suggested that his writings have more value than once accorded them. For example, Ostrowska (2001) points out that the emphasis on the mutual complementarity of components of the social system made structural functionalism a popular way of analysing a socialist society such as Poland, which, since it was not supposed to be conflictual, did not easily lend itself to Marxist theory. In the wider context, Shilling maintains that Parsons' emphasis on the cultural value of instrumental action anticipates the present-day body-conscious, pro-active approach to health and healthcare (2002: 622).

But for now our gaze is upon early medical sociology where Parsons' approach was admired for its endorsement of a distinctly *social model* of illness yet disapproved of for solidifying medicine's power base and ability to set research agendas. As Gold put it, 'the functionalist perspective grants medicine the same defining powers regarding its norms and deviance that medicine grants itself' (1977: 162). By the 1970s, a clear agenda had been set for medical sociology: to liberate understandings of health and medicine from the political straitjacket of the biomedical model. The political economy and interactionist per-spectives which took root in the 1970s and blossomed in the 1980s and beyond provided the wherewithal to put a distinctly different, strongly social and critical, evaluation of medical practice and the power of phy-sicians at the heart of the sociology of health and illness.

The political economy perspective: then and now

The well-spring of the political economy approach is Marx's analysis of the inbuilt structural contradictions of capitalist society, especially the fierce contradiction between the pursuit of profit and the pursuit of health (Waitzkin 2000). But the first health-related contribution came not from Marx, but from his collaborator Engels. In *The Condition of the Working Class in England in 1844* (1993 [1845]), Engels explored the causes and distribution of typhoid, tuberculosis, scrofula and rickets in the population and reached the conclusion that, since they had a direct association with the capitalist social relations of production, medical intervention alone could not eradicate disease.

From the political economy perspective, there is little to be gained by attempting to understand health and healthcare through the activities of individuals or the institution of medicine; they must be placed within the broader political and economic framework of society. In the 1970s, McKinlay set up this framework through the analogy of the game. He argued that:

> one can conceive of medical care-related activities as the game among a group of highly trained players, carefully selected for the affinity of their interests with the requirements of capitalist institutions, which is watched by a vast number of spectators (involving all of the people some of the time and, increasingly, some of the people all the time). And surrounding this game itself, with its interested public, is the capitalistic state (setting the rules by which the game ought to be played before the public), the presence of which ensures the legitimacy of the game and guarantees, through resources derived from spectators, that the prerogatives and interests of the park (finance and industrial capital) are always protected and advanced.
>
> (McKinlay 1977: 464–5)

It is fair to say that, although it has retained its place in the sociology of health and medicine, the political economy approach has tended to dwell more on the edges than at the centre of the discipline. This has not been helped by recurrent declarations of the poverty of neo-Marxist theory. For some, the fall of communism in Eastern Europe in the early 1990s was the death blow to Marxism, which many believed had come to an 'end' itself (Makdisi et al. 1996: ix). Yet more recent events, such as the global financial crisis, environmental disasters and the health repercussions of the booming global biotech industries, have prompted a revitalization of Marxism and the political economy perspective. As Sunder Rajan puts it, capitalism is a restless system, an evolving process which is 'mutable and multiple' (2006: 7). From this vantage point, recent events do not prophesy the end of capitalism but rather 'reconfigurations, new models of development, new spheres of investment and new forms of class power' (Harvey 2010: 11). So we can expect periodic crises both to throw up new health concerns and to contribute to the persistence of longstanding problems which appear in new guises. In what follows, we will explore enduring topics such as the contradiction between health and profit, and the transmission of capitalist ideologies in healthcare, as well as newer concerns such as the drawing of the human body into global health markets.

Profit, environment and health

One of the central contradictions of capitalism is its inherent tendency to 'undermine the very process of interaction with nature' on which it depends (Harman 2009: 307). Part of Engels' (1993 [1845]) legacy was to reveal the devastating health consequences of the smog-filled air, polluted rivers and open sewers of mid-nineteenth-century cities (see also chapter 4 for recent research on place and health). The nature of capitalist production has changed markedly since then but the contradiction between the profit motive and health remains. A stark illustration of this is the illegal dumping of toxic waste on the Côte D'Ivoire in 2006. The ship *Probo Koala* was on its way to the port of Paldiski in Estonia when it entered the port of Amsterdam to refuel and unload its slop tanks. The sample of waste taken by Amsterdam Port Services revealed a significantly higher chemical oxygen demand than it was able to process on its premises. When the cost estimate for processing the waste was revised from €20 to €90 per square metre (m^2), the ship's owner, Trafigura – a Swiss-based company with a turnover of $73 billion in 2008 – requested the waste be reloaded. Once it reached the city of Abidjan, the waste was unloaded by the newly formed company, Tommy Ltd, at a cost of €30 per m^2 and taken by truck to be dumped at various sites in different districts of the city. Local residents were exposed to the waste by skin contact. An estimated 15 people died, 69 were hospitalized and more than 108,000 medical consultations resulted from the incident. Symptoms on the day after the dumping included nausea, headaches, vomiting, abdominal pain, and skin, throat, lung and gastric problems. Trafigura was required to pay €152 million in compensation (UN Human Rights Council 2009).

Environmental disasters, from the 2006 Trafigura incident to Hurricane Katrina in 2005 and the nuclear fallout following the explosion at Japan's Fukushima Daiichi nuclear plant in 2011, ricochet around the world, variously affecting stock markets and threatening the natural environment and human and other life forms far beyond their localities. But as the breach of the levees in New Orleans, Louisiana, in the wake of Hurricane Katrina illuminated, their effects are vastly disproportionate for certain populations. For the politicians, hurricane Katrina was a golden opportunity to clean up, clear out and rebuild the city, while the 'poorest residents were left to drown' or were shut out from largely empty private healthcare facilities as public services floundered under the weight of need (Klein 2007: 408). Naomi Klein uses the term 'disaster capitalism' to depict the link between 'superprofits and megadisasters' (2007: 9). She argues that, under the cloak of the 'War on Terror' post-9/11, the now booming disaster capitalism industry was unleashed to breathe life into the ailing US economy. This included the creation of a global 'homeland security industry' to the tune of $200 billion (in 2006) and the 'privatisation of war and disaster' (2007: 14). Klein reports that hurricane relief in Louisiana was distinctly pro-market with companies snagging lucrative no-bid contracts for reconstruction and the provision of mobile homes. A company contracted to remove bodies ultimately charged the taxpayer $12,500 per victim. Distinctly missing was any attempt to hire local people 'at decent wages to help them put their lives back in order' (2007: 412). Klein concludes that, 'not so long ago, disasters were periods of social levelling, rare moments when atomised communities put divisions aside and pulled together. Increasingly, however, disasters are the opposite: they provide windows into a cruel and ruthlessly divided future in which money and race buy survival' (Klein 2007: 413).

Capitalism and ideologies of healthcare

Today 'the market is "in" everything and seemingly nothing is incapable of being commodified' (Landry and MacLean 1993: xii). Many of us are so dazzled daily by advertisements for the new 'must-have' designer goods that we are blinded to the exploitation embedded in their production and to their limited use-value. As Frank (2004) argues, it is now widely accepted that the for-profit corporate sphere sets the agenda for professional medicine. Physicians become the delivery agents of corporate products, especially in an era where the body has become a commodity itself (as discussed further below). Frank gives the prosaic, but nonetheless still shocking, illustration of New York podiatrists surgically shaping women's feet so that they can buy, fit and look good in their expensive designer shoes. This can be conceived as part of new emerging 'relations between capital and work, bodies and the state, citizenship and social and medical inclusion (and exclusion)' (Scheper-Hughes 2001a: 43).

Political economists and others have long contended that ideologies such as ageism, sexism and racism are played out at the micro-level of provider–patient interactions. We will look at wider illustrations of this in chapter 9, and concentrate here on Howard Waitzkin's argument (2000) that, by subtle processes, the structural roots of suffering within capitalism are depoliticized in doctor–patient encounters. Drawing on Habermas' (1984) concept of 'distorted communication', he argues that through the micro-lens of doctor-patient communication we can observe how problems within medicine originate from and fortify the social contradictions of capitalist society (Waitzkin 2000). He illustrates this through transcripts of medical encounters, which all took place in the US. For example, in one, through an abiding concern with a male patient's return to employment, a physician betrays his definition of health as the ability to work. Another consultation, which concerns a woman with rheumatic disease, menopausal and hearing problems, seems on the surface to be quite egalitarian. But it becomes clear that her symptoms are defined as a problem principally because they interfere with her housework, something she herself vocalizes feeling guilty about. Waitzkin deduces that 'the doctor has several options at this point. He could try to explore and to ease the patient's guilty feelings about her physical limitations; he could also suggest alternative social arrangements, including greater division of labour in housework.' Instead of this he opts for a pharmacological solution and raises the dose of her medication to suppress heart rhythm irregularities (2000: 143). He argues that the physician endorses women's role in capitalism, beneath a cloak of humanistic concern. This is displayed in quite remarkable fashion when, in instructing her to do a bit of exercise during an electrocardiogram, he says, 'could you do some sit-ups for me? . . . Just do a bit, uh, try to get yourself a little bit out of breath . . . try again . . . just scrub one more room' (2000: 134). The point, as Waitzkin discusses, is not that physicians are deceitful, but that they can unwittingly transmit dominant capitalist values which may not be in the interest of the patient. In so doing, they engage in what he calls 'patching', which permits the client's continued functioning in the very capitalist system that so often is the source of their health problems in the first place.

Obesity
Governments in high-income countries direct attention to the proximate causes of illness such as an individual's smoking, diet and alcohol consumption, to the relative neglect of the activities of the capitalist class, the CEOs and directors of companies, rentiers and financial speculators – the very people and their behaviours, so political economists argue, that are the real risk to health (Scambler 2002, 2009). Around the world, some people starve while others reportedly are eating themselves to death as the so-called 'obesity epidemic' takes hold in the West. Solutions to rising rates of overweight and obesity are framed heavily in medical terms and targeted at the individual level. Increasingly the proposed solution is bariatric surgery, which is advertised directly to potential patients in many countries. For example, at the time of writing (in July 2013), the private Spire Hospital in Leicester, England, gave a guide price for gastric band surgery of £7,140 and for a gastric bypass of £10,900. A study of US websites by Salant and Santry (2006) found that obesity is presented as an intractable disease which has physical and emotional consequences that can be remedied only by surgical intervention. If it was portrayed differently as under the control of the individual, the implication would be that they could do something about it and surgery would not necessarily be the best option. Yet, even though surgeons tell patients that dieting doesn't work and obesity is not their fault, the same kind of behaviours as those associated with traditional dieting are deemed crucial to who loses weight and who does not post-surgery (Boero 2010). And, interestingly enough, bariatric surgery generates its own lucrative markets driven by a range of what Monaghan and colleagues (2010) dub 'obesity entrepreneurs', who provide services such as plastic surgery to remove

'redundant skin', skincare products and nutritional supplements and speciality foods like protein powders, drinks and snacks (see also Boero 2010). In sum, those defined as 'obese' are contrarily positioned in the capitalist healthcare economy, pulled towards profitable surgery because it is 'not their fault' yet pushed to assume individual responsibility when outcomes are less than optimal. Distinctly missing in this discourse of responsibilization is any sustained attempt to assess critically and change the activities of the highly profitable fast-food industry and the food consumption that individuals are encouraged to engage in by product marketing (Schlosser 2002).

Neoliberalism, biocapital and the body

Thus far we have brought up to date some of the longstanding concerns of the political economy perspective – namely, *capitalism, the environment and health* and the transmission of *capitalist ideologies of health.* We now enter a relatively new terrain, the economic exploitation of the human body and the extraction of what has been called 'biovalue' (Waldby 2002).

Cooper argues that recent US neoliberal economic policy has been designed to relocate production at the genetic, microbial and cellular level. As a result, 'life becomes, literally, annexed within capitalist processes of accumulation' (Cooper 2008: 19). Drawing on volume III of *Capital* (1974 [1894]) where Marx discusses the relationship between moments of crisis and the devaluation of human life, she shows how capital needs to mobilize and promote the creative forces of human life in order to maximize accumulation but, in the process, undermines life itself. Marx was referring to the exploitation of the late-nineteenth-century worker's body: today's developments in biotechnology, such as cell-based therapies, regenerative medicine, tissue engineering and transplant surgery have the potential to take exploitation to a whole new level. They do not in any simple sense *determine* how we think and act, rather they prosper in the fertile ground of our contemporary perceptions – at least in wealthy economies – of the body as a commodity, a form of physical and economic capital that can be moulded, changed and regenerated (for a wider discussion of the sociology of the body, see chapter 2). In what follows we will focus upon *how* exploitation takes place and *who* is exploited.

'Biovalue' refers to the 'yield of vitality produced by the biotechnical reformulation of living processes' (Waldby 2002: 310). While we tend to think about our bodies at the molar level of organs, limbs, hormones and flows of blood, there is a 'new ontology of life' taking place at the molecular level of 'properties of coding sequences of nucleotide bases and their variations, the molecular mechanisms that regulate gene expression and transcription, the link between the functional properties of proteins and their molecular topography, the role of intracellular components – ion channels, enzyme activities, transporter genes, membrane potentials' (Rose 2007a: 5–6).

There is immense value to be mined at this level of the 'tissue economy' (Waldby and Mitchell 2006). All kinds of tissues, such as blood, cord blood, sperm, eggs, breast and brain tissue, can be placed in tissue banks. Tissue banks can be used therapeutically, for research, or for both. They can be public – such as the UK National Blood Services and Cord Blood (stem cell) Bank – or commercial. Cord blood, which is harvested from the umbilical cord at birth, is a valuable product because it contains haematopoietic stem cells. These cells are pluripotentic, that is, they can differentiate into a number of other tissues. Embryonic stem cells, pluripotent stem cells from the inner cell mass of an early-stage embryo, are even more valuable because they are totipotentic, capable of making *any* other kind of human tissue.

Although the large majority of stem cell therapies are still at the experimental stage, there is an expectation from within biomedical science and from the public that they will eventually be used to treat conditions such as cancer, 'type 1' diabetes, Parkinson's disease, Huntingdon's disease and spinal cord injuries. Richard Branson's Virgin Health Bank (which is partly funded by the biotechnology company Merlin Biosciences) offers two options: so-called 'family banking' where, at the time of writing, parents could store their own child's cord blood for their future personal use for twenty-five years at a cost of £1,695; and 'community banking', where a small amount is kept for family use and the rest is donated to the public, at a cost of £1,195. Nik Brown and colleagues (2011) see cord blood, which frequently trades at £15,000 to £20,000 per unit, as a new currency in the world international blood economy. Cross-border trade is important because of the need to tap into immunity pools for matches between donors and recipients. Some countries have more heterogeneous immunity pools (such as the multi-ethnic UK) than others (such as Japan). The former will have more problems with matches inside the country than the latter.

It might be argued that there is nothing inherently exploitative or health-damaging about stem cell therapies and that tissue banking is a sensible precaution against future health risks. But when stem cells and body parts are treated as 'surplus value', they are ripe for exploitation. As we will see shortly, some people are more able to protect themselves from this than others, but all of us are vulnerable to some degree. Common law assumes that, once informed consent has been given for tissue to be extracted, such as during surgery or childbirth, it is 'abandoned'. Since it is deemed to have no value to the individual, property rights are relinquished. Yet, clearly, tissue can be a source of economic and social value. An oft-cited case from the US is that of John

Moore who sued his physician and several pharmaceutical companies under the charge that they had stolen his spleen during surgery for a rare form of leukaemia and transformed part of it into a commercially viable cell line (Cooper 2008; Waldby and Mitchell 2006).

The market model rests on the premise that, somehow, life can be extended indefinitely. Serious problems occur when, in pursuit of this fantasy, richer patients of the global North 'seek regenerative capacities in the bodies of the poor of the global South' (Waldby and Mitchell 2006: 180). Scheper-Hughes (2001a, 2001b) characterizes this as 'late modern cannibalism'. She relates that, coupled with advancements in medical procedures and biotechnologies, the movement of bodies within global capitalism has 'incited new tastes and desires for the skin, bone, blood, organs, tissue and reproductive and genetic material of the other' (Scheper-Hughes 2001b: 5). The global traffic in organs tends to follow the 'modern routes of capital and labour flows': from South to North, from poor to rich, from black and brown to white, from female to male (Scheper-Hughes 2001a: 45).

The cash-for-kidneys trade, in particular, has grown since the 1980s following the development of immunosuppressant drugs that reduce the need for histo-compatibility between donor and recipient. Some, such as Taylor (2005), argue in favour of a legal trade alongside donation as the only way to solve the donor shortage and relieve suffering. He challenges claims of commodification and exploitation and argues instead for the language of choice and the setting-up of a market system in which vendors can be afforded protection against abuse by purchasers. Others maintain this will never work because 'choice' is meaningless for many. For example, Dickenson (2008) reports of over fifty women from the fishing villages of the Bay of Bengal selling a kidney to rescue their families from debt following the 2004 tsunami. Brokers now act as go-betweens connecting 'third world donors' and 'first world recipients' (Waldby and Mitchell 2006). Reports have emerged of a black market in China where, even though organ transplantation has been resisted for religious and other reasons, allegedly thousands of prisoners are executed annually to provide fresh organs for transplant both at home and on the global market. Becker (1999) likens this to a state execution machine as organs purportedly have been procured for the Communist Party elite. Evidently, markets position people differently in relation to new biotechnologies: some *lose* control over their bodies, selling their organs and other tissues or having them taken, and some *gain* control, as they purchase or are provided with the body parts of others. For Mukta, this '"neo- or postmodern cannibalism" has taken the law of the marketplace to its ultimate end-point, whereby rich bodies can live off desperately poor and suffering bodies, making the "saving" of lives governable by the law of exploitation' (2012: 451).

Medical tourism

Travelling for the benefit of one's health has been practised for centuries; even Marx took the spa waters of Carlsbad and the Isle of Wight, and the thermal springs of Monte Carlo (Wheen 1999). But this has taken on a whole new meaning with the emergence of 'medical tourism' whereby patients, usually from the West, travel to nations such as India, Thailand and Mexico for treatments ranging from cosmetic surgery, to organ transplants, stem cell injections and dental care.

One of the best-known tourist destinations is Thailand's massive 554-bed Bumrungrad Hospital in Bangkok, which revamped itself into a combined 5-star hotel and international medical centre in the wake of the 1997 Asian financial crisis. Brokerage companies such as Planet Hospital pitch 'surf and surgery' holidays in Thailand and 'surgery and safari' breaks in South Africa, all marketed as cheaper options than in the US and as quicker options than in the UK's National Health Service. The company's website shows which surgeons offer what and where in the world. Brokerages also contract with US companies to 'offshore' treatment of their employees to reduce employer insurance costs (Turner 2010).

The globalization of medicine is also apparent in associations with US academic centres, such as Harvard (University) Medical International's link with Dubai Healthcare City. While this kind of co-branding is often presented as a marker of care safety, it needs to be appreciated that a lot of medical tourism is for single episodes of care. A patient from the US, for example, could return home to non-existent or inadequate follow-up care. Moreover, international medical centres can severely drain public-sector care. Thus, public hospitals often find it hard to retain staff in face of higher salaries offered by the global private hospitals (Turner 2010). In India, where private hospitals have expanded since economic liberalization in the mid-1990s, it was estimated that the medical tourism boom would earn the country as much as $2 billion by 2012 (Connell 2006). Yet this occurred in an environment where 40 per cent of the population live below the poverty line with no access to basic healthcare (Cooper 2008). For Buzinde and Yarnal (2012), medical tourism can be understood as a form of neo-colonialism, whereby nations on the global economic periphery better the human security of the nations at the core, such as the US, at the expense of social benefits to their own populations.

Political economy assessed

Buffeted by the significant challenges to its Marxist foundations during the 1990s and into the early twenty-first century, the political economy perspective has garnered new credibility and fresh momentum as a framework within which to analyse health and medicine in an era of significant global economic and social change. Not all of the social scientists whose work is discussed here would necessarily nail their theoretical flag to the mast of political economy, though most draw to some degree on Marx and Marxist concepts in their various critical assessments of the health consequences of contemporary capitalism. Similarly not all would self-define as sociologists of health and medicine. But their exploration of health issues is nonetheless indicative of the diffusion of health concerns into wider sociology and the social sciences, as mentioned in the chapter introduction.

Much like the interactionist perspective to be discussed shortly, the political economy approach is not easily formalized into a set of agreed-upon tenets. However, we can identify two lines of criticism of it as a broad approach. The first concerns how far health problems and health benefits are to do with industrialism and technological development generally or with capitalism specifically. There are questions on both sides of this critical coin. Given that life expectancy rose at the time that capitalism took hold in the West, doesn't this mean that capitalism has promoted health and contributed to the decline in chronic disease (Hart 1982)? In response, it can be argued that the mere fact that two things happen at around the same time does not necessarily mean they are causally linked. Improved life chances are generally ascribed to improved diet, sanitation and housing (see, e.g., McKeown 1976). It may be that the population would have developed even better health if life had not been organized along capitalist lines, particularly as the class divide in health was marked at this time. From the other side of the same critical coin, it can be asked whether blame for the present-day problems identified in this chapter lies more with late industrialism and social and technological advances than it does with capitalism. For example, wouldn't the health risks of nuclear fall-out occur anyway? Won't there always be too few donor organs for those who need them? Possibly, but the response would be that these problems are made infinitely worse because of the corrosive trappings of capitalism, such as the contradiction between the search for profit and safety and health.

The corollary of these responses from the political economy perspective is that health benefits can only be fully realized and damage avoided outside of capitalism. This then raises a second line of criticism: if so many people have so very much invested in the global capitalist economy, how will this situation ever change, especially since, as mentioned earlier, capitalism is ever evolving? Here lies the problem that has haunted Marxist work over the centuries, and which goes far beyond the domain of health and illness. Waitzkin, for example, recognizes that health workers can't deny services to clients, even when they fail to 'attack the deeper roots of their problems' (2000: 201). However, he calls for them to link their clinical work 'to efforts aimed directly at basic socio-political change' (2000: 201). Similarly, Scambler tasks social scientists with raising consciousness by giving greater attention to money and power, exploitation and oppression (2002, 2009), in their research. The rise of anti-capitalist protests sparked at the World Trade Organization meeting in Seattle in 1999, and revived in events such as the anti-G8 protest in Genoa in 2005 and the Unite for Global Change day of protest in cities around the world in late 2011, has led some to identify a nascent movement for change. There have been numerous protests of late, such as those against the tobacco and food industries and environmental hazards, as well as pressure groups protesting against hospital and service closures and advocating for resources for specific health problems (Morello-Frosch et al. 2006; Scambler 2002; Waitzkin 2001). Jean and John Comaroff opine that 'it is unimaginable that innovative forms of emancipatory practice will not emerge to address the excesses of neoliberal capitalism', but 'that is in the future' (Comaroff and Comaroff 2001: 45). More than a decade on from their words, this still seems to be the case.

The interactionist perspective: then and now

For most, interactionism means the 'symbolic interactionism' of George Herbert Mead (1863–1931) and his student Herbert Blumer (1969). Blumer, who coined the term 'symbolic interactionism' in 1937, arguably did more than anyone else to establish Mead's reputation as 'the most innovative alternative to Talcott Parsons' structural functionalism' (da Silva 2007: 71).

Interactionism is not an explanatory theory in the sense of being a testable set of connections between concepts, but rather a 'loosely structured cluster of fundamental ideas' (Lindesmith and Strauss 1969: 1). At its core is the proposition that the self is socially emergent. Da Silva (2007: 3) characterizes this as Mead's dialogic perspective, or his focus on the 'social or communicative nature of the self'. By taking what is called 'the attitude of the other' in social interaction, we are able cognitively to step outside of ourselves and to see ourselves as others see us, through what Cooley (1902) earlier called the 'reflected' or 'looking-glass self'. In so doing, we engage in a kind of 'inner conversation', assuming the attitudes of others and acquiring the ability to see our world from their perspectives. In its most developed form, this involves absorbing attitudes which belong to the 'generalised other', or the wider moral order. A present health-related illustration of this would be adopting the social and moral connotations of obesity – such as gluttony and sloth – and of slenderness – such as restraint and vigour. Language, or the vocal gesture, is crucial to the process of taking the attitude of the other since it provides a strong vehicle for self-reflection. No other gesture or symbol is as successful in affecting the individual in a similar way to how it affects others (Mead 1934 [1972]). By making these points, Mead was insisting that society has priority in the emergence of the self.

With the capacity for reflection, individuals are self-directive – able to select, interpret and bestow meaning upon their interactions with others. But the very fact that they do this in the co-presence of others (either actual or envisaged individuals or groups), means that self-direction is always limited. Constraints come into play – others may not view us in the way that we view ourselves; they may not act towards us in the ways we expect, and the prior actions of others (which we may not be aware of, or may be aware of but are powerless to modify) may set up barriers to our actions. Consequently we are called upon to be 'artful' in our everyday lives by becoming engaged in a process of 'negotiation, impression management, and meaning creation' (Fine 1993: 64).

In a neat turn of phrase, Fisher and Strauss suggest that interactionism is less an 'inheritance passed down through the generations' than a 'long-lived auction house' from which researchers pick whatever elements strike them as valuable and leave the rest behind (1978: 458). To continue the metaphor, Mead's conceptual treasures – such as his insistence that the self emerges socially as we 'take on the role of the other', and his account of how the attitude of the 'generalised other' is incorporated into the self – have become valuable acquisitions for the analysis of such matters as how individuals give meaning to social events (such as childbirth, chronic illness, death), the ways in which they manage changed identities in ill-health, and the 'negotiation' that takes place in formal and informal healthcare settings.

The study of health organizations and the experience of illness

Although there are differences among interactionists, all react against positivistic conceptualizations of organizations which stress their formal structure – particularly technology and rationally defined goals – as a determinant of individual behaviour. The notion of social structure takes on a completely different hue for interactionists. Mead explained that, like individual selves, social institutions

> are developments within, or particular and formalised manifestations of, the social life-process at its human evolutionary level. As such they are not necessarily subversive of individuality in the individual members; and they do not necessarily represent or uphold narrow definitions of certain fixed and specific patterns of acting which in any given cir-

cumstances should characterise the behaviour of ... individuals ... as members of the given community or social group. On the contrary, they need to define the social, or socially responsible, patterns of individual conduct in only a very broad and general sense, affording plenty of scope for originality, flexibility, and a variety of such conduct; and as the main formalised functional aspects or phases of the whole organised structure of the social life-process at its human level they properly partake of the dynamic and progressive character of that process.

(Mead 1934 [1972]: 262–3)

Here Mead simultaneously presents social organizations (such as hospitals, clinics, homes) as flexible and dynamic containers for human agency and as reified actors (institutions act in order to define certain patterns of action and to uphold these definitions). Given this dual conception, it is not surprising that, while sharing a view of human agency as socially emergent and a concern with individual meaning-making, interactionists have conceived of the relationship between social organization and individual action in different ways. A moral alliance with the 'patient's perspective' and a concern that the patient's sense of self be validated (rather than despoiled) by others and that patients should have a greater say in treatment decisions have underlain most research in the interactionist tradition. This in itself signals a concern with undue constraints of various kinds upon individual agency, such as the failure to be heard, or to be allowed to make choices. Indeed, much of the ethnographic work of interactionists has revealed that, in the last instance, there is precious little space for patients (and to a lesser extent health practitioners) to establish their own individual definitions of the situation, and this is largely because of their relative lack of power and resources. A rich array of insights has emerged from research studies into the intricacies of healthcare work in organizations and the delicate manoeuvring that takes place in patient–provider interactions.

Erving Goffman (1922–82) very rarely refers to Mead. Nonetheless, as da Silva (2007: 86) explains, his 'dramaturgical approach to social reality is a brilliant exploration of some of the themes' raised by Mead. Like Mead, he rejected the common perception of the self-contained individual, arguing instead that the self is 'more or less an image cast by social arrangements' (Scheff 2006: 19). Goffman develops a sociology of co-presence, 'of the performances that people put on when they are in one another's presence. It is a social theory that dwells upon the episodic and sees life only as it is lived in a narrow interpersonal circumference', as coming alive 'only in the fluid, transient "encounter"' (Gouldner 1970: 379). In his research, which ranged widely to include the study of mental institutions (Goffman 1961) and the stigma often associated with illness and disability (1963), Goffman 'noticed the riches of the microworld and invented a panoply of terms and phrases to describe them' (Scheff 2006: 17).

It has been argued that it was not individuals per se that interested Goffman. Rather, they engaged his attention because they were a lens through which to observe the workings of social institutions and social orders. Although he viewed the social order as 'fragile, impermanent, full of unexpected holes, and in constant need of repair' (Burns 1992: 26), Goffman's attraction was to the strength of the social order and an exploration of the social rules which govern interaction and impression management. In other words, while active emotion-management and its anticipation was a focal point of his work, it was how this was called forth – almost scripted, it might be said – by social contexts that seemed to concern him most.

In the healthcare context, the surface structure of interaction, such as rituals and ceremonies, was utilized in the late 1970s by Strong in his observational study of paediatric clinics in a Scottish and a US city (Strong 2001 [1979]). Here Strong's concern is not with the feelings, opinions or perceptions of parents and doctors, but instead with the ceremonies that they take part in, the rituals that they enact in the consultation. Each medical encounter is framed by a series of expectations, typically embodied in what Strong calls the 'bureaucratic role format'. This ceremonial form is a collaborative effort, constructed by doctor and parent by avoiding all matters 'not fitting' with the model of an ideal parent and doctor who display themselves as mutually committed to achieving the best for the child under the medical ethos of individual commitment and gentility. Under this form, the doctors in Strong's study actively worked to idealize and sanctify mothers. For example, if a mother was felt to have behaved inappropriately, this was repaired by justifying her actions (offering acceptable excuses for missed appointments, highlighting future good behaviour rather than past misdemeanours). Parents complemented this by idealizing medical competence, assuming the doctor's expertise without question and avoiding reference to errors in judgement and practice. The result of this joint endeavour was the construction of an overt ceremonial order which permitted interaction to proceed as smoothly as possible. Strong points out that, for Goffman, 'people are mere creatures of frames, and what we normally conceive of as a person is reduced to a set of devices for the re-creation and careful maintenance of pre-existing and super-ordinate frames' (Strong 2001 [1979]: 186). Yet at the same time Goffman

> provides us with a quite separate model; one that emphasises the margins of freedom that allow the individual some space for his or her own interests, identity and purposes . . . Rather than being mere puppets, individuals, in this other version, are shown to manipulate frames to

their own advantage . . . to make elaborate copies and parodies of more serious frames, . . . and to distance themselves from frames even while acting within them.

(Strong 2001: 185–6)

In this regard, despite the ritual avoidance of moral indignation in Strong's study, doctors still used strategies to manipulate patients (such as in 'correcting' their opinions and guiding them towards certain behaviours). Patients could also disrupt the ceremonial order, by insistent questioning for example, but this was not very successful given the medical authority invested in the bureaucratic frame. Apparently, the interaction of parent and doctor was quite effectively ring-fenced by the ceremonial order.

In the work of Anselm Strauss and colleagues (see, e.g., Glaser and Strauss 1965; Strauss et al. 1985) the social order is less tightly circumscribed. They argue that the rules, rituals and ceremonies that surround health and healthcare are inherently precarious because they are built on the shaky foundation of a negotiated consensus. The formal institution is a geographical locale, 'a site where persons drawn from different professions come together to carry out their respective purposes' (Strauss et al. 1963: 150). Such institutions do not operate according to rules – indeed, 'hardly anyone knows all the extant rules, much less exactly what they apply to, for whom, and with what sanctions'. Nothing is binding or shared for all time. It is such considerations that led Strauss and colleagues (1963: 148) to 'emphasise the importance of negotiation – the processes of give-and-take, of diplomacy, of bargaining – which characterises organisational life'. Negotiation connotes meaning which develops in the course of interaction; it is through meaning-making that individuals know the world and are able to act effectively in it. Consequently, action in the healthcare context involves a process of definition, that is, defining the context in which one is involved, taking account of the definitions of others and, thereby, negotiating a consensus. This may be fleeting enough to allow one to 'get by' in a particular task or sufficiently long-term to anticipate a changed self or new work policy.

This does not mean to say that social structures are not important – indeed, Strauss (1978) emphasized that they enter *as conditions* into the course of negotiation itself. In what is often dubbed the 'negotiated order approach', the work of Strauss and colleagues involved observational and interview-based studies of the social interaction that surrounds chronic illness, dying and death. In their early research on dying, Glaser and Strauss fashioned the term 'awareness contexts' to conceptualize 'what each interacting person knows of the patient's defined status [as a dying person], along with his [*sic*] recognition of the others' awareness of his own definition' (Glaser and Strauss 1965: 10). A range of forms – closed awareness, suspected awareness, mutual pretence awareness and open awareness – which derived from the authors' fieldwork, depict the contexts in which dying people and those who surround them interact. These are not fixed, but fluid, guiding the interplay between those involved and open to reconstruction as patient, doctor or nurse and others engineer change. Bargaining is central to organizational life, 'every patient . . . wants to get certain things or to have certain events occur; he [or she] coaxes, wheedles, bargains, persuades, hints, and uses other forms of negotiation' to this end (Glaser and Strauss 1965: 94). For their part, staff strike bargains with patients (for example, over nursing regimens or how to deal with relatives) in an effort to achieve a 'job well done' (a humane and acceptable death, for example) (for a wider discussion of death and dying, see chapter 9).

Negotiation is also at the heart of Roth's (1963) now classic study of the timetables constructed in the illness career of tuberculosis (TB) patients, which at the time of Roth's study was surrounded by diagnostic and prognostic uncertainty. Timetables became an important monitoring device which provided patients and doctors with a conception of how long a patient with given disease characteristics should need to spend in hospital. Although Roth found that both patients and doctors grouped patients into categories in an effort to determine when a particular benchmark event in the career (such as taking a gastric culture) should occur, the system of grouping could differ in important ways. Patients used very broad categories, with an individual believing that 'anything that happens to any of the patients in that group . . . can legitimately be used as a reference point for determining what should happen to him [*sic*]' (1963: 36). The physician, in contrast, used more highly differentiated categories, referring to the finer points of clinical tests. Consequently,

> the anticipation of and allowances for the reactions of the other party on both sides of a continuing bargaining system form a dialectic of constant influences operating over a period of time . . . patients constantly press for advancing the timetable; physicians try to resist such pressures . . . The result of these opposing pressures is a continual bargaining between patients and physicians over the question of when given points on the timetable have been reached.
>
> (Roth 1963: 57, 61)

In recent years the notion of the 'negotiated order' has been used to good effect in the study of work 'jurisdictions' (Abbott 1988), especially when they are marked by power differentials, such as those which often exist between physicians and other health professions (e.g. Allen 2001; Nugus et al. 2010; also see discussion in chapter 8)

It should be clear, from what has been said, that research on the organizational context of formal healthcare endorses Mead's contention that the self is a socially emergent form. This insight also contributed to new ways of thinking about 'health behaviour' during the 1970s as sociologists began to replace the traditional 'medical point of view' on appropriate behaviour (e.g., in help-seeking) with a new concern for social actors who, in health and in illness, 'actively sustain their social world in every moment of their interactions with other people' (Cornwell 1984: 19). Most chronic illness researchers attribute the origins of the field in some way or another to interactionism (see, e.g., Scambler and Scambler 2010), and particularly to the work of Anselm Strauss and colleagues (e.g. Strauss and Glaser 1975). Charmaz, a student of Strauss and one of the most influential researchers in this field, contends that studies of the effects of chronic illness on self and identity are a 'magnifying mirror through which problems of the human condition' can be understood (Charmaz 2010: 9). This is ably demonstrated in the following two research examples (a more detailed review of research on chronic illness can be found in chapter 9).

Kelly depicts the tension between the private, inner self and public identity (or the 'public knowable aspect of the person') in his research on individuals who have undergone an ileostomy (surgical removal of the bowel) (1992: 393). He found that, post-surgery, individuals often experience a changed sense of self and body which impinges persistently on activities of everyday life. There may be a dual sense of a negative change in the body (the surgical stoma) and a positive sense of a self that has survived debilitating illness. But the public perception of ileostomy, which 'carries a freight of more or less socially stigmatised symbols associated with dirt, pollution, loss of control and transgression of body margins' (1992: 391), can mean that the individual wants or feels obliged to present an ordinary 'non-ileostomist version of self' to others (1992: 403). The individual's relative success depends on their ability to manage the body (which may be liable to 'let one down') and anticipate the responses of others. For Kelly, these interactive processes underlie Mead's emphasis on 'the ways in which proffered versions of self require legitimation in the process of identity construction, in order to be sustained' (1992: 410).

In a second example, Klunklin and Greenwood (2006) demonstrate the explanatory power of interactionist principles in an interview-based study of the impact of an HIV/AIDS diagnosis on married and widowed women in rural Northern Thailand. They reveal how self-identity as a person with AIDS and all the personal freight that this carries emerges 'in and through social interactions and is modified as definitions of self, the other, and the situations encountered change' (2006: 33). The analysis shows how the women took on the 'role of the generalised Thai village "other"' (2006: 36). Through this, they not only knew how the disease was designated in their villages – as seriously stigmatizing, lethal and highly contagious – but also how to adjust their behaviours, including 'hiding out' to avoid social contact in order to concur with this designation and hence to protect themselves from discrimination. Amongst other things, this involved 'being clean and covered' by concealing dark skin, lesions, and weight loss and 'always presenting themselves in public as clean' (2006: 38).

Interactionism assessed

Interactionism's status as a loose collection of ideas (Lindesmith and Strauss 1969) has been a cause for critical reflection from within its ranks: is this its strength or its weakness? Yes, it has been the well-spring of a cornucopia of research. But what does this add up to theoretically? For example, although highly appreciative of Goffman's work, Scheff concludes that his writing typically is vague to the point of either having no 'thesis at all or one that is so elliptic as to be virtually useless, if not misleading' (2006: ix). Vannini (2008) worries that interactionism is so highly heterogeneous that it has now blended with qualitative research generally, making it invisible and lacking in all-important theoretical brand recognition.

Researchers following in the interactionist tradition commonly engage with Glaser and Strauss' (1999 [1967]) highly influential 'grounded theory', 'a style of analysing data' that 'involves continuous contact between theorising and data collection' (Strauss 1993: 2). This entails developing theory inductively – or ground up – from qualitative data such as in-depth interviews and/or ethnographic observations (now often termed the 'constant comparative method') (Glaser 1965). This follows Blumer's (1969) injunction that symbolic interactionism is not only a theoretical perspective, but also a method. As Charmaz observes, it should be one of interactionism's major strengths that 'theory and method can combine as an integrated whole' (2008: 51). But, all too often, this does not happen. Thus Blaxter (2002) lamented that qualitative research has become 'routinised' and 'trivialised'. Commenting on her work as a journal editor, she remarked, clearly with some exasperation:

> I mean, if I get one more paper which says, 'I looked at these twelve patients by the principles of grounded theory, and here are some excerpts from these interviews', and 'Aren't these excerpts interesting', and 'Look, they think like this' and, 'Bingo, that's the end of my paper', I shall scream, you know! It should be more rigorous than that . . . Sociology is trying to find out how things work, and why things happen, and there must be a 'why' in there somewhere – a 'why' or a 'how' – and if you take the 'why' and the 'how' out, it's no longer sociology.
>
> (Blaxter 2002)

Blaxter is not alone in her concerns. Back in the mid-1980s, Strauss and colleagues worried that 'much that passes for analysis' in qualitative research 'is relatively low-level description' (1985: 295–6). They opined that many research monographs 'are descriptively dense but alas theoretically thin', generating almost no new concepts. Writing more recently, Charmaz has been equally critical of claims made in the name of grounded theory that are actually 'unanalysed description' (2008: 52). It might be argued, then, that although interactionism appears to be flourishing, at least as discerned by the number of publications in its name, this is in stripped-down form. To pick up on the metaphor of the conceptual treasure trove used earlier, might interactionism more aptly be depicted as a cache raided and squandered?

A second criticism commonly levied at interactionism is its alleged neglect of power and politics, which is often associated with its micro-orientation. In his formulation, Mead depicted social life as cooperative. Subsequently, the interactionist approach has been less concerned to endorse the influence of macro-power structures than to demonstrate the operation of power as situational and contingent, an approach which corresponds with the depiction of individuals as conscious agents shaping the social order through interactive processes. This is most evident in the keenly micro-oriented approaches of ethnomethodology and conversational analysis (CA). The objective of ethnomethodology is to reveal how individuals accomplish everyday activities (Garfinkel 1967). It gained momentum in the health field and beyond with the advent of CA which filtered into medical sociology around the late 1970s, most notably in studies of the asymmetry of power in doctor–patient interaction. More recently, CA has expanded to include the wide range of health professionals and their clients, as well as interaction amongst health professionals themselves in a variety of contexts beyond the consultation room (Pilnick et al. 2009; Ten Have 1995).

The value of CA is its capacity to explore the 'fine-grained organisation of health care' through the 'moment-by-moment production of human social life' (Halkowski and Gill 2010: 213) and to reveal and unpack the fundamentally collaborative and contingent nature of communication (Pilnick et al. 2009). Halkowski and Gill draw attention to two key premises. The first is that conversation is 'irremediably temporal in character' (2010: 222). That is, as it unfolds in the 'flow of time', each action – verbal and/or body movement – shapes what follows, even to the extent of affecting talk as it occurs, such as when the interjection or body movement of one person leads the other to change what they are saying or adjust what they are doing. The second is that conversation is fundamentally social. The purpose is to uncover *what* interactants do and *how* they do it, not *why*. Put another way, the objective is not for sociologists to deploy structural factors such as sexism, racism or other power differentials in the manner of Waitzkin (2000), discussed earlier, to account for what is going on in the consultation, but rather to attend closely to the sequence of talk itself and to how participants themselves accomplish the interaction.

Herein lies the problem for many critics not only of CA but of studies inspired by broader interactionist principles; interactionism pays minimal attention to 'how the larger structural features of . . . society influence and perhaps predetermine the limits of the negotiation under investigation' (Day and Day 1977: 134). Wacquant mounts a stinging critique, likening grounded theory to 'an epistemological fairy tale' distinguished by 'theoretical simple-mindedness' (2002: 1481, 1524). He comes to this conclusion after a detailed review of recently published US urban ethnographies, though his remarks are applicable to other studies, such as those undertaken in medical settings. In Wacquant's analysis, ethnographers conjure up moral tales of their respondents' highly troubled inner-city lives with no reference to the social structural forces such as market deregulation and neoliberal values that put them there in the first place. Ethnographers get so close to their respondents that they end up 'parroting their point of view without linking it to the broader system of material and symbolic relations that give it meaning and significance, reducing sociological analysis to the collection and assembly of folk notions and vocabularies of motive' (Wacquant 2002: 1523).

Waquant's corrective is to appreciate that 'every microcosm presupposes a macrocosm that assigns it its place and boundaries and implies a dense web of social relations beyond the local site' (2002: 1524). But Wacquant's critique is not only unwarranted but unnecessary. Interactionists and fellow travellers have raised similar concerns themselves, though in far less vitriolic terms. Thus, Charmaz (2010: 26) refers to 'relationships between social structure, interaction, self and identity' residing 'in the background of many grounded theory works', including her own. She advises that it is now 'time to bring them into the foreground' – that is, to articulate better and make visible the links between local actions and wider social structures.

Conclusions

In theoretical terms, the sociology of health and medicine has travelled a long way in a relatively short period of time. Its practitioners initially sought authenticity by contesting the biomedical model and founded a distinctly social perspective in its place, though, as we have seen, what the social itself consists of is disputed. As remarked upon in the chapter introduction, theories cease to fit as societies change and new approaches are called for. So it is not surprising that, although the underlying theoretical tones of the political economy and interactionist perspectives can still be heard, they have faded somewhat with time.

Broadly speaking, the sociology of health and medicine has taken four turns since its beginning in the last half of the twentieth century. First, in common with the wider discipline of sociology, it has been brought to task for its focus on social factors to the neglect of biology – or, more accurately, neglect of the interaction between the social and the biological. However, as we will see in chapter 2, it is perfectly positioned to contribute to an embodied sociology. Second, even though 'second-wave' feminism developed at broadly the same time as the sociology of health and medicine, and has been entwined with the theoretical and empirical issues explored in this chapter, the contributions of feminism and of gender theories generally have been insufficiently realized until quite recently. Third, traditionally, sociology has sought to understand societies by reference to social laws, and to reveal social structures which position people and institutions as distinct collectivities, such as social classes or genders. For many, this is now seen as outmoded as we have entered a new 'postmodern', or even 'posthuman', age, characterized not by stable structures which work according to social laws, but by flux, indeterminacy, risk and individualism. Fourth, and to some extent encapsulating these three turns, sociology has been turning away from the study of society towards a focus on the global order. It is to these matters that we turn in chapter 2.

2

Contemporary theories of health and medicine in a changing world

All contemporary sociological theories have in common an attempt to rethink the precepts of the discipline in response to the rapidly changing world around us. Although it is a truism to say that disciplines such as sociology are 'in crisis', since such crises seem to be perpetual (and even part of a discipline's vitality), sociology does appear to have found itself facing a crisis of grander than usual proportions since the closing decades of the twentieth century. There is a growing sense that its common object of enquiry, namely 'society', is no longer relevant. Of course, particular societies still exist, but theorists are seriously questioning whether they are a sensible point of reference if we want to understand life in an increasingly globalized world. When we add to this the feeling that sociology presently lacks the finely-honed conceptual tools necessary for the study of contemporary social lives that are indeterminate, fluid and uncertain, then these appear to be troubling times indeed.

Connell argues that 'special privilege accrues to theory which is so abstracted that its statements seem universally true'. Yet theorists really need to 'wear out shoe leather' by 'linking theory to the ground on which the theorist's boots are planted' (2007: 206). Health and the body are highly fertile ground upon which to set our theoretical feet and cultivate the tools fit for the analysis of life in a globalizing world. Although typically not thought of in this way, globalization's effects are highly embodied (Turner 2004). That is, living in an increasingly mobile and networked world has implications not only for our social actions and personal identities, but also for our bodies and our physical and mental health. The body is a ubiquitous topic of enquiry today, but this was not always the case. As discussed in chapter 1, sociology was founded in the mid nineteenth century to deal with 'social matters' which many theorists conceived as distinct from the biological body. This remained the case for well over a century, to around the late 1980s. Since then we have seen a marked and relatively swift 'biological turn in social thought' (Fuller 2006: 118). Accordingly in this chapter we will consider how the 'body and health' have been theorized. We will begin with Foucault's concept of biopower and the new ways of governing the body which have taken hold in Western societies. Then we will explore health and the body in a 'postmodern world'. Here we will contemplate the postmodernist argument that taken-for-granted dualisms such as able/disabled, healthy/sick, are fabricated by modernist sociology and imposed on what the method of deconstruction reveals to be a more fragile, complex and discursively constructed social world. The chapter concludes with a critical reflection on risk, vulnerability and health within what sociological theorists variously characterize as today's 'postmodern', 'runaway' or 'liquid' social world.

Globalization

In the opinion of Burawoy, 'globalisation is wreaking havoc with sociology's basic unit of analysis – the nation-state' (2005: 6). Majority opinion seems to agree with him. We tend to view society through the lens of a region, where entities such as the state, culture and the economy cluster together with boundaries drawn around them (Urry 2000). This applies to those theories we encountered in chapter 1, such as Parsons' structural functionalism where each society is depicted as a closed self-equilibrating system, and interactionism which sees society as a precarious social order based on the negotiation of social actors in specific spaces. Urry maintains that globalization fractures the bounded metaphor of society in a major way. To remedy the problem, he argues that sociology must turn away from its classic preoccupation with 'stasis, structure and order' towards 'movement, mobility and contingent order' (Urry 2000: 18).

Globalization is a slippery concept. In popular parlance it is often equated with the spread of neoliberal economic policies and with 'Westernization', particularly 'Americanization'. While there are elements of this, globalization has no single logic. In fact, instead of moving in one direction, change is multi-causal and multi-dimensional (Beck 2000). Accordingly, emphasis is placed on the unintended and unanticipated consequences of globalization. In Bauman's depiction, it is uncontrolled, operating in a 'vast – foggy and slushy, impassable and untameable – "no man's land" and stretching beyond the design-and-action capacities of anybody's in particular' (1998: 60). Walby uses the metaphor of the wave to help grasp this non-linear and heterogeneous process. She argues that 'social processes developed in one space and time are disembedded and re-embedded in a new one' (2009: 55): 'a wave starts in one temporal and spatial location, builds rapidly through endogenous processes, and then spreads out through space and time to affect social relations in other locations. These events are connected, but not in a simple deterministic manner, passing through networks and social institutions' (2009: 95).

Consequently, creeping Americanization is a superficial veneer; a more significant effect of globalization is to produce greater cultural diversity at local levels (Giddens 2002) or what has become known as 'glocalization' (local places are changed, not homogenized). Yet, as these theorists argue, although globalization's *effects* may be varied and unpredictable, it does have systematic drivers, such as new information and communication technologies, and discernible features, such as heightened mobility and new forms of connectivity between people, all of which have health implications.

Life and health 'on the move'

Many of us now live in a state of perpetual connectivity and movement. With the 'communications revolution' – comprising digital technology, the Internet, the World Wide Web, mobile devices, and so on – our experience of time has speeded up and become dissociated from physical space. This is conceptualized as 'time-space compression' (Harvey 1989). To give a simple example, the best way to communicate with someone the other side of the world used to be to put pen to paper and write a letter. Our letter would have needed physically to travel over large tracts of land for some time to reach its recipient. Today, an email virtually defies this space as it reaches the receiver almost instantaneously with a click of the mouse or touch on a tablet computer. Thus, the connection between time and space is compressed.

As conveyed by Walby's (2009) image of the wave, the notion of movement, and especially 'flow', is central to ways of thinking about globalization. For example, in his theory of the 'network society', Castells argues that social life is now constructed around 'flows of technology, flows of organisational interaction, flows of images, sounds, and symbols' (2010: 442). These flows are supported by the new electronic networks and they link up to network nodes such as particularly influential global institutions and cities. Similarly, Urry (2000, 2007) refers to 'scapes', 'the network of machines, technologies, organisations, texts' that constitute the various interconnected nodes along which 'flows' of peoples, images, money, waste and so on can be relayed across borders. For example, the health arena consists of an increasingly global and interconnected network of 'scapes' such as medical institutions, health-related businesses (the fitness and diet industries, pharmaceutical companies and so on), health-related media (television programmes, magazines), and online or e-health sites, through which a multitude of information, products and people 'flow'. We are even 'on the move' when anchored to physical space as we surf the World Wide Web for health advice, flit through digital TV channels, and connect as 'complex mobile hybrids' via digital media – i.e. machines – to locales in distant parts of the world, which, since they are only a click or touch away, are also quite literally close to hand (Bauman 1998; Urry 2000: 14).

Many readers of this book will experience globalization as the opening-up of the world through cheaper travel and Internet access. Yet, as Bauman relates, the globalized world is a world of contradictions. On the one hand, there is the globally mobile elite for whom 'space has lost its constraining quality and is easily traversed in both its "real" and "virtual" renditions' (1998: 88). These are the people, referred to in chapter 1, who are able to move around the world in the search for personal well-being, healthcare or even an organ for transplant. Connell and Wood (2005) refer to a 'transnational business masculinity' embodied in businessmen who exert power and travel the globe making lucrative deals. But theirs is not a healthy job: long hours, high stress and frequent air travel all take their toll. Their lives and their bodies become a difficult project to be managed (much as they manage projects in their job) by attention to diet, exercise and so on.

On the other hand, there are people who, for reasons such as war or destitution, have no choice *but* to move and to *keep on* moving since they have no safe place to stay (see also chapter 6). Consequently, many of the world's poor 'travel surreptitiously, often illegally, sometimes paying more for the crowded steerage of a stinking unseaworthy boat than others pay for business-class gilded luxuries' (Bauman 1998: 89). The health consequences are not difficult to discern. For example, in early 2011, over fifty Somalis drowned and died fleeing armed conflict in their homeland when their boat capsized in the perilous waters of the Gulf of Aden. Yet, in an apparent paradox, globalization also makes visible the 'world of the locally tied', whose space is actually closing up (Bauman 1998: 88): those people in wealthy nations who to all intents and purposes are barred from moving for economic and other reasons. They must abide whatever changes are wrought on their local communities, including those inimical to mental and physical health (see also chapter 4), while digital media brandish others journeying seemingly at will. It is for these reasons that Bauman and others argue that mobility has become a very powerful stratifying factor.

Illness as world traveller
As Tim Brown (2011) aptly puts it, illness is a world traveller that does not need a visa. Although the passage of disease between countries is not new – witness the bubonic plague (or 'black death'), which

originated in China and haunted Europe from the mid-1300s up to the mid-1700s – today's global networks are an unprecedented and highly fertile conduit for disease. So significant is this that some identify the spread of disease as a new phase in globalization itself (Turner 2004). Not only have many 'old diseases' like cholera, TB and malaria re-emerged, new diseases have appeared such as HIV/AIDS, vCJD, SARs, Ebola fever and the novel influenza viruses H1N1 ('swine flu') and H5N1 (Avian flu).

Health has swiftly moved from the 'rumblings of "low" politics' towards the 'apex of the international security agenda' (Elbe 2010: 2). In 2001, then-Director General of the World Health Organisation (WHO), Gro Harlem Brundtland, remarked that 'in the modern world, bacteria and viruses travel almost as fast as money. With globalization, a single microbial sea washes all of humankind. There are no health sanctuaries' (Brundtland 2001). Though her tone seems extraordinary, it is not unusual. When she became Director General, Margaret Chan remarked that 'traditional defences at national borders cannot protect against the invasion of a disease or vector ... Vulnerability is universal' (WHO 2007: vi). When we add to this the public statements of US President Clinton in 2000 and Russian President Putin in 2006 that HIV/AIDS represents a threat to national security, we must conclude, along with Brown (2011), that 'threat' and 'vulnerability' are the dominant tropes of today's 'global health'.

The securitization of health

But we need to ask: precisely *who* is reckoned to be a threat and *who* is perceived to be vulnerable? Following Wald (2008), if the way we tell stories about disease circumscribes how we think about global health, then the dominant narrative today is one of dangerous people from dangerous places criss-crossing the world (Brown 2011). Even though 'nation' may no longer be a useful point of reference, it is easily – and often emotively – evoked in public health discourse when the intent is to keep infectious 'outsiders' at bay (Craig 2007). Funding travels towards those illnesses deemed security threats to the West / global North, such as HIV, SARs and Avian flu – in other words, to those diseases most likely to trouble the movement of trade and people to high-income nations. But these are not actually the most prevalent diseases in the world – those are conditions such as malaria, schisto-somiasis and onchocerciasis. Nor are they the most common causes of death – those are preventable maternal and childhood deaths, most frequent in the 'developing world'. Typically, the threat narrative also overlooks global vulnerability to illness through the spread of 'unhealthy lifestyles', such as high-fat diets and tobacco use, which typically travel *from* the wealthier *to* the poorer parts of the world and are associated with rising rates of non-communicable diseases such as cancer and heart disease, often *alongside* high rates of infectious disease (Brown 2011; Cockerham and Cockerham 2010). This observation typically falls into the background in the story of 'global health' told from the 'vantage point' of the West / global North (Brown 2011) where, as the aforementioned remarks of then-Presidents Clinton and Putin demonstrate, health has been brought to the heart of geopolitical discourse. In this context, 'fear of infection' easily morphs 'into fear of (bio)terrorism, and then into a fear of the terrorist Other itself' (Labonté 2008: 469).

Warfare

The concepts of the globalization and securitization of health have helped to bring the consequences of war and terrorism into the purview of the sociology of health where once they were absent (Stacey 2002; Williams 2004). In *Frames of War*, Judith Butler (2010) attests to the shared global condition of the precariousness of life. Yet, as she relates, some lives cannot even be apprehended as injured or lost in war when they 'are not first apprehended as living' (2010: 1). The Western media reports almost daily the names of men and women who have died as the result of terrorism, such as in the events of 9/11, and in present-day zones of war. But around the world others remain unnamed and hence ungrieveable: 'Such populations are "lose-able", or can be forfeited, precisely because they are framed as being already lost or forfeited; they are cast as threats to human life as we know it rather than as living populations in need of protection from illegitimate state violence, famine, or pandemics' (Butler 2010: 31).

We can conclude that increased global connectivity directs our attention to the shared vulnerability and precariousness of lives and health around the world. Yet, as discussed earlier, globalization's effects are both contradictory and unpredictable. Consequently, globalization affects us in very different ways (for a discussion of the complexities of gender and health in a global context, see chapter 3). In other words, mobility stratifies. Often the wealthy Western traveller for whom living now means consuming 'in the instant' is driven by desire, constantly 'on the move' (both literally and figuratively), 'looking for, not-finding-it or more exactly not-finding-it-yet' (Bauman 1998: 83), whether this be pleasure, wealth or health. Meanwhile, others are forced either into mobility or sedentariness in hazardous environments which pose a risk not only to health, but to life itself. The over-arching point then is that globalization is essentially an embodied process. And, because 'normative frameworks establish in advance what kind of life will be a life worth living, what will be a life worth preserving', certain bodies are more precariously positioned than others (Butler 2010: 53). To explore this further, we turn to the work of Foucault, particularly his concept of biopower.

Foucault and biopolitics

Baudrillard notoriously entreated us to *Forget Foucault* (2007 [1977]). Fox's assessment of Foucault leads him to conclude that the translation of his ideas to sociology is 'largely vapid' (1992: 429). Cockerham and Scambler consider poststructuralism a 'dead tradition' (2010: 16), though they concede the value of Foucault's ideas for the exploration of health topics. So should we, then, forget Foucault? To address this, we need to ask what distinguishes the approach that has developed in his name and how it has been employed in health research.

Foucault-inspired sociology of health and medicine makes a distinctive break with the more 'traditional' approaches, such as those discussed in chapter 1, which assume that 'whilst knowledge is socially created there exists an underlying truth, a real external world which remains more or less disguised or more or less understood'. 'Traditional' approaches conceive of individuals as active agents in their own personal and collective history and aim 'to expose the social, technical or ideological interests which distort or contribute to the creation of certain types of knowledge' (Nettleton 1992: 136, 149).

In contrast, Foucault sought 'to create a history of the different modes by which, in our culture, human beings are *made subjects*' (Foucault 1982: 777, my emphasis). In his own words, the subject is 'stripped of its creative role and analysed as a complex and variable function of discourse' (Foucault 1977: 138).

As outlined in figure 2.1, Foucault drew a distinction between 'biopower' and the more traditional 'sovereign power'. While the former is bent on 'generating forces, making them grow, and ordering them', the latter is 'dedicated to impeding them, making them submit, or destroying them'. Sovereign power is possessed by people and typically applied in a top-down manner, whereas biopower power is 'a multiple and mobile field of force relations, wherein far-reaching, but never completely stable, effects of domination are produced' (Foucault 1980: 136, 102). As Turner puts it, for Foucault, 'power is rather like a colour dye diffused through the entire social structure' (1997: xii).

From the 1960s up to his death from AIDS-related illness in 1984, Foucault attempted to write a new history of the subject as

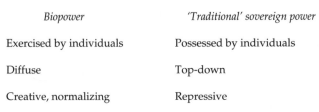

Biopower	*'Traditional' sovereign power*
Exercised by individuals	Possessed by individuals
Diffuse	Top-down
Creative, normalizing	Repressive

Figure 2.1 Conceptualizations of biopower

constituted by disciplinary powers. Contrary to Jewson's (1976) (see chapter 1) argument that knowledge – or in his terminology, different medical cosmologies – developed out of social relations of power between particular social groups (with power shifting from the patient as patron in the late 1700s to medical scientists 100 years later), Foucault's starting point is the configuration of knowledge or *episteme* which constitutes particular subjects during specific historical periods. In *The Birth of the Clinic* (1989 [1963]), he charts the emergence of a new 'clinical gaze'. The key to this change, which took place in late-1700s Europe, was the new-found ability to pinpoint pathology 'in the interior of the body' and to use 'the ever more detailed methods of the [physical] examination to diagnose it' (Armstrong 1983: 2). This shift took place during a period of industrialization, population growth and urbanization. Old forms of control fell away to be superseded by a new kind of governance based upon monitoring of the body, or what Foucault called biopolitics. People were now to be counted and surveyed and new forms of expert knowledge emerged – such as sanitary science, the study of crime and its punishment, and medicine – which all aimed to predict and control populations.

In *Discipline and Punish* (1979), Foucault begins with a description of the torture and public execution of a regicide (killer of a monarch) in 1757 and proceeds to chart the vast changes that took place in Europe over the next eighty-year period. In feudal times, it was practicable to punish only a few wrongdoers as spectacles to discourage the misdemeanours of others. Over the course of the eighteenth century, and with the rise of a larger and more mobile population, this was no longer an effective deterrent. While this kind of sovereign power did not disappear, it became subordinated to the new biopower. This was epitomized by Bentham's Panopticon, a circular building built around a central tower. In this architectural form, prison inmates could not know whether they were being observed from the central tower or not and, consequently, began to police their own behaviour. He argued that whatever part of social life they target, these productive and diffused regimes of individual 'responsibilization' exert a new and unprecedented kind of power upon modern individuals, a form of power potentially more repressive than any that went before. Now there is:

> no need for arms, physical violence, material constraints. Just a gaze. An inspecting gaze, a gaze which each individual under its weight will end by interiorising to the point that he [*sic*] is his own overseer, each individual thus exercising this surveillance over, and against, himself. A superb formula: power exercised continuously and for what turns out to be a minimal cost.
>
> (Foucault 1980: 155)

Here, power operates less through the actions of individuals and social groups and more through norms and technologies which shape the mind and body. So, as Mol points out, while Parsons' doctors exert social control (see chapter 1), Foucault's doctors 'neither oblige people to stay in bed and get better nor to get up and go to work again, instead, they set the standards of normality' (2007: 57). The corollary of this is that, rather than proposing an 'alternative' social model of healthcare to challenge the negative effects of medical dominance, sociologists should seek to understand (and possibly critique) how the power of medicine itself incites the patient to speak *with* the physician in a partnership which emphasizes the social nature of disease (Arney and Bergen 1984; Jones and Porter 1998).

The operation of biopower

The 'obesity epidemic'

For Foucault, biopower operates less by *exclusion and repression* and more by *inclusion and normalization*. The 'obesity epidemic' provides a good illustration of this. In many countries public health is now more about fostering a broader societal ethics of personal responsibility than about health professionals directly instructing people how to 'keep healthy'. Reality television has become a vehicle for this. For example, the programmes of UK celebrity chef Jamie Oliver function like a Panopticon, 'a model of surveillance in which Oliver becomes an omnipresent guard, policing people's everyday lifestyles' (Warin 2011: 28). In the series *Ministry of Food*, Oliver visited Rotherham, a town in one of the most highly deprived areas of England, and tried to teach the inhabitants how to cook and 'eat healthily'. But Warin argues that local people were not really the prime targets here – rather, this and kindred TV spectacles are 'governing at a distance' (2011: 37). This discursive power is productive as people are encouraged to opt into Oliver's mission to improve the health of the nation by improving their own diets. Left out of the frame is any real appreciation that one's ability to adopt a 'healthy diet' is heavily influenced by factors such as socio-economic deprivation (Warin 2011; see also chapter 4 and chapter 9).

According to his website, Jamie Oliver's food programmes are broadcast to forty countries around the world. Here and elsewhere, diet and obesity are represented as global concerns. The WHO (2004b) 'global strategy' on diet and physical exercise emphasizes population monitoring and highlights global connectivity, especially the networks of international bodies, civil society and private organizations (e.g., the food industry) needed to deal with the problem. So while, as far as I am aware, Foucault himself did not write about obesity and largely confined his work to the European context, in principle there is no reason why biopower cannot be conceived of as global in form.

The securitization of AIDS

To give another example, Elbe argues that the securitization of AIDS 'turns international security into a site for the global dissemination of a [Western] biopolitical economy of power' (2005: 405). He discusses the heightening of AIDS surveillance through the sophisticated population monitoring and data collection tools used by global institutions such as the Joint United Nations Programme on HIV/AIDS (UNAIDS). While monitoring activities like these highlight the need for humanitarian responses, such as investment in prevention and healthcare, Elbe maintains that bringing the biological characteristics of a population constantly to light pits the 'healthy (normal)' and the 'unhealthy (abnormal)' against each other and has the potential to position the latter as a sap on the strength and vitality of the former. The negative repercussions could range from extremes such as letting infected populations die, to inadvertently directing scarce resources such as illness prevention campaigns and anti-retroviral therapy (ART) to valued social groups (such as the military). Although Elbe himself does not make this point, the securitization of AIDS might also serve to normalize – that is, make acceptable – the forced sedentariness of HIV-positive populations, thus enhancing the global mobility-based stratification referred to earlier.

The overall point, then, is that, from a Foucauldian perspective, agencies like UNAIDS and WHO do not exercise *repressive* power in dealing with matters such as global HIV/AIDS and obesity – rather, their power is *productive*, monitoring and encouraging bodies to act in certain ways. But, more generally, if (i) power is ubiquitous and diffuse, operating in a capillary manner throughout a society (and, increasingly, globally), and (ii) people are not dupes, then how do they *resist* the effects of biopower? In his final work, the last two volumes in the trilogy *The History of Sexuality* entitled *The Use of Pleasure* (1985) and *The Care of the Self* (1986), Foucault argued that biopower provokes forms of opposition. He became concerned with how individuals fashion their own existence through what he called 'technologies of the self', which 'permit individuals to effect by their own means or with the help of others a certain number of operations on their own bodies and souls, thoughts, conduct and way of being, so as to transform themselves in order to attain a certain state of happiness' (Foucault 1988: 18).

Through self-stylization, such as new bodily expressions, gender displays, 'ethnic identities' and so on, individuals explore the boundaries of their self-identity and engage in an endless task of self-transformation. But McNay (1992) argues that, ultimately, the self then becomes an isolated work of art abstracted from wider political and economic structures, which is far from where Foucault wanted to end up. He was highly critical of the 'cult of the self', yet, in an attempt to 'block the institutional regulation of individuality' (or 'techniques of domination'), he slides into a position which stresses the self-absorbed behaviour of individuals, unable to explain how they may be called out of 'a politics of introversion' (McNay 1992: 178, 191) – in other words, how they might resist.

Should we then 'forget Foucault'? The insights of those who have engaged with Foucauldian ideas, particularly his concept of biopolitics, suggest not. Yet, although Foucault-inspired studies have illustrated how the body is inscribed by power relations, they are 'silent about how the body could be a source of the social, and about the "lived experience" of embodied action' (Shilling 2005: 17). As we are going to turn next to 'the body', we will keep our assessment of Foucault open for now.

The body and the 'lived experience' of health and illness

In Western social thought, body and mind are placed in opposition. Greek philosopher Plato (429–347 BC) described the body thus:

> a source of countless distractions by reason of the mere requirement of food ... liable also to diseases which overtake and impede us in the pursuit of truth; it fills us full of loves, and lusts, and fears, and fancies of all kinds, and endless foolery, and in the very truth, as men say, takes away from us the power of thinking at all.
>
> (Plato quoted in Bordo 1993: 145)

Seventeenth-century philosopher René Descartes maintained that 'my mind, by which I am what I am, is entirely and truly distinct from my body, and may exist without it'. Ergo his now infamous dictum; 'I think, therefore I am' (Descartes 2008 [1637]: 115). On the surface, this seems far-fetched, but his intent was to convey that our bodies are not a constant presence; they change, as we age, lose parts to injury, and so on. Thus, who we *are as a person* is essentially separate from the body. In what became known as Cartesian mind–body dualism, the mind was elevated and the body relegated to the status of mere matter. This cast a very long shadow over Western thought, including the new mid-nineteenth-century discipline of sociology.

The classical sociologists wanted to establish a new discipline distinct from psychology and biology. Perhaps the clearest illustration of this is Durkheim's (1895) identification of sociology's subject matter as 'social facts'. Yet today's commentators point to a 'hidden history' of biology and the body in the classics (see, for instance, Fuller 2006). For example, Marx was highly concerned with capitalism's effects on the worker's body, and in his study of religion Durkheim explored the embodied nature of ritual. But the way we comprehend classical sociology depends on whom we include in the canon. Harriet Martineau

(1802–76) (Martineau 2003 [1844]), 1861) and Charlotte Perkins Gilman (1860–1935) (Gilman 1996 [1898]) – both celebrated sociologists in their own time – paid quite sophisticated attention to the body in their study of society, particularly in relation to women's inequality. Yet this has been written out of history by the casting of male theorists, such as Marx, Durkheim and Weber, as the key players in the founding drama that became sociology (Annandale 2007, 2009; see also chapter 3).

At the time of writing the first edition of this book in the late 1990s, there was a sense of excitement that the then quite new field of the 'sociology of the body' was poised to deliver a newly *embodied* under-standing of social life. In the words of one of the field's prime movers, there has been a 'breath-taking explosion' of interest over the years (Shilling 2005: 1). Even Parsons' work, – which, as we saw in chapter 1, is conventionally regarded as having led sociology towards a dis-tinctly *social* approach towards health and illness – has recently been mined for insights into embodied experience. Towards the end of his life, Parsons (1978: 80) wrote of health as an endowment which lies between the 'intra-organic level' (such as hormones and enzymes) and the 'action level' of society (such as power and language).

As it has grown, the sociology of the body has tumbled into a mul-titude of specific empirical study areas. And so there is not *a* sociology of the body, but rather a 'bewildering array of sociolog*ies* of the body' (Waskul and Vannini 2006: 2). There is a palpable frustration from com-mentators who observe that the body is now everywhere but remains enigmatic and elusive, slip-sliding into view in a variety of guises (Shilling 2005; Williams 2006): the consuming body, the sporting body, the medicalized body, the dying body, and so on. And so the question lingers: just what *is* the body in sociological thought? To address this, we turn to the concepts of embodiment and the 'lived body'.

Embodiment and the 'lived body'

Predating the present-day 'sociology of the body', philosopher Merleau-Ponty (1908–61) emphasized the irreducible fusion of mind and body. He wrote that 'the vision of soul and body is not an amal-gamation between two mutually external terms, subject and object, brought about by arbitrary decree. It is enacted at every instant in the movement of existence' (1962: 88–9). Cartesian mind–body dualism made this difficult to realize in Western thought, but it is unexceptional in many other cultures. For example, Bastien (1985) shows how the Qollahuaya Andeans of Bolivia look to the mountains (or *ayllu*) around them to understand the physiology of their bodies. They project the *ayllu* onto the body using topographical place names that correspond to different levels/parts of the body. Thus, the upper level of the moun-tain has an *uma* (head), *nawi* (eyes) and *wayra* (mouth). The central level has a *sixa* (stomach) and *sono* (heart) and the lower level *chaqis* (legs) and *sillus* (toenails). As one informant explained, 'I am the same as the mountain, Pachamama. Pachamama has fluids which flow through her, and I have fluids which flow through me. Pachamama takes care of my body, and I must give food and drink to Pachamama' (Bastien 1985: 597). So the mountain and bodies have analogous qualities. Sickness 'is a disintegration of the human body similar to the landslide on the mountain and health is restored by feeding the complete mountain', for example, giving coca, blood and fat to its earth shrines. Mind and body are one, 'the body includes the inner self, and experiences are not dualistically conceived' (Bastien 1985: 598).

Although the cultural context is different, theorists have tried to explain how Western experience is also lived through the body's habitual relation to the world. As Leder puts it, 'Just as our physical structure lays the groundwork for our mode of being-in-the-world, so our interactions with this world fold back to reshape our body in ways conducive to health and illness. A medicine of the lived body dwells in this intertwining' (Leder 1998: 125). The concept of the 'lived body' therefore conveys that bodies are *both* biological *and* social. Our bodies have an 'organic facticity', being made up of entities such as genes, blood and bones (Shilling 2005: 198). But we are also possessed of feelings and consciousness which enable us to intervene and make a difference to our environments. These emotions are channelled by and endowed with meaning through culture, but they are seated in the body (Turner and Stets 2005; Turner 2009). And so, as Burkitt asks, 'would we say that we had experienced fear if our hearts did not race and our palms sweat'? Could we be depressed 'without the feeling of physical drag, of everything being just too much trouble to bother about?' (1999: 116). Thinking about the 'lived body' in this way departs from Foucault, for whom, notwithstanding his interest in biopolitics, the body is elusive (Crossley 1996). For, as Shilling (2005) argues, despite drawing our attention to the plasticity of the body, Foucault seems not to accept that this very plasticity has a biological basis that is irreducible to the social. Instead, he construes the body as a product of various social discourses. The disembodied nature of his theory undoubtedly contributes to the 'culturally dopey image of agents' that can be found in his work (Crossley 2006b: 31).

The body expresses emotions formed through our social interactions with others through neuro-hormonal or musculo-skeletal changes which may affect blood pressure or cholesterol levels and develop into conditions such as heart disease or mental illness (Freund 1990). This is how society gets represented in the body; social structures get under our skins. In chapter 1, we discussed the interactionist argument that we become aware of our body and our self through the eyes of others. We become an object for ourselves, as we are for others, because we assume the role of the other (Crossley 2006a). This enables us to perceive ourselves, communicate with ourselves, and act towards ourselves. In so doing, we become objects of our own actions. Charmaz and Rosenfeld detail this in their consideration of chronic illness. They extend the notion of the looking-glass self, or the imagined embodied self in action, to encompass the 'looking-glass body'. The looking-glass body is not only about 'appearances and information control *about* the body', it is also about 'experiences *of* the body and those emanating *from* it' (2006: 38, emphases original).

It has been emphasized in this chapter that present-day analyses of health and illness need to be situated within an intensifying global connectivity. If, as Burawoy (2005), Urry (2000) and others maintain, sociology's point of reference is no longer society, then we should perhaps ask: is the body also now 'postsocietal'? Of course, much like individual societies, the individual body still exists. But, similarly, is it a sensible point of reference for the analysis of health in an ever more globalized world? Whether it is the unusual and extraordinary circumstances of organ procurement or the increasingly ordinary and routine use of global ICT networks, it seems that our health-related experiences and our bodies are formed as much by global, as by national and local, contexts. Formerly envisaged as natural, given and unalterable, many now argue that the body has become a flexible 'project' and the central point of reference in the formation of identity in a 'postmodern' world.

Health in a 'postmodern' world

The terms 'postmodernity' or 'postmodern society' denote a new epoch of history, while 'postmodernism' refers to a new way of 'thinking, feeling and seeing the world' (Clarke 2006: 110).

Postmodernism

Similar to the other theoretical approaches considered here and in chapter 1, postmodernism is not a unitary body of thought, but its different forms do have some shared suppositions. Postmodernists are critical of grand narratives of social progress, such as those of Marx, which position individuals and groups as agents of social change. They seek to uncover how such narratives, and modernist reasoning in general, are highly dependent on binary either/or thinking (Lyotard 1984). For example, we routinely divide the world into men and women (or males and females) and not only start from the premise that men have more in common with each other than they have with women (and vice versa) but assume there is an inherent opposition between the two. The problem is that this 'creates a false appearance of unity by reducing the flux and heterogeneity of experience into supposedly natural or essentialist [i.e. fixed] oppositions' (Flax 1990: 36).

Shildrick argues that modernist thinking constructs 'an inviolable self/body that is secure, distinct, closed, and autonomous' (2002: 51). Thus, while phenomenological accounts (such as that of Merleau-Ponty) appreciate that the 'lived body' is often an absent body in the sense that it is only when illness or disability strikes that the body is felt, or its 'comfortable absence' lost, this in itself betrays an assumption that the integrated and fully functioning body is the implicit standard of phenomenology; any deviations are 'from a singular mode' rather than 'equally valid alternatives' (Shildrick 2002: 49). For Shildrick, the social model of disability, which maintains that if social and political structures were different then disability would lose its negative status, is misguided because it assumes that there are two distinct ways of being in the world – i.e., it rests on the binaries of having / not having and of inclusion/exclusion. She argues that the postmodern theorist's objective should be to lay bare the kind of thinking that maintains this problematic either/or distinction, not to accommodate *to it* by favouring one side (the social) over the other (the biomedical).

Critiquing binary thinking entails the method of deconstruction, which derives from the work of Derrida (see, e.g., Derrida 1982). It comprises:

(1) looking at an imputed opposition (able-bodied/disabled, for example);
(2) showing that the dominant privileged position (able-bodied) is created out of a contrast with the oppressed position (disabled) – that is, we can only conceive of able-bodiedness by conceiving of what it is not: disability;
(3) and, by this method, revealing that what appear to be binary opposites actually are interdependent (since they derive their meaning from an established contrast).

Thus, the elements in binaries always contain traces of their constructed opposites, or what Derrida (1982) called 'différance'. For postmodernists, this is a vital tool with which to challenge existing social arrangements. For example, Shildrick argues that the reason bodily difference is unsettling is 'because it speaks not to an absolute difference between those who are and those who are not disabled, but rather to a deeply disconcerting intimation of commonality' (2009: 3). When the 'monstrous body' – 'hybrid creatures, conjoined twins, human clones, cyborg embodiment and others' – can be made 'other', or 'not me', it poses few problems. But when it begins to resemble us, 'it becomes deeply disturbing' (Shildrick 2002: 2, 3). We are perturbed by the monster because, at the same time as it confirms the normalcy of the enclosed self, it unsettles it by being all too human. The divisions of body and self and other are therefore always under pressure from the liminality of the monster. And this makes us feel persistently vulnerable. To bolster our felt security, we hold others responsible for their illnesses – 'he shouldn't have smoked', 'she shouldn't have driven too fast' – and try to manage our bodies so that they remain 'clean and proper' and on the right side of the problematic border. This is why 'noses are reshaped, warts removed, prosthetic limbs fitted' (Shildrick 2002: 55) – in other words, normalized (see also the discussion of obesity in chapter 9).

Shildrick maintains that once we realize that disability is unsettling precisely because it does not speak to absolute difference, we will recognize that 'it is not simply that some exceptional – paradigmatically disabled – bodies fall short of the normative standards, but that embodiment in general is disordered and uncertain' (2009: 173). The fruitless struggle to secure our existence will then give way to the acceptance of vulnerability and corporeal variety as part of the human condition. Shildrick's (2002, 2009) analysis is illustrative of postmodernist analyses of the contemporary social world. They seek to show that the binary thinking that characterizes modernist theory is politically problematic and that this has blinded us to the heterogeneity and plurality that now characterize 'postmodern' existence (for a discussion of postmodernism and gender, see chapter 3).

Postmodern society and the global 'posthuman' body

What does it mean to say that we are living in a postmodern world? Theorists broadly agree that the sureties of the modern era, such as class positions and gendered and racial divides, have been fractured by the intensive individualism which has accompanied sweeping socio-economic changes in the West (and to some extent globally) since around the 1970s. Referring back to the earlier discussion of health and life 'on the move', ideas about health and the body circulate and transmute as they are transported by the scapes and flows of globalization (Urry 2000: 208). Stacey (2000) links the Western preoccupation with managing the healthy body to global uncertainties. In global journeys to 'find oneself' and in self-help books, individuals from the global North 'are offered hope for a healthier future through a borrowing of beliefs and practices about disease and healing from non-western cultures', in a kind of 'return to nature' (2000: 199). At the same time, global brands such as Coca-Cola, McDonald's, and tobacco companies spread the value systems, cultural identities and aspirations of the global North to the global South (Lee 2005).

Baudrillard, dubbed by Best and Kellner (1991: 111) the 'high priest' of postmodernity, argues that in the shift from a period of modernity dominated by industrial production to a high-technology postmodern world, we enter an era of 'hyper-reality'. Individuals are no longer citizens, but consumers. Under such conditions, there are no stable structures (class, 'race', gender); power is totally dispersed, too dispersed to struggle against. This is why, as mentioned earlier, he advises us to 'forget Foucault' whose argument that power is mobilized through localized discourses fails, in his view, to appreciate that power is, in effect, *dead*, totally dispersed in the implosion of boundaries between the real and the illusory (Baudrillard 2007 [1977]). We are drawn into a simulated form of reality whereby the space between the 'original' object (or signifier) and its 'simulacra' (or signified) crumbles. An example provided by Baudrillard (2009) is the loss (or liberation) of the 'photographic act' in the digital image as the boundary between image and reality evaporates. Applied to the realm of health, we might say that actors who play doctors on television appear more credible to us than our local healthcare practitioners (with whom we are likely to have far less 'contact').

But it is not only that the boundary between image and reality is dissolved, but that the simulated real becomes more real than the 'real'. For example, those in the global North become inured to the 'reality' of ill-health and starvation in war-torn nations. It passes us by; we 'know' about it from digital media feeds, but, living under conditions in which we are bombarded with information, we are unable to take it in. And so we come to accept violence and starvation; for us, it is 'just an image'.

Baudrillard argues that humans are already part of an artificial survival, leaving behind only the trace of the real as a spectral reminder, 'a bit like Lewis Carroll's Cheshire Cat, whose grin still hovers in the air after the rest of him has vanished' (2009: 25). Following Baudrillard, Frank (1992) contends that medicine now deals not with sensual bodies, but simulacra or images of bodies. The traditional doctor's round takes on a new hue:

> It is less for [the physician] to see the patient, than for both patient and physician to assure themselves that the other is still there, each a nostalgic token of the other's productive desire. Real diagnosis takes place away from the patient; bedside is secondary to screen. For diagnosis and even treatment purposes, the image on the screen becomes the 'true' patient, of which the bedridden body is an imperfect replicant, less worthy of attention.
>
> (Frank 1992: 83)

Images of the body displayed on screens are more real than the patient's actual body which is displaced by digital output of angiograms and ultrasounds, CAT scans, graphs showing blood cell counts and serum levels. When, as a patient, he is asked how he feels, Frank writes, 'it is to these that I refer and which refer to me. In the medical simulacrum, I lose myself in my image . . . Hospitalised, I respond to those who ask me how I feel: I do not know how I feel; the tests are not yet back' (1992: 87, 86). Under the sway of medical simulacra, the subjectivity of the doctor disappears alongside that of the patient. No longer productive but transductive, the doctor is merely part of a network of images.

Traditionally, sociology has juxtaposed society and nature in the sense that humans have been set apart from and controlled nature (e.g. Durkheim 1895). But this is no longer sustainable because today's environment is not 'natural', but 'a hybrid, a simultaneous fusion of the physical and the social' (Urry 2000: 210). The rather haunting concept of the 'posthuman', which arises from this milieu, has become a vital part of discussions of health and the body in postmodernity. The most immediately obvious meaning of posthuman is that new information and communication technologies and developments such as bio-engineered prosthetics and nanotechnology are eroding the divide between 'natural and "human-made" phenomena' (Pepperell 2003: 161). This is the notion of the cyborg, described by Haraway (1991) as a leaky figure at the interface of nature/culture and human/machine (for a discussion of cyborg reproduction, see chapter 3). But the posthuman means more than this: it challenges the whole idea of 'human essence' (Toffoletti 2007). Foucault's biopolitics is related to humans and to populations, and agency is attributed to human beings alone; in other words, his theory is anthropocentric. It is also premised on the notion of a 'closed and delimited body' (Lemke 2011: 94). The posthuman form – cyborg, transplant and engineered bodies – therefore clashes with the theoretical approaches of the seemingly ill-matched Foucault and Merleau-Ponty alike, since it places a big question mark over the 'ontological and organic integrity' of humans (Waldby 2000: 44), and with it modernist notions of the body in the thrall of the subject.

Health, risk and vulnerability

The picture developed so far in this chapter is of social lives deeply affected by fast-paced global social change. While some theorists embrace the idea of a *post*modern social world that is presented as a radical break with what has gone before, others are more comfortable to think in terms of a 'new' or 'second' phase of modernity. Thus Beck (1999: 2) refers to a 'first' or 'nation-state modernity' typified by 'collective patterns of life, progress and controllability, full employment and exploitation of nature', and to a 'second modernity' or 'world risk society'. Bauman (2000, 2005, 2007) depicts societies as moving from a 'solid' to a 'liquid' phase of modernity. In Giddens' (2002) assessment, we are living in a 'runaway world'.

The idea of 'liquid' or 'runaway' times brings us back to issues raised at the start of this chapter – namely, the uncontainable nature of globalization and its impact on individual lives and health around the globe. Nomenclature aside, these theorists all agree that this propels risk to the heart of contemporary social life. In his highly influential theory of 'risk society', Beck (1999) highlights the 'globality of risk'. The political economy of health-related risks, such as the health consequences of new migration flows and the search for new markets by global capitalism, were raised in chapter 1. Here we consider another dimension: what the qualitatively new experience of living in a 'risk society' means for health and illness.

While it may seem that risk has always been a feature of life, risk theorists insist that today's risks are qualitatively different from those of the past. Giddens, for example, draws a distinction between two types of risk: external risks which emanate from outside, such as earthquakes, and manufactured risks which arise from our actions on the world, such as global warming. Our age is no more dangerous or more risky than the past, 'but the balance of risks and dangers has shifted. We live in a world where hazards created by ourselves are as, or more, threatening than those that come from outside' (Giddens 2002: 34).

Bauman detects a powerful *ambient fear* born of deregulation of the Western state and individualization. The rolling-back of the state and its protection leaves individuals open to 'vexing volatile and constantly changing circumstances', so much so that fear has 'settled inside, saturating our daily routines' (Bauman 2007: 94, 9). Beck and Beck-Gernsheim identify 'a social impetus towards individualisation of unprecedented scale and dynamism' since the end of the mid twentieth century, which 'forces people – for the sake of their survival – to make themselves the centre of their own life plans and conduct' (2002: 31). Lacking the time and critical space for the necessary reflection to construct linear and narrative biographies, we forge alliances, make deals, but essentially face our troubles alone. If this is the case, then it is hardly surprising that the body becomes a perpetual source of anxiety and vulnerability. Since we cannot control the wider pace of change, we try to control what we can in our individual lives and become 'engrossed in spying out the "seven signs of cancer" or the "five symptoms of depression", or in exorcising the spectre of high blood pressure, a high cholesterol level, stress or obesity' (Bauman 2007: 11). In other words, such actions are substitutes for our wider fears. A vicious circle is produced whereby the more we attend to such matters, the more fear we generate for ourselves. Risk is not only uncontainable, it is self-generating. The result, according to Bauman, is 'harrowing varieties of psychological trauma' such as anorexia and bulimia. With particular reference to the US, he argues that 'more than any other phenomenon, fat encapsulates, condenses and blends the fears emanating from the poorly mapped "frontier-land" stretching between the body of the consumer and the outside world, crowded with incapacitating dangers while simultaneously filled to the brim with irresistible temptations' (Bauman 2005: 96).

Health risks seem to have no end. Risks of contaminated foods, mysterious viral infections, and the stresses and strains of insecure jobs, unemployment and unhappy marriages must be dealt with reflexively as individuals stand alone, looking for security in the face of uncertainty and the implosion of often conflicting information. For example, Katz Rothman's (1988) study of prenatal diagnosis vividly demonstrates the stresses that women experience in a social climate that values knowledge and making informed choices. Women's reasons for refusing amniocentesis (taking amniotic fluid from the uterus to test for genetic abnormalities) – such as a commitment to the foetus/baby, feelings of safety (will the baby be 'normal'?), a sense of fate, or the unacceptability of abortion – are difficult to justify in a world which values the information and 'choice' that an amniocentesis result ostensibly provides. She shows that, far from providing choice and control, amniocentesis creates a 'tentative pregnancy'; fearful of a 'bad result', women cannot embrace their pregnancy, and maintain an emotional distance from the baby/foetus and deny or do not let themselves really feel foetal movements until the test result is available (see also discussion of proto-patienthood in chapter 9).

An illustration: cosmetic breast implants

But dreaming of 'a reliable world, one we can trust' (Bauman 2005: 95) can also mean overlooking risks or casting them aside when arguably they are pertinent. Cosmetic breast implants provide an illustration of this. In 2011, there were 316,848 cosmetic surgery procedures in the US alone, an increase of over 200 per cent from 101,176 in 1997 (American Society for Aesthetic and Plastic Surgery 2012). Surgical procedures like breast augmentation, liposuction and abdominoplasty ('tummy tucks'), as well as non-surgical procedures such as Botox and skin resurfacing, are becoming more and more popular and normalized. For example, Sanchez-Taylor (2011) reports that most of the young British women she studied 'approached cosmetic surgery as consumers, buying teeth from Hungary and breasts from Belgium in a pick-and-mix fashion, searching for bargains in the same way they might when putting together an outfit from the high street'. Any risks to their health were hardly considered. Likewise, for respondents in Fowler's (2009) study of young US women given breast implants as a graduation present, despite their awareness that having implants at an early age would inevitably mean that they would be subject to future surgeries because implants are bound to break, health risks were the least of their concerns,.

Silicone breast implants and their safety have been a source of dispute since the 1970s. Notably, in the 1980s, US multinational company Dow Corning made a multi-million-dollar settlement on a class-action law suit which maintained that its silicone implants caused systemic health problems, such as autoimmune diseases like rheumatoid arthritis and lupus. During 2011 and 2012, controversy raged in Europe over the use of cheap industrial-grade, rather than medical-grade, silicone gel in implants manufactured by the French company Poly Implant Prothèse (PIP), which have been found to have a much higher rupture rate, by a factor of 2–6, compared to other implants. Women in the UK have been advised that, even though the implants are substandard, since there is no evidence of significant risk to health there is no necessity to have them removed unless they have adverse symptoms (Department of Health 2012a). Unwilling to take what they see as a risk to their health, many women with PIP implants have disagreed and have sought to have them removed within the National Health Service (NHS). Given that the majority of implant surgeries took place in the private sector, opinion has been divided on whether the NHS should provide surgery to remove the implants even if medically necessary with many amongst the public arguing that the NHS should not foot the bill for care.

In spite of such scandals, people appear to view cosmetic surgery in general as low-risk and painless (Zuckerman 2010). This seems at odds with the proclamations of Beck, Bauman and others that fears over risks to health are an ever-present feature of our lives. Consent procedures require surgeons to inform their patients about the potential risks of any surgery, but this seems to be easily outweighed by the routinization of cosmetic surgery, its casting as a regular part of consumer behaviour, and its strong association with 'fitness' and success. A glance at hospital cosmetic surgery websites reveals images of young, smiling people. In the manner of Internet holiday offers, in the Summer of 2013 The UK Hospital Group website was offering 'late space availability' with £400 off their procedures. The perceived risk of *not* having surgery – looking 'old' or 'ugly', or failing to take control of one's body and hence life as a whole – is then perhaps felt to be far worse than pain or the possibility of future health risks.

The risk-society thesis assessed

The self-evident ring of truth around the risk-society thesis has protected it from major critique until fairly recently. In his appraisal, Wilkinson draws a distinction between risk as a social dynamic, or trend of our times, and risk as a way in which individuals 'perceive and respond to a host of hazards and conditions of threatening uncertainty' (2010: 8). He argues that it is the former that most interests risk theorists such as Beck. But when we look closely at the latter, theories of risk and uncertainty can seem like castles in the air. He is one of a number of commentators, such as Mythen (2008), who propose that risk research should pay much closer attention to how risk consciousness 'might be shaped, modified, amplified or attenuated within the social dynamics of day-to-day life' (Wilkinson 2010: 61). Yet he reasons that, when researchers do this, they often adopt a technocratic brand of sociology. He particularly calls to account studies of discrepancies between lay and expert views of risk, such as those of patients and doctors, in this regard. Commonly, sociologists are critical of medical professional approaches to risk and seek to show how paying attention to patients' accounts, which are often grounded in the 'lived reality' of social relations rather than technical or probabilistic risk assessments, will promote better healthcare. Wilkinson's concern is that this sidesteps wider matters of power and inequality and promotes the institutional status quo.

Even more critical questions can be raised about the risk perspective. If we – as sociologists and as members of society – become preoccupied with identifying and avoiding risk, we at best overlook, and at worst deny, that vulnerability is part of the human condition. Butler reminds us of the precariousness of life and the inherent vulnerability of the body. In her evaluation, vulnerability implies living socially, recognizing 'the fact that one's life is always in some sense in the hands of the other' (2010: 14). As addressed earlier in this chapter, she contends that to deny this is to consent to the belief that some lives are ungrieveable and hence dispensable, such as in times of conflict and war. Similarly, in Kleinman's assessment, our present-day failure to acknowledge human vulnerability provokes us to act in ways inimical to well-being, which includes the medicalization of human problems. He argues that 'ordinary unhappiness and normal bereavement has been transformed into clinical depression, existential angst turned into anxiety disorders, and the moral consequences of political violence recast as post-traumatic stress disorder' (Kleinman 2006: 9). Furedi (2002: 5) takes a step farther and contends that 'by turning risk into an autonomous, omnipresent force . . . we transform every human experience into a safety situation..' The result, he opines, is passive living and the dissipation of human potential (for a more detailed discussion of medicalization, see chapter 9).

Conclusions

This chapter began by drawing attention to the challenges facing present-day sociological theory. It has been proposed throughout that matters of health, illness and the body are an ideal conduit for the development of sociological theory fit for the twenty-first century.

Increased global connectivity directs our attention to the shared vulnerability and precariousness of lives and health around the world. We have explored many examples of this, from the relationship between new mobilities and health, to the securitization of health, the governance of the body, disability and the 'posthuman' body. A range of theoretical perspectives have been brought to bear on these issues, many of which are revisited in the chapters to come. The established positions of interactionism and political economy retain a firm foothold in the sociology of health and medicine, but increasingly they stand side-by-side with research influenced by Foucauldian social constructionism, postmodernism and theories of liquid modernity and the network society. Additional and influential parts of the mix not yet addressed are feminist and gender theories. These are the subject of the next chapter.

3

Feminism, gender theories and health

Chapters 1 and 2 have explored the historical coming-together of the sociology of health and medicine and the wider discipline of sociology. This chapter continues this theme, concentrating on feminist and gender theories. We will trace the evolution of feminist theories from their eighteenth- and nineteenth-century beginnings through to the ground-breaking work of 'second-wave' liberal and radical feminists from the 1970s onwards. By the mid-1990s, second-wave feminism had begun to seem increasingly out-of-step with gender-related changes taking place in many societies. Most conspicuously, critics became concerned that the focus on social and/or biological difference between men and women was not only outmoded but theoretically and politically problematic. Postmodernists and others instead proposed that both biological sex *and* social gender are multiple and malleable. 'Postfeminist' and third-wave theorists also began to challenge the apparent constrictions of earlier feminist generations. When we add to this the gathering momentum of men's health activism and academic research, the result is a present-day bubbling cauldron of debate over how best to theorize the relationship between gender and all manner of health matters.

Feminist foundations

Although the word 'feminism' was not coined until the 1890s, women were voicing what we would now regard as feminist ideas about health well before this time. In the closing decade of the eighteenth century, Mary Wollstonecraft (often dubbed the 'first feminist') exhorted girls not to undermine their health with mistaken ideals of female beauty and manners; we would hear nothing of women's frailty, she wrote, 'if girls were allowed to take sufficient exercise, and not confined in close rooms till their muscles are relaxed and their digestion destroyed'. She urged the middle-class women of her time, who were induced to 'feign a sickly delicacy' to ensure their husband's affections, to rethink their way of life to save their health (Wollstonecraft 1992 [1792]: 154, 112).

Since women found it extremely difficult to get their ideas into print, and those who managed to do so could expect a backlash for stepping beyond their bounds, fiction became an effective vehicle for feminist ideas. Balin remarks that there is 'scarcely a Victorian fictional narrative without its ailing protagonist, its depiction of a sojourn in the sickroom' (1994: 5). Foreshadowing Parsons' much later (1951) notion of the sick role (see chapter 1), many early feminists presented the sickroom as a 'place of one's own' for women who had little or no personal space within which to rest and recuperate from the pressing physical and mental demands of family life. The sickroom theme is taken up, but with a twist, in the work of American sociologist Charlotte Perkins Gilman (1860–1935).

In her disturbing autobiographical novella, *The Yellow Wallpaper*, Gilman (1973 [1892]) recounts the experience of a young woman who, following a nervous breakdown, is taken to rest in an isolated, broken-down mansion under the 'loving care' of her physician husband. There the character becomes preoccupied by the form of a woman trapped and trying to escape from within the sprawling pattern of the yellow wallpaper that decorates her bedroom. She struggles and tries to break through, but the wallpaper strangles and tortures her. While the character in the novella descends into madness, Gilman herself recovered from a period of mental illness which began shortly after she married and worsened following the birth of her daughter. Her physician, the eminent Silas Weir Mitchell, prescribed his six-week 'rest cure'. He admonished her to 'never touch pen, brush or pencil as long as you live' (Gilman 1963 [1935]). Gilman later wrote that this led her to the edge of utter ruin. So bad did it become that she would 'crawl into remote closets and under beds – to hide from the grinding pressure of that profound distress' (Gilman quoted in Hill 1980: 149). She eventually rejected Weir Mitchell's advice, resumed her academic work, and began to recover. She subsequently chronicled the associations between women's poor health and their situation in life, which she blamed upon the 'excessive sex distinction' created by men which had swept across every act of life in late-nineteenth-century America. She opined: 'when we say *men, man, manly, manhood* and all the other masculine derivatives, we have in the background of our minds a huge vague crowded picture of the world and its activities . . . And when we say women, we think *female* – the sex' (Gilman 1915: 116–17, emphasis original). With these words she meant that, while women are reduced to their biology, men are allowed to be so much more. Under such circumstances women's surrender to mental illness should surprise no one.

The themes taken up by an academic discipline reflect the concerns of the powerful. The shared objective of eighteenth- and nineteenth-century feminists such as Wollstonecraft, Gilman and others was to show that women's ill-health is socially caused, not simply given by their (supposedly) defective biology. This uncovers an alternative to what are conventionally construed as sociology's disembodied origins (discussed in chapter 2). It suggests that there was a nascent embodied sociology from the start in the writing of these women thinkers, which was deprived of the ability to grow by dominance of the intellectual agenda by male thinkers who cast matters of the body and health aside as inferior 'female concerns'.

Many years on, Ann Oakley disclosed that women's discrimination in society was mirrored by concealment in academia. In much sociology, she proclaimed, 'women as a social group are invisible or inadequately represented; they take the insubstantial form of ghosts, shadows or stereotyped characters' (1974: 1). She reasoned that areas of social life which, precisely because of sexism, concern women – such as the domestic sphere – were excluded from the sociological agenda as male sociologists gave their attention to work, industry and the state (all constructed as male – and therefore as the most important – domains of social life) (Stacey 1981). Oakley also argued that sociology gave a distorted picture of women as it tried to fit them into 'pre-defined male-oriented sociological categories' (1974: 4). Her examples included the study of deviance, social stratification, power, the family, and work and industry. Ironically, Oakley failed to include health and illness in her review – in those early days when feminists tended to argue for an awareness of women *within existing* areas of male interest, it seems that health did not get onto the agenda precisely because it was not yet of interest to men.

Thinking about sex, gender and health: feminist differences

Thus far we have seen that feminists struggled to get their ideas taken seriously. As explored in previous chapters, new concepts challenge existing ways of thinking, raise fresh questions and stimulate new research. Arguably, feminism's most potent conceptual weapon to date has been the sex/gender distinction. This now familiar distinction came into currency more than forty years ago and was the well-spring for a wealth of research, principally because it supported the argument begun centuries earlier that women's ill-health is socially constructed, not biologically given. As Oakley put it, '"sex" is a word that refers to the biological differences between male and female: the visible difference in genitalia, the related difference in procreative function. "Gender" however is a matter of culture: it refers to the social classification into the "masculine" and "feminine"' (Oakley 1972: 16).

Akin to those writing about the key concepts considered in earlier chapters, such as 'globalization' and 'embodiment', feminists and others have engaged with the 'sex/gender' distinction in a variety of ways. This raises the pointed issue of how to think and write about different feminist ideas. Since it is fairly common to refer to umbrella types of feminism, such as liberal, radical, intersectional and postmodern feminism, they will be used here, although it needs to be borne in mind that this does not capture all approaches and there are other valid classifications. It is also important to note that, while they do have some internal coherence, these groupings may conceal differences between individual writers. We will begin by looking at liberal and radical feminist approaches which are of long standing in the health field. The case of new reproductive technologies will be used to exemplify their differences. We will then turn to newer gender theories which seek to capture the increasingly complex and contested social relations of gender in the global context, such as intersectional approaches, and transnational and postmodern feminisms.

Liberal feminism

Liberal or equality feminism has its roots in political liberalism. In liberal thought, the uniqueness of human beings lies in their capacity for rationality, and a good and just society is one that allows the individual the potential for autonomy and self-realization. These ideas originated in seventeenth-century England, and took root there in the eighteenth century through the writings of political philosophers such as John Locke (1632–1704). But this vision of the liberal individual did not extend to women. Jean-Jacques Rousseau (1966 [1762]), for example, was adamant that the inequalities between women and men were natural. Mary Wollstonecraft's *A Vindication of the Rights of Woman* (1992 [1792]) was an impassioned attack upon this eighteenth-century vision. She argued for women's parity with men and made a health virtue of their involvement in the public sphere of paid work alongside their responsibility for childrearing.

The emphasis upon realizing equality with men through concerted action, principally within the existing organization of society, is a hallmark of liberal feminist thinking. It travels through time in the works of authors such as Gilman, to the so-called 'second-wave' feminists of the post-World War II period, and into the present. For example, in the highly influential *The Feminine Mystique*, Betty Friedan (1963) stressed women's ability to make rational choices and to act upon them. In this vision men are not the enemy, but rather partners in the search for a more just and equal life. Naomi Wolf views feminism as a 'journey to a social contract that includes men and women fairly' (1994: 83). She responds to feminist poet Audrey Lorde's (1984) dictum that 'the master's tools will never dismantle the master's house', with 'it is *only* the master's tools that can dismantle the master's house; he hardly bothers to notice anyone else's'. Wolf calls upon women to 'walk into the "palace of power", and unapologetically use its mighty resources for change' (1994: 59, 74).

The present-day global face of liberal feminism is gender mainstreaming. Endorsed by the 1995 Beijing platform of the fourth International World Conference of Women, gender mainstreaming has been taken up by agencies such as the UN and WHO, as well as by many national governments. The ultimate objective is to render gender inequality obsolete by identifying and removing 'out-dated gendered ideas and practices' through the use of 'a variety of tools, tactics and techniques' (Zalewski 2010: 6). For those sympathetic to it, such as Walby, mainstreaming shows that feminism 'is no longer an outsider protest movement, but is embedded in institutions of civil society and the state'. The risk, as she appreciates, is that feminism is made invisible within these new mainstreamed 'alliances, coalitions and merged projects' (2011: 24, 148).

Although liberal or equality feminists recognize that biological specificities exist, the argument is that they should not be allowed to make a difference to life experience. This muting of the biological body reflects the privileging of mindful, rational action. As Grosz explains, there is an assumption that men and women have 'an analogous biological or natural potential that is unequally developed because the social roles imposed on the two sexes are not equivalent' (1995: 51). It follows that social factors are at least as important as – and perhaps more important than – biological factors in explaining the health of men and women. For example, in an assessment of women's longer average life expectancy, Verbrugge placed biology fourth in rank order behind 'risk acquired from roles, stress, life styles, and long-term preventative practices'; psychosocial factors (which she related to the possibility that women may report more ill-health than men); and prior healthcare (1985: 173). Equally, discussions of gender mainstreaming pay little attention to the embodied nature of gender inequalities.

The liberal feminist proposition that the route to positive health is through women's access to the more highly valued, male-defined, spheres of life has stimulated a lasting tradition of research on the relationship between the 'housewife role', paid work and health. Some years ago, Betty Friedan (1963, 1981) identified what she called 'the problem with no name': the unhappiness of white, middle-class, heterosexual housewives in the United States. In this, and other writing, she used health statistics to counter the widely held belief that, by entering the workforce, as women were doing in growing numbers, they were seriously risking their health. In Friedan's estimation the exact opposite was true; she argued that women suffer less from serious diseases, such as heart disease, than men because of their better balance of work and home-life. She not only credited feminism for this balance, but also argued that men would benefit from breaking out of the competitive, work-dominated male role (Pollock 2010). Echoing this, Nathanson (1975) proposed that, although paid work can be a source of stress for women, its economic benefits, social support, and the promotion of self-esteem through feelings of accomplishment can enhance mental and physical health. Although much subsequent research has supported this standpoint, benefits can be offset by employer demands for flexible labour at the lowest possible cost, as well as by poorly regulated, health-damaging, work environments (Doyal 2005).

A lot of attention has been given over the years to the health impact of dual or multiple roles – that is, women's responsibility for a combination of paid work and work in the home. Echoing the proposition that it is an optimum balance between social roles that promotes health for both men and women – or what we now often think of as 'work–life balance' – many studies have identified a positive effect of 'multiple roles' upon health, at least as long as time pressures do not tip this over into 'role overload' (Bird and Rieker 2008). However, while many Western women may have the benefits of labour saving domestic equipment and the assistance of husbands, partners or paid help in the home, in the poorest parts of the world they often carry a heavy burden of primary or sole responsibility for domestic work and long hours of health-damaging paid work.

Although research on health status has grown in sophistication, the liberal feminist heritage lives on in the privileging of 'social' aspects of experience to the relative neglect of biology and embodied experience. This often occurs in the absence of any wider theoretical explanation of the particular social relations of gender that give rise to individual 'social role' differences between women and men within societies and communities in the first place. By around the mid-1990s, feminists were arguing with increasing force that, although the distinction between biological sex and social gender is an important weapon in the conceptual armoury needed to fight the historical conflation of women with their (purportedly defective) biology, construing the relationship between sex and gender as more or less arbitrary is unsatisfactory in the analysis of health, which surely has a biological component. As Gatens (1992) has argued, there *is* no neutral body: it is always sexed. This is not to propose that the physical body is essentially given or fixed around biological features (such as genitalia or hormones), but that these features *themselves* are open to cultural investment – that is, biology itself is a social construct, and social gender may have its *genesis* in how we view the body (Gatens 1983) (see also chapter 5). This suggests that, rather than turning away from biology, as liberal feminist-inspired health research has been apt to do, biology needs to be made part of the feminist arsenal.

Radical feminism

Radical feminists have regarded women's biological capacity as the fundamental basis of their physical and mental well-being. From its origins in the 1960s to the present, radical feminism has been a provocative combination of political activism and academic endeavour. The eponymous slogan 'the personal is political' was intended to counter disdain for the numerous local women's consciousness-raising groups that, by the early 1970s, had sprung up across America and elsewhere. Carol Hanisch, who is often credited with putting this slogan into print, explains that consciousness raising was seen by many as 'navel-gazing', as 'personal therapy', and certainly not as 'political': 'they belittled us no end for trying to bring our so-called "personal problems" into the public arena – especially "all those body issues" like sex, appearance, and abortion' (2006 [1970]). It is easy in retrospect to underestimate the potentially life-changing effect of these activities. One of the best-known groups, which started in 1969 and still exists today, is the Boston (Massachusetts) Women's Health Book Collective whose members wrote what was to become the best-selling book *Our Bodies, Ourselves* (*OBOS*) (Boston Women's Health Book Collective 1978), now in its ninth edition (Boston Women's Health Book Collective 2012). As Davis writes, 'above all, *OBOS* validated women's embodied experiences as a resource for challenging medical dogmas about women's bodies and, consequently, as a strategy for personal and collective empowerment' (2002: 224). Consciousness raising was the well-spring for the understanding that, while women and men within the US and elsewhere shared a wider political agenda for change, there was also much that divided them, not least the assumption of many men on the political left that women's interests were at best subordinate to, and at worst a barrier to, wider movements for political change (such as in the class system).

Particular caution is needed when summarizing radical feminism since it is 'susceptible to being presented in ways that make it easy to dismiss it as outdated and over the top' (Zalewski 2009: 14–15). The difference from liberal feminism is, however, very clear. As self-identified radical feminist Robin Morgan puts it, liberal feminism plays by patriarchy's own rules. By assuming that 'imitating establishment men' is good for women, liberal or equality feminism settles for a 'piece of the pie as currently and poisonously baked' (1996: 5). From this perspective, women have not simply been excluded from the rational (male) world of reason; rationality itself has been defined against them by denying the specificity of the female body. Rowland and Klein summarize the radical feminist position, which they support, in two tenets: first, 'women as a social group are oppressed by men as a social group and . . . this oppression is the *primary* oppression for women'; second, it is woman-centred, created 'by women for women' (1996: 11, emphasis original). Of course, the form that oppression takes is highly variable since how patriarchy operates and how it impacts on women (and men) also differs with time and place.

While, as we have seen, liberal feminism has tended to play down women's biological differences *from* men in favour of a focus on social similarities *to* men, radical feminism has taken the biological body as the main site of women's oppression and envisions the route to their liberation in their positive difference *from* men. For example, Mary Daly advocated a new way of being for women that is in harmony with nature, where the force of reason is 'rooted in instinct, intuition, passion' (1984: 7). Her work was notable for its criticism of gynaecology. She wrote that 'there is every reason to see the mutilation and destruction of women by doctors specialising in unnecessary radical mastectomies and hysterectomies, carcinogenic hormone therapy, psychosurgery, spirit killing psychiatry and other forms of psychotherapy as directly related to the rise of radical feminism in the twentieth century' (Daly 1990 [1978]: 228).

Without question, radical feminism vivified popular and academic work on women's health in the 1970s, and its influence continues to be felt today. A very clear agenda was set: to explore the ways in which patriarchy undermines women's health, especially through the male-controlled 'biomedical' approach to healthcare. In the widely read *For Her Own Good*, first published in the late 1970s, Ehrenreich and English (2005) expose the fallacies that women have been asked to accept in the name of science. They write that during the nineteenth century, doctors found uterine and ovarian 'disorders' behind almost every possible female complaint, from headaches to sore throats to indigestion. Women's biological constitution was thus judged so weak that any deviation from the path of marriage, childrearing and homemaking, which comprised women's true and natural vocation, was unhealthful. As Ehrenreich and English (2005) argue, today medical arguments still seem to take the malice out of the oppression of women: what doctors suggest is only 'for their own good'.

Childbirth practices have been a particular concern for radical feminists. Thus, writing in the mid-1970s, Arms likened women giving birth in US hospitals to prisoners, arguing that birth was 'slow and agonising, full of risk, expensive, lonely, demoralising if not demeaning, and heading in the direction that may someday eradicate the need for the woman's body (except her uterus) altogether' (1975: 83). The medicalization of birth, by the induction of labour, the use of foetal monitors, and rising Caesarean section rates, remains subject to criticism worldwide. While healthcare has changed in many countries since the 1970s, the distinction between normal, 'natural, woman-controlled childbirth' and 'abnormal, technological, male/medical controlled birth' continues to influence research agendas today (Annandale 2009).

New reproductive technologies and genetic engineering: 'brutality with a human face'?

New reproductive technologies (NRTs) and genetic engineering are highly contentious ground for radical feminists. Running the gamut from IVF, to gamete intrafallopian transfer (GIFT), egg or embryo donation and surrogacy, through to preimplantation genetic diagnosis and prenatal testing (including sex selection), NRTs throw differences amongst feminists into high relief.

Liberal feminists tend to view NRTs in fairly gender-neutral terms. Consistent with the priority given to individual autonomy and self-realization, to deny women access to reproductive technologies and the opportunity to enter into surrogacy contracts is to limit their democratic and reproductive freedom (Lyndon Shanley 1993; Markens 2007; Shildrick 1997). Many consumer groups make reference to a need on the part of the infertile to give birth to a healthy child as a human right (WHO 2002). Undoubtedly, infertility can be a source of significant suffering for women, especially in pronatalist countries as wide-ranging as the US, Egypt and Israel. However, it can be argued that focusing on the individual diverts attention away from the problems that can arise from the global spread of NRTs, especially to the global South. NRTs can also deflect attention from primary prevention of the major causes of infertility, which are sexually transmitted infections and postpartum complications (Inhorn 2003). What is more they promote a global marketplace for reproductive body parts (sperm, ova, embryos), which renders women vulnerable to exploitation (Gupta 2006), in the manner already discussed in chapter 1.

But the strongest opposition to NRTs comes from the more 'hardline' members of FINRRAGE (The Feminist International Network on Resistance to Reproductive and Genetic Engineering, formed in 1986 and with chapters in twenty countries) who view NRTs as medical violence against women. This expresses the radical feminist position that reproduction is a natural process, inherent in women alone, and that technology is an agent of patriarchy (Franklin 2011; Wajcman 2004). Thus, Raymond (2007) regards most technological reproduction as brutality with a human face. Klein (2008) opines that not only is it dangerous to the health of women and their offspring, but the ultimate aim is to 'create "immortal man" capable of reproducing himself without women – always couched in the rhetoric of "helping": babies for desperate infertile couples; cures for sick people afflicted with severe degenerative diseases' (2008: 159). She argues that life-forms are 'viewed as machines that can be stripped of their biological clocks and reassembled at will . . . combining bits of different women's bodies to create the hope of a test-tube child', a process entirely at odds with the women's health movement's credo, *'our bodies, ourselves'* (that is, our bodies *are* our selves) (2008: 159). Others not necessarily associated with FINRRAGE argue that reproductive genetics promote an individualistic, mechanistic view of the female body. Moreover, women are inappropriately compelled to 'enact a morality of the body which upholds the external population's standard – the desire for conventional (i.e. non-diseased, genetically normal) offspring and the need for citizens fit to be born' (Ettorre 2002: 83).

New worlds of gender, new gender theories

As explored in chapter 1, the relationship between theory and research is reciprocal: theories gradually cease to fit societies as they change and new approaches are called for. Notwithstanding the distinctions between liberal and radical feminism and the research deriving from them, both have approached health and illness through the lens of categorical biological and/or social *difference* between men and women, and the related assumption that both women and men inevitably have more in common with each other than they have potentially dividing them. From this viewpoint, 'differences among women are silenced and differences between men and women privileged; the sameness among women is presumed and the similarity between men and women is denied' (Eisenstein 1988: 3). While this may have made some sense during the 1960s and 1970s when differences between men and women were a palpable feature of most societies, it is a questionable basis for the analysis of life in the twenty-first century in which, in some parts of the world, social relations of gender are fast-changing and growing in complexity and our biological bodies increasingly are conceived of as modifiable rather than fixed.

The early 1990s were a watershed period for feminist theory as, in common with the social sciences in general, and sociology in particular, it was compelled to face up to claims of false universalism. This had, in fact, been brought to public attention more than a century earlier by Sojourner Truth, a black slave, who, to the astonishment of those assembled, stood up at the Women's Rights Convention in Akron, Ohio of 1851 and asked *'Ain't I a woman?'* Her point was that black and white women were treated differently and that black women had the same right to equality with men as white women.[1] It is also important to mention that many white women urged Truth to be silent, for fear that she would deflect attention from women's wider striving for suffrage. As Crenshaw (1989) explains, this speaks of an inappropriate willingness by white women, then and now, to ignore racialized privilege in order to strengthen feminism.

Well over 100 years on, in the mid-1980s, the notion of 'sisterhood' was under direct attack for its assumption of a 'common oppression': its view that all women's bodies and, therefore, their experiences are the same (hooks 1984). Thus, Bryan and colleagues pointed out that when the British women's movement took up the issue of 'abortion on demand' in the 1970s, it had to make known that black women had '*always* been given abortions more readily than white women and are indeed often encouraged to have terminations we did not ask for' (1985: 105, emphasis original). Around this time, it was also made known that the assumption of gender as male/female difference had had the effect of supporting the normative character and irreversibility of that binary, which effectively classed everything outside of it as a perversion and thus obscured non-heterosexual women's health needs (Edwards 2012; Fuss 1989).

Intersectionality and transnational feminism

The concept of 'intersectionality', coined by Crenshaw in 1989, appeals to many feminists because it seems to hold the potential to solve the thorny problem of differences and diversity between women and how they intertwine, but in a way that still seems to speak to all women (Davis 2008). Intersectionality intends to convey that oppressions associated, for example, with gender, class, age, sexuality, race and religion are not simply additive, nor do they necessarily act together in the same way – rather, they often interact in complex ways. So, as Dworkin discusses in relation to HIV/AIDS, although there is a vast amount of evidence that heterosexual transmission contributes significantly to women's risk of infection, there are reasons to question the assumptions that have worked their way into the literature, such as that

> a sex/gender system is constituted by biological women who have one gender role known as femininity (and are hurt by it in the HIV epidemic), while biological men have one gender role known as masculinity (and tend to hurt women with it) . . . [but] individuals do not have singular identities or experiences within social structures that expand or limit social practices, but rather, intersecting ones.
>
> (Dworkin 2005: 617, 618)

The HIV/AIDS epidemic therefore cuts across the 'fault lines of intersectionality' (Dworkin 2005: 618). For example, in the US, 'women of colour' are disproportionately affected (race intersects with gender). And while the overall numbers of men and women affected are about equal, amongst those aged 13–19 females are disproportionately affected (age intersects with gender).

The problem of false universalism extends to the global context. Often notions of 'global sisterhood' or 'global feminism' are euphemisms for a Western – and, in most cases, a North American – liberal version of feminism 'whereby primacy is given to the individual woman and her struggles to realise her potential [and] interventions are centered upon women gaining entrance in the public domain' (Davis 2002: 227). The concept of 'transnational feminism(s)' intends to get away from this. It 'points to the multiplicity of the world's feminisms and to the increasing tendency of national feminisms to politicize women's issues beyond the borders of the nation state' (2002: 296). It signals not only the shared exploitation of women worldwide, but also differences between them. For example, in the case of NRTs and global transactions in reproductive body parts, considered above and in chapter 1, attention is drawn to major divisions between women who profit and women who are exploited. Gupta suggests that 'transnational feminism' prompts us to compare such 'overlapping and discrete oppressions rather than to construct a theory of hegemonic oppression under a unified category of gender' (2006: 34).

Postmodern feminism

While 'intersectional approaches' have grown in popularity, for some – such as postmodern feminists – they are a weak and hence insufficient response to the problem of binarism and false universalism. In the early 1990s, postmodern feminists were mounting an increasingly strong critique of 'modernist' feminist theories. For them, research on women's health from a liberal or radical feminist standpoint gets into severe difficulties because it begins with an *assumption of difference* due to sex and/or gender. The argument is that to take women's difference from men as a basic premise effectively plays into patriarchy's hands. As Grosz expresses it, binary oppositions are inherently patriarchal since their 'very structure is privileged by the male/*non-male* (i.e. female) distinction' (1990: 101, my emphasis). Therefore, if we accept the modernist view that men and women are opposites (irrespective of whether we conceive of sex/gender as biologically or socially based), then women are colluding in their oppression since, under patriarchy, women's 'opposite position' will always be negatively defined. As a fundamental opposition, gendered difference supports other oppositions which attach to it like a magnet – for example, men are rational, women are irrational; women are caring, men are uncaring, and so on. It is through this process that the positively valued 'healthy body' attaches to men and the negatively valued 'sick body' attaches to women.

A different, postmodern, political position is formed through the deconstruction of the binary positions of male/female, man/woman, sex/gender, to reveal that they are artefacts of a modernist worldview rather than apt descriptors of women's and men's experience of health and illness. The objective is to resist closure, not just by elevating the suppressed term (female/woman and all that goes with it) in the manner of radical feminism, but by subverting or destabilizing the hierarchical division itself. This way, commonalities become as important as differences and men can no longer easily be associated with all that is valued and women with all that is devalued (Barrett and Phillips 1992). We are led to conclude that our modernist worldview has blinded us to the heterogeneity and plurality that now characterizes sex and gender in a postmodern world. The idea that social gender flows from biological sex is undone along with the very notion of binary biological difference. In other words, the way that we think about biological sex is exposed as the projection of our socially derived ideas about binary gender (Butler 1990). This shows up the artificiality of binary and fixed ways of thinking about the bodies of men and women. This is not simply an academic narrative. As Martin puts it, 'we are in the midst of a profound sea change in how the body is conceptualised. Ordinary people in all walks of life . . . are working with a conception of a fluid, flexible, ever-changing body' (1999: 105–6).

We can return to the example of NRTs to illustrate the contrasts between postmodern and other feminist perspectives. From a postmodern standpoint, Farquhar (1996) contends that, by arguing either for the transcendence (liberal feminism) or realization (radical feminism) of reproduction as women's telos, modernist feminists shore up conventional binary understandings of bodies (as fertile or infertile) and of family practices. The argument is that NRTs are not gender-neutral (liberal feminism), nor are they an inexorable tool of patriarchy (much of radical feminism). Rather, they are a potential (though not inevitable) source of power for women because they make it possible to transcend the biological body (Haraway 1991). They have the capacity to problematize the basis of self-identity by cutting across 'hitherto entrenched categories of difference (fertile/infertile; young/old; lesbian/heterosexual; and potentially human/animal)', and this underlines the 'instability of modernist homogeneities' (Shildrick 1997: 181). NRTs become an invitation to rethink traditional identity categories and foster openness to new provisional and hybrid ones such as gay and lesbian parenting (Farquhar 1996).

Postmodern feminism has been subject to extensive critical debate, within which two concerns stand out. First, if the differences within men as a group and within women as a group, and similarities between men and women, are as important as what women hold in common, this puts male health and male bodies on the agenda on the same conceptual terms as women's. It is then no longer possible to see men as powerful oppressors and women as victims or survivors in any straightforward way, since the powerful discourses that traverse gender must be recognized. We are led not only to ask whether men are increasingly exposed to the same pressures that women feel, but to begin from the premise that gender as traditionally conceived may not *matter* at all in some circumstances. The second, related, concern is that doing away with sex and gender as binary difference sweeps away not only the patriarchal powers that constructed the difference in the first place, but also the possibility of women's collective resistance. As Bordo (1993) puts it, the protean standpoint of multiple axes of identity can end up as a 'view from nowhere'. If this is the case, then is feminism itself simply an anachronism, a relic of the past?

Feminism: not dead, just different?

For some, feminism is indeed dead, or perhaps dying. Coward (1999) answers the question 'Is feminism relevant to the new millennium?' with a resounding 'No'. Taking the UK as her main point of reference, she argues that the balance of power 'between the sexes' has altered so dramatically that we can no longer talk of patterns of female disadvantage and male advantage. For others, however, if not exactly flourishing, feminism lives on. It just looks very different from the feminisms of the past.

Two very different faces of feminism prevail today. The first is the 'mainstreamed' equality feminism referred to earlier, which is highly successful but much less visible than the feminisms of the past since it is sedimented within institutions (such as the state) and 'hidden within intersecting projects' (such as wider equality policies) (Walby 2011: 148). This face of feminism has been especially popular in the 'developing world' context. The second face is 'third-wave' cultural feminism, particularly evident in the US, which puts a high value on lifestyle, consumption, entitlement, and sometimes sexual display.

No one, as Levy puts it, 'wants to be the archetypical feminist frump at the back of the room anymore, the ghost of women past' (2005: 92). The 'third wave' is a vortex of perspectives which elude easy summary. In her reflection on the lives of US black women, *When Chickenheads Come Home to Roost: My Life as a Hip-Hop Feminist*, Morgan reports: 'how in Oshun's name to capture the nose-ringed/caesared/weaved up/ Gucci-Prada-DKNY down/ultra Nubian alternative-bohemian/beats-loving/smooth-jazz-playing magic of us was something I couldn't begin to fathom' (Morgan 2000: 24).

In *Bitch*, Wurtzel proclaims, 'these days putting out one's pretty power, one's pussy power; one's sexual energy for popular consumption no longer makes you a bimbo' (1998, quoted in Baumgardner and Richards 2000: 141). In gentler tones, Baumgardner and Richards tell their readers, '*we* love Girlie because it makes feminism relevant and fun and in the moment' (2000: 161, emphasis original). But they nonetheless caution that it can also be a trap of conformity to a brand: the invitation easily taken up to 'buy products created by male-owned companies that capture the slogan of feminism [such as on T-shirts], without the power' to go with them (2000: 161). But, according to Aschenbrand, even this can be put to the wider good: 'I was like ... people are constantly staring at our tits because our bodies are objectified ... it follows, then, that we should take advantage of this fact, right? We should reject renting of our bodies as billboard space for odious companies and use them instead to our advantage, to advertise shit that matters' (Aschenbrand 2006: 66). Her company 'body as billboard' (www.bodyasbillboard.com (accessed 15 January 2014)) sells T-shirts carrying the slogan 'Drug Dealer'; the wearer has donated money to buy antiretroviral drugs (ARTs) for children in Africa. It is surely no paradox that Aschenbrand has become her *own* brand.

Cosmetic surgery provides a useful comparative case study of 'modernist', postmodern and even 'postfeminist' feminist positions. For most radical feminists, cosmetic surgery is normalizing, a capitulation to patriarchal ideals of what a woman should look like. This is underpinned by the belief that 'women's bodies are only authentic when they are left alone, and that body practices deny women's real selves' (Pitts-Taylor 2007: 80). However, as cosmetic surgery becomes less expensive and more available to the masses (not just celebrities and the rich), and ideal, slim, young-looking bodies are held up as successful bodies, *ergo* successful women, surgery itself has been normalized. As noted in chapter 1, many do not even seem to see it as a medical procedure. From what is arguably a postmodern or postfeminist position, French performance artist Orlan (2014) has orchestrated numerous cosmetic surgeries on her own body as filmed performances, with the intent not necessarily of beautifying her body, but of experimenting with different identities and making any notion of the natural body obsolete (Davis 1997). But, more moderately, some women opt for cosmetic surgery to 'correct' bodily features – not to be more 'beautiful', just more 'ordinary' (Davis 1995). Equally, they may use surgery to endow the body with the social and economic capital associated with larger breasts, slimmer thighs, a younger face, and so on. Controversially, women often emphasize that their decision to have cosmetic surgery is not fitting into male-defined ideas of what women should look like, but rather a deliberate and well-considered personal choice – in other words, a form of personal empowerment in a postfeminist world: *taking control* not *being controlled*.

From 'women's health' to 'gender and health'

The aforementioned debates make plain that feminist theory is becoming increasingly diverse and internally contested alongside equally diverse and contested changes in women's lives. This can be unsettling. The old analytical tools, such as the binaries of sex/gender, no longer seem as fit for purpose as they once did and new tools have yet to be found. But we should not necessarily see this as a problem. Indeed, on the contrary, it can be argued that this is a period of vibrant change for research on gender and health. In similar terms, feminist research on women's health is being challenged, but also energized, by the growth of men's health activism and academic research.

'Wounded bodies': men's health in crisis?

Whereas 'women's health' was already highly visible by the early 1970s, 'men's health' was not discernible as a topic in its own right until around the mid-1990s. Since then it has become a vibrant field of research with dedicated academic journals, popular magazines, organizations (such as the International Society for Men's Health) and world conferences.

The obvious question to be asked is why was men's health invisible for so long? If privilege is invisible to those who have it, then patriarchy has carried with it an ironic twist: by presenting history as an ungendered and universal process, it has not only concealed women's oppression, but side-lined men's experience *as* men. Thus, at the same time as men's attitudes and behaviours (as healthcare practitioners, for example) are drawn upon to throw light upon women's and girls' health-related oppressions, men's own health-related experiences are cast in shadow. Arguably, the eclipsing of men's health problems has been exacerbated by the longstanding tendency within feminist research to interpret women's disprivilege and poor health against a binary template of men's privilege and good health. As explored in chapter 5, this makes it hard to see men and boys as ill, or as potentially ill. Once men and boys emerged from the shadowlands into the light of health research, policy and practice, the image projected was not one of dominance, but of damage and vulnerability. The word that most often appears alongside reference to men's health today is *'crisis'*. As Robinson argues (and with specific reference to the US), the dominant narrative of white men in decline is 'clothed in a language of crisis', and the texts produced out of the crisis use a 'vocabulary of pain and urgency to dwell on, manage, and/or heal men under siege'. In sum, men are now seen as 'inhabiting wounded bodies' (Robinson 2000: 5, 6).

The crisis narrative rests on the premise of binary difference between men and women, boys and girls. As we have seen, this was also fervently applied by feminists, especially in the 1970s to the early 1990s, to account for *women's* problems. Establishing disadvantage, then, is probably part of legitimating a new field, no matter what the time point in history (Annandale and Kuhlmann 2012). It is an unusual piece of writing, academic or popular, on men's health that does not start with pronouncements and/or statistics showing that, on average, women live longer than men and that men have higher age-specific rates for major causes of death such as heart disease and cancers, and engage in more health-damaging behaviours than women. This is not the discourse of a political fringe, it is at the heart of mainstream practices such as the lobby to create an Office of Men's Health within the US government Department of Health and Human Services (DHHS) (to mirror the Office of Women's Health, set up in 1991): 'Men's health is at great risk. On average, men die 6 years younger than women and suffer higher morbidity rates from the top 10 causes of death. The lives of hundreds of thousands of men will continue to be threatened unless immediate action is taken to combat this growing crisis' (Pennsylvania Department of Health 2011).

Men as 'doubly disadvantaged'

Typically, men's and boys' disadvantage is presented as two-fold: biological and social. First, researchers often point out that anatomical and physiological differences leave male new-borns developmentally from four to six weeks behind their female counterparts; that males are at greater risk from congenital abnormalities throughout life; and that men's lack of oestrogen may render them more vulnerable to heart disease than women (Courtenay 2011; Kraemer 2000). Second, in social terms, men and boys are seen to suffer not only from the need to live up to norms of dominant masculinity, which encourage risk taking (from dangerous driving, to poor diets, to avoiding dealing with the symptoms of illness), but also from the health effects of repressed anger and of coping behaviours such as violence and excessive alcohol consumption in response to gender-related changes in the sphere of education and work that mean we no longer live in a straightforwardly 'man's world' (Kimmel 2009). With reference to the West, Wolfgang Rutz of the WHO argues that 'societal changes seem to affect men more than women', a phenomenon he calls 'societal syndrome' (2004: 22). Despite emerging evidence that it is often women who are the more vulnerable, due to, for example, welfare cuts during the present financial crisis, the men's health movement often taps into a wider popular – and to some extent also academic – assessment that not only are the lives of Western men and women converging, but women are 'winning out' at the expense of men as they 'boundary-cross' into 'masculine social territories and powerscapes' (Atkinson 2008: 71). For example, some argue that men's recent interest in the body is due to it being their only remaining defining source of masculinity (Pope et al. 2000). In his Canadian study, Atkinson (2008: 78) found that men felt under threat, as they put it, from 'younger, smarter and healthier' women. For these men, having cosmetic surgery was a way of reaffirming or regaining a sense of male power, but through traditionally feminine practices.

Wadham (2002) deftly argues that men's health research and policy justifies itself by a strategy of *comparison and equivalence* – that is, by comparing the health of men to the health of women to make the argument that, while the resources accorded to each should be equivalent, they are not. As he discusses, the problem is not so much that comparisons are inappropriate, but that they are often made in a zero-sum fashion with the object of promoting the health needs of men and boys over the health needs of women and girls. Some fairly invidious comparisons appear, such as rates of prostate cancer versus breast cancer, to make the case for equivalence. In sum, in many Western countries in particular, 'a sense of crisis in masculinity and resistance to feminism, and a highly competitive health service environment . . . have encouraged an already competitive and adversarial Men's Health discourse' (Wadham 2002: 80).

Thus, as Schofield (2012) reasons, two gender-based public health constituencies – women's health and men's health – are formed, at the heart of which is a robust binarism between the bodies and experiences of men and women. The main focus of the early 'first wave' (Broom and Tovey 2009) of men's health research has been the hegemonic form of masculinity. As 'the most honoured way of being a man', hegemonic masculinity requires all men to position themselves in relation to it (Connell and Messerschmidt 2005: 832). It is this form of masculinity which usually is seen as the most damaging, both to the minority who live according to its codes and to those who cannot avoid being influenced by it and are subordinated to it (other men and all women). An effect of this has been that, as traditionally male ways of thinking and acting increasingly are seen as inimical to good health, health has become 'feminized'. In other words, '"masculinity" has come to be defined as a barrier to health', while 'feminine attitudes such as willingness to consider oneself as vulnerable and "at risk", and to seek help' are 'validated as desirable characteristics for both men and women' (Lee and Frayn 2008: 115). So we seem to have witnessed a major turnaround: from holding up masculine attributes as the norm of the healthy individual (which so concerned the early feminist thinkers discussed at the start of the chapter) to where the 'healthy body is now more likely to be described in conventionally feminine terms' (Moore 2010: 96). Yet it is debatable whether women are healthier than men, and it is far from a given that women are more attentive to their health or more willing to seek help when ill than men. Neither is it self-evident that men are less healthy than women or more reluctant to seek help (for an empirical discussion of these matters, see chapter 5).

While much of men's health research remains wedded to binary thinking, more and more researchers are now pointing out that masculinity is far from singular, fixed and binary in form. Instead, it is multiple, fluid and variable: as Courtenay puts it, masculinity is 'a complex, dynamic, and ever-changing concept, enacted differently in different contexts' (2011: viii). This parallels the identification of fluid and multiple forms of femininity amongst women, briefly discussed earlier. The problem, as with studies of women's health, is how to capture this theoretically. Social scientists, the media, and men and women themselves are giving names to a growing catalogue of different types of 'masculine' and 'feminine' identity and practices existing side-by-side. From 'metrosexuality', 'ubersexuality,' and 'transnational business masculinity', to 'Girlie', 'grrrlpower' and many more, these tags are attempts to pin down and make sense of highly complex gender-related changes within communities, and their new associated expressions of identity.

I have argued elsewhere (Annandale 2009) that the rigid gender orthodoxies that prevailed up until around the last quarter of the twentieth century in much of the West are breaking down and being reconfigured in new ways. The older, more traditional, binaries of sex and gender – distinct male and female bodies, distinct male and female social experiences, in work and family life, for example – persist, and are even hyper-accentuated, but exist alongside fluidity and diversity (especially amongst, but not confined to, younger people). For example, consumption patterns which were traditionally very highly gendered, such as smoking (male) and dieting (female), are increasingly 'opened up' to both men and women. This is not to say that men and women are now equal (though that may be the case for some, in some domains of life), but rather that far more complex patterns of equality and inequality are apparent. As we will see in chapter 5, these are written not only on the surface of the body, but also into the biological body in the experiences of morbidity and mortality. While these changes may seem to belong to the West, it would be mistaken to think that they are not being felt in various ways in other parts of the world too.

A global gender order

Globalization is often inappropriately construed in gender-neutral terms (Doyal 2005). Yet local gender orders often require analysis on a global scale (Connell 2009). As pointed out in chapter 2 and discussed further in chapter 7, although globalization must to some extent involve the interconnection of societies, it has no singular logic. Rather than moving in one direction, change is multi-causal and multi-dimensional (Beck 2000; Walby 2009). Consequently, we would expect the health experiences of men and women in different parts of the world to be influenced by the network of global companies and the flow of diseases around the globe, but not necessarily in the same way or with the same consequences.

When we think about globalization and health, we usually have in mind how economic and cultural globalization is affecting the health of men and women. As just noted, it is easy to assume that changes to traditional gender orders are a phenomenon of the affluent global North, which is not the case. For example, research for the World Bank on the experience of 'poor men and women' in fifty countries (e.g. of Sub-Saharan Africa, North Africa, South Asia, Eastern Europe) points to high levels of 'gender anxiety' around household changes brought about by globalization: 'Economic hardship is forcing poor people to adapt to new environments and, in turn, these adaptive actions are forcing wrenching change in gender roles in households in both subtle and obvious ways' (Narayan 2000: 176). Changes such as women going out to work due to the loss of traditional male jobs are not usually accompanied by changes in gender norms. As a result, 'values and relationships are being broken, tested, contested, and renegotiated in silence, pain, and violence' (2000: 175). The inability to fulfil the male role of provider can precipitate anger and frustration, and negative coping behaviours such as alcoholism. Women can then end up taking on more work, often in the informal, unregulated sector, in low-income, low-status jobs which are a risk to health. But this is not totally generalizable; some men may be willing to take on domestic and caring work and, despite their workplace vulnerability, women may gain confidence as they start earning and retaining cash incomes.

So we can see that globalization impacts upon health through changing gender roles. In turn globalization's impact on health also has knock-on effects on gender roles and attitudes. For example, Doyal (2005) points out that, as more women become ill and die of HIV/ AIDS, so traditional gendered support systems atrophy and men (especially young men) and boys are beginning to take on domestic and caring responsibilities that they once would have considered inappropriate. In their research in KwaZulu Natal, South Africa, where rates of HIV/AIDS are amongst the highest in the world, Montgomery and colleagues (2006) found that, while women appear to be able to cross the traditional male breadwinner / female homemaker line in a way that has been incorporated into the dominant discourse on family life, men's crossing of the gender divide into what has traditionally been seen as women's work continues to be perceived as deviant. Yet these authors found men not only caring for their own children but also assuming a fatherhood relationship with children who were not their biological offspring (as uncles, grandfathers, older brothers). This was largely invisible and hence unrecognized as prevailing norms about gender roles and responsibilities within households worked against the recognition within the community of such involvement, focusing attention instead on men's inability to meet their traditional obligations as economic providers.

Conclusions

Social relations of gender clearly are changing in many societies and this has especially been felt in many Western countries over the last couple of decades. Theories premised on the assumption of binary difference between men and women and the privileges and disprivileges that go with this have begun to seem out of date as commentators emphasize that social relations of gender and gender identities are now far more fluid and complex. This does not necessarily mean that men and women are now equal (though in some domains of life in some places, they may be) – indeed, new forms of inequality may be arising at the intersections of gender with ages, ethnicities or sexualities, for example, all of which have implications for health and healthcare, as we will see in coming chapters.

4

Socio-economic inequalities in health

The 21st-century world is characterized by extremes of poverty and wealth, scarcity and abundance. Differences between rich and poor nations are growing, regional inequalities are increasing within many nations and, at the local level, pockets of poverty thrive amidst affluence. As argued by Krieger and Davey Smith, 'we literally embody the world in which we live, thereby producing population patterns of health, disease, disability and death' (2004: 92). Patterns of morbidity and mortality are a stark and often surprisingly swift barometer of the impacts of economic and social change upon people's lives.

This chapter begins by drawing attention to continuities in the long history of research on health inequalities. It then charts trends in economic inequality since the mid-1970s and their association with changes in population health. We will then see that, although the *evidence* for an association between people's socio-economic circumstances and their health is compelling and now largely accepted, *explanations* are hotly disputed and politically charged.

'Social murder': the historical foundations of health inequalities research

The overall prosperity brought about by industrialization and social invention during the nineteenth century heralded unprecedented fortune for some, but untold misery for others. In England, for example, 'For millions, entire lives – albeit often very short ones – were passed in new industrial cities of dreadful night with all too typical socio-pathology: foul housing, often in flooded cellars, gross overcrowding, atmospheric and water-supply pollution, overflowing cesspools, contaminated pumps; poverty, hunger, fatigue and abjection everywhere' (Porter 1997: 399).

Analyses of population-level differences in health were aided by the new discipline of medical statistics and, in Britain, by the establishment in the 1830s of the Registrar General's Department for the registration of births, marriages and deaths. Using the health of those in the best-off districts of England as a comparative benchmark, William Farr (1807–83) was able to determine that people in worse-off areas were dying unnecessarily. These findings influenced social reformers such as Friedrich Engels, who came to the conclusion that the relationship between capitalism and health was 'social murder': 'society in England daily and hourly commits what the working-men's organs [organizations], with perfect correctness, characterize as social murder, . . . it has placed the workers under conditions in which they can neither retain health nor live long; . . . it undermines the vital force of these workers gradually, little by little, and so hurries them to the grave before their time' (Engels 1993 [1845]: 107).

Despite rising prosperity and tremendous improvements in the overall health of people in affluent nations in the almost 170 years since Engels and others were writing, little has been achieved in reducing the health *gap* between rich and poor; indeed, it has been widening in many nations. To explore this, we need first to look at the economic changes that have been taking place since the mid-1970s.

Economic inequality

There are a number of ways of measuring economic inequality. One of these is the Gini coefficient. Figure 4.1 charts changes in the Gini coefficient between 1979 and 2009–10 for Britain (values range from 0 to 1: the higher the Gini coefficient, the higher the level of inequality). It shows dramatic rises in inequality over the 1980s, dips in the mid-1990s, followed by further rises and peaks to reach a historic high of 0.36 in 2007–8. It is of note that the most recent figure for Britain is higher than for most other European countries, but lower than for the US, which had a Gini coefficient of 0.469 in 2009–10 (DeNavas-Walt et al. 2011).

Figure 4.2 demonstrates that disposable incomes have risen steadily in the UK since 1988/9, but at a faster rate at the top than at the bottom of the income ladder. When adjusted for household size and composition (in order to take account of differing demands on resources, which is called equivalization), the incomes of households in the ninetieth (or top) percentile have diverged significantly from the median (or mid-point of the distribution, above and below which 50 per cent of people fall) over time.

There is strong evidence of the 'transmission of poverty' between generations. For example, Blanden and Gibbons (2006: ix) found that teenage poverty not only doubled the odds of being poor young

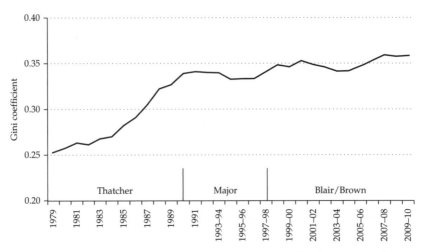

Note: The Gini coefficient has been calculated using incomes before housing costs have been deducted.
Source: Wenchao et al. (2011: fig 3.7)

Figure 4.1 The Gini coefficient (GB)

adults for those growing up in 1970s Britain, it also doubled their odds of being poor in the year 2000 when they were in their early forties.

Assessments of economic inequality by reference to where households or individuals are placed relative to others are useful for charting changes over time. They are less useful for identifying people living on low incomes or in poverty. For instance, using the classification in figure 4.2 would mean 10 per cent always being defined as poor. Consequently, most developed nations specify a 'poverty line' which sets an income threshold as a fraction of the population below the median income. This involves a subjective judgement about 'where, and how, to draw a line between those in poverty and the rest' (Alcock 2006: 67). For example, European countries generally set the poverty line at 60 per cent of equivalized median household income after the deduction of housing costs (because those on low incomes tend to spend a high proportion of income on housing). This is a measure of *relative poverty* since the poverty line changes year on year, and households are compared against general rises in income. By this measure, the number of people living in poverty in the UK increased dramatically during the 1980s, more steadily in the early 1990s, then stabilized or fell up to 2004–5, after which it has begun to increase again (Wenchao et al. 2011). Focusing on the 18-month period of reces-

£ per week at 2008/09 prices

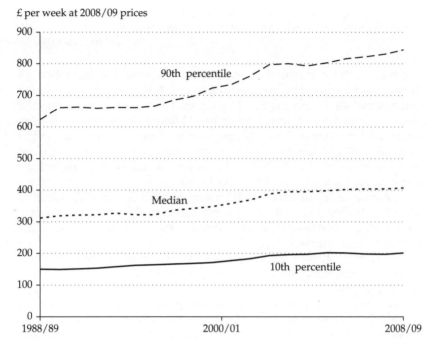

Notes:
1 Adjusted to 2008/9 prices using the retail prices index less council tax/domestic rates.
2 Equivalized household disposable income before deduction of housing costs, using OECD equivalization scale.
3 Data for 1994/5 to 2001/2 are for Great Britain only.
Source: Department for Work and Pensions (DWP), ONS (2011: fig. 2)

Figure 4.2 Distribution of real[1] household disposable income[2]: United Kingdom/Great Britain[3]

sion in 2008 and 2009 in the UK, Parekh and colleagues (2010) report 5.8 million people living in 'deep poverty' (household incomes below 40 per cent of the median).

Others have argued that it is equally, if not more, important to look at *absolute* poverty, specified in terms of lack of access to the minimum subsistence to sustain life – such as food, shelter and clean water. As Alcock discusses:

> On the face of it this is a contradiction in terms – how do those without enough to live on, live? The answer, according to the absolute poverty theorists, is that they do not live for long; and if they are not provided with enough for subsistence they will starve, or – perhaps more likely in a country such as Britain – in the winter they will freeze. Indeed every

winter a significant number of older people ... do die of hypothermia
because they cannot afford to heat their homes adequately.

(Alcock 2006: 64)

Others still maintain that in affluent societies the definition of
'human need' should be assessed not in absolute terms, but in relation
to the population concerned and their views about what constitutes the
'necessities of life'. Research from the Millennium Survey of *Poverty
and Social Exclusion in Britain* (Pantazis et al. 2006) showed that people
from all walks of life tend not to restrict necessities to basic material
needs such as food and shelter, but rather broaden them to include
social activities such as celebrating birthdays and having the money
for a hobby or leisure activity (Pantazis et al. 2006: 89–122). Ideas of
what constitutes 'necessities' have expanded over time – that is, they
are relative to contemporary conditions rather than fixed to absolute
subsistence, or 'staying alive'.

As Alcock's (2006) illustration of hypothermia suggests poverty
impacts differentially on population groups. In 2009–10, 15.6 per cent
of old-age pensioners (1.8 million), and 29.1 per cent of children (3.8
million), in the UK were living below the 'poverty line', many in severe
poverty (Wenchao et al. 2011). Variations between countries show that
'there is nothing inevitable or insurmountable about child poverty
rates; they reflect different national policies interacting with social
changes and market forces' (UNICEF 2005: 3). Finally, it is important
to appreciate that poverty unduly affects people with disabilities,
of whom around 30 per cent (about 1.5 million people) live in relative poverty in the UK, about double the rate of non-disabled people
(Parckar 2008).

Wealthier and healthier?

The foregoing discussion indicates that, although Western nations
are getting wealthier, the gap between rich and poor is increasing. A
similar association is found for the health of populations. There have
been dramatic improvements since the nineteenth century when life
expectancy at birth for British men and women was only 41 and 43 years
respectively. By the first decade of the twentieth century this had risen
to 49 and 52 years. The pace of change quickened during the twentieth
century to reach just over 77.5 years for men, and around 81.5 years
for women by 2008 (Fitzpatrick and Chandola 2000; ONS 2011). These
upward trends are mirrored in other affluent nations. For example, the
life expectancy of Australians grew by 43 per cent between 1901–10 and
2006–8: from just under 59 to almost 84 years for women, and from just
over 55 to just over 79 years for men (AIHW 2010). Mortality rates have
also fallen in affluent nations. Between 1979 and 2003 in the UK, overall

age-standardized[1] mortality rates decreased by 38 per cent in males (from 1,331 to 814 per 100,000) and by 29 per cent in females (from 798 to 567 per 100,000) (Bajekal et al. 2006: 167–8). Years of 'disability-free life expectancy' have also increased over the period, suggesting that people are not only living longer, but living longer in better health.

However, these encouraging trends mask not only the persistence of socio-economic inequalities in health since modern records began but that they have been worsening, especially since the mid-1970s. Generally the reason for this is that rates of improvement in wealth and in health have been faster-paced in higher socio-economic groups than in lower socio-economic groups. Before we look at some of the evidence for this, we need to review briefly how researchers measure socio-economic status in relation to health.

Measurement issues: social class
It is often mistakenly assumed that concepts and measures are inter-changeable and somehow tap into the same underlying constructs of advantage/disadvantage. As Bartley remarks, 'we use oversimplified and poorly thought-out concepts and measures of socio-economic position at our peril' (2004: 22). The most commonly used measures in the UK have been occupationally based, the most familiar being the Registrar General's social classification (RGSC) which, although periodically revised, dates back to 1911. It generates six categories based on occupational skill levels, with an implicit understanding that these relate to the general standing or prestige of occupations. Despite its conceptual vagueness, the RGSC has yielded consistent gradients in health status over a great many years. As Bartley astutely observes, it 'is a bit like aspirin: everyone knows that it works, but nobody knows why'. Moreover, 'just as knowing about the effectiveness of aspirin has not helped to understand the causes of migraine', this does not take us very far in explaining health inequalities (Bartley 2004: 32).

The RGSC remains important for looking at trends over time. However, it was superseded in the 2001 census by the National Statistics Socio-economic Classification (NS-SEC). NS-SEC was introduced to enhance the possibility of *explaining* associations between socio-economic differences and other aspects of life, such as health, and to do so by being conceptually clear. It aims to better 'reflect the socio-economic structure of twenty-first century societies and the major shift in the UK economy from manufacturing to service industries' (White et al. 2007: 7). Whereas RGSC is based on an assumed hierarchy of skill and social standing, NS-SEC is rooted in employment relations and conditions. It originates in the work of the sociologists Erikson and Goldthorpe (the 'Erikson–Goldthorpe schema') who distinguish between two ideal-typical forms of employment contract, the 'service contract' and the 'labour contract'. Those working under a 'service contract' tend to have a high degree of autonomy, to be highly trusted (since they are not easily monitored) and to have salary increments and opportunities for career progression. By contrast, work under a 'labour contract' is more easily monitored, payment is closely tied to hours of work, there is less likelihood of career progression and job security is lower (Erikson and Goldthorpe 1992). An adaptation of the Erikson–Goldthorpe schema, NS-SEC collates occupations into seven groups defined by a set of criteria (such as job security, how people are paid, whether they have pay increments, whether they have autonomy in when they start and leave work, and influence over designing work tasks). An eighth category covers those who have never worked and the long-term unemployed. The originators explain that NS-SEC

> defines *structural* positions that can be seen conceptually to exist independently of the individuals who occupy those positions at any particular time. The positions condition and shape the lives and the life chances of their occupants. That is, the life chances of individuals and families depend mainly on their position in the division of labour and the material and symbolic advantages that derive from it.
>
> (Rose and Pevalin 2005: 18, emphasis original)

Although occupation is a powerful indicator of socio-economic position, it has practical limitations. While it is possible to code those not in work, such as the unemployed, retired and long-term sick, to their past occupation (if they have one) or to the occupation of the 'head of household' (if there is one), this is not always a good indicator of an individual's current circumstances (for the particular problems in relation to women, see chapter 5). For this and other reasons, researchers commonly use indicators such as education, income, material assets and home ownership, or a series of indicators combined into an index. Indices are routinely used in studies of geographically defined populations or areas. An example is the Carstairs Deprivation Index consisting of the proportion in an area of unemployed males, overcrowded households, households with no car, and households where the occupation of the 'head of household' is RGSC IV or V (see, e.g., Morgan and Baker 2006). Areas are typically defined by existing boundaries such as local authority and electoral wards in the UK, and by states, counties or census-tracts in the US. As we will see later in this chapter, studying *both* the socio-economic characteristics of individuals *and* the characteristics of the areas in which they live makes it possible to explore the interaction of individual and structural factors in the production of health inequalities.

Measurement issues: health and illness
Health and illness are just as difficult to conceptualize and measure as socio-economic circumstances. For the majority of people, we can be

certain that age of death is objective and accurate. Self-reports of health pose more problems since it is quite difficult to know exactly what they are measuring and hence how reliable they are. However, the strong associations that have been found between general measures of self-rated health – such as whether people assess their health as 'good', 'fair' or 'poor' – and future mortality (Idler and Benyamani 1997) suggest a degree of 'accuracy' in personal assessments. Self-assessments are not predictors in any simple causative sense. A self-assessment is more likely to 'predict' death when, for example, the individual is aware that they have coronary heart disease and when we know that coronary heart disease is likely to be the cause of their death, than when death is the result of random violence. But the overall argument is that, whether intuitively or in a more consciously reflective way, people arrive at their own assessments which seem appropriately to reflect the state of their bodily conditions (Jylha 2009).

A particularly useful recent development has been composite measures, or what are termed 'health expectancies', which combine age at death with measures of health during a person's lifetime. Two of the most common 'health expectancies' are 'disability-free life expectancy' (DFLE) and 'healthy life expectancy' (HLE).

With these points about measurement in mind, we now turn to look at some of the evidence for the widening socio-economic gap in health.

The widening gap

Table 4.1 shows that, although life expectancy at birth improved for both men and women in all RGSC groups in England and Wales between 1972–6 and 2002–5, the gap between those at the 'top' and the 'bottom' remained. The column on the far right also shows that men and women in non-manual occupations (classes I–IIInm) had greater average increases in years of life expectancy than those in manual occupations (IIIm–V).

A baby boy born in England and Wales in 1981–3 had a 47 per cent chance, and a baby girl a 66 per cent chance, of surviving to age 75. For those born in 2004–6, this had risen to 66 per cent and 77 per cent, respectively. However, as illustrated in table 4.2, this masks significant differences between geographic areas. For example, we can see that only 51.7 per cent of males born in the Manchester area in 2004–6 could expect to live to age 75, compared to 78.1 per cent of males born in East Dorset in the same period. We can also see that the difference between those areas with the highest and lowest chances of survival increased by just under 6 per cent for males between the time periods, indicating growing inequality.

The persistence of a severe North–South divide in England recently

Table 4.1 Life expectancy at birth (years) by social class, England and Wales

Occupational social class (RGSC)	1972–6		2002–5		Diffs between 1972–6 and 2002–5, at birth	
	Men	Women	Men	Women	Men	Women
I Professional	71.9	79.0	80.0	85.1		
II Managerial and technical/ intermediate	71.9	77.1	79.4	83.2	8.0	5.2
IIInm Skilled non manual	69.5	78.3	78.4	82.4		
IIIm Skilled manual	70.0	75.2	76.5	80.5		
IV Partly skilled	68.3	75.3	75.7	79.9	6.8	4.8
V Unskilled	66.5	74.2	72.7	78.1		

Source: derived from ONS, *Trends in Life Expectancy by Social Class, 1972–2005*, www.statistics.gov.uk/statbase/Product.asp?vlnk=8460 (accessed 23 July 2008)

Table 4.2 Local areas with the highest and lowest probabilities of survival of males to age 75, England and Wales

	1981–3		2004–6	
	Highest area	Lowest area	Highest area	Lowest area
Males	57.8% (East Dorset)	37.1% (Manchester)	78.1% (East Dorset)	51.7% (Manchester)
		Difference 20.7%		Difference 26.4%
Females	74.5% (Crawley)	57.8% (Burnley)	80.9% (Monmouth- shire)	67.4% (Blaenau Gwent)
		Difference 16.7%		Difference 13.5%

Source: derived from Wells and Gordon (2008: tables 1 and 3)

has been shown by Hacking and colleagues who report an average northern excess mortality of 13.8 per cent over the period 1965 to 2008 (Hacking et al. 2011). These general trends are replicated in many other countries. For example, the life-expectancy gap between the least and most deprived areas in the US increased from 2.8 years in 1980–2 to 4.5 years in 1998–2000 (Singh and Siahpush 2006).

As these life-expectancy data show, death rates have been falling across all socio-economic groups. However, as we have noted, the rate of improvement has been sharper amongst non-manual occupational groups, contributing to the growing socio-economic divide. In the UK, the major contributor to this trend appears to be growing disparities amongst men. Table 4.3 shows that the mortality ratio of RGSC classes

Table 4.3 Trends in all-cause mortality by social class, 1986–1999, men and women aged 35–64 (directly age-standardized rates per 100,000 person years*)

Social class	1986–92		1993–6		1997–9	
	Men	**Women**	**Men**	**Women**	**Men**	**Women**
I&II	460	274	376	262	347	237
IIIn	480	310	437	262	417	253
IIIm	617	350	538	324	512	327
IV & V	776	422	648	378	606	335
Ratio IV&V: I&II	1.69	1.54	1.71	1.44	1.75	1.41

Note: * Age standardization adjusts for the effects of any differences in age distributions of different occupational groups.
Source: derived from White et al. (2003: tables 1 and 2)

IV&V to classes I&II grew from 1.69 to 1.75 for men between 1986–92 and 1997–9, while for women they declined slightly over the same period (although it is important to note that significant class differences still exist amongst women at each time period). Again, these differences are not confined to Britain. Mackenbach and colleagues (2003) found that relative inequalities in death rates increased during the 1980s and early 1990s across six European countries. This was due to faster proportional mortality declines in higher socio-economic groups, especially improvements in cardiovascular disease mortality, as well as increases in some causes of death in lower socio-economic groups.

Research on male British civil servants of different grades 'from mandarin to messenger' suggests that social position has differential effects as people age. Using a composite measure of physical health, Chandola and colleagues (2007) found that, as the civil servants aged, the gap between lower and higher grades grew. Thus the average physical health score of a 'high grade' man at age 45 in 1991–2 was almost 53, which was about the same as a 'low-grade' man 4.5 years younger. Yet the average score of a 'high-grade' man aged 70 in 2002–4 was almost 48, about the same as a 'low-grade' man 8 years younger. This suggests that people lower in the occupational hierarchy tend to 'age more quickly'.

The major causes of death in wealthy nations are heart disease, cerebrovascular disease and cancer. The widening gap for all of these causes of death for men in England and Wales during the 1990s was strongly associated with swifter declines in all of these causes of death amongst RGSC groups I and II. The picture for women is more complicated. Deaths from ischaemic heart disease declined by similar levels for all RGSC groups over the period; deaths due to cerebrovascular disease fell in groups IIIn, IV and V, but increased slightly in groups I, II and IIIm; while lung cancer deaths fell slightly in classes I and II, but stayed very high in groups IV and V (White et al. 2003).

Research on morbidity – that is, the state of people's health during their lives – generally also shows that people in lower socio-economic groups report worse health than those in higher groups. This is evident from both occupation- and area-based measures. Thus, data on prevalence of self-reported longstanding illness from the 2011 General Lifestyle Survey of households in Britain shows a clear gradient across the three aggregated NS-SEC groups (of the household reference person), with 29 per cent of those in the 'managerial and professional group', 35 per cent of those in the 'intermediate group', and 38 per cent of those in the 'manual occupations' group reporting a longstanding illness (ONS 2013). Drawing on 2001 census data, Rasulo et al. (2007) ranked small areas (wards) in England and Wales according to the Carstairs Deprivation Index referred to earlier. They found a clear step-wise gradient, with rates of 'poor health' amongst both males and females about three times higher, and rates of 'limiting long term illness' about two times higher, in the most deprived compared to the least deprived area.

Specific health conditions

There is also evidence of increasing socio-economic inequalities in specific health conditions. Two examples of current concern are lung cancer and obesity. Lung cancer rates have been declining amongst both men and women, but more swiftly amongst higher socio-economic groups. Between 1986–92 and 1997–9, male lung cancer death rates in England and Wales declined by 45 per cent amongst RGSC non-manual groups, but only by 31 per cent amongst manual groups. The equivalent figures for women were 40 per cent and 24 per cent (White et al. 2003). Given the strong association between smoking and lung cancer, it is noteworthy that smoking has also been declining, but at a faster pace amongst higher socio-economic groups (Babb et al. 2006).

However, turning to other conditions, it is predicted that, if current trends continue, obesity will soon overtake smoking as the primary cause of preventable death (Moon et al. 2007). Paradoxically, obesity is socially patterned along the same lines as hunger was in the nineteenth century, being much more prevalent in England in lower socio-economic groups and those living in more deprived areas (Mackenbach 2008). This trend is forecasted to continue in future years (Zaninotto et al. 2006). Obesity is associated with major illnesses such as heart disease and diabetes, which themselves are strongly related to socio-economic status. Diabetes is particularly important given that its incidence is rising, especially amongst lower socio-economic groups and in more deprived areas (Department of Health 2006). Turning to mental health, Dorling documents rising depression among adolescents in unequal affluent countries. As he puts it, the 'average North American child by the late 1980s was already more anxious about life than some 85 per cent of North American children in the 1950s' (2010: 277). He puts this down to growing insecurity fostered by a more competitive society.

Global health inequalities

So far we have been concerned with health inequalities *within* affluent countries. It is also important to consider inequalities *between* countries. As Moser and colleagues write, 'since the late 1980s the world has not only failed to become a more equal place in terms of mortality, but it has actually become less equal' (2005: 205). Some commentators connect these changes directly to the spread of neoliberal globalization policies, such as economic deregulation and associated reductions in welfare spending, that have been promoted by the G-20,[2] transnational corporations and multilateral institutions, such as the World Bank and International Monetary Fund since the 1980s (Schrecker et al. 2008; De Vogli 2011) (see wider discussion in chapter 1).

It is not simply that life expectancy has been rising more rapidly in some countries than others. Since the global distribution of wealth became more and more unequal during the 1980s, many of the countries of Africa and of Central and Eastern Europe have actually witnessed a downturn in life expectancy and an increase in mortality. World Health Organisation (WHO) statistics show that, between 1990 and 2007, nineteen countries (notably in Sub-Saharan Africa) experienced falls in life expectancy at birth (WHO 2010). This is a major turnaround from the trend of rising life expectancy and worldwide convergence since the 1950s (Leon 2011). Individuals living in many countries of Africa can expect to live only into their forties. In 2009, life expectancy at birth for males and females respectively was 47 and 50 in Zimbabwe and in Afghanistan. This can be compared to the countries of Europe where the equivalent life expectancies were 78 and 82 in the UK, 80 and 83 in Iceland, and 77 and 81 in Denmark (WHO 2011a). It is also salutary to note that life expectancies in many African countries today are equivalent to or lower than those of mid-nineteenth-century England referred to earlier in the chapter. The AIDS burden has been a significant contributor to this.

In Europe, the most significant differences are found between the western and eastern parts of the region. WHO data for 1980 to 2000 show a dramatic increase in the life-expectancy gap between the fifteen countries of the western part of the European Union (EU), the fifteen central and south-eastern European countries (CSEC) and the twelve countries that constitute the Commonwealth of Independent States (CIS, the former USSR) (WHO 2003). As we can see in figure 4.3, the pattern for the CIS is remarkable. The improvements of the mid-1980s

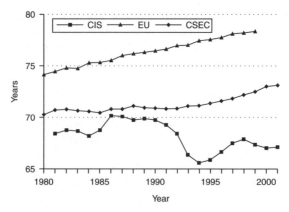

Figure 4.3 Life expectancy at birth (CIS, EU, CSEC)

are generally attributed to anti-alcohol campaigns introduced in the USSR in 1985, and deteriorations to the fall into deep economic crisis in the mid-1990s. Eastern Europe has been a natural laboratory within which to observe just how swiftly economic and social change is marked on the social body through changes in health. The same holds for Zimbabwe. In the 1950s, average life expectancy was in the fifties; by the early 1980s this had grown to the early sixties. Thereafter it plummeted to such an extent that people can now expect to live only into their late forties / early fifties. In 2008, *healthy* life expectancy (HLE) in Zimbabwe was only 40 years for men and 38 years for women, statistics not too far out of line with other countries of Sub-Saharan Africa (WHO 2010). Once the breadbasket of Africa, Zimbabwe is now a famished land ravaged by poverty and AIDS.

The discussion so far makes clear that, no matter how it is measured, the association between inequality and health is indisputable. This has been most clearly illustrated by the swift and unequal impact of global economic change upon particular groups of people both within and between countries. However, a vital question remains: exactly how are health inequalities between social groups produced?

Explaining health inequalities

Theorizing inequality

When seeking to explain health inequalities in affluent societies, we face the not-inconsiderable challenge of identifying the dynamics by which socio-economic inequalities become rooted in the individual and the social (collective) body. This involves specifying the health-related constraints and choices that arise for particular individuals and communities from global, national and local-level change. In order to do this, we need to reflect on the form that social inequality takes and whether it may be decoupling from occupation.

According to Beck (2002), social class is a 'zombie category', actually dead for some time, but revived and inappropriately kept alive – if barely – within sociology, particularly in Britain. This encapsulates a generalized sentiment that class as traditionally conceived is outmoded. It is crucial here to distinguish between *class* and *inequality*: the majority of sociologists are insistent that inequalities persist – and, indeed, may be hardening – but many believe that they cannot be understood in class terms, since classes – that is, collectivities leading lives distinct from, and in conflict with, other classes – no longer exist.

People's identities used to be very closely tied to their employment. To paraphrase Beck and Beck-Gernsheim (2002: xxiv), in the past, if you knew a man was an apprentice in a car manufacturing company, then you more or less also knew what he earned, his opinions and how he talked, the way he dressed and what he did in his spare time, what he read and how he voted. These connections have been swept away by the growing individualism that has accompanied wide-scale economic change from the mid-1970s. The decline in manufacturing and rise of the knowledge economy has meant more part-time working, more temporary and flexible labour, more self-employment, chronic unemployment and workless households. Places of employment are shifting from 'being dense, often rigid, pyramidal bureaucracies to more flexible networks in a constant state of inner revision' (Sennett 2000: 176). As we saw in chapter 2, Bauman depicts this process as a shift from a 'heavy' or 'solid' to a 'light' or 'liquefied' modernity: to a world of more freedom, but also of radical uncertainty, a world of 'ever deepening wealth-and-income gaps between the better off and the worse off sections of the world population, and inside every single society' (2001: 114).

Bauman argues that, even though inequalities manifest in economic terms, this is too narrow a frame of reference. He refers to 'a political economy of uncertainty', the defining feature of which is 'ambient fear', as even those in seemingly secure positions are chronically aware and ever fearful of becoming part of the large reserve of the poor. So, even though individualism may be culturally mandated, there is a yawning gap between 'the right of self-assertion and the capacity to control the social settings which render such self-assertion feasible or unrealistic' (Bauman 2002: xv). A culturally significant illustration is the cult of celebrity fed by 'reality' TV shows whereby individuals are encouraged to believe that they can 'make it' – often through visible and fierce competition against others – when the actual 'reality' is abject, and often public, failure. Speaking more generally, instead of meaning less

UNIVERSITY OF WINCHESTER
LIBRARY

inequality between individuals and groups, the release from class may actually mean more. The main point is that these inequalities are not self-evidently collective in form.

For these reasons, Beck believes that you cannot relate occupation-ally based measures (such as RGSC and NS-SEC) 'to how people live and think, eat, how they dress, love, organise their lives and so on. If you are interested in what is going on in people's minds and the ways of life they are leading, you have to get away from the old categories' (Beck 2002: 207). This corresponds with the wider 'cultural turn' within sociology in which class is construed as an active process, something which 'is *done* (in both "public" and "private" arenas) rather than a system into which we are slotted' (Lawler 2005: 804, emphasis original). Much of this way of thinking derives from Bourdieu's (1984) notion that classes are produced and reproduced though hierarchies of taste or cultural preference. Here 'culture is not a product of class relations but is itself a field in which class relations operate' (Savage 2000: 106). People are aware of class: it is a benchmark with which they make sense of their lives, but they are hesitant to use class labels because doing so would undermine their 'aspiration to be an individual agent, not programmed to act in any particular way' (Savage 2000: 113). Yet, amongst others, Savage argues that these processes are systematically driven. Thus, he concludes that the 'culture of individualization' actu-ally permits the processes producing inequality to operate in a more naked way than before, since 'it allows the creation of a society that routinely reproduces social inequality at the same time as deflecting the attention ... sideways rather than upwards and downwards, so making the issue of inequality largely "invisible" and somehow "uninteresting"' (2000: 159). Based on their recent research in Britain, Savage and colleagues (Savage et al. 2013) identify a new phase of 'cultural class analysis' which de-couples class from occupation in favour of a multidimensional model based on the interplay between three dimensions of capital – economic, social and cultural (Bourdieu 1984). In 2011, they conducted a large-scale web survey – the *Great British Class Survey* (www.bbc.co.uk/science/0/21970879, accessed 28 January 2014) which was publicized by the BBC (British Broadcasting Corporation) – and face-to-face interviews. They asked respondents a large range of questions to tap into the three forms of capital, includ-ing about their leisure interests, musical tastes, food preferences, social ties, income and savings. Using the statistical technique of latent class analysis, they identified seven classes: the 'elite', the 'established middle class', the 'technical middle class', the 'new affluent workers', the 'traditional working class', the 'emergent service sector', and the 'precariat'. While they found some expected fits with occupation – e.g. barristers and judges fall only into the 'elite' class – some occupations occurred across classes, such as care workers who were found in the 'traditional working class', in the 'emergent service sector' and in the 'precariat'. The researchers highlight the capacity of their schema to reveal the cultural and social barriers that operate in Britain and draw particular attention to the capacity of their schema to register the existence of a distinct and sizeable (6 per cent of the population) 'elite' who have very high economic capital, high social capital and very highbrow cultural capital, and an even more sizeable 'precariat' (15 per cent of the population) who have poor economic capital, and the lowest scores on every other criterion.

Explanatory models

Most of the theoretical debates about class discussed above are not directed towards health; they are nevertheless important because their concerns surface in various guises in recent attempts to provide explanations for health inequalities.

In the 1980s, the *Black Report* on inequalities in health (Townsend and Davidson 1982) proposed four explanations for health inequalities: artefactual (differences are statistical artefacts, or errors due to the way the research was carried out); natural or social selection (health influences social class position, rather than the other way round); cultural/ behavioural (individual lifestyles and habits are the most important); and material (high and low income and their consequences directly affect health). Although they came down firmly in favour of material explanations, the *Black Report* authors did not so much dismiss other explanations as place them at the margins. The four-fold framework had a huge and politically charged influence on debate that continues to this day (see Berridge 2003). Although researchers have now pretty much moved away from the 'competing' explanations of the *Black Report* to explore the 'interrelation between and contribution of different types of explanation' (Blaxter 2010: 117), the flames of debate have not dampened. If anything, they have intensified as researchers have advanced new syncretic theories to explain the dynamic interplay between individuals and the complex social environments in which they live their lives.

Visual models are often used to tease out the interplay between the individual and social structures in relation to health. One of the most recent high-profile examples comes from the WHO's Commission on the Social Determinants of Health (CSDH 2008) (see figure 4.4). The CSDH accounts for the distribution of health and well-being in society through the impact of material circumstances, levels of social cohesion, psychosocial factors, behaviours and biological factors upon different groups of people as they are distinguished by socio-economic position, education, occupation, income, gender, ethnicity/race, and so on. It relates the degree of stratification in these groups to the structural

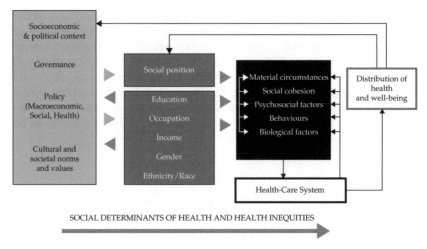

Source: Solar and Irwin (2007); CSDH (2008)

Figure 4.4 Commission on Social Determinants of Health conceptual framework

drivers of the socio-economic and political context of a society, how a society is governed, its social policies, and its cultural and societal norms and values.

The merit of a model such as this is that it situates individuals within the constellation of wider influences upon their health. Such models are an advance on theories which seek to explain health inequalities *either* by reference to distal or 'upstream' societal influences *or* by reference to proximal or 'downstream' factors closest to the individual, such as their 'biological constitution' or 'individual lifestyles' (Krieger 2008). Couched at a high level of theoretical abstraction, they are intended to stimulate the research imagination and to guide enquiry rather than to specify the exact empirical pathways that produce health inequalities. However, Krieger maintains that most fail to fire the research imagination. What we need, she maintains, is iconoclastic iconography that 'readily sparks instant and vivid insight into the causal processes at play', which are the 'skewed distributions of power and resources in society' (Krieger 2009: 1102, 1003). Under the banner of 'ecosocial theory' Krieger aims to convey the myriad pathways through which social inequality becomes biologically embodied, and produces health inequalities (Krieger 2001, 2008, 2009). This discussion highlights that although there is wide-scale agreement that pitting the individual against society, the social against the biological, and the cultural/social against the economic/material is far less useful than studying their interaction in the production of health inequalities, major differences remain in how researchers theorize the social processes involved. We now turn to a critical analysis of present debates, beginning with the recent interest in embodiment.

The embodiment of health inequalities

Biology has had an uneasy place in health inequalities research, particularly in the early days when it was felt that any suggestion of biological influence might smack of eugenics. The sequencing of the human genome, or so-called 'book of life', in the first decade of the twenty-first century has encouraged the belief that our fate is in our genes. Biological determinism is premised on the belief that 'human lives and actions are the consequences of the biochemical properties of the cells that make up an individual' which, in turn, are determined by the genes that each individual possesses (Pilnick 2002: 19). The result is a highly individualized depiction of society in which health inequalities are a direct consequence of inherited ability. Social scientists have countered such reductivist and fatalistic accounts by emphasizing biological plasticity and the importance of the interaction of the human organism with its social environment. Thus Dickens argues that 'perhaps the most satisfactory way forward is to consider the human organism . . . as consisting of a set of potentials, capacities and developmental tendencies. These are genetically inherited. But how, indeed, whether, these work out in practice depends on the social and physical environment' (Dickens 2000: 80).

How can we relate this to health inequalities? Mackenbach provides an explanation as follows. For the genetic constitution of an individual organism (or genotype) to have a role two conditions must be fulfilled. First, socio-economic status must be associated with one or more genotypes, and second, these genotypes must be 'causally involved in the occurrence of health problems, either directly (by an effect on the occurrence of disease) or indirectly (by an effect on determinants of disease)' (Mackenbach 2005: 269). Causality could work in two directions. Congenital abnormalities of the foetus, which are more common in lower socio-economic groups, could follow from the mother's social exposure to noxious influences in pregnancy, such as through her workplace or cigarette smoking. However, Mackenbach suggests that causality is more likely to run in the reverse direction;– that is, from the genetic to the social – as certain 'given' personal attributes which are markers of health, such as general intelligence, personality and mental fitness, indirectly influence health by 'selecting' people into different socio-economic groups through educational and occupational opportunities, and, in later life, shape health behaviours, such as exercise, diet and the use of health services. Even so, he makes clear that in overall terms, the part played by genetics in the generation of health inequalities is 'rather distal and probably modest' (2005: 271). Most commentators believe that even where genetics does play a role in health problems, its contribution will be highly complex and difficult to establish. In Holtzman's assessment, this complexity 'makes it virtually impossible that the genetic variants will be concentrated in any social class and transmitted more to children of that class than to children of another class' (2002: 535).

Whether genetic explanations falter in part for want of research or entirely from inherent flaws is not yet clear. In any event, biology is about more than genetics. It concerns the interaction of the whole organism with its social environment. There is wide agreement that it is crucial to tease out just how this occurs if we want to understand health inequalities. Tarlov (1996: 84) identifies the processes by which individuals in different social groups 'receive messages about their social circumstances, convert the information into perceptions, and then translate these perceptions into biological signals that are anteced-ents to disease' – or what he calls the 'sociobiological translation' – as a great new frontier for science. The recent upsurge of research on the life course has been very useful in this regard because it allows us to explore the temporal sequencing of social and biological processes, and therefore to begin to sort out cause and effect, not only in relation to changes over individual lifetimes but also in relation to changes in the societies in which people live out their lives.

Life course analysis

It makes intuitive sense that things which happen to us early in life affect our health later on. Thus, serious illnesses in infancy are likely to shape later life chances in direct or indirect ways. Similarly, our health at older ages may have been affected in some way by our social origins and earlier pathway through life. Commonsensical though these prem-ises are, they have been difficult to study until very recently because they require not only detailed data collected over the potentially long course of individual lives, but also several sets of data following people who were born and grew up during different historical periods set some time apart. The British cohort studies which are following people born in 1946, 1958, 1970 and 2000 are invaluable in this regard. In order to conduct detailed statistical analyses, we need reasonably large numbers of health conditions and incidences of illness and death. The association between illness and ageing means we are reliant upon cohorts getting older. Survivors of the 1946 birth cohort are now in their late sixties; the 1958 cohort their mid-fifties; and the 1970 cohort their early forties. As we saw earlier, on average, people in Britain have been living into their seventies and beyond over this period. This means that, even now, we are dealing mainly with 'premature' morbidity and mortality (Blane 2006).

The life course approach is useful because it enables us to explore the 'dynamic interplay between the changing individual and a changing social context' (Schoon 2006: 23). Again, while this is easy to appreciate in principle, it has been difficult to study empirically (Blaxter 2003; Schoon 2006). A useful starting point is to try to assess the contribution that childhood socio-economic status makes to later health. Using cohort data relating to various causes of mortality and morbidity, researchers have reached the general conclusion that childhood socio-economic status (typically measured by parental occupation) retains a strong influence on health even after controlling for achieved adult socio-economic status. For example, Kuh and colleagues (2002) measured the cumulative death rate of the British 1946 cohort and found that, by age 54, those in more disadvantaged positions in childhood were around twice as likely to have died than those from more advantaged origins. The effect of father's RGSC remained significant even after taking into account the individual's own RGSC and whether they owned their own home or not. Turning to morbidity, Power and colleagues (2007) found that, for the 1958 birth cohort at age 45, statistically significant differences in high blood pressure, body mass index (BMI), depression and anxiety, and chronic pain, by childhood RGSC, were attenuated, but did not go away, when adult RGSC was taken into account. This body of research suggests that childhood socio-economic status casts a long and gloomy shadow over later life for those born into disadvantaged circumstances. But it does not tell us what the social processes are that actually link socio-economic status and health over the life course.

Different life course models
The life course is a wide canvas (Graham 2002) which researchers have tended to frame in different ways. Broadly speaking, there are two main models. The first is the *'biological or critical periods model'*, which proposes that negative events during critically salient developmental periods may permanently alter health trajectories over the life course (Kuh and Ben-Shlomo 1997). This model has two strands. In the first strand, 'biological programming' is argued to have a direct effect on health in later life, irrespective of any intervening factors. Congenital and genetic conditions are examples. Growth before birth in particular is identified as a critical and unique period in which most elements of organ growth are completed. For example, under-nutrition and poor delivery of oxygen to the foetus *in utero* are believed to lead to permanent changes in the physiology, metabolism and structure of the body, which heighten the risk of birth defects, such as spina bifida, and the onset of conditions such as respiratory and cardiovascular morbidity later in life (see Barker 1998). It seems unlikely, however, that such developmental processes are entirely independent of social context.

For example, the neural tube is formed very early in the developmental process, even before most women are aware that they are pregnant, and is highly sensitive to lack of vitamin B, which can cause defects such as spina bifida. As Bartley puts it, 'in households where money is short, even for these few weeks, the damage will be done' (2004: 132). Equally, low birth weight, a known risk for later health, is strongly associated with maternal factors such as raised blood pressure, cigarette smoking and excess alcohol consumption, all of which are more common amongst expectant mothers in poorer socio-economic circumstances (Galobardes et al. 2004).

The second strand of the biological or critical periods model proposes that the influence of development in infancy upon later health is indirect. Here the argument is that certain 'given' psychological characteristics, such as cognitive ability and coping ability, tend to favour *both* better socio-economic status *and* better health. At the present time, there is a fair amount of interest in the role that IQ might play in this (see, e.g., Batty et al. 2006). But, as Bartley (2004) explains, even if psychological characteristics were to explain half of the differences in adult ill-health between socio-economic groups, this would still leave the other half to be explained by other factors such as the social hazards that people face as they go through life.

A second life course model is the *'accumulation of risk model'*. The argument here is that links in a chain of disadvantage (which vary in their specific nature, duration and intensity) accumulate over the life course. A magnet-effect tends to occur as lower early-life socio-economic status attracts other negatives for health, with people being more susceptible to risk at certain critical periods of life, such as when they leave school, and start or retire from work. In their follow-up study of biomarker data from seven different physiological systems (e.g. lipid metabolism, cardiovascular) drawn from US adults, Gruenewald et al. (2011) show how the experience of socio-economic adversity across the life course harms multiple biological systems or, as they put it, how biological systems 'weather' negatively through wear and tear.

The accumulation of risk model is conceptually distinct from the biological or critical periods model in that it places much greater emphasis on the causal importance of social factors. But these approaches are not necessarily distinct in reality. As Graham puts it, 'disadvantage during critical periods in early life can direct children into developmental and educational pathways which increase risk of disadvantage in adulthood, with this chain of risks exposing individuals to further cumulative effects' (2002: 2008). It is also possible that, for some health conditions, *specific exposures* matter more, while for others *accumulative effects* are more important (Galobardes et al. 2004). For example, it is probable that early exposure to the *helicobacter pylori* (a virulent bacterium), associated with deprivation, is significant for adult stomach cancer. Yet for lung cancer, the influence of early socio-economic position is much reduced when adult socio-economic position is taken into account, suggesting that it is the accumulation of later-life experience that matters more (Power and Kuh 2006).

Age cohorts
So far, we have been concerned with changing lives largely in isolation from changes in the wider society. Historical events, such as the introduction of the National Health Service in the UK, and Medicare and Medicaid in the US, changes in state benefit entitlements, and the onset of global economic recession, will impact people differently, depending not only on their age but on when they were born and where they grow up and live. This is known as cohort-specific effects. Comparative cohort analysis is powerful because it enables us to explore how the dynamics of inequality change as lines of advantage and disadvantage are differently drawn in different socio-historical time periods. It 'extends our reach beyond individual life courses' to the 'societal processes that are reshaping them' (Graham 2002: 2009). For example, the 1958 British birth cohort grew up in an age of liberalization, optimism and relative affluence. Most had completed their education before the onset of the economic depression of the late 1970s and could expect to find jobs when they left school. In contrast, the 1970 birth cohort were hit by the recession and collapse of the housing market (Schoon 2006). The latest 2000 UK birth cohort are growing up not only in an economic downturn, but 'in the face of growing individualization and flexibility and new family structures' and with unprecedented question marks over intergenerational commitments to care for others at the start and end of life (Dex et al. 2005: 11). Almost a quarter of these 'Millennium babies' started out their lives in poverty (Dex et al. 2005).

Time will tell how these 'Millennium babies' fare, but it is likely that the widening and deepening of social inequality discussed earlier in the chapter will be just as crucial for them as for earlier cohorts – if not more so. A review of the research literature supports the worrying conclusion that, despite overall improvements in material conditions of life generally, mortality is higher after childhood deprivation in more recent than in earlier cohorts (Galobardes et al. 2004). This is backed up by an analysis of the 1958 and 1970 birth cohorts which shows that those born in 1970 'who were experiencing socio-economic adversity, appear to be more disadvantaged relative to other children in the same cohort than similarly affected children in 1958' (Schoon 2006: 72). Schoon suggests that the stronger association between early socio-economic disadvantage and poor psychological well-being when the 1970 cohort reached their early thirties, compared to when the 1958 cohort reached the same age, could mean that those in material deprivation from the younger cohort are a more extreme group relative to their peers than the earlier cohort, reflecting the social polarization of society between the time periods in which they grew up (Schoon et al. 2003). Life course research therefore demonstrates that, in order to understand health inequalities, we need to look beyond the characteristics of individuals to the wider socio-economic dynamics of society.

Health, place and social capital

If it is possible to identify the influence of seemingly distal factors such as the dynamics of change in inequality on the health of individuals, it should be easier still to pinpoint those which are figuratively and literally closer to home, such as the places where people live. Most of us are familiar with the quip 'location, location, location' in response to the question of what to look for when buying a home. It suggests a strong relationship between neighbourhood and economic value. Although some things are hard to miss, such as a nuclear power plant on our door-step, the 'health value' of a new neighbourhood is much less likely to be on our mind when weighing up the pros and cons of where to live. But there is a body of evidence which indicates that neighbourhoods do indeed have 'health value'. Physical features (such as air quality, noise levels, environmental pollution, housing stock), local resources (green spaces, type of food outlets, quality of health services) and the socio-cultural environment (crime levels, networks of community support) – factors which themselves are associated with housing values – all also affect health. Symbolic dimensions such as an area's reputation are important too because they influence the feelings of those who live there, as well as who moves in and out, such as employers and investors. For example, research by Bush and colleagues (2001) found that people living close to a steel and petro-chemical plant in a disadvantaged area in the North of England were discredited with the self-same characteristics as the place where they lived and known locally as 'Smogs'.

Research on health and place stems back to the mid-nineteenth-century studies referred to earlier in the chapter. It has been re-kindled in attempts to identify whether the places where people live have independent influences upon health over and above the characteristics of the individuals who live in them. This is what is thought of as the relative significance of *compositional* and *contextual* variations in health. *Compositional variation* results from the attributes of individuals who make up the population of an area. A purely compositional explanation would be that similar types of people will have similar health experiences no matter where they live (Curtis and Rees Jones 1998). *Contextual variation* would be found when people with more or less the same individual characteristics (e.g. income, RGSC) show varying health depending on where they live. The interest in contextual variation follows the longstanding sociological premise that collectivities – here, people in areas – are more than the sum of their parts; they have, as Durkheim (1895) argued, a reality *sui generis*. The intuitive sociological appeal of context framed in these terms might explain the interest in so-called 'area affects' upon health. Research has been aided in this quest by the statistical technique of multilevel modelling which makes it possible to distinguish between different levels of aggregation of data in analysis. For example, it enables us to take account both of individuals' education levels and the level of education in an area as a whole. Generally speaking, research has tended to find a residual effect of area (context) once compositional effects are taken into account (Macintyre et al. 2002). Much of this research relies on data collected at one point in time, known as cross-sectional analysis. But in a recent longitudinal analysis, following cohorts of people of different ages living in different areas of Glasgow in Scotland over time, Ellaway and colleagues (2012) found that, after controlling for individual socio-economic status, those in poorer neighbourhoods reported poorer health at younger ages than those in more affluent areas.

From their review of published research Pickett and Pearl (2001) conclude that most research has found a significant statistical association between at least one measure of social environment and a health outcome. Nonetheless, they report that 'contextual effects were generally modest and much smaller than compositional effects' (2001: 111). Thus, it seems reasonable to conclude that, although 'where you live matters to health outcomes ... it is less influential than who you are' (Mohan et al. 2004: 6).

Social capital

When considering the influence of local areas upon health, it is important to distinguish between those factors which are material in form (such as housing quality or income levels) and those which are less tangible, such as social cohesion and civic trust. Interest in the latter has been stimulated by the outpouring of research on social capital and health. The notion of social capital can be traced back to the early nineteenth century when de Tocqueville (1967 [1835, 1840]) identified voluntary associations as a defining feature of American life, and Durkheim (1970 [1897]) drew an association between the levels of social integration and moral regulation in society and the magnitude and types of suicide. More than a century later, Robert Putnam characterized US society as suffering from a pervasive 'civic malaise'. He was concerned about the decline in connections amongst individuals and a loss of social networks and the norms of reciprocity that they foster. Putnam conceived of two forms of social capital: *bonding* (or exclusive) social capital, which refers to networks that are 'inward looking' and reinforce exclusive identities and homogeneous groups (such as country clubs or gangs), and *bridging* (or inclusive) social capital, which refers to networks that are 'outward looking' and potentially 'encompass people across diverse social cleavages' (such as youth groups or Neighbourhood Watch schemes) (Putnam 2000: 22).

Putnam's own illustration of what we might now call the influence of 'area level social capital' on health came from the study of Roseto, a small Italian-American community in Pennsylvania. From the 1950s to the 1980s, researchers noticed something puzzling: 'Rosetans just didn't die of heart attacks' (Putnam 2000: 329). Their age-adjusted heart attack rate was less than half that of their neighbours. Why could this be? Research showed that the usual explanations of diet, exercise, weight, smoking, family history and so on could not explain it – indeed, Rosetans seemed to have somewhat more than their share of these risk factors. Rather, the explanation was found in the tightly knit nature of the community. Roseto had been founded back in the nineteenth century by a group of people from the same village back in Italy. Once in the US, they had created a mutual aid society, a labour union, churches, youth groups and sports clubs. Conspicuous displays of consumption were scorned and 'family values' and 'good behaviours' reinforced. Life in Roseto harks back to a bygone age, which is precisely Putnam's point: as socially mobile young people began to reject the 'tight-knit Italian folkways', the heart attack rate became analogous to that of neighbours in similar towns (Putnam 2000: 329). There are, of course, few communities like Roseto; the point is that the work of Putnam and others stimulated researchers to look more generally at the associations between social cohesion and health using the concept of social capital.

Social capital is a slippery concept which is difficult to define and measure. It concerns norms such as trust, social responsibility, civic responsibility and social connectedness that cannot be directly observed (Mohan et al. 2004). Consequently, they tend to be studied using aggregated data of individual perceptions, such as feelings of trust, and experiences of membership of social networks. Sometimes measures which are independent of people's reports are also included, such as actual crime rates rather than fear of crime, for example (Blaxter and Poland 2002).

From around the 1990s, researchers began to explore whether variations in social capital might help in the explanation of area inequalities in health. This seam of research was pioneered by Kawachi and colleagues who used US states as the area measure. For example, in a study of thirty states between 1986 and 1990, they found that lower social capital (measured by levels of feelings of civic trust and density of organizational membership) was associated with both higher state-level income inequality and increased mortality risk (Kawachi and Kennedy 1997). This suggests that variations in social capital may mediate (or help to explain) the link between area-level material factors (such as income inequality) and the health of populations. However, as Kawachi and colleagues have themselves noted, it is questionable whether states are a meaningful unit of analysis for area effects. Consequently researchers have begun to look at smaller areas. For example, in a study of mortality in Chicago neighbourhoods, researchers found that social capital (as measured by reciprocity, trust and civic participation) was associated with death rates even after adjustment for neighbourhood material deprivation (Lochner et al. 2003). However, a study of English electoral wards found that a wide range of measures of social capital did not account substantially for variations in mortality between wards. Even where modest effects were found they were attenuated when area-level deprivation, individual socio-economic status, and health-related behaviours (like diet and cigarette smoking) were taken into account (Mohan et al. 2004).

The experience of place
Although research on social capital takes our understanding of place beyond material factors, it is often hampered by weak theoretical conceptualization of place. The inclusion of structural-level variables, such as measures of social capital, helps to counter methodological individualism, but an inappropriate determinism can be fostered when factors such as average education level, average income or levels of trust in an area are deemed to 'influence disease outcomes in a uniform fashion across space and that these types of variables comprise context' (Frohlich et al. 2001: 778). Increasingly, researchers believe that, rather than trying to separate out *compositional* and *contextual* effects, we should see them as interdependent. Places are not just containers in which social processes play out; they actively contribute to these processes in a dynamic manner (Curtis 2004). We therefore need to appreciate the dynamic interaction between people and places: 'people make places and places make people' (Tunstall et al. 2004: 7). In other words, individuals are not only affected by the social contexts within which they live their lives, they themselves constantly re-create the social conditions which make these contexts possible (Frohlich et al. 2001).

It is here that the difference between space and place becomes important. 'A "space" describes *where* a location is, while a "place" describes *what* a location is' – place is to space as home is to house (Tunstall et al. 2004: 6, emphasis original). So, while the characteristics of the areas in which we live are important, how we relate to them matters just as much, perhaps more. This means we need to grasp the tight 'intertwining of people and place' (Williams 2007: 13). This necessitates reaching down to the fine grain of health inequality that is not easily captured in large-scale surveys. For example, the meaning of distance goes beyond the simple sense of physical distance such as kilometres between one place and another. Whether there are quality affordable food outlets near to home is likely to matter more to an elderly person who finds it difficult to get around than to a younger person who can get on one or more buses to go to the shops. Such illustrations may seem prosaic, but they are crucial to people's ability to maintain their health.

Research is beginning to tease out how people relate to place and how this influences not only their health, but how they conceive of inequalities. For example, Popay and colleagues (2003a) conducted in-depth interviews with adults in two relatively advantaged and two relatively disadvantaged areas in the North of England. They found that people's ideas of 'proper' places – that is, where they wanted to be – were influenced by the characteristics of areas (e.g. safe streets, access to shops) as well as by the behaviours of people in those places (e.g. community spirit, sense of trust, social networks). The experience of 'improper' places often led to adjustments that were not good for health. Thus a lone mother described the impact of her environment as follows:

> the doctor has put me on Prozac[3] a few months back for living here. Because it's depressing. You get up, you look round and all you see is junkies . . . I know one day I will come off, I will get off here. I mean I started drinking a hell of a lot more since I've been on here. I drink every night. I have a drink every night just to get to sleep. I smoke more as well.
>
> (Popay et al. 2003a: 68)

The researchers found that material deprivation was related to poor health and health behaviours, but that the route between the two was influenced by people's potential to (re)construct a positive identity for themselves despite their poor environment. The ability to do this was associated with their personal biographies and their capacity to construct finely differentiated categories that localized the problems of place and associated them with 'others'. This process of 'othering' may explain why, in this study, people in disadvantaged areas were reluctant to accept the existence of health inequalities. Even though they gave vivid accounts of the association between health and material disadvantage, they wanted to avoid the moral connotations of assigning negative attributes to their own places and the people living in them (Popay et al. 2003b). Respondents squared the apparent mismatch with the belief that individual strength of character and moral control can protect people from poor health. As Williams explains: 'what people know is not simply datum for epidemiological or sociological extraction. It *co-constitutes* the world as it is, and helps social scientists to understand *how* structures determine health' (2003: 146, emphasis original). The lay conception that individuals can 'see their way out' may seem fanciful, but it is not that far removed from recent attempts by social scientists to use concepts such as 'personal resilience' to explain why some people adapt positively in the face of adversity – in other words, how they beat the odds (see Schoon 2006).

It has been stressed throughout this chapter that inequalities in health are the embodiment of societal dynamics. The not-inconsiderable challenge for researchers is illuminating the social processes through which this occurs. This involves identifying the interplay between social structure and individual agency, and capturing the dynamics of individual and collective lives; paying attention to material factors (such as socio-economic status); and also to seemingly less tangible factors such as people's perceptions of place and of others. We saw earlier that the widening of health inequalities in affluent societies since the middle of the twentieth century is associated with rising overall affluence alongside a hardening of inequalities between people. These changes are cultural as well as economic in form, and involve the development of new social identities and new social hierarchies alongside the simply economic ones (Bauman 2000; Beck 2002). As part and parcel of this process, we are led to ask: what matters most for health inequalities in wealthy societies? Is it absolute differences in the material circumstances of people's lives? Or could it be that perceptions of relative differences between people now matter more?

Relative inequality and health

Health differentials are not just between those at the top and the bottom, or 'haves' and the 'have nots': 'they run all the way down the social scale from the most to the least privileged, covering everyone in between' (Marmot 2005: 36). This 'fine grain' or 'continuous gradient' poses a challenge to explanations which depend on the causal significance of absolute levels of deprivation below which health is likely to be affected. Rather, the fine grain suggests that the social processes which generate health inequalities operate *right across the social scale*. Work by Michael Marmot, Richard Wilkinson and others, suggests that relative deprivation may be more important than absolute deprivation, and that the social processes at work may be psychosocial in kind.

Wilkinson and Pickett (2009) maintain that rich countries face a profound paradox between material success and social failure. For poor countries, the higher the gross national income per head (a measure of living standards), the longer is the average life expectancy of the population. But as societies get richer during the process of economic and social development, further increases in living standards not only gradually lose their power to improve standards of health, the tendency is actually slightly reversed and health gets worse. How can it be that, within a country like the US, people who have a household income of less than $17,000 have worse health than those whose income is $34,000 (and those who have $68,000 have better health still), and yet for the country as a whole, a 'national income of £34,000 per person does not seem to buy better health than having $17,000'? (Marmot 2005: 67). The answer is that it is not how much money you have in *absolute terms*, but how much you have *relative to others*. Thus, 'in the rich countries, it is now the symbolic importance of wealth and possessions that matters. What purchases say about status and identity is often more important than the goods themselves. Put crudely, second-rate goods are assumed to reflect second-rate people' (Wilkinson and Pickett 2009: 30).

These sentiments are far more than individual in form, they are generated by a corrosive sense of inequality that impacts negatively on social relations between people, and relate to the ambient fear that Bauman (2002) associates with 'liquid modernity', which affects everyone to some degree. As Dorling puts it, 'wealth does not shelter you or those you love from despair. Should you be rich and live in a rich unequal country, your children are far more likely to suffer from mental illness than you were' (2010: 306).

In the opinion of Wilkinson, 'the central issue facing modern societies – affecting the health, happiness, and quality of life of all of us – is the quality of social relations' (2005: 285). As inequality has grown within rich societies, anti-social behaviour, stress and mistrust have increased, while sociability, social support and trust have decreased, all with direct consequences for health and longevity. In support of this thesis, researchers report data which show that it is not the richest societies that have the best health, but those that are the most socially cohesive and demonstrate high levels of trust. Japan, which has the longest life expectancy in the world, has a much narrower income gap between the most and least affluent people than any other rich market society (Marmot 2005). Conversely, less egalitarian societies such as the US and UK show lower levels of trust and higher rates of hostility and homicide, alongside higher levels of obesity, mental illness and mortality (Wilkinson and Pickett 2009). Levels of social capital – here measured at the societal level – are often proposed as the 'intervening variable which completes the chain of causative reasoning connecting income inequality and health' (Mohan et al. 2004: 7).

Biological pathways

But how exactly does *felt* inequality generate poor health? Evidence from naturalistic monitoring during everyday life using ambulatory heart monitors and biochemical analysis of saliva (to assess neuroendocrine function), suggests that it is not acute traumatic stressors such as life events that damage health, but rather constant, often low-grade, stress. Steptoe draws an analogy with cigarette smoking: 'a single cigarette has an acute effect on biological function that soon dissipates with no lasting consequences. But a cigarette every thirty minutes, every day, every month, every year for decades has a profound effect on health. The same may apply to the responses observed in psychobiological studies' (Steptoe 2006: 166).

So, although the bodily effects of phenomena such as low – compared to high – felt control in the workplace may be small, they add up over time. The lives of persons in lower-status positions are more likely to be characterized by exposure to chronic life stressors at work, in the family and in respect of finances and resources. Freund points out that these stressors are not only psychosocial but also material (e.g. the actions of our bodies in certain physical milieus, such as work environments). This demonstrates the melded nature of 'mindbody' in relation to health inequalities (Freund 2011).

In biological terms, the psychosocial explanation rests on the identification of neurohormonal pathways between social status and bodies (Freund 2011). Psychosocial factors, such as felt inequality, 'stimulate biological systems via central nervous system activation of autonomic, neuroendocrine, immune and inflammatory responses' (Steptoe 2006: 103). In studies of macaque monkeys, it is possible to hold material factors, such as diet and environment (e.g. access to water, food and space), constant while manipulating social status by moving monkeys between groups. Research has shown that animals in low-status groups develop significant risks to health, such as increased atherosclerosis, unfavourable ratios of high- to low-density lipoprotein cholesterol, insulin resistance and a tendency to central obesity (Wilkinson and Pickett 2009). Although we need to be cautious when transferring results from animal experiments to humans, this suggests that when people experience chronic stress, and when they have little control over their lives, their health begins to suffer. For example, obesity levels are higher in more unequal societies (only 2.4 per cent of adults are obese in Japan, compared to 30 per cent in the US), which Wilkinson and Pickett (2009) associate with the consumption of high-fat- and high-sugar-content foods – so-called 'comfort eating'- that feelings of stress and lack of control associated with relative or felt inequality often provoke.

Critical evaluation

This approach, which has become known as the 'psychosocial explanation', has generated some of the most querulous debates in research on health inequalities in recent years, most notably in contrast with 'neo-material explanations'. In simplified terms, 'neo-materialists', such as Coburn, Lynch and Navarro, contend that health inequalities result above all from the direct effects of inequalities in material conditions over which people have little choice, such as occupational hazards, poor housing and childhood deprivation. Those who favour the 'psychosocial explanation', such as Marmot, and Wilkinson and Pickett, maintain that health inequalities are the psychosocially mediated effects of relative deprivation, in the manner already discussed. To give a flavour of the jostle and parry of debate, we can consider statements from each side. Thus Marmot and Wilkinson remark: 'If, in the spirit of neo-materialism, you gave every child access to a computer and every family a car, deal with air pollution, and provide a physically safe environment, is the problem solved? We believe not. The psychosocial effects of relative deprivation including control over life, insecurity, anxiety, social isolation . . . remain untouched' (Marmot and Wilkinson 2001: 1234).

Lynch and colleagues use the metaphor of airline travel to punch home the significance of material factors as follows:

> Differences in neo-material conditions between first and economy class may produce health inequalities after a long flight. First class passengers get, among other advantages such as better food and service, more space and a wider, more comfortable seat that reclines into a bed. First class passengers arrive refreshed and rested, while many in economy arrive feeling a bit rough. Under a psychosocial interpretation, these health inequalities are due to negative emotions engendered by perceptions of relative disadvantage. Under a neo-material interpretation, people in economy have worse health because they sat in a cramped space and an uncomfortable seat, and they were not able to sleep. The fact that they can see the bigger seats as they walk off the plane is not the cause of their poorer health.
>
> (Lynch et al. 2000: 1202–3)

Despite this stand-off, each side accedes that the other has merit. That is, most neo-materialists do not deny that psychosocial factors may play a role, and most psychosocial theorists do not reject the influence of material factors. Rather, the issues are where the *origins* of health inequalities lie and the causal sequence of influential factors. Thus, in a critique of the psychosocial explanation, Coburn (2000) argues that we should be less concerned about how relative income inequality leads to lowered social cohesion and trust (with all the negative implications for health) and more with how *both* income inequality *and* lowered social cohesion are the product of the neoliberal market economy that has held sway since the late 1970s (see also chapters 2 and 7). While Coburn (2004) explains that he wants to encompass and go beyond the psychosocial explanation, Navarro argues that the emphasis on social capital within the psychosocial explanation is *itself* indicative of the expansion of neoliberalism imported into the social sciences. He maintains that the psychosocial explanation is underpinned by the premise that 'individuals need capital in order to compete or better survive in a competitive world' (Navarro 2004: 672). Moreover, he argues that income is construed as a consumption category with no recognition of where it comes from – namely, the particular form of capitalist power relations in the sphere of production (Navarro 2002). Along similar lines, Muntaner and Lynch (2002) argue that Wilkinson shies away from what causes economic inequality in the first place. However, Wilkinson responds that he is not unaware of, nor does he dispute, the role of neoliberalism; nor is he guilty as accused of 'a conspiracy to *de*politicise and *de*socialise health issues' (2000: 97, emphasis original). Rather, he questions the attempt of Coburn (and, by extension, others) to by-pass the role of relative income inequality. He believes that this is inadvisable when health inequalities are evident not only between the 'top' and 'bottom' but at all levels in-between – that is, when they are to do with more than absolute material deprivation. These different positions are sociologically interesting in their own right and also in terms of their policy implications for how health inequalities might be reduced.

Reducing health inequalities

Since health inequalities are socially caused, there is nothing inevitable about them. Even so, 'developing strategies to reduce health inequalities is a daunting task' (Mackenbach 2006: 245). The general dearth of evidence on 'what works' has made it very difficult to design and implement policy interventions.

As noted earlier, the *Black Report* of the early 1980s was a watershed for inequalities research. However, it received a frosty reception from the then-new Conservative government in the UK, which, under Margaret Thatcher, was highly disinclined to acknowledge any existence of health inequalities (see discussion in Berridge and Blume 2003). Although research continued during the 1980s, there was, unsurprisingly, a distinct lack of political will to do anything with the findings. The Acheson inquiry (Acheson Report 1998) which was set up by the new Labour government of 1997 was similar to blueprint policy developments in other countries, such as the Netherlands, Sweden, Norway and Finland (Mackenbach 2006, 2010; Vallgårda 2010). It was intended to identify priority areas for policy development and became the backbone of a health inequalities strategy which relied on a series of national inequalities targets. England is a useful point of reference because it was the first European country to implement a policy to reduce inequalities in health in 2007. Despite some partial success, it failed to reach its targets of reducing by at least 10 per cent: (i) the gap between the fifth of areas with the lowest life expectancy at birth and the population as a whole; and (ii) the gap in infant mortality between 'routine manual' occupational groups and the rest of the population by the year 2010 (Department of Health 2007a; Dorling 2010; Mackenbach 2010). Mackenbach (2010) identifies several reasons for this, including a poor match between policies and targets. Thus, for example – though important – preventable deaths due to fuel poverty and homelessness are relatively rare, or, in relation to child poverty and education, were likely to occur sometime in the future (not by 2010).

The focus on 'the worst' and 'the rest' has been criticized for leaving a lot of society untouched and failing to address the wider social gradient (Wilkinson 2007). As Dorling (2013) relates, although inequalities harm the poor most, they also harm the rich. This was emphasized in the Marmot Review (2010) of health inequalities in England, *Fair Society, Healthy Lives*: 'Focusing solely on the most disadvantaged will not reduce health inequalities sufficiently. To reduce the steepness of the social gradient in health, actions must be universal, but with a scale and intensity that is proportionate to the level of disadvantage' (Marmot Review 2010: 15).

Many critical analysts are also concerned that, instead of tackling 'upstream' economic and cultural forces, UK government policy has been focused at local levels and directed towards individuals. For example, during the early days of office after the 2010 national election, the Coalition (Conservative and Liberal Democrat) government showed an enthusiasm for so-called 'nudge thinking' – that is, nudging people to make 'healthy choices' and change their health behaviours, such as diet and exercise, as a mechanism for health improvement (Department of Health 2010a). As Graham (2012) discusses, most policies and interventions in the UK and beyond are far more concerned with individuals and their lifestyles than they are with social environments and population-level threats to health equity, such as tobacco use.

If the root cause of health inequalities is economic, the solution seems clear: reduce income inequalities and increase the living standards of the worst-off in society. Thus, the CSDH (2008), referred to earlier, put forward a series of ambitious policy recommendations, including tackling the inequitable distribution of power, money and resources. A number of commentators have argued that what we need is a fundamental redistribution of income or wealth (Carlisle 2001; Dahlgren and Whitehead 2006; Shaw et al. 1999, 2005), or new forms of economic organization, such as employee-ownership (Wilkinson and Pickett 2009). But others believe that, although they are important, such changes would not fully solve the problem. Thus, Wilkinson argues that 'we need not only to tackle national issues of inequality, pay differentials, and "fat cat" salaries, but also to think about the nature of personal interactions and what makes people feel valued and appreciated, rather than put down and annoyed' (2005: 316). Consequently, he recommends not only income redistribution policies, but also policies to reduce differentials before redistribution, through developments such as codes of practice that stop advertisements that encourage invidious social comparisons, appeal to 'exclusivity' and suggest that 'without whatever it is, we are second-rate people, and trying endlessly to create dissatisfaction with what we have or what we are' (2005: 317).

Conclusions

The explanatory thread running through the fabric of research on health inequalities is clear enough: social polarization is leading to a hardening of health inequalities both within and between societies. However, this is complex and tightly woven, making it difficult to unpick the different theoretical strands and to identify their relative contribution to the overall picture. Although they have not entirely disappeared, the dualisms which once drove explanations – such as 'individual or structural' factors, 'social or biological' factors, 'culture or material' factors – have begun to break down in recent years as researchers have appreciated the need to explore their interaction in the production of health inequalities. The move away from static to more dynamic conceptualizations of individual lives and the characteristics of the communities and the wider society in which they are embedded has made clear that the warp and weft of health inequalities is in continual production and hence subject to change. The not-inconsiderable challenges to social scientists who seek to interpret the picture are to capture these processes in their research, and to identify effective policy interventions.

5

Gender inequalities in health

The connection between the social relations of gender and the health of men and women worldwide is enduring and strong. The experiences of people living as geographically and culturally far apart as the affluent countries of Western Europe and North America, the transition countries of Eastern Europe and the ravaged lands of Zimbabwe are irrevocably shaped by the gender arrangements of their own societies and the global economy of which they are a part:. 'Being a man or a woman . . . is not a pre-determined state. It is a *becoming*, a condition actively under construction' (Connell 2009: 5, emphasis in original). We must therefore seek to understand gender inequalities in health dynamically, by paying attention to how societies change over time.

This chapter begins by establishing the importance of biological sex and social gender for understanding the health of women and men. From this foundation, we explore international differences in life expectancy and causes of death and how they have changed over time. Through this we begin to build a picture of the intricate and multifaceted nature of the connections between gender and health. This leads us to question over-simplistic assumptions that the health of women and men can be explained in terms of binary difference. The picture grows in complexity in the next section of the chapter where we address the vexed question of who tend to be sicker during their lives, men or women? The chapter concludes by looking at gender and socio-economic status as intersecting influences upon health.

The social and the biological

As we saw in chapter 3, as far back as the eighteenth century feminists were arguing that male advantage depends on equating women with their (defective) bodies. Feminists countered with two claims: first, women are no more (or less) determined by their biology than men are; and, second, that the image of women's biology that patriarchy has presented to the world is grossly misconstrued. The sex/gender distinction was intended as an analytic device, but, in actuality, researchers ended up not only by referring to sex and gender as if they are separate, but also by framing them as competing explanations for any health differences found. Although the focus on the social causes of ill-health stimulated a seam of highly valuable research, it had the unfortunate consequence of relegating biological sex to the realm of 'scientifically verifiable fact' (Fausto-Sterling 2003: 123), with researchers proceeding 'as if biological differences between men and women are either minimal or largely irrelevant' (Rieker and Bird 2000: 107).

Biology as 'sex difference'

We live in an age in which biological determinism is highly fashionable, and have become accustomed to the notion that genetic differences explain the health of men and women. Yet, when closely investigated, many prominent claims for sex-related differences in genetic associations – such as for diabetes mellitus, multiple sclerosis and hepatitis C virus infection – are either insufficiently documented or spurious (Patsopoulos et al. 2007). While we are able to identify and counter the crude Genes 'R' Us story of gender and health (Birke 2003), biological determinism has crept back into research in more subtle guises. Epstein (2007) identifies a new trend which he dubs the 'inclusion-and-difference' approach. It is driven by two substantive goals: 'the *inclusion* of members of various groups generally considered to have been underrepresented previously as subjects in clinical studies; and the measurement, within those studies, of *differences* across groups with regard to treatment effects, disease progression, or biological processes' (Epstein 2007: 6, my emphasis).

Inclusion is motivated by the quite understandable desire to confront the historical privileging of the male body and male experience as the 'gold standard' in medical research and practice. But it has had the unfortunate consequence of foregrounding women's *differences* from men (and vice versa). The 'inclusion-and-difference' approach has provided fertile ground for the growth of 'gender-specific medicine', a movement defined by one of its founders as 'the science of the differences in the normal physiology of men and women and the ways that they experience disease' (Legato 2003: 917). 'Gender-specific medicine' aims to turn attention away from 'old school' views of health as a 'limited feminist', or 'boutique issue', towards a 'new science' which 'embraces the entire organism' and includes men as well as women within its remit (Legato 2002, 2003). Much of the momentum for this derives from the influential US National Institute of Medicine report *Exploring the Biological Contributions to Human Health. Does Sex Matter?* (Wizeman and Pardue 2001). This report views biological sex as 'generally dimorphic' and explicitly sets out to focus on 'sex-based differences, versus similarities' under the assumption that 'they are more likely to successfully demonstrate the need for further research and lead to greater understanding of the significance of sex in human biology and health' (2001: 17, 2).

The growing trend of 'gender-specific medicine' is significant for how we understand patterns of morbidity and mortality because, despite professing inclusivity, it actually 'reinforces a problematic notion that each individual belongs to a category that can be diagnosed and treated accordingly' (Epstein 2007: 254). This is problematic because 'biological sex is *not* an either/or – not at the anatomic, the hormonal, or the chromosomal levels. There are no truly dichotomous variables in nature, and ... there is no precise or fully satisfactory biological means of demarcating all males from all females' (Epstein 2007: 236, emphasis in original). An additional problem of the growing 'sex difference' trend is the supposition that biological sex is basically given and fixed, when the reality is that 'findings of so-called biological difference do not imply a claim of immutability or inevitability' (Fausto-Sterling 2003: 125). Therefore we need to think in terms of how biological processes and social processes are *intertwined* in the production of gender differences and similarities in health.

The interaction of biological sex and social gender

'There are relatively few conditions which affect the health of men and women which are not influenced by biology in some way, even if this influence is minor' (Payne 2006: 22). For example, male sex makes men vulnerable to prostate disease, and female sex makes women vulnerable to cervical cancer and cancer of the womb. Biological differences may also play a role in conditions which *both* men and women experience. Thus, lung function matures more slowly in the male foetus, which gives rise to more respiratory distress syndromes and lung-related injuries in male newborns (Snow 2010). Gene expression seems to render women more vulnerable to lung cancer, since they have higher rates of this condition at the same level of smoking (Snow 2010). Conversely, female sex hormones help reduce the risk of coronary heart disease in women in their 'reproductive years' due to the protective effects of oestrogen on the arterial walls of the heart, serum lipid profile and cholesterol levels. The male hormone testosterone, however, can have untoward effects, such as reducing immunity, which increases men's risks of viruses and parasitic infections (Payne 2006).

The crucial point, however, is that these biological factors do not *determine* the health of men and women, boys and girls. The actual impact of any biologically shaped advantages and disadvantages of males and females 'will be mediated by gender-related factors – such as health behaviours, access to social and economic capital, which can affect stress, or the availability of health-promoting resources' (Payne 2006: 15). In other words, sex and gender are mutually constructed. Specifying just how biological sex and social gender interact is far more easily said than done. Sen and Östlin explain that 'the interactions between nature and nurture are probably more complex in the case of gender equity in health than in almost any other aspect of social hierarchy' (2010: 1). The human body does not passively unfold from some preformed blueprint but evolves dynamically in relation to its environment (Fausto-Sterling 2005: 131). As a result, 'social factors can overrule or even negate biological propensities' (Baunach 2003: 332). This occurs across the lifespan, whether long or short, and often results in higher prevalence of illnesses for girls and women, even if it does not necessarily culminate in their earlier death (Sen and Östlin 2010).

The examples of 'missing women' and HIV rates show that social relations of gender mediate both women's biological hardiness and their vulnerability. For Sen, low valuation of women means that millions are 'missing' around the world. If, as he maintains, 'women are hardier than men and, given similar care, survive better at all ages – including in utero', it is indeed curious that about 5 per cent more boys than girls are born around the world (Sen 1992: 587). The ratio of women to men exceeds 1.05 in countries such as the UK, France and the US. Yet in many 'third world' countries, especially those of Asia and North Africa, the ratio is 0.90 or below. Sen (1992, 2003) concludes that these 'missing women' are accounted for by the gender discriminatory practices of sex-specific abortion (female foeticide), neglect of female health, and poor nutrition in infancy. HIV rates illustrate how such practices can also exacerbate biological vulnerability. The biological body puts women at higher risk of seroconversion during unprotected sex with an infected partner since, amongst other things, the greater area of mucus membrane exposed during sex provides a fertile environment for the virus to enter the body, and micro-tears that occur in vaginal tissue increase the risk of male-to-female transmission. But, crucially, around the world, it is the *social* relations of gender, notably women's lack of control over sexual activity, that really matters, because it is this that puts women at risk of exposure to the virus in the first place (Gilbert and Selikow 2012: 215).

As Snow points out:

> our widening exposure to historical change and variations across different societies underscores the fact that gender identity is mutable and amenable to social messaging. To the extent that chromosomal sex

dictates human capability, it would appear to provide an impressive array of options for 'doing gender', suggesting that our species, at the least, is highly adaptive to experimentation and adoption of new habits.

(Snow 2010: 65)

In other words, social relations of gender interact with the biological body to produce certain configurations of morbidity and mortality in different times and places. This is made very clear in international differences in life expectancy.

'Gender convergence' and 'gender divergence': international differences in life expectancy

Women outlive men in virtually all countries of the world today. However, as the data in table 5.1 show, the *extent* of this longevity varies considerably from just one or two years in Sierra Leone and Bangladesh, to five years in the US, and 12 years in the Russian Federation.

When we reach back in history, we find that things used to be quite different. Studies of sixteenth- and seventeenth-century European villages provide evidence of a *male* longevity advantage (Shorter 1982). From the mid-1880s, and for most of the period up to the beginning of the twentieth century, the difference between the death rates of boys and girls in general was 3 per cent or less, and even showed a pattern of female disadvantage up to the late 1880s (OPCS 1992). This was even

Table 5.1 Life expectancy at birth in selected WHO member states, 2011

Country	Life expectancy at birth (years)	
	Males	Females
Australia	80	84
Bangladesh	69	70
Bulgaria	71	78
Finland	78	84
France	78	85
Hungary	71	79
Iraq	65	72
Russian Federation	63	75
Sierra Leone	46	47
Sudan	60	64
United Kingdom	79	82
United Republic of Tanzania	58	61
United States of America	76	81

Source: WHO (2013)

more marked for children aged between 10 and 14 amongst whom, aside from just a few years when rates were equal, boys had a 3 to 8 per cent advantage right up to the mid-1930s (OPCS 1992). For adolescents (aged 15–19), female excess mortality persisted into the late nineteenth century. This has led historical demographers to conclude that any biological advantage conferred on girls and women is easily damaged by the impact of economic scarcity in patriarchal societies. For example, Johansson (1977: 35) argues that the construction of gender 'made it temporarily hazardous to be a young female during a period of accelerated social and economic change' in mid-Victorian England. This was especially the case in the countryside where female excess mortality spanned the ages 5 to 64. As paid employment in the agrarian sector declined with the enclosure movement and technological change, jobs got increasingly scarce for women. Johansson (1977) hypothesizes that, as women's economic value declined, families may have found it prudent to invest in the health of males. Then, as urbanization proceeded apace, and women were able to obtain work in the cities, excess female mortality disappeared.

As Gita Sen and colleagues explain, 'together, gender systems, structural processes and their interplay, constitute the gendered structural determinants of health'. However, 'how they manifest through beliefs, norms, organisations, behaviours, and practices can vary' (Sen et al. 2007: xii). We should therefore expect significant variation in different parts of the world. Globalization and fast paced gender-related changes within and between societies are reflected internationally in changing configurations of mortality and morbidity. While these are not easily summarized, some broad global trends can be highlighted through the lens of decreasing and increasing 'gender gaps' in life expectancy.

Western countries: increasing life expectancy and a decreasing 'gender gap'

The 100 or so years from roughly the 1880s to around the 1970s were a period of gradually increasingly female longevity advantage in the West. In England and Wales, for example, the number of extra years, on average, that a female might expect to live at birth, compared to a male, rose from around 2.0 years for those born in 1841, to 3.6 years for those born in 1910, to 4.4 years for those born in 1950, and culminated in the largest difference to date: of 6.3 years for those born in 1969 and 1970 (ONS 2009a). This is mirrored elsewhere. For example, the longevity advantage grew from 3.6 years for Australian females and from about 3 years for Canadian females who were born at the start of the twentieth century, to a projected 7.0 and 7.1 years respectively for those born in the early 1980s (AIHW 2008; Statistics Canada 2001).

This seems to have marked a historical peak for the West as the female longevity advantage gradually began to erode from the closing

Table 5.2 The 'gender gap' in life expectancy in Western countries (years)

	1980	2002
UK	6.0	4.7
USA	7.4	5.4
Sweden	6.0	4.4
Finland	8.5	6.6
France	8.1	7.4
Iceland	6.5	3.9
Australia	7.0*	4.9

* 1980–2
Sources: Gjonça et al. (2005); AIHW (2006); Council of Europe (2005: tables 4.3, 4.6)

Table 5.3 Residual life expectancy at selected ages, Sweden and UK

Sweden

Year	At birth			Age 45			Age 65		
	M	F	*diff.*	M	F	*diff.*	M	F	*diff.*
1980	72.8	78.8	**6.0**	30.4	35.4	**5.0**	14.3	17.9	**3.6**
1990	74.8	80.4	**5.6**	32.0	36.8	**4.8**	15.3	19.0	**3.7**
2003	77.9	82.4	**4.5**	34.4	38.4	**4.0**	17.0	20.3	**3.3**
Over period	**5.1**	**3.6**		**4.0**	**3.0**		**2.7**	**2.4**	

UK

Year	At birth			Age 45			Age 65		
	M	F	*diff.*	M	F	*diff.*	M	F	*diff.*
1980	70.8	76.9	**6.1**	28.5	33.9	**5.4**	12.9	17.0	**4.1**
1990	72.9	78.5	**5.6**	30.3	35.0	**4.7**	14.0	17.8	**3.8**
2002	75.9	80.5	**4.6**	33.0	36.8	**3.8**	16.1	19.1	**3.0**
Over period	**5.1**	**3.6**		**4.5**	**2.9**		**3.2**	**2.1**	

Source: Council of Europe (2005: tables 4.3, 4.4, 4.6)

decades of the twentieth century. Average life expectancy is increasing for males and females alike, but, as table 5.2 shows, the 'gender gap' between them has been decreasing. Table 5.3 gives statistics for 'residual life expectancy' – that is, 'life left' at different ages, using the examples of Sweden and the UK between 1980 and 2002/3. It shows that both males and females gained years over the period and that this occurred at each selected point in the lifecourse (birth, age 45 and age 65). But, alongside this, we see a reducing female/male gap. The data also show that this decreasing gap reflects larger 'male gains' at all age points as summarized by the differences 'over the period' on the bottom row of the table. Indeed, between 1980 and 2003, the life expectancy of Western European men as a whole increased by 6.5 per cent and that of women by only 3.5 per cent (White and Cash 2004). In the US, men gained 3.4 years of average life expectancy between 1990 and 2005, yet women gained just 1.6 (National Center for Health Statistics 2010). Although, on the face of it, these differences seem small, the important point is that they may mark a significant new historical trend.

Generally speaking, *healthy* life expectancy falls as life expectancy increases, reflecting the burden of illness that often accompanies older age. So, although, on average, women still live longer than men, their 'extra years' are not in the main spent in good health. As men's life expectancy increases, we might also expect them to accumulate less-healthy years. It is therefore noteworthy that research from the Netherlands found men's overall life expectancy not only *grew more* than women's between 1989 and 2000, but was accompanied by greater gains in *healthy* life expectancy (Perenboom et al. 2005). A similar trend is reported for the US (Bird and Rieker 2008).

Many affluent Western societies have been going through striking gender-related changes as erstwhile distinctions between the experiences of men and women have been breaking down since the mid-1970s. Women are often positioned as the major beneficiaries of the new 'knowledge economy' that has accompanied the decline in manufacturing and the rise of the service industries (Walby 2007, 2011). Such changes are regularly depicted as part of 'gender convergence' or, as it is more popularly put, 'men becoming more like women and women becoming more like men'. It is quite common now for conventional masculinity to be viewed as health-damaging, and traditional femininity as health-enhancing. Consequently, there is an expectation that 'if men quit conventional masculinity, or if women adopt it', sex differences in life expectancy will decrease (Månsdotter et al. 2006: 616). We have already seen that the reducing 'gender gap' in life expectancy may in some significant part be due to 'male gains' and 'female losses'. So, does this mean that gender-related changes in Western society are advantaging men and disadvantaging women? We can look at this by briefly exploring changes in major causes of death.

Major causes of death in Western countries
The major causes of death in affluent Western societies are circulatory disease (including heart disease and stroke) and cancer. Death from circulatory diseases has declined significantly since the 1950s. But although overall they have higher rates, the decline has been more pronounced amongst men than amongst women since the 1970s (e.g., for the UK, see Scarborough et al. 2011). Cancer mortality rates have

declined far more slowly in general over the last thirty or so years. But here too there are male/female differences. To take the UK as an illustration, male cancer deaths peaked in 1984 at 2,897 per million and then fell to 2,111 per million by 2007. By comparison, female death rates peaked later, in 1989, at 1,905 per million, and then gradually fell to 1,567 per million by 2007 (ONS 2009a). Overall rates conceal variations in trends for different kinds of cancer. Lung cancer incidence and mortality rates, for example, also remain higher for men than women, but the timing of peaks and troughs is quite different. Taking the US as an example, male age-adjusted death rates for cancer of the lung, bronchus and trachea rose enormously from the mid twentieth century, to peak at 91.1 per 100,000 of the population in 1990, and thereafter began to fall to reach 67.0 in 2006. Meanwhile, death rates for women lagged about twenty years behind and plateaued as recently as the year 2000 at 41.3 and, at 40.0, remained close to this in 2006 (National Center for Health Statistics 2010). A recent analysis of temporal trends reveals that the relative risk of deaths from lung cancer, chronic obstructive pulmonary disease (COPD), ischaemic heart disease, strokes and all causes are now nearly identical for female and male smokers (Thun et al. 2013). The incidence of malignant melanoma (skin cancer) has risen steadily since the middle of the twentieth century. Incidence varies by gender across countries. In some, it is higher amongst women and in others, amongst men (there is considerable variation amongst European countries, for example). However, taking Great Britain as an illustration, while age-standardized rates for females are higher than for males, and more than quadrupled from 3.9 to 16.4 per 100,000 of population between 1975 and 2009, male rates increased more than six-fold from 2.5 to 16.1 over the same period. Moreover, death from the disease is now, and has always been, higher amongst men (Cancer Research UK 2011). Alcohol-related deaths, such as those from chronic liver disease and cirrhosis, have been rising in a number of Western countries. In England, for example, male rates have escalated since the 1970s and have remained consistently higher than rates for women. But female rates rose from amongst the lowest in the European Union (EU) in 1971 to above the EU average by 2003 (Department of Health 2008).

These trends tell us that while, generally speaking, Western men are still 'worse off', there have been noteworthy gender-related changes. By and large, and with the exception of skin cancer, things have been improving more quickly for men, and more slowly for women, which is likely to be a significant contributor to the reduction in the 'gender gap' in life expectancy. Circulatory diseases, many cancers, and cirrhosis of the liver are associated with the very lifestyle and health behaviour changes that have accompanied so-called 'gender convergence'. The obvious example is lung cancer where 'the smoking patterns of yes-

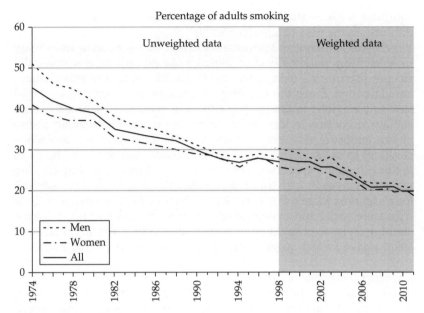

Notes:
1 For 1998 unweighted and weighted data are shown for comparison purposes. Weighted data are not available before this point.
2 The survey was not run in 1997/98 or 1999/00. A liner trend has been drawn between the data point before and after these years.
Source: General Lifestyle Survey-Office for National Statistics

Figure 5.1 Prevalence of cigarette smoking by sex, 1974 to 2010, Great Britain[1, 2]

teryears are showing up now as the incidence of lung cancer starts to narrow between men and women' (Toh 2009: 400). Social prohibitions on women's smoking began to loosen in the West in the 1920s and 1930s. The narrowing longevity gap began in the 1970s, by which time women born in the early decades of the twentieth century would be around 60 years old and already subject to the negative health effects of smoking. By comparison, male smoking rates and lung cancer deaths were already declining by the 1970s. Moreover, although male smoking rates historically have been higher, presently there is little difference between men and women in many Western countries. For example, figure 5.1 shows that 21 per cent of men and 20 per cent of women aged 16 and over smoked in Britain in 2010. In Sweden, which by official measures is the most gender-equal country in the world (Hausmann et al. 2009), for those aged 15 and over, more females than males report smoking daily (at 15.0 per cent and 14.3 per cent respectively) (OECD 2011). Since girls now actually smoke more than boys in some Western countries such as the UK and Sweden, these trends are unlikely to diminish in the near future (NCSR 2007).

Whereas smoking and lung cancer draw our attention to an increase in behaviours potentially detrimental to health amongst women, the steeper rise in male skin cancer incidence directs us towards changes amongst men. Since the majority of melanomas are caused by exposure to ultraviolet radiation, sun exposure and indoor tanning mainly explain recent trends. Men and women seem more or less equally aware of sun exposure risk, but men are less likely to wear sun-protective clothing, to use sunscreens and to seek shade, and are more likely to get burnt. New expectations of the desirable tanned/healthy-looking male body co-exist with traditional male attitudes to risk. The main site for melanoma in men is the trunk (mid-back) while for women it is the legs. Here social and biological factors interact: different male/female clothing styles expose different parts of the body to risk and mid-back lesions have a much worse prognosis (Wizeman and Pardue 2001).

Changing gender identities and health
As discussed in chapter 3, contemporary Western lives are laced with contradictions as the old binary orthodoxies of gender break down and are reconfigured in new ways. Traditional masculine and feminine gender roles and gender identities – including new forms of hyper-accentuated femininity and masculinity – co-exist with gender identities which involve taking on attributes typically associated with the so-called 'opposite sex' (although this varies considerably by factors such as age, social class and ethnicity). While this means gender is more malleable than was the case even a decade ago, there are still heavy limitations on what is socially acceptable. This is readily apparent, for example, in moral panics over the health-related behaviours of young women and men. UK readers, for example, will be familiar with tabloid headlines decrying the 'binge drinking culture' amongst young women. Interestingly, the 'hedonistic girl' who breaks feminine codes by aping the behaviour of men (Lyons and Willott 2008) is a problem because she encroaches on traditionally male domains – public spaces and the pub (Day et al. 2004; Jackson and Tinkler 2007).

Kimmel documents the equally difficult terrain that boys traverse as they become men in the US: 'As the economy has shifted from a culture of production to a culture of consumption men experience their masculinity less as providers and protectors, and more as consumers, and "ornaments". Many men feel "downsized" – both economically and emotionally, they feel smaller, less essential, less like real men' (Kimmel 2008: 17–18). This has been argued to have triggered a backlash amongst some men as they seek to recreate the very traditional identities and lifestyles that can endanger health (Kimmel 2009; Nayak 2006). But men are not all alike; 'at any given historical moment, there are competing masculinities – some hegemonic (idealized, preferred), some marginalized, and some stigmatized – each with their respective structural, psychological and cultural moorings' (Sabo and Gordon 1995: 10). This suggests that, rather than framing discussion in terms of 'convergence' or 'equality', we should fine-tune our analysis to the complex and multifaceted patterns of gender-related similarity and difference that are emerging in the West (Annandale 2009).

Sub-Saharan Africa: decreasing life expectancy and a decreasing 'gender gap'

So far we have seen that, in affluent Western countries, life expectancy has been increasing and the 'gender gap' has been decreasing. Literally and figuratively worlds away, many countries of Sub-Saharan Africa have *also* experienced a decreasing 'gender gap' in life expectancy. But the reasons for this decreasing gap could not be more different from those in the West. Table 5.4 shows that in Sub-Saharan Africa the life expectancy of both men and women decreased between 1990 and 2007 and that, in some countries, the reason for the reduced 'gender gap' was that women lost more years than men. Since then, with the significant exception of Cameroon, life expectancy has risen and the gap has attenuated somewhat with women generally gaining more years than men. However, the period 1990–2011 as a whole generally shows a decreasing gap of 'female advantage'.

It has been argued that women are the 'shock absorbers' in globalization processes, soaking up the increased violence and brutal economic conditions that accompany the 'changing political economy of nation states in the global order' (Sen et al. 2007: xiv). Although Sub-Saharan Africa has seen sustained growth, it still has the lowest value for all regions of the world on the UN Human Development Index (HDI) (UN 2013). By reference to the Gender Inequality Index (GII), it is the most

Table 5.4 Changing life expectancies (LEs) in Sub-Saharan Africa

	LE men			LE women			LE gap			Healthy LE 2007	
	1990	2007	2011	1990	2007	2011	1990	2007	2011	Men	Women
Botswana	64	56	64	68	56	67	4	0	3	49	46
Cameroon	55	51	51	58	52	54	3	1	3	45	45
Chad	48	46	50	50	47	53	2	1	3	40	40
Ghana	57	56	62	60	58	65	3	2	3	49	50
Kenya	58	53	58	63	56	61	5	3	3	47	48
Namibia	60	58	64	65	61	66	5	3	2	52	53
Zambia	52	45	54	55	47	56	3	2	2	39	40
Zimbabwe	57	45	53	63	44	55	6	−1	2	38	39

Source: WHO (2009, 2013)

gender-unequal region of the world (UN 2013). As explained earlier, any biological advantage that women may have in life expectancy is attenuated when they bear the brunt of harsh economic policies alongside gender discrimination (Bird and Rieker 2008: 95). This is reflected in 'healthy life expectancy' in Sub-Saharan Africa which, as table 5.4 shows, differed very little between men and women in 2007. In Botswana, it was actually lower for women.

People in the region suffer the same major causes of death in older age as their Western counterparts, such as coronary heart disease (CHD) and cancer. Different patterns are found for specific diseases. A major contributor to the increasing 'gender gap' in the West is cigarette-related deaths. Such deaths are very low for both men and women in Sub-Saharan Africa, although the region is positioned on the upslope given recent promotional activities by tobacco companies (Pampel 2008). The decisive difference between Sub-Saharan Africa and the West is heightened vulnerability to death at younger age, or *premature death*. Women are highly vulnerable to maternal mortality, which, by definition, occurs in the reproductive years. While, in the industrialized countries, the lifetime risk of maternal death is 1:4300, the equivalent statistic for Sub-Saharan Africa is a staggering 1:31. It is even higher in some countries, such as Chad where the risk is 1:14 (UNICEF 2011). Women are also at exceptionally high risk of premature death due to armed conflict and HIV/AIDS.

Women's vulnerability: armed conflict and HIV/AIDS
In 2006, with just 13 per cent of the global population, Africa experienced over 40 per cent of the world's conflicts (Handley et al. 2009). Much of this conflict has been taking place within national borders, involving militia units and rebel groups, rather than the armed forces of sovereign states (Jacobson et al. 2000; Lamb et al. 2004). We tend to think of war deaths as combatant deaths which disproportionately affect men and boys, but in actuality, worldwide, over ten civilians are killed for every combatant, and the majority of these are women and children (Lamb et al. 2004). Moreover, civilians increasingly are targets rather than accidental victims. Left without legal protection and financial resources, women are especially vulnerable to sexual violence during times of war as their 'bodies are used as a means to undermine, disgrace, and challenge the perceived enemy – amongst other atrocities, women have been deliberately raped and infected with HIV' (Lamb et al. 2004: 15).

Sub-Saharan Africa is the region of the world most heavily afflicted by HIV/AIDS. Women are disproportionately affected, accounting for 60 per cent of cases. This is atypical given that women make up 50 per cent of cases globally (UNAIDS 2010). In some countries, and for some ages, gender disparities are stark. Thus in Kenya, 15- to 19-year-old females are 3 times, and 20- to 24-year-olds 5.5 times, more likely to become infected than their male counterparts (UNAIDS 2010). In households living in poverty due to HIV/AIDS, trading sex often is the only way to survive. Girls whose parents suffer or have died from AIDS are vulnerable to trafficking for their labour and to sexual violence. For example, during the Sudanese civil war, 50,000 girls were captured by government forces and kept as sex slaves in the northern territories (Lamb et al. 2004). More generally, AIDS-related human rights abuse occurs in rape inside and outside marriage and other forms of sexual violence that are associated with poverty, unequal property and inheritance rights, and poor access to education and healthcare (Human Rights Watch 2003). Cultural constructions of 'hegemonic masculinity' and 'hegemonic' or 'emphasised femininity' can be a lethal combination, since expectations of the 'real man' 'encourage and legitimate multiple partners and sexual violence' and oblige women 'to be obedient to their male partners and to focus on men's sexual pleasure, even if it increases their own risk of HIV infection' (Gilbert and Selikow 2010: 195).

In sum, the 'gender gap' in life expectancy in Sub-Saharan Africa has occurred alongside the intensification of the poverty–violence–AIDS nexus which has a bearing on the population as a whole, but has disproportionately affected women.

Countries experiencing an increasing 'gender gap'

In distinction to the West and to Sub-Saharan Africa, there are countries that have experienced an *increasing* 'gender gap' in life expectancy. In common with their counterparts in the majority of the countries of the world, Russian women have longer life expectancies than men. However, average life expectancy *worsened* for both men and women between 1980 and 2007. As table 5.5 shows, this was accompanied by an increasing 'gender gap' which is accounted for by the fact that *men's* life expectancy worsened more than women's did over the period (Gjonça et al. 2005). Hungary has also seen an increasing 'gender gap'

Table 5.5 Some countries with an increasing life-expectancy gap between 1980 and 2007

	LE gap	
	1980	**2007**
Russian Federation	11.6	13.0
Hungary	7.2	9.0
Japan	5.4	7.0

Source: figures for 1980 from Gjonça et al. (2005); figures for 2007 from WHO (2009)

in life expectancy. But in contrast to the Russian Federation, this has occurred in the context of a gradually increasing life expectancy for both males and females and is explicable by larger gains for females over the period (Gjonça et al. 2005). Finally, although it is obviously a very different society, analytically, Japan mirrors Hungary: life expectancy has been rising for both men and women (to become the highest in the world) and the increasing 'gender' gap is mainly accounted for by swifter improvements for women.

'Vodka and a rope': the Russian federation

At age 75 for women and only 63 for men, the 'gender gap' in *healthy* life expectancy in the Russian Federation is now the largest in the world (WHO 2013). Eastern Europe has been a natural laboratory within which to observe just how swiftly economic and social change is marked on the body through changes in health. We have seen that deaths from circulatory diseases generally, and CHD specifically, have been declining in the West. In contrast, in the Russian Federation, CHD deaths amongst people aged 35–74 rose by 26 per cent for women and by a substantial 45 per cent for men, between 1982 and 2002 (British Heart Foundation 2005). There have also been dramatic increases in all forms of violent deaths, including homicide and accidental poisoning amongst men (which includes alcohol-related deaths) (Cockerham 2000). Statistics such as these have led researchers to refer to a 'mortality crisis' and a resulting generation of 'missing men' (Stuckler et al. 2009).

Much of male mortality in Russia is attributed to high levels of cigarette smoking and alcohol consumption; 25 per cent of women and just under a massive 60 per cent of Russian men reported daily smoking in 2009 (WHO 2011b). Research shows that middle-aged, working-class men have been particularly vulnerable to the rapid and brutal market-related socio-economic changes of the post-Soviet period (Cockerham 2000). This has included the collapse of heavy industries and agricultural production coupled with increased cultural emphasis on men's role as providers (Kay 2006). In Russian society, rises in heavy alcohol consumption, smoking and other health-damaging behaviours, such as violence against women, tend to be framed as almost natural compensatory behaviours: a reassertion of masculinity in response to self-perceived subordination (Pietilä and Rytkönen 2008). Indeed, Kay argues that men's health has become a metaphor for a society 'gone wrong': 'It is as if the degeneration of a nation can be best typified by the image of the self-pitying [male] drunk, defeated by circumstance, spiralling into an early grave' (Kay 2006: 1). Men, it might be said, can't cope and respond with 'vodka and a rope' – in other words, with suicide (Kay 2006).

While this prevailing narrative has a ring of truth, as the statistics show, there are cautionary notes to be sounded. First, there is a danger that 'male failure' has become normalized as the 'way things are', making it difficult to recognize different ways of being amongst men. Kay's (2006) research reveals the challenges men face but also makes clear the historic legacy of self-responsibility and determination that still permeates Russian culture. Second, the focus on 'male failure' can render women's problems invisible (Hinote et al. 2009). Popular belief holds that women have been protected from the worst consequences of market change because they have the 'natural resort' of the home and family (Pietilä and Rytkönen 2008: 1078). But with the collapse of Soviet communism, many – often younger – females may be adopting behaviors such as higher levels of alcohol consumption 'either as a personal statement against a formerly masculine-dominated social system or against the traditionalist Soviet order, or as a way of exercising agency or individual choice in an increasingly uncertain time' (Hinote et al. 2009: 1260). So, as with Western societies, the situation is more complex than appears at first glance.

Gender and morbidity: who is sicker?

The preceding discussion has established two important things. First, gender inequalities in health are highly responsive to changing socio-economic and cultural circumstances. This tells us that any differences and similarities observed cannot be explained by biology alone. Second, the social production of patterns of major mortality resulting in death is a complex process which cannot be captured through the simple lens of binary difference. This becomes even more apparent when we turn from mortality to morbidity.

While we would expect there to be a connection between morbidity and mortality in regard to the major causes of death we have looked at so far, this tells us relatively little about a person's health during their lifetime because it significantly overlooks the burden of ill-health due to non-fatal acute and long-term chronic conditions. Age at death is a relatively robust indicator and historical data enable us reliably to review trends over time. In contrast, 'health, disease and illness are, like every other human experience, social constructs; they are categories which have been named, defined and codified by human beings' (Blaxter 2010: 30). Health and gender are interconnected aspects of identity. As Saltonstall (1993: 12) puts it, 'the doing of health is a form of doing gender' and the meaning of gender changes as societies change. This makes it very difficult to track patterns of morbidity over time since any observed changes could reflect changing thresholds of 'what counts' as illness and in symptom reporting amongst men and women. The study of gender and morbidity therefore presents numerous challenges to the researcher.

'Women are sicker and men die quicker'?

For a substantial period of time from the early 1970s, research was pre-occupied with the apparent paradox that although 'women are sicker', 'men die quicker' (Nathanson 1977). In other words, while, on average, women live longer than men, they tend to be (or appear to be) sicker during their lives. As noted in chapter 3, researchers have tended to approach this seeming conundrum through the lens of social roles and the health benefits (through 'role enhancement') and harms (through 'role stress') of combinations of paid employment and domestic and childcare responsibilities. Potential harms to women's health from the 'dual role' of paid work and domestic work has been a running thread through research which, generally, has found that Western women benefit from the income and social contact that paid work provides, although inevitably this varies significantly by factors such as marital status, whether they have children, and the kind of work that they do (Klumb and Lampert 2004).

This research has thrown useful light on the associations between the circumstances of men's and women's lives and their health. However, its conceptual lens is often quite limited. Using categories such as male/female, married / not married, in paid work / not in paid work is economical and practical, but it also imposes 'boundaries that do not reflect [the] unclear distinctions' of people's lives (Fuchs Epstein 1988: 337). As discussed in chapters 2 and 3, we have tended to view the world through the lens of binary oppositions which endow gender roles with a heavily scripted and binary character. This has spilled over into assessments of research findings, such that 'negative (read: not statistically significant) findings tend not to be reported, or if they are, they are not able to counter all of the pre-existing research which shows differences between women and men. Sex differences are magnified, the duality of these "differences" is reinforced, and our attention is turned away from the common humanity which men and women share' (Kandrack et al. 1991: 588).

Although these words of warning were not heeded immediately, researchers now increasingly argue that suppositions of women's higher morbidity – or the 'women are sicker' aspect of the 'gender paradox' – have been erroneously perpetuated because of in-built assumptions of binary difference in research designs (see Gorman and Ghazal Read 2006; Payne 2006). For example, Macintyre and colleagues recount that, when they presented their research highlighting that female excess morbidity is not universal at an international conference, 'several listeners afterward told us that they had not found the "expected" gender differences in self-reported health in their surveys, but had never drawn attention to this because they assumed it was due to a peculiarity in their sample or social setting, or to some other "anomalous" circumstance' (Macintyre et al. 1996: 623). This does not mean to say that there are no gender inequalities in morbidity – rather, to paraphrase Macintyre and colleagues (1996), things are not as simple as they seem: in other words, that inequalities may not necessarily line up across neat divides of traditional social roles and experiences.

Presently, self-reported gender differences in health in adulthood appear to be relatively small in the West (Bartley 2004; Payne 2006). To take Britain as an example, although for the large majority of years between 1972 and 2009 self-reports of longstanding (chronic) illness inclined modestly towards women, the overall picture was more of similarity than difference (ONS 2011). Similarly, Australian data on self-assessed health for 2001 to 2007–8 show minimal or no differences (AIHW 2010). Inevitably, the picture gets more complex when we look at different age groups. Several studies show that relative equality in childhood gives way to higher levels of self-rated physical and mental illness amongst females in adolescence (see e.g. Torsheim et al. 2006; West and Sweeting 2003), and that differences attenuate in older age (see, e.g., McCullough and Laurenceau 2004). Differences also arise for specific conditions. Thus data from several countries show that, despite little difference in overall self-rated general health, older women suffer more from arthritis and rheumatism than their male counterparts (ONS 2009b; Wadman et al. 2008).

Although rates of mental illness do not differ much overall by gender (WHO 2004b), there are some notable differences for specific diagnoses with, for example, women diagnosed more often with depression and eating disorders, and men with antisocial personality disorder, and drug and alcohol abuse (Ussher 2011). Cultural variations in what counts as symptoms of mental illness make international comparisons difficult. However, a study reporting data for people aged 18–65 from twenty-five countries in 2006/7 revealed higher rates of depression amongst women (Van de Velde et al. 2010). A survey of people in England aged 16 and over living in the community found higher rates of the majority of mental disorders amongst women for 'common mental disorders' (including depression and anxiety), eating disorders, schizophrenia and bi-polar disorder, and suicidal thoughts. Only personality disorder was more common in men (McManus et al. 2009). Suicide rates are also consistently higher amongst men in England and elsewhere (see McPhedran and Baker 2008; ONS 2010). Even so, the question remains as to how far any differences and similarities are biologically based or reflect differences in the conditions of men's and women's lives and/or their relative willingness to report and act on symptoms. Diagnostic bias on the part of health practitioners may also play a role.

In light of these mental and physical health statistics, researchers often 'resolve' the 'gender paradox' by concluding that any 'excess' morbidity experienced by women may be very debilitating, but is not sufficiently serious to cause death (Verbrugge 1988).

Men as 'reluctant help-seekers'

Data from many Western countries show that women make more visits to their general practitioners' / doctors' offices and emergency departments and receive more home care than men. However, this varies by age with the peak of female visits generally occurring between ages 16 and 44; that is, the 'reproductive years' – with more similar, or even higher, rates for men after age 75 (see NCHS 2010; ONS 2009b). Age variations aside, much has been made of men's alleged tendency to fail to seek help or to delay seeking help for health problems. Indeed, as 'gender and health' research has rounded out to include men, the 'reluctant help-seeker' has become emblematic of the wider state of men's health. Thus, under the assumption that early detection and treatment of conditions can save lives, delay in help-seeking is quite often linked by researchers and commentators to men's shorter life expectancy.

As explained earlier, health is a form of 'doing gender' (Saltonstall 1993) and men's seeming reluctance to seek help is taken to be part of 'doing masculinity'. Courtenay contends that men are under greater pressure than women to meet 'societal prescriptions, such as the strongly endorsed *health-related* beliefs that men are independent, self-reliant, strong, robust and tough' (2011: 143, emphasis original). Consequently, 'when a man brags, "I haven't been to a doctor in years", he is simultaneously describing a health practice and situating himself in a masculine arena' (2011: 145–6). A growing body of research bears witness to this. However, although researchers now often recognize that masculinity is expressed in various forms, static, stereotypical measures of masculinity that perpetuate 'the myth of what it means to be masculine' are still built into studies (Galdas 2009: 65). Galdas reasons that research needs to get away from this to address how masculinity is actively constructed as part of the help-seeking process.

There are several recent illustrations of this sort of approach. For example, research with a wide range of men in Scotland found that, although there was widespread endorsement that seeking help was a threat to masculinity, particularly amongst those who were younger and healthy, some men embraced help-seeking when it would assist in preserving masculinity, for example when it would help them to keep working or when it would restore valued aspects of masculinity, such as sexual performance. As one man said, 'if you have a problem that gets in the way of sex, you get it sorted pretty quick' (O'Brien et al. 2005: 513). Farrimond's (2012) study of high socio-economic status men aged 20 to 60 in England found that help-seeking was framed as a form of 'taking action' and being 'in control'. Research with Welsh men and women in their twenties found that, even though talking about health was associated with vulnerability and lack of control, which was incompatible with masculinity, there were men who not only talked about health to each other but were 'also able to recognise their own vulnerability' (Charles and Walters 2008: 129). Consequently, a close review of the literature reveals 'a more intricate picture than popular stereotypes . . . might suggest' (Galdas 2009: 65).

We also need to consider the implications of the narrative of the 'reluctant help-seeker' for the study of women's use of health-care. Men's 'delay' in help-seeking is really only meaningful through a contrast with women's 'readiness' to seek help (Annandale and Hammarström 2011). This can render women's experience invisible as it is simply presumed that, in contrast to men, they are more attentive to the body, more accepting of 'weakness' and 'will go to the doctor more readily and will consult with less serious complaints' (Hunt et al. 2012: 241). This may not be the case at all. For example, stereotypes of heart attacks as a 'male problem' have contributed to women's misinterpretation of their own symptoms and to fatal delays in seeking care (Galdas 2009). Finally, it needs to be borne in mind that in many countries the prospect of seeking care in the first place falters on the ability to pay. In many low-income countries, girls and women are unable to take their own decisions about seeking care and families invest less in their care than men's, even though they may have greater need (Sen et al. 2007).

We have seen that there is no simple answer to the question of whether women are sicker than men (or vice versa), not least because research itself is suffused with a priori assumptions which steer research in some directions and not others. Moreover, as noted earlier, gender and self-assessments of health are so intricately connected that cause and effect are not easily disentangled. The only conclusion that can be reached with any degree of confidence, and then only for the West, is that women tend to report more symptoms of minor psychological illness, some somatic complaints (like tiredness, headaches, muscular aches and pains) and functional limitations than men (Bartley 2004).

Gender and socio-economic status

So far, we have approached gender as if it stands alone, when in actuality it intersects in complex ways with other factors, such as socio-economic status and ethnicity. In this final section of the chapter, we will look at the association between gender and socio-economic status (gender and ethnicity is referred to in chapter 6).

Chapter 4 showed the robust association between socio-economic status and health. But how, if at all, does this vary by gender? Despite the putative convergence raised earlier, the lives of Western men and women still differ in a number of ways, which subjects them to different social exposures, both materially and culturally (Hunt and Batty 2009). In spite of women's increased labour-force participation, horizontal and vertical segregation remains. On average, women are paid less than men and they are still mainly responsible for childcare and the home. As Hunt and Batty remark, 'as both occupational and material wealth are common bases for examining socio-economic inequalities, these differences in labour market engagement and reward suggest that we might expect to see different patterns of socio-economic inequalities for men and women' (2009: 142).

As we saw in chapter 3, there is now no shortage of assertions that socio-economic status and gender should be approached as complex and intersecting rather than as separate or additive processes (Acker 2006; Crenshaw 1989). However, when it comes to health, actual research on these intersections is still relatively scarce. Commonly, research on socio-economic status and health looks at men only, or controls for sex in analysis, 'as if it is "noise" and there is some pure, ungendered, relationship between risk factor and disease which one wishes to uncover' (Macintyre 2001: 283). We also need to acknowledge that the conventional use of male samples does not mean that men's *gender-related* experience is in sight. Indeed, much of this research is gender-blind. As Lohan (2009) discusses more widely, there is a schism between the literatures on men and masculinity and on health and health inequalities.

Women and class gradients

The limited existing research generally has found that the magnitude of socio-economic gradients is sharper for men (Bartley 2004; Hunt and Batty 2009). In other words, differences in mortality and morbidity between the top and bottom of the socio-economic hierarchy, and intervals between, tend to be greater for men than for women. For example, Saurel-Cubizolles and colleagues (2009) studied mortality rates for men and women aged 30–64 in France in the late 1990s using individuals' own occupational group and educational level as measures of inequality. Inequality was expressed as 'relative indices of inequality' (RIIs), which is the ratio of the mortality rate for the lowest occupational or educational level to that of the highest. They found higher RIIs in relation to education for men at 2.96 (compared to 2.62 for women) and 6.08 for occupation for men (compared to 3.42 for women). As noted, findings of this kind generally hold for other affluent developed countries. Breast cancer is one condition (another being melanoma) for which a 'reverse class gradient' is observed – that is, the incidence of the condition is greater amongst women higher up the socio-economic ladder. Since breast cancer is a leading cause of death, it has been suggested that it could account for at least part of the weaker socio-economic gradient for women, though the fact that survival tends to be higher amongst middle class women diminishes the power of this explanation (Bartley 2004; Saurel-Cubizolles et al. 2009). Despite shallower gradients for all-cause mortality, CHD mortality consistently shows stronger socio-economic gradients for women than men (Hunt and Batty 2009; White et al. 2003). There is also a stronger socio-economic gradient for obesity for women in many Western countries (Wilkinson and Pickett 2009).

Gender and the widening inequality gap

In chapter 4 we saw that, although life expectancy has been improving for men and women in Western countries, the gap between them has been widening as economic inequality has grown. However, the widening gap has been due to changes for men more than for women. To give some examples, economic inequality (measured by poverty group)[1] grew for both men and women in Britain between 1992–4 and 2001–3. But, while for men this was accompanied by a rise in the difference in life expectancy between the top and the bottom poverty group from a 4.73-year gap to a 4.97-year gap, for women the difference between top and bottom remained stable over the period (Shaw et al. 2005). The gap between the local authority areas (LAs) of England and Wales with the highest and lowest probabilities of survival to age 75, between 1981–3 and 2004–6, increased by 6 per cent for men (from a 21 per cent to a 36 per cent gap), but by only 1 per cent for women (from a 17 per cent gap to an 18 per cent gap) (Wells and Gordon 2008). Finally, inequalities in life expectancy between the least-deprived and the most-deprived of US counties classified into ten groups of approximately equal population size were not only greater for men than for women in 1980–2 and in 1998–2000, but the magnitude of the difference increased over time more for males than for females (Singh and Siahpush 2006).

Explanations

These differences tend to be reported but not explained. So why, with some exceptions, does research find that socio-economic gradients are shallower for women than men? It is hard to imagine that socio-economic inequality matters less for the health of women than for men. Could the shallower gradient therefore be an artefact of the way that socio-economic status is measured? It has been argued that traditional occupational measures such as the UK Registrar General's social classification (RGSC), discussed in chapter 4, are problematic because they are based on a male occupational structure and consequently fail to differentiate between the jobs that women do (Pugh and Moser 1990). Given that women are more likely to move in and out of the job market when they have children, occupational class is also more likely to 'line up' with other dimensions of in/equality, such as material circumstances, for men than for women (Bartley 2004). Alternative asset-based measures, such as availability of amenities, pose problems because, in actuality, some women may have little access to assets like cars. Equally, lack of amenities which appear at first glance to be communal may have different significance for women and men. For example, having no hot water means something different to the man who uses it to wash and shave in the morning and the woman who is responsible throughout the day for childcare, washing clothes and cleaning the house (Payne 1991).

Given these concerns, it is intriguing that the first study to explore socio-economic status and mortality using the UK National Statistics Socio-economic Classification (NS-SEC) found clear gradients amongst women aged 25–59 in England and Wales in 2001–3 (Langford and Johnson 2009). As we saw in chapter 4, while RGSC is based on an assumed hierarchy of skill and social standing, NS-SEC reflects employment relations and conditions by distinguishing between those working under a 'service contract', who tend to have a high degree of autonomy, to be highly trusted (since they are not easily monitored), to have salary increments and opportunities for career progression, and those who work under a 'labour contract' whereby payment is closely tied to hours of work, there is less likelihood of career progression, work is more easily monitored, and job security is lower (Erikson and Goldthorpe 1992). The authors used women's 'own' NS-SEC and, for those who were married, a 'combined' classification of own and husband's NS-SEC (representing household circumstances). For 'own NS-SEC', they found a steadily increasing mortality gradient between NS-SEC class 1 (Higher managerial and professional occupations) and class 7 (Routine occupations), with the exception of a drop for class 4 (Small employers and own account workers). The gradient was even stronger for the 'combined' measure.

Reflecting on why NS-SEC seems to yield mortality gradients when other occupation-based measures do not, Langford and Johnson (2009) suggest that 'own' NS-SEC captures women's employment relations – which are associated with inequality, such as stress at work due to lack of autonomy and poor rewards – and that 'combined' NS-SEC taps into women's access to wider socio-economic resources. Although not referring to health, Acker maintains that, in industrialized countries, class divisions between women are becoming greater as 'more and more women enter well-paid professional and managerial jobs while a majority of women remain in low paid "women's jobs"'. She stresses that social class is 'emergent in practices', remarking that 'people are not located in class structures, but enmeshed in class relations' (Acker 2006: 2, 8). It is therefore feasible that, with its emphasis on employment relations, NS-SEC and similar measures may better capture 21st-century health inequalities amongst women. However, more research is needed to test this.

Even so, we need to extend our theoretical vision beyond individual-level quantitative measures, such as occupation, to capture fully the relationship between gender, socio-economic status and health. We need to connect the experience of health to wider forms of possible oppression – in other words, to bring the gendered societal context into the frame (Inhorn and Whittle 2001). Moss opines that 'contexualising studies in historical and geopolitical frameworks is the next big step' for research on gender equality (2002: 659). Chapter 4 explored the relative importance of the spatial contexts of people's lives for their health, over and above the composition or attributes of individuals who live in a geographical area. However, research which explicitly builds such measures of macro-level 'gender context' into analysis has been fairly limited to date. In one such study, Chen and colleagues (2005) modelled the relationship between women's status and autonomy at the US state level and depressive symptoms, taking account of the characteristics of individual women who lived in (or composed) the state, such as age, ethnicity, income, education and employment status. They found that, although women with lower socio-economic status had more symptoms, *all* women benefited from living in US states which were more equal – that is, the contextual effects of the macro-level gender context were important influences. Drawing on individual-level data for persons aged 15 or over in the European Social Survey of twenty-five countries for 2006–7, Van de Velde and colleagues (2013) found that macro-level gender equality – measured by political participation and decision-making power, and power over economic resources (estimated earned income) – was associated with lower levels of depression in *both* women and men. In other words, 'it neither amplifies nor diminishes women's disadvantage in depression' (Van de Velde et al. 2013: 694). However, a study of Sweden which hypothesized that those municipalities which were more gender-equal would show a convergence between men's and women's life expectancy and sickness absence from work – Backhans et al. (2007) – found, contrary to expectations, that living in municipalities that were more 'gender equal' in economic terms (measured by average incomes, and relative poverty) was associated with *worse* health for both men and women. They aver that, even though Sweden can be described as fairly gender-equal, 'the direction of change has primarily been one where women have expanded into previously male-dominated areas, while less change has been seen in men's behaviour' (2007: 1901). Consequently, they suggest that there may be an 'unfinished equality' which is damaging 'for women, who have become more burdened, and for men, who have been reluctant to change and who, as a group, have lost many of their old privileges' (2007: 1901).

Most research which uses structural (areal, societal) indicators of gender equality or gender inequality has been concerned with women's health. Perhaps this is because, as Wilkinson and Pickett (2009) argue, more unequal societies seem more masculine and women's status tends to be worse in more unequal societies. It is therefore interesting that research by Stanistreet and colleagues (2005) found an association between high levels of patriarchy and higher mortality for men. Drawing on data for 1995 for fifty-one countries around the world (excluding Africa), they found 'the higher the rate of female homicide [taken as an indicator of patriarchy], and hence the greater the indicator of patriarchy, the higher is the rate of mortality among men' (Stanistreet et al. 2005: 873). They conclude that 'oppression and exploitation harm oppressors [men] as well as those they oppress [women]' (2005: 874). From the different perspective of relative deprivation theory (which has paid scant attention to gender to date), Zheng and colleagues argue that relative deprivation has more of an impact on the self-rated health of men than that of women in the US. They suggest this is because men experience more negative work-related stress because they 'are more embedded in competitive settings' (Zheng 2009: 1339). They maintain that women, by comparison, are more protected by kin-based and other social networks. Somewhat ironically, this takes us right back to the early days of research on gender and health in the 1970s, referred to at the start of the chapter, but with a twist since, at that time, one of the central concerns was that it was women's very exclusion from this 'male world' of employment that was detrimental to their well-being.

Conclusions

This chapter has demonstrated that research on gender inequalities in health defies the easy summaries that often appear in the literature even today. To be sure, on average women do still live longer than men around most of the world and, by some measures in some study samples, their health is worse than that of men. However, when we dig more deeply, we find that the differences and similarities between the health of men and of women are both exceedingly complex and highly responsive to social context and social change. This became clear in the analysis of the changing 'gender gap' in life expectancy in various parts of the world. The limitations of trying to capture the association between gender and health status through the simple lens of binary difference was evident in the discussion of morbidity, where we found that the often-posed question, 'Who is sicker: men or women?' is not easily answered because research is often suffused with gendered assumptions which steer it in some directions for men and others for women. Moreover, given that gender and self-assessments of health are so intricately connected that cause and effect are not easily disentangled, the question is not the right one to pose anyway. Finally, we have seen that gender does not stand alone as an influence upon health – rather, it intersects in complex, but as yet relatively unexplored, ways with other social factors such as socio-economic status.

6

'Race', ethnicity and health

Chapters 4 and 5 highlighted the lively and contested nature of debate around social class and gender inequalities in health. We have seen that global economic and social restructuring has prompted sociologists to reflect critically on whether social class as traditionally conceived is eroding, to be replaced by new forms of stratification. Similarly, the customary tools of feminism which stress the dichotomous character of gender are no longer fit for the analysis of today's highly complex health inequalities as they concern both women and men. The capacity of sociologists of health to engage empirically with these debates has been hindered by a dearth of the necessary conceptual and methodological tools to match theoretical advances. This is equally apparent when we turn to ethnicity and health where researchers are wrangling over the contentious concepts of 'race', ethnicity and racism. Even so, new energy has been injected into research on ethnicity and health in recent years as it has responded to the rise of new racisms and ethnonationalisms, reflected critically on the growth of 'racial profiling' in medicine, and engaged with wider social science debates on ethnic identities which have replaced former ways of thinking about ethnicity as a static personal trait of individuals with a more dynamic and socially constructed approach.

This chapter begins by looking at the racialization of the body, the ascendance of racial categories, and the recent re-emergence of 'racial medicine'. This leads us to reflect critically upon the definitions and classifications which are the pillars for the collection of data on ethnic groups. We then examine the associations that have been observed between various health outcomes and ethnic groupings from survey research, taking the UK and the US as our focus. This will reveal the considerable heterogeneity in health experience between ethnic groups and highlight that minorities are not simply disadvantaged on all dimensions by comparison to the 'general population'. Finally, we will deliberate upon how observed differences might be explained through a consideration of the association between socio-economic and cultural factors and racism.

Bodily imprints: the birth of modern racism

Although the idea of 'race' first appeared in the English language in the early 1600s, it was not until the late 1700s that it began to be used in Europe and North America to name and explain phenotypical (to do with the observable characteristics of an organism) differences between human beings. By the mid-1800s, the notion that there are a number of distinct 'races', each with a biological capacity for social development, was firmly etched on to the scientific and popular consciousness (Miles 1994). Colonial expansion of the West and the recognition of 'difference' that this entailed, coupled with the rise of science, provided a firm foundation upon which to build a new 'race science'.

The visibility of the body makes it a crucial site for marking differences between people. For example, in the aftermath of terrorist attacks in the US on 9/11, on the Madrid underground in May of 2004 and on the London transport system in July 2005, body markers such as skin colour, hair texture and facial features have become the basis of a troubling new 'racial vigilance' (Gibel Azoulay 2008). Although they present in different forms, the origins of present-day ideas of 'race' lie back in the seventeenth century. This was the time during which the new, docile, objective and observable body of Cartesian mechanical philosophy (see chapter 2) first gave itself up to be 'analysed, categorised, classified, and ordered with the cold gaze of scientific distance' (Goldberg 1990: 302).

Given its concern with the body, medicine has always been a medium for the exercise of the racial classificatory gaze. As we saw in chapter 1, the new clinical medicine began to develop in the latter part of the eighteenth century and was fairly well established in the industrializing nations by the early nineteenth century. In the wake of Darwin's work culminating in *On the Origin of Species* (Darwin 1859), the eminent physicians of the day sought out racial differences in physiology, anatomy and health. A belief in the superiority of the 'white race' was used to justify subordination of 'coloureds' by such means as immigration control and slavery (Bhopal 1988).

This is illuminated by the medical debate on slavery in the US Southern states. In her analysis, Krieger (1987) takes us back to the early 1800s, to when the US was the greatest slave carrier of the world. Many physicians of the time hired their services to plantation owners and inspected slaves for auction at the block. Notions of innate racial difference found clear expression in medical studies of the day. Krieger discusses a text by one Dr Pendleton of Sparta, Georgia, who, in 1849, argued that the reason why twice as many blacks as whites died of tuberculosis was that they were not suited to the cold of even Georgia's warm climate. He omitted to make any reference to a life of slavery in which men and women were 'forced to live in crowded, poorly heated, leaky cabins without adequate clothing or blankets and were overworked to boot' (1987: 263). Faced with the problem of why it was the 'coarse muscular Negress' rather than the 'delicate white female' who had more miscarriages, Pendleton ignored the social causes of overwork in favour of an explanation based on miscarriages resulting from 'the unnatural tendency of the African female to destroy her offspring' (quoted in Krieger 1987: 264). In 1850, Dr Sammuel Cartwright, an ardent defender of slavery, authored an infamous article entitled 'Diseases and physical peculiarities of the Negro race', wherein he proclaimed the natural status of the 'Negro' as slave and professed to have discovered the 'ultimate physical basis of black inferiority: their inability to consume as much oxygen as whites, a consequence of certain "peculiarities" of the black nervous system' (1987: 268). He went on to declare that this oxygen insufficiency predisposed slaves to lethargy, the only antidote to which was forced labour.

By the 1850s, the voice of 'black' physicians entered the fray. One of the most outspoken was Dr John Rock, who sought to replace the existing medical science and its biological rationales for slavery with a social model which emphasized 'the white man's desire for cheap labour' (Krieger 1987: 271). This was taken up by Dr James McCune Smith who argued that traits which appeared to be innate were a product of the social environment: hence the diseases of slaves were the effect of racism, rather than being caused by 'race'. The ongoing debate between the reductionist medical science of many white physicians and their nascent black detractors took a new turn in the aftermath of the Civil War as slaves were turned from property into people. But, as history bears testimony, racism did not die with the abolition of slavery. Indeed, it lived on in subsequent 'discoveries' by science and medicine.

One of the most horrifying twentieth-century manifestations of 'scientific racism' was the aiding and abetting of Nazi racial policies by the psychiatrists and anthropologists who provided the 'scientific' evidence for racial and genetic inferiority of Jews, and the involvement of physicians and nurses in the classification of mental patients and those of 'inferior races' for sterilization, forced labour and death. Referring back to the 1800s, Gilman (1991: 38) writes that 'there is no space more highly impacted with the sense of difference about the body of the Jew than the public space of "medicine"'. In an intriguing analysis, he explores how pathologies attributed to the 'Jewish foot' marked men out as unfit for military service and, thereby, for full citizenship. In this process, 'the foot became the hallmark of difference, of the Jewish body being separate from the body politic' (1991: 44). This spread to the wider body as the sign of the 'limping Jew' was read into a number of diagnostic categories of nineteenth-century neurology. For example, intermittent claudication (manifest in chronic pain and tension in the lower leg, resulting in stiffness and inability to move the leg) was seen as the cause of an inhibited gait and ultimately as a sign of the inherent constitutional weakness of Jewish people.

Race and biology

The examples of slavery and Nazi medicine highlight how the body is marked by racial discourse through the complicity of medical science. Skin colour, head shape, body size, smell, hair texture and other phenotypical features were the markers of the gaze of medical science which professed to be cold and objective (Goldberg 1990). We now know that there is no genetic basis for racial classifications – indeed, most genes occur identically in all human beings: 'human genetic variation is real', 'but the overall amount of measured genetic differentiation between populations is meagre' (Graves and Rose 2007: 186). Moreover, human physical characteristics are not correlated with each other in ways that reflect genetic relatedness. So we cannot necessarily infer that the genetic relatedness of individuals within populations means that they are certain to share the same phenotypes (Graves and Rose 2007: 183). Rather, complex phenotypes are the result of the interaction between genetics and the social and physical environments in which people live their lives.

In chapter 5, we considered the quandary of what Epstein (2007) calls the 'inclusion and difference' paradigm in relation to gender. We saw that the push to include members of hitherto unrepresented groups has intensified a felt need to take difference into account in medical research. In the case of 'race', this has led (mainly in the US) to fractious debates over 'racial profiling' for medical purposes. In 2005, the US Federal Food and Drug Administration (FDA) approved a new drug for the treatment of heart failure (BiDil), which is prescribed for black Americans. Epstein questions whether such developments are 'a victory worth savouring in a long struggle to bring medical attention to the excluded and the underserved?' Or do they reflect a limited understanding of 'the social and biological production of bodily difference, which may not only harm human health but also inappropriately reinforce ideas about the reality of essential differences between groups'? Epstein lines up with the critics, arguing that health inequalities are first and foremost a massive *social* problem, and that 'focusing on biological differences is not the way to address them' (Epstein 2007: 204). He contends that racial profiling in medicine leads to the improper treatment of the patient who does not live up to the stereotype of his or her phenotypical 'racial group'. But, for our purposes, perhaps his most important point is that racial profiling clouds the relationship between the social and the biological and hence 'interferes with our attempts to understand and eliminate health disparities'. Epstein explains that when racial differences are attributed to biology and genetics, social and cultural causes of health inequalities are no longer recognized. In the case of heart disease, for example, this directs our attention away from the social factors that cause cardio-vascular disease in the first place (Gibel Azoulay 2008: 59).

Ethnic classifications

The language of classificatory schema is the medium through which we actively construct 'race' and ethnicity. It is hardly surprising therefore that terminology has occasioned considerable debate within the social sciences and beyond. For example, the 'ethnicity question' which first appeared in the 1991 UK census was the outcome of almost twenty years of deliberation, initially on its desirability and then on the form it should take (Coleman and Salt 1996). So, before we look at recent health-related research, it is important to reflect on the vocabulary that shapes it.

Definitions of race and ethnicity are a challenge to health researchers, not only because they are politically charged, but also because they are not always understood in the same way in different countries, are subject to change over time, and can reinforce racialized ways of thinking (Bradby 2012; Bradby and Nazroo 2010). State-sponsored enumerations date back to 1790 when the US began its decennial censuses and they soon became a defining feature of most European and New World states (Kertzer and Arel 2002). Since census classifications are a desire on the part of the modern state to represent and control populations, they have weighty political consequences: as Foucault (1980) identified, knowledge is power (see chapter 2). To give a historical example, in the nineteenth-century American South, white privilege was preserved through the 'one-drop rule' (known also as 'hypo-descent') whereby people with black and white parents were treated as black. This protected white privilege before the law and in popular culture (Bradby and Nazroo 2010; Graves and Rose 2007). Today, numerical supremacy is used to justify political ownership of resources such as land and the forced eviction of minorities through 'ethnic cleansing' in various parts of the world.

The term 'ethnicity' is usually taken to represent self-identity with a culture (Bradby 2012). Yet, as Kertzer and Arel (2002) discuss, the compulsion to divide people into racial categories based on the belief that identity can be objectively determined through ancestry often means that race and ethnicity get blurred. We see this in the US

Table 6.1 UK population by ethnic group, April 2011

Classification		Percentage
White	White British	80.5
	Irish	0.9
	Gypsy or Irish traveller	0.1
	Other	4.4
Mixed/multiple ethnic groups	White and Black Caribbean	0.8
	White and Asian	0.6
	White and Black African	0.3
	Other Mixed	0.5
Asian / Asian British	Indian	2.5
	Pakistani	2.0
	Bangladeshi	0.8
	Chinese	0.7
	Other Asian	1.5
Black / African / Caribbean /	African	1.8
Black British	Caribbean	1.1
	Other Black	0.5
Other ethnic group	Arab	0.4
	Any other ethnic group	0.6

Source: ONS (2012)

official classification which divides the population into four 'races': White, Black, American Indian / Alaskan Native, and Asian or Pacific Islander. Hispanic people are described as an ethnic group, rather than a 'race' (Bartley 2004: 149). The present-day UK census classification (see table 6.1), mixes nationality, country of birth, language, and skin colour. Here and elsewhere, 'black and white are pseudo-racial categories, referring, rather inaccurately, to perceived skin colours, but Indian, Pakistani and Bangladeshi are all legal nationalities although they may also be regarded as ethnic categories. Chinese is a nationality, but it is also an ethnic description as well as a linguistic group, and so on' (Skellington 1996: 26).

Since the admixture of census categories is replicated in various ways in other schema, if we wish to engage with survey statistics the latitude for avoiding racialized classifications is minimal. This makes it appropriate to ask whether the categories are simply another way of essentializing and naturalizing difference, or – to put it another way – are they a euphemism for 'race' (Ratcliffe 2004)? Slippage between the terms 'race' and 'ethnicity' is evident in the hybrid language we often see in research, such as 'race/ethnicity' (Bradby 2012). Moreover, although we might seek to separate race and racism conceptually, in reality this is hard to do. As Goldberg (2009: 9) puts it, 'race is the glove in which the titanic, the weighty, hand of racism fits. The cloth may be velvet but it is studded with spikes and soaked in blood.'

We might also object that fixing racialized identities under labels, no matter how nuanced they are, inevitably does violence to the sheer complexity of the ethnic identities that are forged by individuals themselves. In the process of data analysis, the underlying meaning of a variable like 'ethnic group' can get lost as ethnicity is reified and health outcomes are frozen into static stereotypes with minimal consideration for the processes of power and racialization that are complicit in their construction. What is more, as we will see later in the chapter, there is the accompanying risk that 'ethnic' culture gets construed as the *cause* of health differentials (Karlsen 2004).

Notwithstanding these sizeable problems, many social epidemiologists, health sociologists, policy makers and others are prepared to live with the inadequacies of classification because they feel that this still is the best way to reveal the realities of oppression that ethnic minorities often experience. So, as this chapter itself reveals, if we wish to draw upon existing research data there is no choice but to employ their lexicon.

Minority ethnic groups and aspects of health status

Even today in the UK, there is a dearth of good-quality large-scale survey data containing the measures of general health and specific health problems which would give us the opportunity to look at ethnic minority groups alongside the majority 'white' population (Karlsen 2004). Until the 1991 census and the inclusion of the so-called 'ethnic question', only data on country of birth were collected. The implication before this time was that racial and ethnic minorities were 'foreign', even though most were actually British citizens (Bradby and Nazroo 2010). The UK still does not make nationally collected mortality data available by ethnic group. However, there are some data that enable us to develop at least a partial picture of the relationship between ethnicity and health status.

Table 6.2 shows the percentage of people in England reporting a longstanding illness that limits their activities by ethnic minority group and the general population (that is, everybody including ethnic minorities) in 1999 and 2004, separately for men and women. The data are age-standardized. This is necessary because ethnic minority groups tend to be younger than the general population, and younger people tend to be healthier. Age-standardization therefore removes the possibly of under-estimating ill-health in ethnic minority populations. The first thing to notice in the table is the significant variation by ethnic group. Some groups fare much better than the general population, such

Table 6.2 Self-reported limiting longstanding illness, 1999 and 2004, by age within minority ethnic groups, and gender, England (%; age-standardized)

		Black Caribbean	Indian	Paki-stani	Bangla-deshi	Chinese	Irish	General popula-tion
Men	1999	24	21	22	30	14	29	25
	2004	24	23	20	24	9	26	23
Women	1999	27	25	23	22	12	27	26
	2000	28	19	30	21	10	23	27

Source: NHS Information Centre (2004). Copyright © 2013, re-used with the permission of the Health and Social Care Information Centre. All rights reserved

Table 6.3 Self-reported 'bad / very bad' health, by ethnic group and sex, 2004 (age-standardized)

	Men(%)	Women(%)
General population	6	7
Irish	10	5
Indian	9	8
Black Caribbean	9	11
Pakistani	10	15
Bangladeshi	15	14
Chinese	4	3

Source: NHS Information Centre (2004: fig. 2B). Copyright © 2013, re-used with the permission of the Health and Social Care Information Centre. All rights reserved.

as Chinese men and women, who have much lower rates of illness. Rates for Bangladeshi women are also relatively low, as are those in Indian women in 2004 (but not 1999). In contrast, Pakistani women had noticeably higher rates of illness in 2004, as did Bangladeshi men and Irish men in 1999.

Table 6.3 presents self-reports of 'bad / very bad health' in England by ethnic minority group. Once again we see that Chinese men and women fare well in comparison to both the general population and other ethnic minority groups. In contrast, reports of poor health are relatively high amongst Bangladeshi men and women and amongst Pakistani women. In relation to the discussions of gender differences in morbidity in chapter 5, it is interesting to observe that, although percentages vary, there is no consistent pattern of higher self-reports of illness amongst women than amongst men (and we can note that the rate for men is double that of women amongst the Irish).

There are also notable differences in mental health. Figure 6.1 shows risk ratios of poor self-assessed mental health amongst ethnic

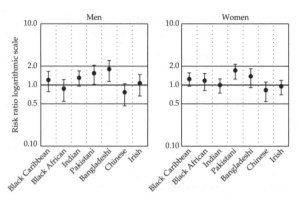

General population = 1.0. Error bars indicate 95% confidence limit

Source: NHS Information Centre (2004). Copyright © 2013, re-used with the permission of the Health and Social Care Information Centre. All rights reserved.

Figure 6.1 High GHQ scores, by minority ethnic group

minority men and women (using the GHQ12, a general measure of mental well-being). A risk equivalent to the general population is represented by the X-axis (i.e. a value of 1.0). So any figure above 1.0 represents a higher risk and a figure below 1.0 a lower risk of mental ill-health for the ethnic group in question, compared to the general population. For example, a risk ratio of 2.0 would mean that the group concerned has twice the risk of mental ill-health. Interestingly, there is little variation by gender, except for Black Africans amongst whom women have a higher, and men have a lower, relative risk of mental ill-health than the general population. It is notable that both Pakistani and Bangladeshi men and women have higher rates than the general population. The 'misery of Asian women' has been a particular concern of the research literature, where it has been suggested that relatively high rates of primary care consultations for physical conditions such as musculoskeletal pain denote the so-called 'somatization' of mental ill-health: in other words, that Asian women present their mental distress as bodily symptoms. However, as Rogers and Pilgrim discuss, assuming 'that physical distress is "really" a mental illness may reflect a form of Western cultural imperialism on the part of the psychiatric profession' (2010: 103).

We need to be sensitive to the likelihood that self-assessments of health and responses to them are influenced by cultural beliefs and practices. For this reason, we should be wary of assuming that the self-assessments of 'poor' health are equivalent to each other. This point, which has already been made for gender inequalities in health (see chapter 5), may be particularly important when making comparisons between ethnic minority groups and the 'general population'.

Table 6.4 Life expectancy at birth by race and sex, United States, selected years, 1990–2010

Year	White			Black or African American		
	Male	Female	*Gender gap*	Male	Female	*Gender gap*
1900	46.6	48.7	2.1	32.5	33.5	1.0
1950	66.5	72.2	5.7	59.1	62.9	3.8
1960	67.4	74.1	6.7	61.1	66.3	5.2
1970	68.0	75.6	7.6	60.0	68.3	8.3
1980	70.7	78.1	7.2	63.8	72.5	8.7
1990	72.7	79.4	7.1	64.5	73.6	9.1
2000	74.7	79.9	5.8	68.2	75.1	6.9
2006	75.7	80.6	4.9	69.7	76.5	6.9
2010	76.5	81.3	4.8	71.8	78.0	6.2

Source: NCHS (2010, 2012)

That said, while we can pick out what appear to be consistent health disadvantages for some groups, such as Pakistani women and Irish men, the most striking finding is the considerable diversity, even within those commonly grouped as South Asian (Indian, Pakistani, Bangladeshi).

To consider mortality, we turn to US data. Table 6.4 depicts differences in life expectancy for males and females, for selected years between 1900 and 2010. The first thing to notice is that even though life expectancies have risen for all groups, the life expectancies of black or African males and females are consistently lower than those of their white counterparts at all time points. In chapter 5 we looked at the reducing 'gender gap' in life expectancy in affluent Western nations such as the US from around the 1970s/1980s. The data in table 6.4 provide us with the opportunity to explore any variations by 'race'. Data for both groups show the familiar gender pattern, although the timing of the peak female advantage and the extent of this advantage varies. Thus, for whites, the peak is 1970 when the gap favouring women is 7.6 years. The peak gender gap for black or African Americans is in 1990 and, at a remarkable 9.1 years, is considerably larger. After 1970 and 1990 respectively, the 'gender gaps' begin to reduce, though it has to be noted that the female advantage for Black and African Americans in particular was still high at 6.2 years in 2010. Although we can only speculate, it is possible that this reflects high mortality amongst black and African American males.

Table 6.5 presents age-adjusted death rates for selected causes for the population as a whole (All population) and for African Americans, Asian Americans and Pacific Islanders. Although they are only a one-year snap-shot in time, there are noticeable differences. Thus

Table 6.5 Age-adjusted death rates for selected causes of death, per 100,000 population, United States, 2006

	All population	African Americans	Asian Americans and Pacific Islanders
All causes	776.5	982.0	428.6
Heart disease	200.2	257.7	108.5
Cancer	180.7	217.4	106.5
Diabetes	23.3	45.1	15.8
Unintentional injury	39.8	38.3	16.9
HIV disease	4.0	18.6	0.6

Source: NCHS (2010)

African Americans have higher rates of death than the overall population for all causes except unintentional injury. In contrast, Asian Americans and Pacific Islanders have lower rates for all causes. The differential death rates from 'HIV causes' warrant particular mention since the rate for Asian Americans and Pacific Islanders is just 0.6 per 100,000 people, compared to 18.6 for African Americans. Again, these data highlight the considerable heterogeneity of experience across ethnic groups.

'Race', ethnicity and socio-economic inequalities

Although the data we have looked at are useful, they tell us nothing directly about the *reasons* for the differentials observed. As we saw in chapter 4, socio-economic status has been in the conceptual spotlight as protagonists propose different explanations for health inequalities, such as relative and absolute deprivation. Contained within this debate is the question of whether class should be approached as a collective identity or whether it is now more appropriate to think in terms of a range of inequalities which distinguish relatively autonomous individuals along a number of axes (occupational, cultural) which are unlikely to align to form a strong *collective* economic or social identity. Research on ethnicity and health is both paralleled and cross-cut by these concerns. We will explore this first of all by looking at the relative significance of class and ethnicity in the production of morbidity and mortality differences.

'Race' *or class, or 'race'* and *class?*

This subheading is borrowed from the title of an article by Navarro (1989) in which he dissents from any reduction of social class to 'race', from the political standpoint that to think in terms of racial divisions effectively weakens the class solidarities that traverse the 'black–white' divide. Others also spurn reductionist explanations but from the vantage point of not subsuming 'race' under class or socio-economic status. For example, Ahmad (1993: 31) argues that there is a 'danger that a radical field of "race"/health research will encourage material reductionism where all phenomena are reduced to material disadvantage or class oppression'. But, as Krieger (2003: 197) writes, it is a fallacy to frame debate as 'either/or' – instead, we need to think in terms of 'both/and'. So, ultimately, we must find a way of exploring the potentially combined influences of 'race' and class upon health status.

Research has begun to show quite convincingly that social and economic inequality underpins much of the observed ethnic/racial inequality in health that we have observed (Nazroo 2010). Thus, socio-economic inequality is 'part of the casual pathway that links race to health' (Williams 2012: 283). But there is also an *added burden* of race over and above socio-economic status that is linked to poor health (Williams 2012). As Grimsley and Bhat put it some years ago, minority ethnic groups appear to 'endure working-class health inequality and then some' (1988: 201).

We see this in figure 6.2, which is an analysis by Nazroo (2010) of six health differences for three broad ethnic groups. The data are drawn from the UK Fourth National Survey of Ethnic Minorities collected in 1993–4. They are presented as the relative risk of each ethnic group for each of the health conditions. Of most interest are the changes in the relative risks once socio-economic status (measured by standard of living) is taken into account. We see that 'in all cases the risk for each ethnic minority group compared with whites is reduced once the socio-economic control has been applied' (Nazroo 2010: 121). This suggests that socio-economic factors contribute to ethnic inequalities in health. However, as Nazroo explains, the data also raise the possibility that other factors play a role too because, 'for most groups and most outcomes, differences remain once the adjustment for the socio-economic indicator has been made' (2010: 122). Drawing on life-expectancy data for those aged 25 in the US, Williams (2012) reports that whites live five years longer than blacks. However, for both groups, variations in life expectancy by socio-economic status (as measured by income and education) are larger than the overall black–white difference. Thus, high-income blacks live 7.1 years longer, and high-income whites live 6.8 years longer, than their lower-income counterparts. For both blacks and whites, as income level rises, health improves, but there are black–white differences in life expectancy of at least 3 years at each income level. In sum, these (and other) studies show that socio-economic

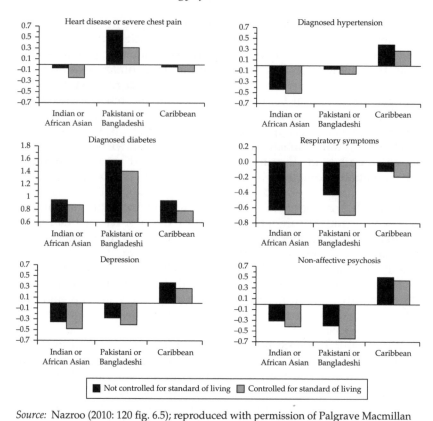

Source: Nazroo (2010: 120 fig. 6.5); reproduced with permission of Palgrave Macmillan

Figure 6.2 Reduction in relative risk of ill-health (compared with whites after controlling for standard of living) (UK Fourth National Survey of Ethnic Minorities)

factors play a major part in, but do not fully account for, health inequalities between ethnic groups. To put it another way, there is a residual effect of race after socio-economic status is controlled for (Williams 2012). Much more research is needed to express the precise mechanisms that link socio-economic status and health. For example, it is highly likely that factors associated with racism, such as discrimination, are antecedents of socio-economic inequality and also materialize in habitual everyday social harm to individuals (Ford and Airhihenbuwa 2010). It is also worth noting that, to date, most research employs the language of socio-economic status (SES) differences, as measured by income or education. This means that social class is ultimately reduced to indicators of material advantage/ disadvantage, losing its potential connection with any sense of group identity.

Racism and health

Racism is chameleonic in its nature: sometimes overt (as in racist violence), sometimes more guileful and expressed through a variety of coded signifiers which 'produce a racist effect while denying that this effect is the result of racism' (Solomos and Back 1994: 156). However, at its core, racism can be defined as any argument which suggests 'the human species is composed of naturally occurring discrete groups in order to legitimate social inequality' (Miles and Brown 2003: 83). Since it has many guises – indeed, it is more appropriate to refer to racisms than to racism – it can be argued that there is little merit in trying to treat racism as a separate factor that can be parcelled out in analysis, whether this is in relation to material or to cultural determinants of health, or to both. Rather, as Andrews and Jewson put it some years ago, racism should be viewed as 'integral to whatever analysis that is developed' and the question posed not whether it operates but when, where and how (1993: 149).

'Scientific racism' is now accompanied by a newer 'cultural racism' which exerts no less power and is no less repressive because it swaps the language of biology for that of culture. As already noted, racism is plural in form and highly adaptive to the changing contours of modern society. Although fluid and unstable, typically racial identities are constructed in an attempt to naturalize the difference between 'belongingness and otherness' (Hall 1992: 255). For example, although it did not draw explicitly on biological differences, Gilroy contends that the 'popular' racism of 1980s and 1990s Britain was based on a preoccupation with drawing lines of inclusion and exclusion between people. By this process, he writes,

> Britons are invited to put on their tin hats and climb back down into their World War II air raid shelters. There they can be comforted by the rustic glow of the homogeneous national culture that has been steadily diluted by black settlement in the post War years. The unsullied culture can be mystically reconstructed, particularly amidst national adversity when distinctly British qualities supposedly emerge with the greatest force and clarity.
>
> (Gilroy 1990: 266)

These sentiments have not gone away, they just resurface in new guises, such as anti-Muslim sentiment. As Miles and Brown (2003: 164) put it, 'when Muslims become a racialised group, an amalgam of nationality ("Arab" or "Pakistani", for example), religion (Islam) and politics (extremism, fundamentalism and terrorism) manifests in Orientalism, Islamophobic and racist discourses'.

Many have pointed out that survey research faces serious challenges when measuring racism and its effects (see, e.g., Krieger 2003;

Nazroo 2010). Racism can be overt, but also 'everyday' and insidious, which is less easy to 'get at' in quantitative research. That said, many studies have found that racism powerfully undermines people's health through 'social ostracism and blocked economic opportunity' (Brondolo et al. 2009). It is argued that the experience of discrimination triggers stress responses in the individual that are inimical to health. For some health outcomes it is possible to identify the biological mechanism involved in stress responses. In the case of preterm birth, for example, the increased production of neuropeptide corticotropin-releasing hormone (CRH) in the placenta plays a role in initiating labour in response to maternal or foetal stress (Lauderdale 2006). Post 9/11 in the USA, many persons perceived to be Arabs were subject to harassment, hate crime and workplace discrimination. Lauderdale studied the risk of preterm birth and low birth weight (less than 2,500 grams) in California over two time periods: the six months *post 9/11* (1 October 2001 to 31 March 2002) and the equivalent period the *previous year* (1 October 2000 to 31 March 2001). She found that, while there were no differences in birth outcomes in the two periods among all women in aggregate, Arabic-named women experienced an elevated risk of adverse outcomes compared to equivalent women who gave birth a year earlier. For example, they were 34 per cent more likely to have a low-birthweight baby in the later period (Lauderdale 2006).

Studies of self-reported racial discrimination show a strong association with various aspects of poor health in many countries. Mental health appears to be particularly affected. For example, after controlling for age, gender and socio-economic status, Karlsen and colleagues (2005) discovered that personal experience of interpersonal racism (verbal or physical attack on the respondent or their property), discrimination in the workplace, and perceiving racism in the wider society each had an independent effect on the risk of anxiety disorder or depression and psychosis amongst Caribbean, Indian, Pakistani, Bangladeshi and Irish ethnic minority groups in England.

Mental illness is complex and manifests in various forms. However, one consistently highlighted statistic is that 'Caribbean' people in the UK are three to five times more likely to be admitted to hospital with a diagnosis of schizophrenia than white people, and rates are even higher than this for young men (Nazroo 2010). The reasons for these high rates are hotly debated. As Nazroo (2010) explains, given that low rates of psychotic illness are found in the populations of Jamaica and Trinidad, and rates are higher amongst those born in the UK than amongst migrants, they are unlikely to be genetic. Hence researchers posit links between high illness rates and the combination of racist discrimination and socio-economic disadvantage. Health services have also been directly implicated. There is a strong tendency for white people to interpret black people's behaviours as signs of insanity and danger. 'Caribbean' patients are far more likely to reach the mental health system via the police, the courts and prisons, and to experience more harsh and invasive forms of treatment (such as electro-convulsive therapy), than other people. Rogers and Pilgrim remark that 'at each point of the processing of the criminal justice and mental health systems there appears to be a staged increase in discrimination' (2010: 96).

It has been customary to attribute high rates of illness to the cultures and genes of the people in the ethnic categories with these higher rates (Nazroo 2010). This is typically framed as difference from some often unarticulated 'white' norm. This strikes a chord with broader, popular forms of discrimination that take as axiomatic that 'minorities could and should change their culture in favour of the majority' in order to fit in better; that is, they are seen as 'authors of their own disadvantage', and their culture is the cause (Bradby and Nazroo 2010: 115). Examples abound, but one of the most notorious is the case of so-called 'Asian rickets'. Rickets, which is caused by vitamin D deficiency, is a known disease of poverty. In 1940s Britain it was tackled among the white population via the fortification of margarine. However, when a high prevalence was observed amongst South Asian school children in the 1970s it was explained in terms of un-British eating and living habits and a (possible) genetic deficiency in absorbing vitamins into the blood stream or in synthesizing sunlight (Reed 2003). The given solution was adopting a 'British diet' and lifestyle. Thus rickets, a disease of poverty, probably related to the poor conditions migrants faced when entering Britain, was racialized through a cultural inscription among 'Asians' (Ahmad 1993: 21).

There are many other illustrations of how cultural 'difference from us' is manifest in healthcare. We have already touched upon mental health, but some of the most troubling examples over the years come from reproductive healthcare. For example, in their research on Somali refugees' experience of maternity care in London, Harper Bulman and McCourt (2002) found that, even though interpreter services were available, they were rarely used. Instead, many women had to provide their own informal interpreters. This could mean relying on men. Thus one respondent spoke of calling on the services of her neighbour: 'He was a man and he was not my brother or husband, and when they were checking me I asked him to go out, but I really needed to understand everything because I was really scared. I had already had two miscarriages, and I was scared to have another' (respondent quoted in Harper Bulman and McCourt 2002: 370–1). Racist perceptions of the body and cultural stereotyping led the midwives in the study to conclude that the Somali women were 'more natural' and so they would rarely have epidurals for pain, though they would take 'gas and air' (entonox). However, the women themselves reported that the option of pain control was not raised with them.

Even though it is difficult at present to build a complete picture of the role healthcare might play in producing ethnic differences in health, studies such as Harper Bulman and McCourt's (2002) and many others on the treatment of various health conditions reveal problems in access to services and the quality of care received. For example, the US Institute of Medicine report *Unequal Treatment: Confronting Racial and Ethnic Disparities in Health Care* revealed 'remarkably consistent' racial and ethnic inequalities 'across a range of illness and healthcare services' (Smedley et al. 2003: 5). These are wide-ranging and include 'racial differences' in the receipt of diagnostic tests for cancer, antiretroviral treatment (ART) for HIV/AIDS and revascularization procedures for heart disease, and provision of rehabilitation services. The authors of the report associate these differences with the operation of the US health system and 'discrimination at the individual, patient–provider level' (Smedley et al. 2003: 4). Even though the UK's NHS provides universal free access to care, it is not immune from similar racial biases (see Nazroo 2010).

Medicine and health education can be criticized for an 'intellectual apartheid' in their conceptualization of minority ethnic groups as carriers of problematic cultures and 'exotic' illnesses (Bradby and Nazroo 2010). Ahmad (1996) forcefully points out that, when researchers employ simple, rigid and essentialist notions of culture, they pursue a politics of victim blaming as minority communities are construed as a danger to their own heath. As he continues, the corollary is that they need to be 'saved' from their own cultures and encouraged to become more 'like us'. Sorely missing is any recognition that culture can be a source of support, strength and well-being. Ahmad maintains that, frozen in time and space and linked to health only through its difference from an often undisclosed 'white' standard, the world of culture and medicine in relation to minority ethnic groups has been that of 'lifeless, limp, cellophane-wrapped and neatly tagged cultures, rather than one of living and lived in cultures with all their vitality, complexity, complementarities and contradictions, cultures that are empowering, changing, challenging and flexible – cultures that are real' (1996: 199). Yet, as Reed (2003) shows in her study of the health choices made by British Asian mothers in the English city of Leicester, ethnicity and culture are part of a complex web of influences on health choices. Culture is dynamic and it 'changes to incorporate fresh ideas and perspectives as people develop new ways of responding to their environments' (2003: 5).

In much the same way that patriarchal privilege is indiscernible to many men, so too is 'white' privilege invisible to many white men and women. 'Whiteness' is 'unmarked and unnamed', as only 'Others' are seen to carry 'culture'. Whiteness, therefore, is a 'space defined only by reference to those named cultures that it has flung to its perimeters' (Frankenberg 1993: 231). It is not surprising, then, that many white people do not perceive themselves as having an ethnicity at all (Karlsen 2004), and it would seem that many researchers do not either. As Frankenberg relates, any consideration of Afro-Caribbean women will 'probably address race and culture; a study of white women . . . probably will not' (1993: 18). The pervasive tendency to homogenize 'white' ethnicity is arguably part and parcel of its invisibility. Thus, in the UK – with some limited exceptions, such as attempts to understand the health of Irish and Polish people – white ethnicities remain largely unexplored in the context of health.

A number of problems follow from the use of 'white' culture as an unarticulated standard from which to judge minority ethnic culture and health, the most important of which, as already mentioned, is the tendency to subsume people under an oppressive and deterministic cloud of cultural difference. Research shortcomings are brought clearly to the fore when *only* minority ethnic cultures (beliefs, attitudes, behaviours) are considered (Karlsen 2004). There is, for example, merit in Pierce and Armstrong's (1996) research on the beliefs that older Afro-Caribbeans hold about diabetes. In their study, individuals came across as unsure, perhaps even confused about what diabetes is and its implications for their long-term health. However, the authors tend to set this against a rather authoratorial medical 'truth' of the disease, in the face of which the 'lay' voice is almost bound to be 'confused' (not only if it is that of predominantly older Afro-Caribbean men, but also if it is that of various majority 'white' ethnic groups). The authors recognize that any attribution of the accounts of their respondents to "ethnic beliefs" must be tentative in the absence of any empirical comparisons, but still feel able to conclude that 'a number of views were expressed that clearly did seem to reflect a specific and different ethnic culture' (Pierce and Armstrong 1996: 99). The question that arises, of course, is: different from what?

Multiculturalism and ethnic identity

Chapter 2 raised the health implications of the increased global flow of goods, finance and people around the world. The migration of people from one country to another occurs for different reasons. It can be voluntary, such as for educational reasons (e.g. overseas university students) or employment reasons, or involuntary, owing, for example, to civil war, ethnic oppression and political persecution. Involuntarily uprooted people seek refuge outside their homelands (refugees) and in new locations away from their homes within their countries (internally displaced persons living in camps). As peoples are dispersed from their homelands, diasporic communities have been formed in cities around the world (see Braziel 2008). For Giardina 'the new millennia nation-state now composes an increasingly hybridized population in which practices of identity construction are no longer bound by the physical borders of nation-state formations' (2003: 66). In Hall's assessment, this enables racism to be rescued from 'otherness' and used to show that 'we all speak from a particular place, out of a particular history, out of a particular experience, a particular culture, without being contained by that position' (1992: 258). This mirrors the argument in relation to class, discussed in chapter 4: that we live in a culture of individualization in which class as collective identity is diminishing to be replaced by more fluid self-stylizations, which, in relation to ethnicity, link to the hybridi-zation of 'ethnic' identity. Ratcliffe remarks upon the oft-given example of British South Asian youth:

> at home they may speak Urdu, Hindi or Punjab and dress quite happily in accordance with their family's wishes. In the public sphere, however, they may have carved out a rather different persona, with Anglo-Asian or African-American-Asian overtones. Black street styles are common in most towns and cities in Europe and the US, irrespective of an indi-vidual's origins or heritage.
>
> (Ratcliffe 2004: 28)

Drawing on this more 'fluid' sense of identity seems to be an effec-tive way of tackling the problems that arise when an individual's health status, health beliefs and health behaviours are rather uncritically 'read off' their assigned 'ethnic group' (in both quantitative and qualitative research). However, the option to choose one's ethnicity does not apply equally to all. As Bradby and Nazroo argue in relation to the US, many whites are able to choose which ethnic group they do or do not align with (Scottish, Swedish, Italian and so on) as well as whether they adopt its cultural practices, such as the celebration of particular holidays: 'this is the crucial difference between race and ethnicity; for suburban whites, ethnicity lacks social costs, provides enjoyment, and is chosen voluntarily, none of which is true for non-white Americans' (2010: 117). Equally, it is the invisible/'unproblematic' character of white ethnicity and the power position that goes with it that makes it possible for celebrities and others to adopt markers of 'black culture', something which is far less easily done in reverse by ethnic minori-ties (Karlsen 2004; Lury 2000). As cautioned by Smaje, 'no amount of strategic manipulation alters the direction of the racist's fist' (1996: 142).

The challenge then is how to avoid *both* the essentialism of ethnic categorization *and* undue relativism. Karlsen argues that ethnicity is 'in no way predetermined, objective or absolute'; since it 'is based on belief, it must be subjective' (2004: 110). But, as she continues, this does not mean that it is individualized. So, even though we may choose how we define our ethnic group, our sense of membership comes from being able to distinguish the group to which we feel a belonging from others, and from how those in other groups view our group in turn. Karlsen quite appropriately remarks that 'the need to be sensitive to the contextual nature of identity alone makes it hard, if not impossible, to operationalize underlying concepts in the relatively crude measurement systems required by a quantitative study' (2004: 114). While carefully crafted qualitative studies of illness experience might be expected to get round this problem, as Ahmad and Bradby (2007) point out, such literature is lacking in relation to ethnic minority groups.

Conclusions

This chapter has sought to demonstrate that social science research on 'race' and health status suffers from a number of problems. Somewhat ironically, research has uncovered the racist ideologies of medicine, both past and present, but has yet to develop fully adequate conceptual tools for the study of 'race' and health inequalities. The categorizations that are employed in survey research are questionable at best, and in qualitative research there has been a tendency to reduce ethnic minority cultural categories to static and unchanging entities that 'determine' health beliefs and behaviours. However, sociologists of health and medicine are beginning to engage with the wider social science literature on 'race' which currently points to the seeming paradox of a concurrent hardening of racism alongside emerging 'ethnic diversity'. The fact that fixity seems to co-exist with fluidity, both empirically and in the conceptual frameworks of social scientists, raises two significant issues. First, racism itself is packaged in a variety of ways and is highly adaptable to changing circumstances. Second, it alerts us to the fact that individuals are never wholly slaves to ascribed 'ethnic identities'. Together, these points are highly relevant to the exploration of health inequalities of various kinds since they suggest that we should seek out the theoretical tools that will enable us both to recognize the impact of racisms of various kinds upon health, and also to explore the ways in which the cultural and material resources of individuals from both minority and majority 'ethnic groups' facilitate and impede good health.

7

Health systems and healthcare in transition

In the discussion of 'health and medicine in a changing world' in chapter 2, it was argued that it is useful to situate the experience of health and illness within the context of economic and cultural globalization. This applies equally to the examination of health systems, the focus of the present chapter. We begin by looking at the rollback of state or public provision of healthcare in favour of the free market principles associated with global neoliberalism that is taking place in many countries worldwide. For many observers, this represents a shift away from the collectivist values of civil society towards an ethos of individualism and consumerism (Gorsky 2008; Tritter et al. 2010). This is explored in more depth in the second part of the chapter through a consideration of recent changes in the UK and US health systems. Around the world, many governments and other stakeholders are promoting the values of citizen engagement and individual patient choice. This is intended to stimulate plural markets of competing healthcare providers, which is assumed to bring about more efficient and effective care. Consequently, in the third part of the chapter, we analyse the complex meanings accorded in health policy agendas to 'patient choice', by asking how far individuals and social groups are actually empowered.

Conceptualizing health systems

Following Hunter (2008), health systems can be defined as the wide constellation of institutions and actors, within the public and private sectors, engaged in the maintenance, restoration and improvement of health. The World Health Organisation (WHO 2011c) emphasizes that, to be effective, the configuration of health systems needs to be collaborative, multi-level and co-produced by a wide range of actors, including the state (e.g. ministries, parliaments), society (e.g. citizens, businesses, community groups) and supranational organizations (e.g. the United Nations and the European Union). The sheer complexity of health governance has led the WHO and others to dub it a 'wicked problem'. As the originators of this term explain, a 'wicked' problem is not ethically deplorable – rather, it is one which defies easy solution because it is embedded in a complex open system (Rittel and Webber 1973: 160). It has no 'quick fixes' or simple solutions (WHO 2011c). Many commentators maintain that to develop an accurate understanding of how health systems work we need to abandon traditional linear ways of thinking wherein 'big problems can be broken down into smaller ones, analysed, and solved by rational deduction' (Plsek and Greenhalgh 2001: 625). Rather, public health issues, such as health inequalities and obesity, require system-level approaches and solutions (Hunter 2009; WHO 2011c). Hence it is argued that we need to adopt system-level thinking which conceptualizes public policy domains as ever-evolving and uncertain: as complex adaptive systems which, to be successful, require intersectoral and partnership working (see, e.g., Commonwealth of Australia 2007). From this perspective, healthcare systems are envisaged as fluid and as properties of other complex adaptive systems (see Kernick 2004; Sweeny and Griffiths 2002). For example, as discussed in chapter 1, health is bound up with foreign policy-making and shaped by decisions made in other policy areas such as food security, the environment and poverty alleviation strategies. The conceptualization of healthcare as an open complex system accords with Castells' (2010) portrayal of the 'network society' and Urry's (2000, 2007) depiction of 'scapes' or the network of technologies and organizations that make up the interconnected nodes along which 'flows' of people, money and ideas traverse national borders (see chapter 2). In sum, similar to how 'globalization' has challenged sociologists' erstwhile focus on society as a unit of analysis, the considerable evidence that health systems worldwide are influenced by a set of global economic and cultural changes signals that we should think beyond the nation state.

While we can identify a set of *shared influences* upon health systems, there is no one simple line of convergence towards common arrangements for financing and delivery. As we will see later in the chapter, the US, UK and many other health systems are grappling with mutual problems of an ageing population, increased need and demand for care and the rising costs of providing it. Equally, their way of dealing with these problems is through a balance of market competition and managed care. But the notion of an eventual common arrangement is doubtful because it involves submerging or trivializing the differences between cultures that have shaped different economic and political regimes, in many cases for centuries (Gray 2002). Hence a gamut of convergences and divergences are apparent internationally (Stevens 2010: 434). Health systems take their form from how a society defines and deals with issues of health and illness (Mechanic 2004a; Stevens 2010). For example, in some countries, such as the UK, health has been traditionally viewed as a collective good, while in others, such as the US, with its underlying cultural preference for independence, autonomy, choice and activism, it is more commonly thought of as a commodity. These cultural factors influence how a population responds to proposed changes to their health system.

Globalization, neoliberalism and health systems

Neoliberalism is widely recognized to be the world's dominant politico-economic policy framework (Connell 2010). It can be defined as a project of economic and social change involving the transfer of economic power and control from governments to private markets and the injection of market competition into areas such as education, housing and healthcare which, in many Western countries, were once part of post-World War II welfare states (Centeno and Cohen 2012). While we cannot put a precise date on it, neoliberalism is usually interpreted as a response to the period of structural crisis in the 1970s when, from mid-decade, the US and UK and other Western societies witnessed lower rates of financial accumulation and growth, rises in unemployment, double-digit inflation rates and growing macro-economic instability (Duménil and Lévy 2011). Often associated with the economic policies of the 1980s conservative governments of US President Reagan and UK Prime Minister Thatcher, neoliberal economic policies have encouraged financial deregulation and the opening-up of free trade and opportunities for large investments by wealthy countries in regions of the world where social conditions afford high returns. Since neoliberal policies are global in reach and globalization is furthered by the tenets of neoliberalism, neologisms such as 'neoliberal globalization' or 'global neoliberalism' are commonly used to depict such processes.

Macro-economic policies, structural adjustment and healthcare access

Up to the end of the 1970s, the prevailing approach to improving health worldwide was to strengthen public health systems, especially access to primary healthcare. This was the stance of the highly influential WHO Alma-Ata Declaration of 1978, which deemed access to healthcare to be a human right. The Washington-based World Bank (WB), International Monetary Fund (IMF) and other agencies turned away from this standpoint in the 1980s as they adopted monetarist policies prioritizing the achievement of macro-economic stability via constraints on the growth of money supply (inflation) and on public spending over other social development goals (CSDH 2008; Rowden 2009). Supranational agencies such as the IMF, World Trade Organization (WTO) and the WB have been key players in the spread of global neoliberalism in the health field. Often their influence is indirect, comprising the development of trade and investment agreements negotiated at bilateral, plurilateral and multilateral levels and the associated promotion of market-oriented structures and regulatory reforms (Tritter et al. 2010). The market-like approaches that have come to the fore include the introduction of user-fees alongside the expansion of private sector provision and public–private partnerships. Governments are no longer seen as providers of care, but as stewards. This is reflected in recent WHO thinking which relates that 'the state must play new roles and become much more involved in problem-solving as a broker, catalyst, animator, educator and partner in much more participatory, "flat" processes' (WHO 2011c: 70).

Since the 1980s, billions of dollars of global financial aid has flowed from rich countries such as the US, the UK, the Netherlands, Sweden and Ireland to low-income countries to tackle the HIV/AIDS epidemic (Rowden 2009). In 2012 alone, money from the Global Fund to AIDS, Tuberculosis and Malaria (launched in 2002 at the UN General Assembly Special Session in New York) amounted to $3,619,166,176 (Global Fund 2012). While many programmes like the Global Fund have strengthened donor aspects of health systems, higher levels of per person government spending and much larger and stronger health systems and workforce are also needed within the most affected countries. For example, Sub-Saharan Africa, which has 11 per cent of the world's population, is home to 64 per cent of HIV/AIDS and has only 3 per cent of the world's health workers, many of whom are sick with the disease themselves (Rowden 2009). Rowden argues that is it hard to build the capacity to treat people when health systems are weakened by the neoliberal policies of institutions like the WB which promote individual user-fees, private-sector provision and the deregulation and decentralization of services.

As a major lender for development projects, the WB has been a considerable force in healthcare in developing countries. It was established from a gathering of Allied nations to discuss post-World War II reconstruction in Bretton Woods, New Hampshire, in 1944 (the Bretton Woods Accord), and draws on money from private financial markets and donations from the wealthy countries of the world. Much of the money used to provide loans to low-income countries has been directed towards health. Arguably the most controversial of WB policies, which began in the 1980s, has been the pressure upon low-income countries to adopt structural adjustment programmes (or SAPs). This follows the Washington Consensus, a term used after 1989 to describe a set of economic policies of the IMF, WB and US Treasury for developing countries, which includes opening up to external trade and investment, and public-sector contraction and privatization (Prah Ruger 2005). In a nutshell, as a condition of the receipt of foreign aid and loans, structural adjustments involve lowering trade barriers, selling-off state-owned assets, and cutting public-sector budgets and public-sector workforces (Rowden 2009).

The WB's standpoint is that structural adjustment stabilizes economies, promotes investment and generates long-term economic growth. Others argue to the contrary, claiming that it leads directly to chronic underfunding of local public-sector services, collapsing domestic industries in the face of cheaper imports, rural–urban migration, reduced health budgets (and less money for health workers) and the reduction of access to services for local communities (Pfeiffer and Chapman 2010; Rowden 2009).

Oxfam (2009: 2) singles out user-fees as 'the most inequitable way of paying for health care' since they reduce service use and prevent poor people accessing care. For example, when user-fees were introduced in Rwanda in 1996, take-up of health services halved. In Kenya, the introduction of even a modest US$0.75 charge for an insecticide-treated bed (a net to combat malaria) reduced demand by 75 per cent (Oxfam 2009). The user-fee model is premised on the assumption of individuals as rational economic actors who maximize their health by seeking healthcare when they experience symptoms. This neglects the very large research literature from within the health and social sciences which shows very clearly that it is not this straightforward since cultural values and socio-economic constraints play a major role in how people interpret symptoms and are enabled to act upon them (see wider discussion in chapter 9).

For example, research in the Ganjool region of the Senegal River Delta in Sub-Saharan Africa by Foley (2008) reveals the structural violence wrought on the community following the state-sponsored imposition of user-fees for healthcare and the commercialization of agriculture. The creation of a dam upstream led to the salinization of soil and the undermining of livelihoods in the local community. Young men were forced to move out and work as migrant fishermen away from home for eleven months of the year. This had the consequence of shifting the household economic power-base away from its traditional seat amongst older men to the younger migrant workers. The effect was that older men often sought to re-exert their power by failing to acknowledge serious illness in young men in the family and by withholding healthcare from them, sometimes with tragic consequences. Foley (2008) points out that, since they are based solely on economic logic and construe people simply as rational economic actors, neo-liberal policies, such as those followed in Senegal, fail to appreciate the social complexities of vulnerability to disease and help-seeking behaviour.

International trade agreements
The impact of neoliberal economic policies is also felt in the wealthy countries of the global North. WB, IMF and WTO policies are enacted by international law through the multilateral General Agreement on Tariffs and Trade Legislation (the free trade agreement, or GATT, of 1994) to which all 157 current member countries conform. Trade agreements within Europe and beyond have guaranteed four market freedoms: the movement of goods, services, people and capital (Tritter et al. 2010).

GATT is a potential challenge to the sovereignty of national governments over policy-making in relation to public health and the provision of health services. For example, under the regional North American Free Trade Agreement (NAFTA) of 1994 between Canada, Mexico and the US, services established for public purposes are exempt from free trade legislation. However, the controversial Chapter 11 of NAFTA includes an investor's rights instrument under which foreign investors can sue national governments if they encounter trade barriers adversely affecting their operations (Waitzkin 2011). For example, Canadian healthcare is publicly funded for the most part, but most services are provided by the private sector. The expansion of private-sector involvement raises a question over whether services are any longer established for public purposes, which potentially opens the door to foreign companies.

The cultural and political dimensions of neoliberalism
Global neoliberalism is more than economic – there is also 'deep transformation of culture at work' (Connell 2010: 27). Long ago, Nye Bevan, architect of the British NHS, exposed the problems which arise from commercialism in healthcare. In *In Place of Fear*, published in the early 1950s, he characterizes the free NHS as opposed to the 'hedonism of capitalist society' (Bevan 1952: 81). He regarded the NHS as 'a triumphant example of the superiority of collective action and public initiative applied to a segment of society where commercial principles are seen at their worst' (1952: 85). Tellingly, Bevan opined that abuse would occur if private commercialism was allowed to impinge on the Health Service.

Centeno and Cohen argue that the normalization of markets as inescapable natural laws of social life has now penetrated popular culture and elevated the 'sanctity of individual choice' to 'the highest priority' (2012: 331). Arguably, the acme of this is the US health system which grew out of this dominant philosophy and continues to be profoundly influenced by it (Blank 2012). But it also finds expression globally and at every level: from state policies on how healthcare should be funded; in the importation of private-sector management practices which cast governments as regulators and purchasers rather than providers of healthcare and the public and patients as consumers, alluded to earlier in the chapter; and in health policies which stress individual responsibility. With these points in mind, we turn now to look at the commercialization of healthcare, taking recent changes in the UK and US health systems as case studies.

Healthcare and commercialization

Policy analysts categorize health systems into different models. In simplified form, we can refer to three types:

- The *NHS or Beveridge model* (after William Beveridge, engineer of the British post-World War II welfare system), which pertains to the UK, Italy and the Nordic countries. Here most aspects of care are provided free of charge at the point of service, funded through taxation. Canada's Medicare system also falls broadly into this model.
- The *social insurance or Bismarck model* (after Chancellor Otto von Bismarck, architect of the late-nineteenth-century German welfare system). Patients and their employers pay an insurance premium into a Sick Fund which contracts with various healthcare providers. As well as in Germany, this pertains to a wide range of other countries such as Austria, France, Hungary, Japan and Taiwan.
- The *private reimbursement model* is epitomized by the USA. Unless paying directly out-of-their-pockets, patients need to obtain private insurance, paid for by their employers and/or by themselves, to cover their care. Medicare (healthcare for individuals over the age of 65) and Medicaid (means-tested healthcare for individuals and families with low incomes), which were established in the 1960s, provide a minimal safety net for some individuals. The federal Emergency Medical Treatment Act of 1986 requires hospitals to provide Emergency Department care, regardless of ability to pay, for those with serious emergencies.

Rising costs and drivers for change

Despite the different mechanisms for providing care, within all of the above types governments are seeking to curb costs by finding a balance between competition and managed care, while at the same time endeavouring to improve access and quality (Stevens 2010). As Hunter relates, health systems inevitably face a set of competing goals: equality of access, quality, and cost containment (also termed 'cost-efficiency'). These form a 'three-legged stool' that is very hard to balance (Hunter 2008). The reasons are largely self-explanatory: improving access and enhancing levels of care have the capacity to drive up costs and, conversely, cost-savings have the potential to reduce access and to compromise quality of care.

Cost reduction runs through the deep veins of contemporary health reform. It is salutary to reflect that the founders of the post-World War II British NHS fully expected that expenditure would decline once the existing backlog of unmet need was catered for through the new free Service. In reality, expenditure has risen year-on-year since the first year of operation. At 2010/11 prices, net expenditure for the UK in 1948/9 was £6,843 million. By 1975, it had reached £31,853 million and, by 2010/11, £122,220 million (Office of Health Economics 2011, 2012). Rising costs of healthcare in the UK and beyond are attributed, on the *demand side*, to a combination of ageing populations, greater numbers of people living with chronic illnesses (including in younger age), increasing public demand associated with rising expectations, and attempts by governments to widen access; and, on the *supply side*, to medical progress and associated advances in technologies, including drugs (Appleby 2012; Ham et al. 2012). The data in table 7.1 for selected OECD (Organisation for Economic Co-operation and Development) member countries show that costs as a percentage of GDP rose considerably between the 1960s and 1970s and 2009/10, with a remarkable close to 250 per cent increase for the USA (see also discussion of healthcare rationing in chapter 9). Data for countries beyond the OECD show similar trends. For example, between the year 2000 and 2009, the percentage of GDP spent on health rose from 6.1 to 12.1 per cent in Cuba; 2.8 to 8.4 per cent in Iraq; 5.1 to 12.1 per cent in Liberia; and from 2.8 to 3.4 per cent in Bangladesh (WHO 2012). At the time of writing, the most recent OECD data for European Union countries suggest that the global economic recession which began in 2008 may be acting as a brake on spending as cash-strapped governments have curbed

Table 7.1 Rising healthcare expenditures as % of GDP, selected countries

	1960	1970	1980	1990	Most recent	Annual growth 2000–2009 (or most recent year)
Australia	3.7	–	6.1	6.7	9.1 (2009)	4.9
Germany	–	6.0	8.4	8.3	11.6 (2010)	1.7
Japan	3.0	4.4	6.4	6.8	9.5 (2009)	2.6
Sweden	–	7.1	8.6	8.2	9.6 (2010)	3.2
UK	3.9	4.5	5.6	5.9	9.6 (2010)	5.5
US	5.1	7.1	9.0	12.4	17.6 (2010)	5.4
OECD average						4.5

Source: OECD, *Health Data 2012 – Frequently requested data*

outlays to cut budget deficits. Thus while, with an increase of 46 per cent, health spending per person grew two to three times faster than incomes in many countries between 2000 and 2009, between 2009 and 2010 it fell by 0.6 per cent. Although this decrease is small, it marks the first time health spending has fallen in Europe since 1975 (OECD 2012). Nonetheless, we should interpret this with caution – first, because it is for EU countries only, and, second, it is too soon to tell whether this is the start of a trend or a temporary blip.

Many governments are seeking to achieve efficiency savings without cutting their health budgets. Thus, in its most recent comprehensive *Spending Review* covering 2010 to 2014/15, the British government committed to real-term spending increases of 0.4 per cent each year, but mandated that the NHS will need to make efficiency savings of £20 billion to deal with rising demand and the costs of new technologies (HM Treasury 2010). Concerns like this are far from new. Indeed, they can be tracked back to the global economic crisis of the 1970s referred to earlier in the chapter and the so-called 'fiscal crisis of the state', resulting from the structural gap between state expenditure and revenue (O'Connor 1973), which precipitated the rise of the neoliberal economic policies already discussed.

The revolt of the payers: managed care and beyond

Be it governments, social insurance funds or private insurance companies, those who pay for healthcare are trying to rein in costs by what is known as managed care. This is a broad rubric originating in the US to refer to organizations which use a range of structures and utilization strategies to reduce unneeded services and lessen costs (Mechanic 2004a). By the late 1960s, the US was witnessing a 'revolt of the payers' (Relman 2010). Up to then, payers, principally insurance companies and employers covering premiums, had pretty much accepted bills from doctors and hospitals. Prepaid managed care insurance plans sought to exercise an element of control over what care was provided and by whom. HMOs (Health Maintenance Organizations), which took off in the 1970s, were the first widespread form of managed care. They were distinctive in providing payers with a pre-paid package of services – in other words, care was not open-ended – and in requiring patients to select their provider from a panel of primary care doctors under contract to the organization and paid on a per-capita basis. HMOs 'managed' by involving case managers (usually representing insurance companies) to approve patient referrals to specialists and approve procedures and hospital admissions.

However, it was not long before patients began a revolt of their own, not on the basis of costs, but due to care restrictions. Anxieties about rationing also came to the fore. In actuality, since they effectively ration by lack of insurance, it is private reimbursement and fee-for-service payments that ration care most. However, the patient revolt arose because managed care made choice limitation *transparent* – 'in popular parlance, it was "in your face" rationing' for the middle classes (Mechanic 2004a: 78). An undercurrent of the backlash was perceived damage to cherished values of patient choice and physician autonomy (Mechanic 2001, 2004a).

The British NHS can be considered as a form of managed care; the state is the payer and, historically, general practitioners (GPs, primary care doctors) have acted as gatekeepers to services, such as referral to hospitals and other providers for out-patient, diagnostic and in-patient services, as well as to community-based services and access to drugs. Clinical autonomy was built into the NHS from its inception in 1948 when, in a successful bid to buy off medical opposition, GPs were permitted to remain as independent contractors (rather than becoming salaried employees) and consultants given generous salaries and time for private practice. Whatever other merits and demerits clinical autonomy may have (see discussion in chapter 8), it been the bane of numerous governments because it put treatment decisions almost totally in the hands of clinicians who had no incentives to restrict their spending.

Attempts to reverse NHS spending began in earnest with the supply-side health system reforms to the NHS of the 1980s and early 1990s (Tritter et al. 2010). A key development was the Conservative government's *NHS Management Enquiry* (known as the *Griffiths Report*) (DHSS 1983) which aimed to inculcate a 'business culture' by putting a new cadre of general managers, rather than doctors, in control. However, research showed that this did little to tame medical power and spending – indeed, Harrison and colleagues (1992) found that most managers did not even seem to *expect* doctors to change. Although highly controversial at the time, the Griffiths reforms were mild by comparison with what was to come. By the mid- to late-1980s, there was a distinct sense that the NHS was in acute crisis as the media drew more and more attention to cancelled operations and bed closures. In late 1987, the Presidents of the Royal Medical Colleges publicly said that the NHS had reached breaking point. Early in 1988, Prime Minister Thatcher announced that a ministerial group had been set up to review the operation of the NHS. This resulted in the Government White Paper *Working for Patients* (Department of Health 1989), and the NHS and Community Care Act of 1990. Healthcare would remain free at the point of access, but the crucial – and, looking back, momentous – change was the introduction of an 'internal market' into healthcare, whereby Health Authorities (which previously had been providers of care in their own hospitals) and some general practitioners became purchasers (initially known as 'fundholders') of elective (planned) care on behalf of their patients. Purchasers, who would hold the purse-strings, were expected to become more cost-conscious by holding providers to account for spending and quality. Of course, this was not a market in any true sense – indeed, it was often referred to as a 'quasi-market' or 'mimic-market' – not least because, realistically, purchasers could contract only with local hospitals. Also as part of the 1990 Act, hospitals were encouraged to opt out of local authority control and to become self-governing NHS trusts.

The idea of an 'internal market' grew from the theories of US economist Alain Enthoven, the architect of US managed care in the 1980s, referred to above. The resemblance to the UK reforms is clear from his later enunciations of managed care or 'managed competition', which, in his own words, 'divides providers in each community into competing economic units' and uses 'market forces to motivate them to develop efficient delivery systems' (Enthoven 1993: 30). However, recent retrospective reviews of the evidence have found it difficult to identify wholesale efficiency savings and quality improvement from the internal market in the early to late 1990s. For example, the Civitas organization concludes that the 'beneficial outcomes that classical economic theory predicts of markets, including provider responsiveness to patients and purchasers; large-scale cost reduction; and innovation in service provision' were not realized (Civitas 2010: 10).

Thus, the managed care reforms of the 1980s and early 1990s seemed to do little either to reduce run-away costs or to improve access and quality of care. For some commentators, the reason is self-evident: payers may have an incentive to reduce the amount of care provided (unnecessary or otherwise), but when commercial profit sits at the heart of a health system there will always be a motive to increase expenditure, and equity and quality will always take a backseat (Pollock 2004; Relman 2010; Tritter et al. 2010; Tudor Hart 2010). Nothing has happened in the ensuing years to diminish the commercialization of the US and UK health systems – indeed, it has continued apace. In the next section of the chapter, we explore this through a condensed analysis of policy reforms and attempted policy reforms in each country from the mid-1990s through to the present.

Enhancing markets: the British NHS

Before looking at recent changes in the British NHS, it is important to be aware that healthcare within the constituent countries of Great Britain began to diverge in the late 1990s. Referendums in 1997 established a devolved Scottish Parliament and the National Assembly for Wales (Cynulliad Cenedlaethol Cymru). While political power over matters such as taxation, national defence and foreign policy still rests with Westminster, authority over healthcare (and other matters such as education) is now devolved to Scotland and Wales. The NHS remains a unitary system in the sense that it is funded from general taxation, but there are now significant differences in how it is organized. England has been the vanguard in adopting market-style competition. At the time of writing, the Scottish and Welsh systems are based more on partnership working between stakeholders, rather than a 'purchaser–provider split' (Hunter 2008). By way of illustration, the Bevan Commission (2011) highlights that Wales is following a path in healthcare that differs from many countries of Europe; instead of competition, it values what are defined as the moral principles underlying collective, planned provision. Thus the discussion of commercialization that follows will focus on England.

The political will to drive through habitually unpopular health reforms in England results from an underlying belief within all of the main political parties that the public does not really mind who provides their care, as long as it is free (Hunter 2008; Tudor Hart 2010). The purchaser–provider split instituted by the NHS and Community Care Act of 1990 was a crucial foundation for the further commercialization of the NHS which began in the later part of that decade (Tritter et al. 2010). Policy analysts are agreed that the New Labour government of Prime Minister Tony Blair, which came to power in 1997, picked up from where the Conservative government of John Major (Margaret Thatcher's successor in late 1990) left off. New Labour proposed a new politics of the 'third way' to capture a novel social contract different from 'old Labour's' centralized planning and the free-market enthusiasms of the outgoing Conservative government (Blair 1998). Advisor to the Blair government sociologist Anthony Giddens maintained that public institutions, like the NHS, could no longer be harnessed to the state which, in a knowledge economy, is inadequate in the provision of public goods and services. He argued that the political left had 'to get comfortable with markets, with the role of business in the creation of wealth, and the fact that private capital is essential for social investment' (Giddens 2000: 34). Echoing neoliberal ideas, Giddens endorsed the theorem 'no rights without responsibilities', and proposed that the role of government should be to foster the social capability of individuals to contribute to their own well-being, not to provide it for them.

The first major policy statement from New Labour, the government White Paper *The New NHS* (Department of Health 1997) endorsed a 'third way' between command and control and 'the divisive internal market of the 1990s' (Department of Health 1997: 10), characterized as 'partnership working'. This was accompanied by a 'modernization agenda' intended to shift from the central control of public services towards local accountability, steered by targets and measured outcomes (Klein 2010). As Hunter explains, this instituted a 'terror-by-target culture' (2008: 38), the legacy of which is still keenly felt today. The internal market ostensibly was removed as fundholding was replaced by primary care groups and then (after 2001) large Primary Care Trusts (PCTs), which were given responsibility for managing budgets for health and social care for their patients in the community and making contracts with hospitals and other providers. Effectively this made all GPs into 'fundholders' (Gorsky 2008; Pollock 2004).

Thus, at the start of the twenty-first century, the situation could be characterized as: 'the internal market is dead, long live the internal market' (Hunter 2008: 68). This was evident in the next major policy documents, *The NHS Plan* (Department of Health 2000a) and the Health and Social Care Act of 2001, which coupled a commitment to increase NHS funding and capital investment over the following four years with a new concordat between the NHS and private providers and the promotion of public–private partnerships. To quote from the document, 'for decades there has been a stand-off between the NHS and the private sector providers of healthcare. This has to end' (Department of Health 2000a: 96). This would work two ways: the private sector could provide critical and elective surgery and immediate care for NHS patients, and the NHS would review the potential for the private sector to provide services, such as pathology and diagnostic imaging. This was followed in 2002 by Foundation Trusts (FTs), a new structure for hospitals which remain formally part of the NHS but are independent legal entities (public benefit corporations) freed from government control, but subject to monitoring. They can raise capital from both public and private contractors and invest profits back into services. At the time of writing, all English hospitals were expected to become FTs by 2014.

In their public embrace of a plurality and diversity of providers, Klein (2010) considers these reforms to be a tectonic shift in the NHS. For others, too, they marked a distinctive movement along a path embarked upon back in the 1980s, towards privatization. High-volume, low-risk treatments, such as cataract surgery, knee replacements, hernia removals and some diagnostic tests, were 'unbundled' from the NHS, and Independent Sector Treatment Centres (ISTCs) – privately owned walk-in (i.e. without an appointment) and treatment centres (some within NHS hospitals) – were set up in 2002/3 under the NHS logo to reduce waiting lists, increase service capacity and extend patient choice. This created a number of openings for private providers, including companies limited by shares, such as Virgin Care and Care UK (Allen et al. 2011). Research by Waring and Bishop (2012) on ISTCs providing day surgery found that, while most staff welcomed a better work environment and better equipment, their service managers were mostly concerned with making profits for their parent companies – clinical staff were told that they should work like a car factory or supermarket.

Another significant development in the mid-2000s was the signing by GPs of a new General Medical Services contract, under which they could choose to provide just essential care or offer a wider range of services, such as contraception, vaccination, minor surgery, or the management of more complex medical conditions. For the first time, they were able to opt out of providing out-of-hours care (with a 6 per cent loss of income). A full 90 per cent of GPs did just that. In the opinion of Leys and Player (2011), the government took this as an opportunity for the private sector, especially since the Alternative Provider of Medical Services (or APMS) contract of around that time allowed PCTs to contract with social enterprises and private providers as well as general practices. By the summer of 2010, 227 GP surgeries were being run by private companies such as Virgin Assura (now Virgin Care) (Leys and Player 2011). By the mid-2000s, reports began to emerge of private companies winning contracts to run GP services when they came up for tender. One of the most controversial was in Derbyshire where United Health Europe was chosen as the preferred provider over a local GP's bid (Tudor Hart 2010). As of 2009 it was reported that over 20 commercial companies were running well over 200 GP surgeries (Davidson and Evans, cited in Allen et al. 2011: 83). Towards the end of the decade, Hunter questioned whether the public was 'sleep-walking into an NHS that will be different from that with which they are familiar. The brand and the logo may stay the same but increasingly they are a façade behind which a very different, hollowed out, NHS is taking shape' (Hunter 2008: 117–18). These were prophetic words. In the summer of 2010, just three months after assuming office, and making no mention of NHS reform during the election campaign – even shunning 'big bang' reorganization and speaking of reform fatigue (Hunter 2011) – the new Coalition (Conservative – Liberal Democrat) government launched what many identified as the most contentious reforms (Department of Health 2010b) in the history of the NHS (Pollock and Price 2011).

Critics of the Health and Social Care Act which eventually received royal assent in March of 2012 (and took effect on 1 April 2013) were especially concerned by the repeal of existing legislation, in place since 1948, which required the government to provide a comprehensive service by providing a specified list of services throughout the country. They feared privatization and further fragmentation of services (Pollock et al. 2012). Debate was so heated that the Act was halted in mid-legislative process to 'pause, listen and reflect' on public concerns. Ham (2012) likens summarizing the contents of the eventual Bill to paraphrasing *War and Peace* on Twitter, but the crux is the setting up of geographically based Clinical Commissioning Groups (CCGs) (212 were in place at the time of writing). CCGs are budget-holders (controlling 60 per cent of the NHS budget) which, under 'any qualified provider' provision, are expected to enable patients to choose health and social services not only from NHS providers, but also from the for-profit private sector and not-for-profit third sector (charities and social enterprises). They are overseen by the NHS Commissioning Board which takes a lead in quality improvement through the commissioning process. A new regulator, Monitor, is intended to ensure that the health sector acts in the interests of patients and to prevent anticompetitive behaviour. As Dorling and others have pointed out, CCGs are 'not simply metamorphosed PCTS'; they hold powers which once belonged to the Secretary of State for Health. Crucially, the legal duty to provide comprehensive healthcare passes from government to local commissioners and providers (Dorling 2013: 84).

Responsibility for public health, including health needs assessment and health improvement, has moved from the NHS into local government, where Health and Well-being Boards are tasked with promoting the integration of local government and NHS organizations, the private sector and other providers (Department of Health 2011a, 2012b). Allied reforms in social care also emphasize 'local markets' and the removal of boundaries between the NHS, LAs, and third-sector and private-sector provision (Department of Health 2012c). The role of the third sector, particularly local charities and voluntary groups, in health and social care is nothing new – it stems back to pre-NHS days. What *is* new, however, is the active encouragement for the third sector to compete for contracts from CCGs alongside the NHS and private sector (Ham 2009). A reading of the inclusion of the third sector is that it makes 'any qualified provider' policies more palatable to the public than if they concerned the private sector alone.

The third sector
The 'third sector' is an umbrella under which sit not only charities and voluntary groups, but also social enterprises (businesses with a social mission towards which they reinvest profits). A range of government schemes have encouraged NHS staff to set up social enterprises. Indeed, the White Paper *Equity and Excellence: Liberating the NHS* stated: 'we aim to create the largest social enterprise sector in the world' (Department of Health 2010b: 5). As Mohan puts it, social enterprise might be described as 'the iron fist of the market encased in the velvet glove of community ownership' (2009: 88). On the one hand, social enterprises and charities might hold out an alternative trajectory to the expected move of national for-profit providers into health and social care in the UK. But, on the other, change in the landscape means that many charities have lost longstanding local relationships with former commissioners (the PCTs) and are finding it hard to survive in a cash-strapped economy (Dickinson and Miller 2011). If NHS services fail to meet local needs it is unlikely that the private sector will step in to provide unprofitable services, and charities may end up struggling to pick up the pieces.

Assessments differ on the likely future of the British NHS. For some it is heading at accelerating pace towards privatization (Leys and Player 2011; Pollock 2004; Tudor Hart 2010), while others opine that the low scale of private involvement belies this (Ham 2009, 2012). But while it is clear that healthcare in England is becoming increasingly commercialized, as Moody (2011) discusses, the barrier to 'true' competition is the predominance of state funding and free delivery. As we will now go on to explore, US healthcare is very different from that in England.

Protecting markets: the US insurance-based system

Earlier in the chapter, US healthcare was identified as fitting the *private reimbursement model*. Historically, unless paying directly out of their pocket, most patients have needed to obtain private insurance, paid either by their employers or by themselves, to cover their care. Recent US history is littered with failed reform attempts, stemming back to the early part of the twentieth century. Democrat Harry Truman, President between 1945 and 1953, who was the first to support a scheme whereby the federal government would provide comprehensive, compulsory national health insurance financed mainly through general taxation (a single-payer scheme), experienced a vitriolic reaction from pro-market Republicans, insurance companies and businesses (employers). This was the period of the Cold War and marked anti-communist sentiment. The American Medical Association (AMA) averred that national insurance would make doctors slaves and referred to White House staffers as 'followers of the Moscow party line' (AMA quoted in Altman and Shactman 2011: 103). This highlights, albeit it in particularly strong terms, a leitmotif running through US healthcare reform attempts over subsequent years: the dominant philosophy of individual rights and individual responsibility (Cockerham and Cockerham 2010). As Blank (2012) expresses it, seemingly Americans want no constitutional constraint on access to care or on their ability to access high-cost and high-technology medicine with no limits. This is underpinned by a reluctance to give up individual needs for the collective good.

The John F. Kennedy Administration of the 1960s implemented Medicaid and Medicare legislation (mentioned earlier in the chapter) and Senator Ted Kennedy sought without success to implement a Bill to introduce a single-payer system. The 1970s witnessed a policy shift from expansion of services to the cost-control reform attempts referred to earlier, such as HMOs, which were introduced under the Republican Administration of Richard Nixon. In 1974 Nixon pursued a Comprehensive Health Insurance Program (CHIP) which was less far-reaching than the earlier Kennedy Bill and based on a mandate for private insurance cover. This too was defeated, not least because of the Watergate scandal, which eventually led to his resignation in the face of impeachment. The next significant reform endeavour did not come until the ill-fated attempts of the Bill Clinton Administration of the 1990s. It is instructive to note that, by this time, the corporate world, which had been opposed to health system reform in the 1960s, was becoming increasingly concerned by the rising costs of employee insurance cover. Chrysler, for example, had seen its healthcare spending rise from $432 million in 1985 to $702 million in 1988 – this added up to a healthcare expense per car of $700, double the costs incurred by manufacturers in France and Germany and triple those in Japan. Public-sector costs for Medicare and Medicaid were also soaring (Altman and Shactman 2011). Initially at least, this favourably disposed businesses towards the 1993 Clinton Health Policy Task Force plans. Task Force Chair Hillary Clinton later wrote of rising healthcare costs 'sapping the nation's economy, undermining American competitiveness, eroding workers' wages . . . and eroding the national budget' (Clinton 2003: 144). The Clinton plan rejected a single-payer model in favour of a quasi-private system, that is, 'managed competition' (broadly based on the Enthoven model referred to previously). As Clinton put it, the object was to rely on 'private forces to drive down costs through competition' via capi-tated or pre-paid health plans (2003: 150). Altman and Shactman (2011) opine that the plan stumbled on the fact that it would change the way that people received healthcare – not only might they need to change their doctors, but also their insurance companies. Small insurance com-panies feared for their existence. The Health Insurance Association of America opposed the reforms with a hugely successful $3.5 million TV campaign featuring the characters Harry and Louise, catapulted, as the caption read, to *Sometime in the Future*. Sitting in their kitchen, Harry and Louise discuss how people need to pick their insurer from a few healthcare plans, which is 'no choice at all'. Recalling the high value on individual rights referred to previously, it is hard not to concur with Altman and Shactman that the Clinton plan failed because it was seen as 'too much change and too much government' (2011: 83).

It is apparent therefore that, over the decades, US health reform has been blocked by fears of 'big government', 'socialised medicine' (Marmor and Oberlander 2011) and the opposition of business inter-ests, such as the insurance industry. President Barack Obama took office in 2009 at the start of the world financial crisis, a recession and high unemployment, although the challenges from interest groups had not gone away. However, he was eventually able to pass into law the Patient Protection and Affordable Care Act of 2010 (hereafter, 'the Act'). Upon its passing, twenty-one states almost immediately mounted legal cases on the grounds of unconstitutional violation of the rights of states and individuals *not* to purchase insurance (Light 2010). However, in July 2012, the Supreme Court ruled the Act constitutional.

The Act is complex and contains very many more provisions than can be detailed here (for a summary see Kaiser Foundation 2010). The basic elements are: from 2014 almost everyone has been required to have private health insurance or pay a fine; those in receipt of Medicaid will be enrolled in largely federally subsidized state programmes provided by private insurers; and employers with more than 200 employees are required to enrol them in insurance plans that they offer, though employees can opt out of these to buy their own coverage. Under the 'individual mandate', the rest of the population – and here there are notable exceptions, such as undocumented migrants – will be required to buy insurance through new state Health Exchanges, monitored by state governments, which are modelled after those already in place in Massachusetts (since 2006). To assist those who find it hard to pay for insurance, refundable tax credits are available for individuals who buy an insurance plan from an Exchange and have a household income of between 133 per cent and 400 per cent of the federal poverty line. Penalties will be levied against those who do not purchase insurance. While, as we have seen, past attempts at reform faltered due to the vested interests of the insurance industry, the individual mandate is a potential boon to the insurance industry as it is likely to bring a pool of young, healthy people with government subsidies to offset the costs of older sicker people (Light 2010; Quandango 2010).

It is estimated that the Act will provide coverage for 32 million people who otherwise would not have insurance. It is important, however, to reflect on what it does *not* change. 'Structurally it makes no inroads into the private, competitive nature of the industry' of healthcare (Moody 2011). In other words, it does relatively little to alter the way that healthcare is delivered in the US, and healthcare remains a highly profitable business (see also discussion in chapter 1).

Patient choice and citizen engagement

Thus far, it has been emphasized that the promotion of markets has been at the heart of neoliberal health policy reforms throughout most of the world since the latter part of the twentieth century. In the West, this has been accompanied by a new form of governance at the heart of which are 'discriminating consumers' and 'accountable professionals' (Newman and Kuhlmann 2009). Hence, in this final section, we will look at the growing emphasis on patient choice, which, as the principal driver of a plural market of competing providers, has become the lifeblood of cost-reduction strategies, commercialization and drives for greater efficiency and improved quality across much of the West.

The appeal of enhancing 'patient choice', 'patient and public involvement' and other similarly designated strategies is that they are malleable in how patient identities are construed (Milewa 2009) and can be called into the service of many different ends that are not necessarily compatible (Newman and Kuhlmann 2009). For example, ideologies of democratic public engagement can grate against economically motivated 'consumerist' approaches (Gibson et al. 2012). These points form a backdrop against which to consider how 'patient involvement' has been formulated in policy agendas over the last twenty or so years. With specific reference to the UK, Dent refers to a shift over the period from an emphasis on individual 'consumers' of services in the quasi-market of the 1990s, to 'patient choice' in the 2000s, to the present concern with 'citizen voice' (Dent 2006a, 2006b; Dent et al. 2011). When user-involvement is premised on individual 'patient choice', the assumption is that the healthcare market empowers them through the ultimate option of 'exit'. In other words, there is an assumption that the user will endorse patient-friendly and efficient services. Their reward will be high throughput (cost effectiveness) while, conversely, 'poorly performing' hospitals will be held to account and potentially lose business (Dent et al. 2011).

The *Patient's Charter* of the early 1990s was the first major attempt to nurture health service consumers and to forefront individual rights in the UK (Department of Health 1991). It was abolished in 2000, but the central thread of the activist individual exercising their personal choices, assessing the receipt of services and holding providers to account when things go wrong or are not as good as they feel they should be remains. For example, the late 2000s saw the launch of an *NHS Constitution*. The most recent version of 2013 refers to a series of rights, pledges and responsibilities (Department of Health 2013a). But this has been accompanied by a policy emphasis on 'people exercising democratic choice as part of a larger set of democratic relations' (Dent 2006b: 457). For example, Patient and Public Involvement (PPI) forums which were set up in 2003, and their successor from 2008, LINKs (Local Involvement Networks), endeavoured to seek the experience of local people, including healthcare providers, and to monitor and help shape services via a focus on local spaces. The latest arrangement, with broadly the same agenda, is HealthWatch, which came into being in 2013. The self-evident challenge of ventures like these is that of representativeness, since it is often, though not exclusively, people with social capital such as education (the middle classes) and time (those retired from employment) who take on such roles.

These shifts, which so far have been discussed mainly in relation to the UK, are reflected in wider policy turns. Thus, the WHO refers to a set of 'new, complex relations between the state and society', wherein factors such as participation and accountability become 'engines for innovation' (WHO 2011c: viii). This is dubbed a 'whole-of-society' approach and links back to points made towards the start of the chapter – namely, that the governance of health systems needs to take a systems-wide approach. Citizens are conceptualized as 'co-producers' of health in a context of 'diffused governance'. The term 'co-producer', again, is one which can be invested with many meanings, ranging from acting as health activists (for example, in protesting against health-damaging environments or advocating for particular services), sharing the financial costs of care, taking some responsibility for keeping healthy, through to sharing decision-making within consultations, and undoubtedly still more. An illustration, from the UK but originating in California, is the Expert Patients Programme (Department of Health 2001) which began in 2002 as part of the then Labour government's endeavours to situate persons with chronic illnesses as the key decision-makers in their own care (Bury 2008). More recently, during the protracted legislative process which eventually culminated in the passing of the Health and Social Care Act of 2012, government spokespersons adopted the slogan 'no decision about me, without me', which, it was asserted, 'must be hard-wired into every part of the system – from the legislation through to each and every encounter between a patient and a healthcare professional' (Department of Health 2011b: 6). As many commentators have pointed out, while this might seem laudable in principle, on closer inspection concerns become apparent. Thus Tritter and colleagues point out that for many patients an opportunity or requirement to identify and direct their own doctors is both 'alien and alarming' (Tritter et al. 2010: 46). People make sense of their health within the complex social contexts of their lives. As we saw in the very different context of the Ganjool region of the Senegal River Delta (Foley 2008) earlier in the chapter, the notion of the all-knowing, all-calculating, rational consumer of the economic market reflects neither how people deal with their illness nor how they seek to protect their well-being (Tritter et al. 2010). Moreover, as Mol explores through the study of diabetic care, 'choice has to be doubted because, when it comes to it almost nobody (ill or healthy) is any good at it' (2008: 6).

Conclusions

In this chapter, we have explored the significant changes taking place in health systems around the world. A constellation of policy actors, including governments, businesses, civil society organizations and supranational organizations, are seeking to reform health systems to reduce costs and enhance effectiveness by extending markets and patient involvement. The variability in how people gain access to care, how it is delivered, and by whom, is partly explainable by historical exigencies and partly by the cultural and political influences that shape policy-making in different countries. These issues will be important now as we turn, in chapter 8, to consider, amongst other things, new forms of governance of health professionals.

8

Professions in transition

Anyone who has ever known doctors well enough to hear medical shop talked without reserve knows that they are full of stories about each other's blunders and errors, and that the theory of their omniscience and omnipotence no more holds good among themselves than it did with Moliere and Napoleon.

(Shaw 1980 [1911]: 15)

High-profile, catastrophic failures of care resulting from poor clinical practice and organizational environments inimical to high-quality healthcare suggest that playwright George Bernard Shaw's connection between the omniscience and omnipotence of the medical profession and blunders in practice is as pertinent today as it was over 100 years ago. Yet one thing certainly has changed, in a world of social media exposés and an increasingly health-literate public, sheltering confidently behind 'divine omniscience' is far more hard to imagine.

This chapter begins by looking at the influential concept of 'professional dominance' which was coined in the early 1970s and subsequently motivated discussions on the power of medicine as a profession. We will consider whether this power has been eroded with new forms of governance that have accompanied the commercialization of health systems discussed in chapter 7. Concurrently, we will reflect on the analytical difficulty of determining what counts as evidence of declining professional power, and upon the resilience of the medical profession. We will look at challenges arising from managerialism and the introduction of 'new public management' principles into healthcare, and from changes in the healthcare division of labour, especially the changing nature of nursing work. The final part of the chapter then turns to recent scandals in patient care resulting from internal regulatory failures within medicine. We will conclude by reflecting on whether public trust in medicine is declining and analyse deliberations by the medical profession and others in the wake of such failures on how best to craft a 'new professionalism' appropriate for the twenty-first century.

The power of medicine: three phases of critical thinking

Sociological thinking on the power of medicine has gone through three overlapping phases wherein commentators have: (i) depicted the *autonomy and dominance* of medicine; (ii) reflected on whether it is appreciably in *decline*; and (iii) highlighted its *resilience*.

Medical autonomy and dominance

Eliot Freidson's concept of 'professional dominance' so successfully captured the collective imagination of several generations of sociologists that it continues to serve as the lens through which debates on the power of medicine are reflected. Writing in 1970, he remarked that 'the professional has gained a status which protects him [*sic*] more than other experts from outside scrutiny and criticism and which grants him extraordinary autonomy in controlling both the definition of the problems he works on and the way he performs his work' (Freidson 1988 [1970]: 337).

State-sponsored monopoly over diagnosis and treatment through licensing and credentialing afforded physicians a pre-eminent place in the healthcare division of labour: 'Where we find one occupation with organised autonomy in a division of labour, it dominates the others. Immune from legitimate regulation or evaluation by other occupations, it can itself legitimately evaluate and order the work of others. By its position in the division of labour we can designate it as a *dominant profession*' (Freidson 1988: 369, emphasis original). Thus, as Freidson (1988 [1970]) and others (e.g. Starr 1982; Willis 1983) proposed, professional power derives from *autonomy* (the ability to control one's own work activities) and from *dominance* (control over others in the healthcare division of labour). Writing in the 1970s, Freidson concluded that, together, they 'give the professions a splendid isolation, indeed the opportunity to develop a protected insularity without peer among occupations lacking the same privileges' (1988 [1970]: 369).

As outlined in chapter 1, Parsons (1975: 271) regarded the physician's 'institutionalised superiority' as an essential part of the successful treatment of the patient. However, for Freidson this is the 'critical flaw' of professional autonomy; it encourages 'a self-deceiving view of the objectivity and reliability of the knowledge and of the virtues of its members' (1988 [1970]: 370). Errors of practice go undetected, alternative views of health and illness are excluded, and other health practitioners

UNIVERSITY OF WINCHESTER
LIBRARY

are denied the capacity to work independently and in ways that may not be favoured by medical doctors. In the final chapter of *Profession of Medicine* (1988 [1970]), he declared it was time for medicine's autonomy to be tempered, and proposed several means of achieving this, including changes in how physicians are trained and mechanisms for reviewing their work. Changes over subsequent decades have far surpassed those urged by Freidson over forty years ago, prompting some to refer to – and, perhaps unexpectedly, to bemoan – the considerable waning of medical autonomy and dominance.

Declining autonomy and dominance

Mainly with reference to the US, McKinlay and colleagues argue that the twin processes of loss of state sponsorship and increased dominance of healthcare by global financial interests have led to seismic changes in the practice of medicine since its zenith or 'golden age' of the 1930s through to the 1950s (McKinlay and Arches 1985; McKinlay and Marceau 2002). As discussed in chapter 7, in the US and beyond, the penetration of markets into healthcare and emulation of private-sector styles of management have intensified health professionals' accountability to other groups, such as proprietors and managers working at their behest (Hunter 2008; Tritter et al. 2010). Also governments have recast patients as consumers exercising choice and holding professionals to account.

McKinlay and colleagues portray this as the 'corporatisation' (initially termed 'proletarianisation') of medicine. They argue that, with the golden age of medicine now long past, physicians powerlessly await 'the next corporate onslaught' (McKinlay and Marceau 2002: 410). They predict, for example, that, within twenty years, primary care doctors will have disappeared in the US due to: the shedding of state responsibility for care (which historically supported self-determined billing via third-party reimbursement); declining incomes; the ascendance of non-physicians (such as nurses) in the healthcare division of labour; the decline of the 'full service doctor's visit' consequent upon the growth of walk-in clinics in high footfall venues such as shopping malls; and the decreased dependence of patients with chronic conditions, such as diabetes, on primary care doctors, owing to home self-monitoring technologies, such as blood glucose meters (McKinlay and Marceau 2008: 1487).

How should changes be deciphered?
There is widespread agreement that the erstwhile partnership between medicine and the state has been fractured by neoliberal policies which promote plural markets, transfer control over clinical decision-making from doctors to other healthcare practitioners and managers,

and advance patient consumerism – all under the assumption that increasing professional accountability will furnish better care (see, e.g., Coburn 2006; Dingwall 2008; Willis 2006). The crucial question, however, is: does this add up to corporatization? Most commentators reach the conclusion that this thesis misses the mark (see, e.g., Timmermans 2008). Even so, as Willis (2006) rightly observes, how we interpret the present and likely future of medicine rests on whether we conceptualize its glass as 'half full' or 'half empty'. For example, as we will see later in the chapter, governments have been easing the boundaries between the health professions, but this doesn't mean that they no longer exist (Willis 2006), or that medicine cannot exploit and benefit from changes by shedding less desired work to others. As we saw in chapter 7, many governments are extending patients' choice and voice as part of the expansion of healthcare markets. This can be a way of holding physicians to account, yet equally, patients may align with their physicians – in arguing for access to rationed services, for example – which may bolster professional dominance vis-à-vis the state (Dent 2006b; Klein 2010; Kuhlmann and Burau 2008). In other words, the same broad indicators – such as the promotion of a more flexible workforce and consumer voice – can be read in alternate ways. Most observers conclude that, although recent changes mean medical power is not what it once was, this doesn't mean that the profession has lost or will lose its dominance and autonomy (Coburn 2006; Dingwall 2008; Willis 2006). In fact, on the contrary, many point instead to its resilience (e.g. Allsop 2006; Freidson 1994; Timmermans 2008).

The resilience of the medical profession

Freidson remained a critical observer of changes in healthcare during the period after *Profession of Medicine* was published in 1970. He particularly drew attention to the profession's capacity to resist inroads into its autonomy and dominance through a process of *re-stratification* (Freidson 1994). Whereas different specialisms and ranks used to act as presumptive peers, the divisions between them have heightened and become far more visible and obvious. Hence, he argued that we have witnessed 'the magnification and formalisation of . . . relationships into a considerably more overt and consequential system of stratification which can no longer be protected by the face-saving norms of traditional professional etiquette' (1994: 144). Internal cohesion diminishes as the profession divides into a *rank and file* and a tripartite disciplinary, educational and administrative *elite* in an attempt to stave off external control (Freidson 1989). He maintained that, at the *corporate* level, physicians are still in control of those things which confer autonomy: control over credentialing (training and the right to practise) and the monitoring of practice standards. It is the rank and file – that is, the vast majority of doctors working with patients in the community (such as general practitioners) and in hospitals – who bear the brunt of these changes. Consequently, elites 'subject everyday practitioners to unprecedented surveillance and evaluation . . . they are empowered to impose concrete economic sanctions, in some cases as severe as suspending their license to practice' (Freidson 1989: 216).

As Dopson and colleagues explain, although surveillance by elites through 'evidence-based medicine' and the use of practice guidelines may be 'irksome and resisted to some extent', it may still be more acceptable than managerial control (2003: 323). Freidson (1994) maintained that even the rank and file of doctors have infinitely more discretion in their daily tasks than people who work in other fields. Although weakly supported by detailed empirical evidence to date, commentators habitually point out that medicine is characterized by contested knowledge and contingencies of practice. For example, a convincing argument is put forward in *How Doctors Think* by Jerome Groopman (2007), a practising oncologist and professor at Harvard Medical School. Groopman probes the highly challenging question, 'what goes on in a doctor's mind as he or she treats a patient?' (2007: 3). Addressing this, he laments the turn towards the following of preset algorithms and practice guidelines in the form of decision trees in the diagnostic process. He evaluates that their rigidity 'risks having the doctor choose care passively, solely by the numbers'. He opines that 'statistics cannot substitute for the human being before you; statistics embody averages, not individuals' (2007: 6). Thus medicine is depicted 'at its core' as an uncertain science (2007: 7). Sociologists have argued that this black box of the complexity and uncertainty inherent in the treatment of bodies is a forceful barrier to managerial control (Freidson 1994; Tousijn 2006) which – evidence-based medicine and clinical protocols notwithstanding – makes it unlikely that diagnostic and treatment decisions will be externally controlled in the foreseeable future.

The 'feminization' of medicine

Freidson and his contemporaries first drew attention to the problems of medical power during the late 1960s and early 1970s, which was much the same time that male dominance in healthcare was being linked with the oppression of women (Annandale 2009), but they gave no recognition that male dominance and medical dominance might be connected. Rather, deliberations on medical power took place in gender-neutral terms, something which largely still continues today (Riska 2008, 2010). Yet, as we will now consider, the gender composition of the profession is directly relevant to the status of medicine

In the post-Soviet states, women have outnumbered men in the medical profession for decades. For example, they have comprised

70 per cent of the profession in Russia since the 1930s, and make up 87 per cent of physicians in Lithuania today (Harden 2001; Riska and Novelskaite 2011). However, as in other countries, the medical profession is horizontally (by specialism) and vertically (by hierarchical position) stratified by gender (Riska 2010). In Russia, 'feminization' resulted from pro-natalist policies which expected women both to produce new workers and to work for the economy. Industrial-sector jobs were deemed a risk to motherhood, while work in healthcare was not. These protectionist policies were overlain with essentialist gendered expectations that medicine is suited to women's biological closeness to nature and gentle disposition (Harden 2001). This 'feminization' of medicine occurred under strong subordination of the profession to the state (as a salaried occupation) and in the absence of independent professional medical associations (Riska and Novelskaite 2008, 2011) – that is, under the very conditions deemed conducive to corporatization in the West today (Hafferty and McKinlay 1993).

No matter the time and place, if male dominance is assumed, the entry of women into the profession in ever-growing numbers is almost bound to be taken as a marker of declining prestige and power. Hence it comes as no surprise that 'feminization' has evoked panic over the status of medicine. In Britain, women have been the majority of medical school entrants since the early 1990s, and in 2010 they made up 56 per cent of medical students; 62 per cent of those in the first clinical foundation (F1) year; and 42 per cent of registered doctors (GMC 2011). Extrapolating from current trends, women will comprise the majority of the NHS medical workforce sometime between 2017 and 2022. This trend is mirrored in other Western European counties, but weaker in Australia, Canada, New Zealand and the US. In contrast, women constitute less than a quarter of physicians in less affluent countries, such as those of Africa and Asia (Elston 2009).

Public debate was sparked in Britain in 2004 when the President of the Royal College of Physicians, Carol Black, expressed the opinion that the 'feminization of medicine' would downgrade the profession and endanger its future. The line of reasoning by those advancing this argument is that maternity leave, family-related career breaks, and the desire for what has become known as work–family balance leads women into a limited number of 'accommodating' specialisms – such as general practice, rather than surgery, for example – and to less engagement in medicine's professional bodies than men. This culminates in the supposition that if medicine is female-dominated, it will fail to function effectively. There are several reasons to question this. As Elston (2009) analyses for the UK, the rate of change towards a female majority is likely to be moderated by inflows of international medical graduates who, historically, have been predominantly male. Also, for good or ill, the preference for traditionally male specialisms from men and female specialisms from women is likely to continue, and men are still likely to rise and fill the top positions in the profession. But, as Riska highlights, the culture of medicine is rarely addressed in these discussions. She argues that, instead of asking what will happen if medicine becomes feminized, we should be inquiring: 'What is there in current medical work that requires new skills and why is it that mainly women are drawn into this new context?' (2008: 13). Workforce policy changes towards more part-time and flexible working could ease women's progression into traditionally male specialisms, overturning the argument that feminization is an inevitable challenge to the standing of medicine and its capacity to deliver quality care.

In most Western countries, the elite – male and female alike – are also mostly white. In the UK, for example, NHS consultants (the most senior doctors) are predominantly white, while Black and Minority Ethnic (BME) physicians make up the largest sub-group amongst non-career grades (GMC 2011). It is important then to appreciate that increased stratification within medicine is likely to impact disproportionately on women and minority ethnic physicians.

Re-stratification beyond the West
Further insight into re-stratification processes and their likely consequences can be gleaned by looking comparatively and beyond affluent-Anglophone contexts. Although the research base is fairly limited to date, we can reflect on two contrasting illustrations. The first concerns primary care physicians in England and California, and the second the medical profession in Zimbabwe. In her US–England study, McDonald (2012) found that most English 'rank and file' GPs, whose income rests substantially on meeting 146 indicators of quality of care, responded favourably to actions by colleagues – 'chasers', or the administrative elite in Freidson's terms – aimed at ensuring their work was geared towards meeting targets, and they did not feel that this impacted negatively on their autonomy. Their Californian counterparts, in contrast, were far less positive. They felt ill informed about the relationship between performance targets and their personal payments and questioned the accuracy of data.

In her study of Zimbabwe, Mutizwa-Mangiza (1999) explains that the former colonial Rhodesian state sheltered the white settler medical profession in a number of ways, such as by refusing to recognize the qualifications of doctors trained in the US and Europe; by denying training to blacks; by rejecting a recommendation of the 1946 Saints Commission that a national health service be established; and by expanding their private market. The subsequent policies of the post-colonial independent government of Zimbabwe of 1980, such as free healthcare, legalization of traditional medicine, and the adoption of a bonding contract for nationally trained graduates, were a potential threat to physicians' economic interests and practice autonomy. But, in actuality, the state was impeded by the threat of strikes by junior doctors, by the neoliberal policies of the IMF and World Bank, and by the pressure from British- and US-owned multinational corporations which resisted any changes likely to curtail their financial interest in the country (for a wider discussion of IMF and World Bank policies, see chapter 7). Physicians' practice autonomy endured in the absence of regulatory bodies, and medical consultants retained the right to treat private patients in and outside of government hospitals, in an environment with very few procedures to ensure that they worked according to contracts. Unlike in many Western countries, physicians in administrative positions identified more with the rank and file, partly as a result of high turnover of those in high positions and partly because of the small community of physicians in the country (Mutizwa-Mangiza 1999). These two illustrations highlight that re-stratification is a complex process that plays out in different ways in different contexts.

Countervailing powers and jurisdictional claims

Rather than ruminating on whether physicians are dominant / not dominant, autonomous/dependent and so on, Light (1995, 2000) counsels us to conceptualize the medical profession as subject to *countervailing powers* (a concept which stems back to the eighteenth-century French philosopher Montesquieu). This directs our attention away from a trajectory with a propositional endpoint (such as corporatization) towards groups jockeying for position in a game of move and countermove. Analysis then concerns 'the interactions of powerful actors in a field where they are inherently interdependent yet distinct. If one party is dominant, as the . . . medical profession has long been, its dominance is contextual and eventually elicits counter-moves by other powerful actors, not to destroy it but to redress an imbalance of power' (Light 1995: 26).

This resembles Abbott's (1988) influential conceptualization of professions as an interdependent *system*. The crux of Abbott's thesis is that control over tasks, the key organizing feature of professional life, is established by competitive claims in such arenas as the legal sphere, the media and the workplace. Various settlements arise between groups, which create temporary stabilities in a process of competition for jurisdiction. Given that most jurisdictions are uniquely held, professions constitute a system, since 'one profession's jurisdiction pre-empts another's' (Abbott 1988: 87). Abbott explains how 'vacancies' and 'bump chains' arise as external forces open or close areas for jurisdiction and as existing or new professions seek out fresh ground. From this perspective, there is 'no long-run equilibrium in the professional world' – rather, 'tasks are continually changing, jurisdictional weaknesses continually being challenged' (1988: 91). The analysis of professions as a system invites a dynamic analysis of interconnecting groups within organizational fields, such as hospitals, clinics and community settings (Casalino 2004). It also helps to contextualize debate and thereby counteract what, by the early 2000s, was seen by many as the weak explanatory power of the 'corporatization' thesis, due to its abstract and ideal-typical character (Numerato et al. 2012). With these points in mind, we turn now to look at the changing relationship between physicians and management, and between physicians and other healthcare providers.

Physicians and management
Chapter 7 explored how the transfer of healthcare from governments to private markets is transforming global health systems. A significant and much-discussed element of this has been the diffusion of neoliberal 'new public management' (NPM) techniques into healthcare at all levels, from government departments to Local Authorities to the organizations in which care is delivered. NPM is a broad umbrella term under which a series of interlinked developments are clustered, including the harnessing of performance management to targets, an emphasis on change management and flexible working (casualization), and the promotion of cultural values of leadership and self-regulation (Ferlie et al.1996). This ethos is supported by supranational agencies such as WHO (2011c), which contrasts NPM to traditional 'managing' with its hierarchically distributed authority located within specialized bureaux and functions dictated by the stable, exhaustive rules of the state.

The stereotype of the manager as a petty bureaucrat, slavishly adhering to 'paperwork' prompts not only clinical managers but also general managers (those who work in healthcare but are not health professionals) to shun the label of 'manager' as part of their professional identity (Harvey et al. 2014; Hyde et al. 2012). Perforce, there have been attempts to replace the pejorative term 'manager' with a new vocabulary of 'leadership'. In the UK, for example, the influential charity the Kings Fund (2011, 2012) advises that medical 'leadership' should be embedded at the 'systems' level of health organizations to encourage physicians to interpret their role as involving far more than the care of the individual patient. As Martin and Learmonth (2012) explain, 'leading' has an attractive, heroic, air which may appeal to clinicians who would not wish to associate themselves with 'managing'. But as these and other authors point out, this is more than a change of vocabulary; it promotes the 'responsibilization' of practitioners at all levels of the organization, including front-line care, as they are encouraged to adopt a new subjectivity which incorporates the values of performance and quality (Dent 2006b; Martin and Learmonth 2012).

The language of leadership is the most recent in a series of moves across health systems internationally to transform how medical work takes place. To take Britain as an example, although physicians have been encouraged to 'manage' their own work actively since the Ministry of Health's 'cogwheel' reports (so named after the cover image) of the late 1960s, until the early 1980s the NHS was characterized by 'consensus management' through multidisciplinary teams, facilitated by administrators. The *NHS Management Enquiry* led by Sir Roy Griffiths, referred to in chapter 7, replaced consensus management with a more 'thrusting and committed' general management (DHSS 1983: 12). Griffiths supported the notion of generic management skills, maintaining that differences between NHS management and business management were greatly overstated (DHSS 1983; Strong and Robinson 1990). Consequently, managers were brought in from the private sector, and existing administrators, doctors, nurses and other clinical staff were re-trained in private-sector practice (Currie and Brown 2003).

The declaration that the nearer the management process gets to the patient, the more important it becomes for the doctors to be looked upon as the *natural managers*, conveyed the expectation that doctors would *want* to manage (DHSS 1983). But, almost regardless of the terminology used to describe it, most health professionals have recoiled from the medical-manager role. It draws them away from their clinical work and distances them from their peers who can regard them as having 'gone over to the dark side' (Harvey et al. 2013). This helps to explain why research has tended to portray the medicine–management relationship as inherently oppositional and to ask whether the new managerialism *has* or *has not* contributed to a decline in professional dominance. This way of thinking has come under criticism in recent years for framing physicians *either* as 'victims' oppressed by strategies of control such as managerialism *or* as 'artful dodgers' 'seeking to contest the spaces and contradictions of market and audit cultures' (Gleeson and Knights 2006: 279). Numerato and colleagues (2012) argue that analysis has been unduly ring-fenced by the dominant *hegemony/ resistance framework* – that is, the hegemony of managerialism and the resistance of medicine – which fails adequately to convey how practices of adaptation, negotiation and resistance are *co-produced* in various institutional contexts via the interplay of structure and agency. This has been explored empirically by Waring and Bishop (2013) in their study of physicians working in two English ISTCs (as discussed in chapter 7, ISTCs are part of the NHS but privately managed). Both Centres were engaged in the hyper-rationalization of work, involving strong top-down performance management, such as targets for turnover, profit and market share, and step-by-step instructions on decision-making and interaction with patients. Waring and Bishop found that non-clinical executives tended to see doctors more as technicians than as experts. However, the way doctors reacted to this regime depended on their position and resources. For some senior doctors, it was highly unwelcome and there was some evidence of resistance – for example, by starting an operating theatre list late or disregarding check-lists. However, most acceded to targets and metrics and participated in the review of their own performance in relation to others. Still others accepted the ISTC's approach as part of the overall marketization of healthcare, with some even viewing it as good training for their future. But most of those who supported the ethos held formal management or leadership positions and worked closely with non-clinical managers, who relied on their 'buy-in' to foster the compliance of their colleagues. Some had links with the parent company through financial invest-ment or share ownership. Waring and Bishop explain that they then 'seemed motivated to better manage their rank-and-file colleagues to increase operational productivity and, in turn, advance their own financial positions and careers' (2013: 155). They argue that, by virtue of their position, these doctors neither resist nor are subject to mana-gerial hegemony – rather, they co-create with management within the environments in which they work. Thus the physician elite and management *together* establish a basis for evaluating, even if not closely monitoring, the work of the rank and file. As Kuhlmann (2006) writes more generally, although the medical profession tends to be seen as a conservative force, its actions can actively advance more hybrid forms of regulation which amalgamate managerialism and professionalism, making them not only adaptive but also transformative.

Contested domains: medicine and other health workers
As explained at the start of the chapter, traditionally medical domi-nance has been strongly associated with control over others in the healthcare division of labour, including patients and alternative prac-titioners of various kinds. But this has been changing in recent years as neoliberal policies have opened up the boundaries between medicine and other groups through skill-mix changes. Alternative practition-ers are a diverse group, ranging, for example, from crystal healers, to aromatherapists, to herbalists, osteopaths and chiropractors. As some groups have sought to professionalize by the development of self- or statutory regulation, they have become potential market competitors to the exclusionary practices of orthodox medical practitioners, especially as complementary and alternative medicine (CAM) becomes increas-ingly popular. Yet as Saks (2003) discusses, these developments are perhaps best viewed as a rapprochement between orthodox medicine and at least some areas of CAM. For example, in the US, orthodox medicine incorporated osteopaths when there were intern (junior doctor) positions to be filled (Saks 2003).

The profession most discussed in relation to medical dominance in the division of labour, however, has been nursing. Nursing has always been divided along hierarchical lines. This has been part of its complex professionalizing strategy as professional elites have sought to shed nursing of its female-gendered, handmaiden image (Hallam 2000). It has become increasingly fragmented as the 'new professionalisers' steer some segments of the profession towards high-expertise work, while the majority are 'shaped as flexible workers' (Wrede 2012: 483). Such workers often include nurses from resource-poor countries, such as the Philippines, who have migrated in large numbers to the USA, UK and other wealthy nations experiencing workforce shortages as home-trained nurses have exited the profession in response to low pay and hard working conditions.

Breaking boundaries between the health professions has been a central plank of many government policies internationally. For example, the limitations on junior doctors' working hours by the European Working Time Directive has led to medical workforce shortages in countries such as the UK. The UK's NHS 'modernization' agenda has emphasized that healthcare providers should no longer be thought of in terms of 'different professional tribes' but as 'teams of people', and that the work that they do should be flexible according to skill, not job title (Department of Health 2000b: 9, 2002a). This lines up with nursing's own professionalizing strategies, which have sought to enhance practice autonomy and upward mobility by putting the qualified nurse at the centre of the healthcare division of labour as the key carer, through such developments as primary nursing and the 'named nurse'. New 'extended' and 'expanded' roles had become the orthodoxy by the early 2000s (Allen 2001). Extended roles can be seen as a kind of labour substitution whereby allied health professionals, such as nurses and occupational therapists, take on work tradition-ally the prerogative of doctors and, in turn, support workers assume some of their work. Doctors generally are happier to shed work that is considered mundane or uninteresting. Often this involves task-based activities, such as venepuncture, the siting of IV lines, inserting can-nulas and suturing. This can be seen as work de-skilling, especially when undertaken in isolation from wider processes of care. In contrast, expanded roles involve up-skilling through new named roles, such as clinical nurse specialist, nurse practitioner and nurse consultant. Here nurses move into 'medical territory' which can take them closer to biomedicine and away from nursing's traditional holistic care of the patient. Davies (2000) has cautioned nurses against embracing the heavily male-gendered model of profession that typifies medicine and management. She dubs this the 'lone hero model of masculinity' which is characterized by mastery of knowledge, unilateral decision processes, autonomy and self-management, individual accountability and detachment. She encourages nurses instead to develop a 'new professionalism', shaped by gender and based on interdependence with colleagues and patients, an engaged and committed stance towards clients, and an investment of self in the clinical encounter.

In practice, developments in nursing roles are likely to combine elements of the extended and expanded approaches, depending on particular work contexts and the nature of working relationships with doctors and others. Research within the 'negotiated order' perspective (discussed in chapter 1) by Allen (2001), for example, draws attention to the 'jurisdictional ambiguity' created by new roles. She highlights that it is nurses, not doctors, who are expected to be the malleable workers in the system, and whose willingness to blur boundaries is subject to abuse through work-overload. Yet, equally, research in an English Casualty department and an Emergency Admissions Unit (EAU) by Annandale and colleagues (1999) has shown that nurses' enactment of extended roles is fluid and responsive to what is happening within a work environment. In Casualty and the EAU there is little that staff can do to control the numbers of patients coming through, but they must deal with the flow in and out. As a nurse remarked, 'Here we tend to tell the doctor to do it himself unless we know it's going to delay everything'. Thus, nurses would undertake tasks such as taking blood or suturing in order to speed things up. Equally, they would retreat from such tasks when it was busy, falling back instead on the more traditional nursing tasks of admitting patients and doing observations of vital signs. This could cause consternation for doctors who found it hard to deal with what one junior doctor referred to as a 'half-way house approach' to extended roles: 'If they've got the time, they do it. If they've not got the time, they get the doctors to do it, whether he or she has got the time or not, which is not really fair because at the end of the day, I have to do it, whatever. And to have someone say, "well, I'll do it today, but I won't do it tomorrow", it's quite irritating' (junior doctor quoted in Annandale et al. 1999: 149).

Thus far in the chapter we have addressed the challenges to professional dominance arising from the twin forces of the marketization of health systems and the retreat of state support for medical autonomy and dominance associated with neoliberalism. While some, such as McKinlay and Marceau (2002, 2008), interpret this as leading to the 'corporatization' of medicine – in other words, to a trajectory of ultimate decline in professional power – the majority of commentators point instead to its resilience. Through a series of interconnected developments encapsulated by the rubric of re-stratification, Freidson (1994) argues that professional elites are able to hold on to power at the corporate level by increased governance of the rank and file. The complexity of this process is evident in the intricacies of changing boundaries between medicine and management and between medicine and nursing. As already discussed, a danger of upholding professional dominance is that errors of practice go undetected and malfeasance unpunished. Re-stratification is a potential way of dealing with this through internal governance, often in collaboration with managerial practices. But even though this may be a necessary component of protecting professional dominance, it is not necessarily sufficient for the protection of *patients*. The public trust which historically has underpinned professional autonomy has been deeply questioned in the wake of high-profile failures of internal regulation in recent years. Indeed, increasingly, patients are being drawn into medical regulation to protect their own care.

Medicine under fire

As the quotation from Bernard Shaw (1980 [1911]) at the beginning of the chapter indicates, an awareness of medical error and patient harm goes back many years. Yet there was little recognition of – or perhaps willingness to acknowledge – the extent and seriousness of this until as recently as the early 1990s when there began a period of major turbulence around patient trust and the failure of the medical profession to protect patients from incompetence and malfeasance (Vincent 2010). As Stacey aptly put it, the 'dam which held back the collective expression of patients' sorrow and anger' burst (2002: 269).

In the UK, one of the most shocking revelations was the case of GP Harold Shipman, the most prolific serial killer in the country's history, who is estimated to have killed at least 236 of his patients over many years (he died in prison, never having admitted his guilt) (Shipman Inquiry Fifth Report 2004). Gynaecologist Rodney Ledward was struck off the medical register for, amongst other things, highly incompetent surgery going back over fifteen years. He nonetheless maintained he was a perfectly capable surgeon who had done a first-class job (Ritchie 2000). It came to light that the deaths of around thirty children at the Bristol Royal Infirmary might have been avoided if staff had heeded the mounting evidence of excess mortality and poor surgical skills of two paediatric heart surgeons (Kennedy 2001). A pathologist at the Royal Liverpool Hospital was struck off the medical register for conducting autopsies without parental consent and retaining the organs of a large number of children (Redfern 2001). In the US, the media drew attention to several tragic cases of death from incorrect drug doses, drug mix-ups and wrong site surgery (Vincent 2010).

Historically, the state has delegated responsibility for protecting the vulnerability of the patient to the doctor, on the assumption that patients are incapable of understanding or judging their expertise, that doctors are especially virtuous and trustworthy, and that doctors are willing to take action when one of their number falls short (Dixon-Woods et al. 2011). Expectations such as these have been embodied in collegial self-regulation. The scandals described above were the catalyst for major changes in medical regulation in the UK as it became apparent that imperatives of collegial cooperation, failure to act in the face of suspected abuse and poor practice of peers, and fear of the consequences – such as being drawn into a stressful and drawn-out formal disciplinary process against a colleague, if one did speak out – had obstructed the disclosure of major failings (Dixon-Woods et al. 2011: 1455). Far more stringent controls over licensing and ways of dealing with complaints were introduced, and doctors lost their majority position on the regulatory body, the General Medical Council (GMC) (Department of Health 2007b).

Yet all of these cases in various ways point not only to the failings of individuals, but also to 'systems gone wrong'. To borrow and extend an analogy from Dixon-Woods et al. (2011), individual bad apples are the result of a rotten orchard. The framing of error as a systems-level, rather than individual-level, problem is evident in the US Institute of Medicine report *To Err is Human: Building a Safer Health System* (Kohn et al. 2000). Similarly, the UK Department of Health's response to the Bristol scandal emphasizes that the NHS needs to learn from evidence of 'poor organisation, failure of communication, lack of leadership, paternalism and a "club culture" and a failure to put patients at the centre' (Department of Health 2002b: 1). Yet, over ten years on from the Bristol Report, catastrophic failures of care recently came to light at the Mid Staffordshire NHS Hospital Trust in England. The government report which followed (Department of Health 2013b) detailed appalling suffering by patients treated with callous indifference by nurses; understaffing and untrained staff undertaking inappropriate roles, such as triage in Accident and Emergency; and a wider organizational culture geared towards achieving financial targets at the expense of quality of patient care. The report's author, barrister Robert Francis, severely admonished doctors for failing to speak out on behalf of patients and hence for colluding in a culture which tolerated abysmally low standards of care (*British Medical Journal* 2013).

It is particularly telling that the failings in the Mid Staffordshire Trust were brought to light by patients and their relatives, not by doctors and nurses. Research on the front-line of care shows that patient safety is not a unidirectional achievement of staff but co-accomplished within the patient–provider relationship as patients identify risks and ask questions (Hor et al. 2013). As we saw in chapter 7, citizens are now often conceptualized as 'co-producers' of health in a process of diffused governance (e.g. WHO 2011c) and called upon to hold health professionals to account. The present discussion suggests that this now extends to patients securing the safety of their own care, underscoring the point that they are crucial workers in the healthcare division of labour and not just bodies to be worked *on* (Olesen 2002). For example, one of the principal reasons why oncologist Groopman (2007) wrote the previously mentioned book *How Doctors Think* was to propose that, when patients and their loved ones know not only how doctors think, but also how they *fail* to think, they can become partners in the process of reaching the right diagnosis and treatment. Several of the case stories presented in the book relate occasions when it was the patient's realization of what was wrong in a 'life or death' situation that led the doctor to set them on the right path to recovery.

Trust

The above discussion speaks to a crisis in the wider cultural authority of medicine. As has been emphasized throughout this chapter, medicine's position of dominance in the healthcare division of labour and authority to direct its own work is a privilege conferred by others. At the heart of this lies trust. As captured in the time-worn cliché, 'Trust me, I'm a doctor', the inherent uncertainty in the application of scientific knowledge in the treatment of the human body makes trust an essential ingredient in the doctor–patient relationship. For Mechanic, it 'provides the glue that makes cooperation possible without costly and intrusive regulation' (2004b: 1418).

Opinion polls show high levels of trust in doctors, at least relative to other occupations. For example, in 2013, 89 per cent of British adults said that they generally trust doctors to tell the truth, compared to 21 per cent trusting bankers, 18 per cent politicians and 64 per cent 'ordinary men and women' on the street (IPSOS Mori 2013). However, wider research, including some from outside the UK, suggests that this reflects 'interpersonal trust' or 'embodied trust' in one's 'own' doctor, not trust in the health systems and organizations in which they work – or 'institutional trust' – which typically is much lower (Calnan and Rowe 2006; Hall 2006). For example, research in England in the early 2000s by Calnan and Sanford (2004) found that the highest levels of *dis*trust were found not in relation to doctors and nurses, but to matters connected to the organization and provision of care, such as cost cutting and waiting times. Notably, trust in healthcare managers was very low. In reference to the US, Illingworth (2005) has argued that aggressive managed care plans that limit physician autonomy in decision-making in relation to patient treatments have the potential to undermine patient trust in the doctor–patient relationship.

Thus, research suggests that, despite high-profile failures to detect and deal with incompetent, misguided and malicious individuals, rising rates of complaints and litigation, and a generalized lack of trust in the health systems in which they work, patients and the public still continue to trust their doctors, if not healthcare organizations and managers. This has bolstered claims from within the medical profession itself that a new, reinvigorated social contract with society should be firmly based in a *partnership with patients*. As we will now go on to explore, this partnership is envisioned not only as the foundation for improved healthcare, but also as a natural political alliance in the fight against managerialism and marketization – that is, against the very processes which, as we have seen, challenge professional dominance.

The 'new professionalism' and the partnership message

A new ideology of 'professionalism', which emerged in the early 2000s and has grown thereafter, has been embraced 'with almost religious fervour' (Hafferty 2003: 136). As Askham and Chisholm (2006) remark, defining what the new professionalism stands for has become an industry itself, spawning a legion of articles, books and reports from professional bodies in a numbers of countries, such as Canada, the US and the UK. However, it has two interconnected objectives: to regenerate values such as honesty, integrity, and altruism within the profession, and to warn the public of the dangers of dismantling professional autonomy.

Richard Horton, editor of the prestigious medical journal the *Lancet*, admits that what he calls the collusive relationship between medicine and the state has worked against patient interests at times, and accepts wider-scale regulatory failures in Britain (2005). Nonetheless, he cautions that, although the dimming of the profession's flame will be welcomed by critics of professional power, the endemic demoralization of doctors 'is creating a cold front of danger that threatens the public's health' (2005: 1985). In *Hippocratic Oaths, Medicine and its Discontents*, medical consultant and author Raymond Tallis (2004) writes that distrust-fuelled regulation on the part of governments is not only wasteful of resources, it will provoke a backlash, such as defensive and inappropriate practices by physicians (such as over-testing and unnecessary referrals), which are not in the patient's interest.

This begins to explain the entreaties by medical elites to the public for a new partnership with medicine. For example, Donald Irvine, ex-President of the British GMC, connects the renaissance of 'medical professionalism' with a broad alliance of 'thoughtful doctors, sociologists, and lay people seeing that unrestrained consumerism, commercialism, and managerialism could easily strip the profession of its ethical core' (2006: 49). While such authors place a responsibility on doctors to change by forgetting obsolete notions of mastery and unbounded knowledge (Horton 2005; RCP 2005), the public is asked to accept the inherent uncertainties of medical practice (Horton 2005; Tallis 2004). As Miles (2002) discusses with reference to the US-driven

Charter on Medical Professionalism (*Annals of Internal Medicine* 2002), the grounding of the 'new professionalism' in physician frustration with market dynamics of healthcare and appeal to public support jars somewhat with the Charter's three stated 'fundamental principles': of patient welfare, patient autonomy, and social justice. He argues that if it is truly these principles that are at stake, then we might expect more explicit attention to matters such as global health inequality and access to care. And, as Hafferty discuses more generally, although commercialism is condemned in the 'new professionalism', 'it continues to flourish within the entrepreneurial domains of clinical and research medicine', such as in the sale of patients into clinical trials, and in the transformation of biomedical discoveries into marketable products (2006: 299) (see also discussion in chapter 1).

Some social scientists have joined forces with medicine in criticisms of neoliberal modes of governance of the professions and the distrust that it engenders. For example, a number have reasoned that a decline of institutional trust in the medical profession discourages patients from using healthcare and inhibits the disclosure of important information, while encouraging unnecessary 'shopping around' (Rowe and Calnan 2006; Hall et al. 2001). At a higher level, it has been argued that, since health systems are part of the fabric of a country, a trust-based health system helps to build social cohesion (Gilson 2003). Social theorist Richard Sennett (2008) draws a connection between commercialization and competition and the decline of the basic human impulse of the worker's desire, no matter what the job – woodworker, musician, doctor – to do a job well for its own sake. He contends that, at the higher level, the tacit skills of 'the craftsman' are learnt through the embodied process of doing and reflecting on one's craft. Much like the physicians already cited, he argues that such necessary skills in dealing with patients are being stymied by the imposition of standardized guidelines for practice and constant, churning organizational changes (such as in the British NHS). In these and other deliberations, we begin to see a sympathetic account of the dangers of challenges to medical power from social scientists. Arguably, the period of sociological critique of medical dominance described earlier in the chapter has yielded to the upholding of professionalism as a normative value (Evetts 2006).

The 'third logic' of professionalism

In his final book, *Professionalism: The Third Logic*, published in 2001, Freidson (who died in 2005) identifies three ideal types or logics of the control of the professions (none of which exist exclusively in concrete reality): *bureaucracy* (control by management); the *market* (control by consumers); and *professionalism* (occupational self-control). The book is not just about medicine; it concerns the professions generally, but the use of medicine (and US medicine specifically) as an illustrative case has meant that it has been taken up particularly by those concerned with health. Thus, in the third logic of professionalism, it is health workers themselves (not managers, not consumers) who determine what work is performed and its relation to the work of others. Freidson asks what will happen if the logics of bureaucracy and market are followed? His answer is that quality of service will suffer through the minimization of discretion in practice as the individual needs of patients are forced into standardized administrative procedures. He maintains that knowledge development will be narrowed as it becomes increasingly directed to what industry and the public feel they want: 'I believe that the emphasis on consumerism and managerialism has legitimised and advanced the individual pursuit of material self-interest and the standardisation of professional work which are the very vices for which professions have been criticised, preserving form without spirit' (Freidson 2001: 181). As this quotation signals, he claims that the spirit or soul of professionalism will be lost if professions become 'merely technical experts in the service of the political and cultural economy' (2001: 121). Doctors will lose their independent moral voice in society, their 'ideology of service'.

Professionalism, or the 'third logic', has a strong ideological component based on transcendental values and the profession as a secular calling. In Freidson's assessment this claim to professionalism should be promoted because it ensures that doctors' rights to apply knowledge and skill are not abused and allows them to claim independence of judgement and freedom of action. In the evaluation of some, a nefarious consensus dialogue has emerged between medical elites and erstwhile critics of professional dominance, such as Freidson. Brint, for example, argues that, since the 1970s and *Profession of Medicine* (discussed at the start of the chapter), Freidson 'travelled 180 degrees, leaving the party of critics of professionalism and joining the party of its defenders' (2006: 103).

Conclusions

In this chapter we have seen that political winds of change have swept forcefully over the power of the medical profession since Freidson and others first wrote on professional dominance in the 1970s. Many within the higher echelons of the profession are likely to see it as an ill wind indeed. As to whether this means that medicine is losing its professional dominance, it is hard to reach a definitive conclusion. If we return to the notion of countervailing powers, as Light (1995) explains, medical dominance is contextual and eventually elicits countermoves by powerful actors, in this case by the neoliberal state intent on rebalancing power as a way of reigning in healthcare costs and addressing lapses in care quality. Social scientists, such as Freidson in his later work (2001), lament what they see as the negative consequences of its systematic dismantling, such as the loss of the medical profession's independent voice on behalf of the patient and as a progressive force for change. Although writing some years ago now, Stacey (1992) argued that the organized medical profession has, on significant occasions, been an effective public ally voicing opposition to government policies over issues such as nuclear waste and restrictive abortion laws. As we have seen, medical elites are themselves seeking an alliance with patients as a counterweight to onslaughts by governments on their autonomy. But much of this dialogue has taken place at a rather abstract level of medicine as a corporate body. In the final chapter of the book, we build on the issues raised here and in chapter 7, on the structure of health systems and the place of physicians, nurses and others, to explore how healthcare is delivered and the experience of health and illness.

9

The experience of health, illness and healthcare

The screen is black and white and we hear the faint sound of what seems to be snoring. A white rectangle of light suddenly silhouettes the form of a woman who has just opened a door. A man is revealed, dressed in medical scrubs and lying on a gurney. It is Dr Mark Greene, dead asleep at five a.m., being awakened to care for his first patient of the day. The patient turns out to be his friend and co-worker, Dr Doug Ross, who has just reeled into the hospital, quite drunk, and is in immediate need of chemically-induced sobering. Greene reluctantly gets up. It is another long and very full day in the ER.

(Pourroy 1996: 7)

So begins 24 hours in the life of a Chicago Hospital Emergency Department in the ground-breaking, award-winning TV drama series *ER*, which aired between 1994 and 2009. As the day unfolds, the script reveals

a scaffolding that collapses, injuring twelve; an eight-year-old with a bleeding ulcer; a thirteen-year-old with an ectopic pregnancy; a nurse who has taken an overdose of drugs; and more than a dozen other major and minor crises. In between these emergencies fall the everyday routines of filling out paper work and having lunch with a spouse. Chaos is juxtaposed with calm; sunshine gives way to snowfall, which gives way to rain, and lengthy scenes keep tempo alongside the merest glimpses of plot and character.

(Pourroy 1996: 7)

It seems that the hyper-reality of the Baudrillardian nightmare (see chapter 2) is replacing the reassuring face of bedside medicine of yester-year as images of patients transported in search of hospital beds, rationing of care, staffing crises, vulnerable doctors and incompetent practice dominate our cinema and TV screens and the print media around the world.

Yet perhaps not so much has changed. Consider, for example, another drama from an altogether different time and place. In *The Doctor's Dilemma: A Tragedy*, George Bernard Shaw (1980 [1911]), winner of the Nobel Prize for Literature, whose views on the medical profession we also touched upon in chapter 8, satirizes medical practice in early twentieth-century England. As the play opens, Sir Colenso Ridgeon, a well-known London Harley Street doctor, has just received a knighthood for discovering a cure for tuberculosis, a mortal illness at the time. The remedy, opsonin, is vitally sensitive to the phase of the disease: when the patient is in the negative phase, you kill; when he or she is in the positive phase, you cure. The drama unfolds as Ridgeon and five of his colleagues deliberate the latest trumpery cures and careers to be made by the discovery of fashionable new surgeries. Medicine's moral failings, explicitly linked by Shaw to private practice, dominate the plot as the doctors are forced to make a decision about whom to treat with the drug, since they are only able to treat ten people (Shaw never makes clear why this is the case though it seems to be related to the time and skill needed to administer the remedy (Allett 2001)).

The concerns of Shaw's drama reflect the dilemmas of present-day medical practice in a quite uncanny way: morality, clinical uncertainty and questions of who should be treated and who not, are as high on the agenda now as they were over 100 years ago. But they are being played out in a globalized social world light years away from Shaw's early twentieth-century England. Moreover, they are overlain with complex social inequalities and debates on entitlement to care. The present-day experience of health, illness and healthcare can be approached in terms of a tension between, on the one hand, the premium that is increasingly placed on reflexivity and personal choice (over issues as wide-ranging as how to 'keep oneself healthy' and the treatment options for a particular disease) and, on the other hand, the moral responsibility actually to make these choices and the constraints that surround decision-making for both patients and healthcare providers.

Within the confines of this chapter, there is the opportunity to discuss only a limited number of ways in which this tension impacts on the experience of health, illness and healthcare. We begin by looking at the experience of illness, starting with a discussion of death and dying. We then explore lay concepts of health and social representations of health and illness, paying particular attention to the search for meaning in illness and the insight that this provides into the contemporary social condition. We then turn to medicalization, contested illnesses, and the construction of 'patients-in-waiting' through population screening and genetic testing. The chapter closes by returning to the dilemmas raised by Shaw all those years ago, by addressing the question of who gets treated today, and why?

Death and dying

It is often remarked that Western societies hide death away from everyday experience as the large majority of deaths occur in hospitals and care homes. It is for this reason that a number of prominent analysts (Ariès 1981; Becker 1973; Elias 1985) consider them death-denying. Bauman, for example, argues that, unable to contemplate the end, we have 'fought death tooth and nail'. Never quite believing in the end of death, we have pushed it back tiny bit by tiny bit, making it an event without a cause as we diffuse the 'perennial horror of mortality' by dissembling it into an infinite chain of particular preventable causes, such as diseases that can be conquered and avoided by lifestyle changes (Bauman 1993: 28, 29). The argument goes that when death is pushed to the margins of life, life itself begins to lose meaning. For the philosopher Heidegger (1962 [1927]), since we can never know death, the thing that matters is its effect on life. Hence, it is essential that we comprehend our finality in order to live a good life.

Yet, as Walter (1994) points out, in contemporary Western societies, we seem to deny death, yet increasingly talk (and write) about it. This is particularly evident when celebrity figures, such as writers, actors, journalists, politicians and sports stars, declare and publicize their impending deaths in the media (see Seale 1998). As discussed in chapter 2, it has been proposed that the 'responsibilization' that accompanies the spread of neoliberalism has encouraged people to make themselves the centre of their own life plans, literally for the sake of their survival (Beck and Beck-Gernsheim 2002). Walter proposes that, in a culture of individualism that values a unique life, 'the requirement that I live my life my own way is increasingly being extended to a requirement that I die and mourn my own way' too (1994: 2). Thus he maintains that the modern 'revival of death' is an attempt to resolve the contradiction of the visible public side of death (the insurance industry, funeral business, stylized media display) with its private side (grief that is usually hidden away). A resolution is achieved by making the public side of death more personal, something which is exceedingly important to us because the rational bureaucratic approach to death (hospital-based, under medical control, a relatively impersonal funeral service) is hard to tolerate when such a premium is placed on the unique individual.

Some years ago, Seale (1998) drew attention to the 'pathography genre' of representing death in the British broadcast media through the example of well-known presenter Melvyn Bragg's television interview of the then-dying playwright Dennis Potter in 1994. He argues that the interview reveals the uniquely elevated authority that accompanies the marginal or liminal status between life and death. Thus Potter discourses on 'the deficiencies of the living' and presents 'projects for restructuring the world he will leave behind' (Seale 1998: 130). More recently Walter (2009) has explored the complex tensions between the public/private boundary of death and dying through an analysis of the public response to the dying of 27-year-old British reality TV *Big Brother* star, Jade Goody, from cervical cancer in 2009. Goody's dying seemed to defy the three key components of the sequestration of death thesis. First, in death and dying, the body is hidden from view. Goody put her own dying into the spotlight. She invited the media to witness and chronicle her dying in words and pictures which populated TV screens and newspapers. Her self-given reasons for this were that she wanted to earn money to support her sons after her death and to raise awareness of the need for cervical cancer screening amongst women. Second, the sequestration thesis maintains that death and dying is cut off from ordinary routines of life. On the contrary, Goody's experience of dying was woven into the everyday lives of those who witnessed it almost daily in the media. And third, while sequestration involves privatized dying, Goody chose to make the meaning she gave to her illness and dying public. Yet Walter (2009) points out that, although this seems to challenge the sequestration thesis, those who witnessed the spectacle knew full well that it was not the norm; indeed, it could be argued that it only served to highlight that usually dying is different from this, which shores up the private/public boundary that continues to mark the dying process.

Goody's death symbolized one of the most valued features of a 'good death' today: that the dying person has agency – in other words, that they control their own dying process (Kellehear 2009). Hence a 'good death' has become associated with preparation, such as advance directives, getting one's legal and other affairs in order, and active negotiation with doctors and other health workers about what will happen in our care. Although this resonates strongly with the individualization and responsibilization of life, as Kellehear explains, 'theories of agency locate these activities, obligations and responsibilities in a dying person who is usually conscious enough and has time enough to execute them' (2009: 4). Although this may be the popular image, it is not the reality for many people.

The debate in Western, especially Anglo-American, societies, over openness and secrecy about death and dying was first highlighted in sociology by Glaser and Strauss (1965). The main concern has been the increasing institutionalization and medicalization of death and dying. Up to the early twentieth century, barring accidents, people would usually die at home (Howarth 2007). In the current century, around one-fifth of deaths occur in the domestic home and four-fifths in hospitals, care homes and hospices. Gomes and Higginson (2008) have suggested that if this trend continued then less than 10 per cent of people would die in their homes in 2030. This is despite the preference of most people to die at home. The hospice movement arose as an attempt to provide home-like care for dying people (mainly cancer patients) and to provide support for people dying at home. In Britain, for example, it seems also to have had some success in improving the quality of care in hospitals. However, the recently well-documented lack of sensitivity and depersonalized care in UK hospitals (referred to in chapter 8) means that, at best, such amelioration is partial and vulnerable to set-backs (Department of Health 2013b).

As the discussion thus far signals, much of our understanding of dying is based on research on people dying from diseases of affluence, such as cancer and heart disease – in other words, most of what we know comes from *illness-related* dying in the West. Generally left out, no matter where they live, are those who die in vegetative states, from dementia, from poverty, from incarceration. Thus Kellehear depicts most dying as disenfranchised, 'not recognised by medical, political or international authorities but occurring anyway in far greater numbers than appear in hospices or cancer wards' (2009: 14). Similarly, Howarth (2009) explains that, when death is thought of globally, a dichotomy usually comes to mind: in affluent countries, people die of the 'top killers' of cancer, heart disease and stroke; in developing countries, they die of infectious diseases, such as malaria, TB, AIDS and measles. She agrees that this is to some extent accurate, though the spread of 'Western lifestyles' associated with high-fat diets and tobacco has led to rising rates of non-communicable diseases in developing countries, and global mobility has been associated with the re-introduction of infectious diseases like TB into industrialized countries (see discussion in chapter 2). But above all, this dichotomy overlooks politically motivated dying – disenfranchised deaths in Kellehear's (2009) terms – through war, 'ethnic cleansing' and starvation. Here we are reminded of Butler's argument, touched upon in chapter 1, that some lives cannot even be apprehended as injured or lost in war because they 'are not first apprehended as living' (2010: 1) They are seen as lives not worth knowing and, in the context of the present discussion, as deaths not worth understanding.

On the face of it, the experience of dying seems to be very personal – nowhere more so, it would seem, than in contemporary Western society with its stress upon the authority of the self amid competing ideas about how illness should be understood and treated. Yet this co-exists with strong normalizing forces which structure our experience – the imperative to make one's own choice being a rather ironic illustration of this. Out of these multiple realities, people fashion their own understandings of health and illness. These wider issues will be taken up in the next part of the chapter as we consider the experience of health and illness.

Social representations of health and illness

It is a sociological common-place to point out that we seem to know health only as a lack, as the absence of disease. As we saw in chapter 2, chiefly this is because the body only becomes a subject of conscious attention when afflicted by symptoms such as pain or weakness; otherwise it is an absent presence (Lawton 2003). Even so, if, along with Gadamer, we ponder on the enigma of health, we are prompted to ask: 'is it not an extraordinary thing that the lack of something, although we do not know precisely what it is that is lacking, can reveal the miraculous existence of health?' (Gadamer 1996: 74). As Gadamer goes on to explain, we can try to define someone's health by standard values, but given that at least some degree of deviation from whatever values you impose is likely to occur for almost all people, all we will end up doing is making the person ill. Equally, notions of the 'normal' – normal weight, normal blood pressure, normal energy levels and so on – only raise the question, 'Normal for whom?' (Blaxter 2010). So, health is indeed likely to be known when it is unsettled, but since people have radically different life experiences, what this means is likely to be subject to substantial variation.

The difficulty of uncovering the meaning of health helps explain why there are relatively few studies of health compared to studies of illness, which are legion. In the early 1990s, research from the British Health and Lifestyles Survey found that over 10 per cent of respondents could not answer the question 'What is it like when you are healthy?' For a minority, more often the elderly, this was because 'I am never healthy, so I don't know', but, more frequently, health was quite simply the 'ordinary': a norm that is difficult to describe (Blaxter 1990: 19–20). As one woman struggled to articulate, 'I don't really know. Sometimes I do feel less healthy, but I can't say that I feel what it is to be healthy at other times' (1990: 20). In-depth qualitative studies have grouped people's representations of health in a number of ways. One of the best-known of these is Claudine Herzlich's (1973) now-classic study of middle-class people in France. From her analysis of in-depth interview data, she derived three dimensions of health, which could co-exist in any one account. First, she found 'health in a vacuum', that is, health as the simple absence of disease. Much like Blaxter's (1990) respondents, this was not a positive account since people could not say what health was, only what it was not: 'not being ill'. Second, they referred to 'health as reserve' or capital asset. The 'reserve' was expressed as physical robustness and the potential to resist attacks of illness, for example. Third, they spoke of 'health as equilibrium' or a positive state of well-being, articulated through representations such as the body as a well-oiled machine or as being at ease. In their review of the wider body of published research some years later, Shaw Hughner and Schultz Kleine (2004) found that these broad themes were still fairly generalizable, though textured by the different social contexts in which various studies were carried out. Thus, lay definitions encompass two negative views of health: as the absence of illness and as the ability to carry out daily activities; and two positive views of health, as 'achieving harmony and equilibrium in daily life' and 'the freedom to live life to the fullest' (2004: 415). In each of the positive views, health is far from a given – rather, it is something that needs to be achieved or to be striven for. However, some societies view health neither as 'absence of illness' nor as something striven for by the individual. For example, amongst the Cree people of northern Quebec, concepts of health are synonymous with collective Cree social and political well-being, which is bound up with a life on the land (Adelson 1998). The term 'health' has no meaning – rather, wellness is expressed as *miyupimaatisiim*, or 'being alive well'. 'Being alive well' is distinct from the degree of a person's own biological morbidity and constituted from both within and outside the boundaries of the individual body. Thus one can speak of being well and unwell at the same time. Significantly, 'being alive well' incorporates 'being Cree' and serves as a point of opposition to encroachment on the land by the postcolonial 'whiteman'. Hence health encompasses a larger strategy of identity and constraint (Adelson 1998). This illustration shows that the notion of health as the absence of disease is a Western product of biomedical ways of thinking.

If the prevalence of biomedical knowledge makes health hard to know in the West, what about illness – is that any easier to fathom? The answer seems to be a definitive 'yes'. Chiefly this is precisely because biomedicine has provided us with a ready language of interpretation, one that individuals all, to a greater or lesser degree, become familiar with as they grow up and engage with modern healthcare systems. This is complemented by a media-saturated environment which exposes us to a constant loop of television programmes, films, news articles and online communications about problems of health and the body. Illness, it seems, is something that we relate to quite readily. To return to Herzlich's (1973) classic study, in Western societies people seem to represent illness in three ways. Like representations of health, people can hold combinations of these, and one or the other may be more or less salient at any one time. The first representation is 'illness as destructive'. Although this is likely to vary according to the nature of the illness and whether it is expected to be short-term (an acute episode) or long-term (a chronic or terminal illness), illness involves temporary or long-term loss since things that are valued often have to be given up. The second is 'illness as occupation'. Since, as we have seen, health tends to be seen as something that needs to be striven for, it is not surprising that people represent illness as something that absorbs or occupies you as you have to fight against it. Third, and perhaps less expectedly, some people saw 'illness as a liberator', something that opens up a new world unlike anything one has experienced before. We will return to this particular representation of illness again later when we look at the experience of chronic illness.

Although we have begun to detect connections between how we think about health and how we think about illness, thus far we have been conceiving them as separate phenomena. Yet, even in Western societies, saturated with biomedical thinking, this is unlikely to be the reality of people's experience. Research consistently shows that definitions of 'health' can accommodate a fair amount of discomfort and disability. Thus, it is not uncommon for people to report that they are in good health while simultaneously referring to often quite severe functional limitations (Blaxter 2010; Cornwell 1984). Equally, as the previously referred-to notion of 'illness as liberator' conveys, people can find new positive life experiences in illness. It is for this reason that philosopher Havi Carel advises that we move away from thinking about health and illness as 'mutually exclusive opposites, towards a continuum or a blend of the two' (2008: 78). Writing from the perspective of her own rare, very debilitating illness, she employs the concept of *'health within illness'*, arguing that, much as 'episodes of illness can occur within health, an experience of health within illness is a possible, if often overlooked, phenomenon' (2008: 77). She maintains that 'health within illness' is enabled by our ability to adapt to more limited capabilities and by the creativity that arises from the novel challenges occasioned by serious illness (see also discussion of chronic illness, below). But, as Carel and others also address, we make sense of and live with illness not as individuals but as part of families, social networks and wider societies. So how we interpret and cope with our own illnesses is also bound up with how others respond to illness and those who are ill.

Morality and responsibilization

'Acting like a sponge, illness soaks up personal and social significance from the world of the sick person.' This quotation from Kleinman's (1988: 31) study of illness narratives draws attention to two things. First, making sense of illness is simultaneously to make sense of the wider social world around us, and, second, sense-making is often highly metaphorical. Metaphor takes on a unique role in illness, shaping our perception, our identities and our experience. The language that we use to refer to diseases affects how people deal with their conditions and how others treat them (Lupton 2012).

Moral meanings – what is deemed right or wrong human behaviour or character – have been associated with health and illness throughout modern history in the simple but very powerful sense of equating health with goodness and illness with badness. It is not uncommon, for example, for someone who feels ill to say, 'I feel bad.' Conversely, beauty and positivity are often taken to be the same as healthiness. This should not surprise us since, as Saltonstall writes, 'the experience of self as body and body as self constitutes the human experience, and as such, is saturated with notions of moral action and responsibility' (1993: 9). A fine illustration of this is Cornwell's (1984) classic study, *Hard Earned Lives*, which explores concepts of health amongst working-class people in the East End of London. Her respondents spoke about three kinds of illnesses: 'normal illness' (e.g. childhood illnesses such as tonsillitis, stomach aches, colds and flu); 'health problems' (such as arthritis, skin problems or symptoms of menopause); and 'real illness' (major disability and potentially life-threatening conditions, such as cancer and cardio-vascular diseases). Crucially, in their view, only 'real illnesses' were legitimate illnesses. Thus the threshold on what counts as illness was set very high. People neither wanted to define themselves as ill nor wanted others to do so for them, for the reason that illness was a strong threat to moral reputations, which were closely bound up with the ability to work. Hence, as Cornwell writes, for her respondents: '"Good people" are not only hard-working, they are also cheerful and stoical and, if they feel ill, they prefer to work off their symptoms rather than give in to them. "Bad people", on the other hand, are people who will not work (malingerers) and who are also likely to be hypochondriacs who waste valuable medical resources' (Cornwell 1984: 133).

Longstanding views such as these live on in contemporary Western societies, but are overlain with new emphases. The more health is envisaged as something to be achieved – indeed, as something that we are individually *responsible* for – the more it becomes an essential part of our identity. As Crawford discusses for the US, but we can generalize more widely: 'individual responsibility for health has become a model of and a model for the neoliberal restructuring of American society' (2006: 419). Health, it seems, now has to be produced and maintained as a moral duty (Beck and Beck-Gernsheim 2002). There are many illustrations of this such as Skolbekken and colleagues' (2008) interview-based study of the experience of bone-density measurement amongst Norwegian women aged 55 to 75 years. The respondents (who were interviewed in 2001) felt that in their grandmothers' day people could not help suffering from osteoporosis as it was a result of the harsh conditions of their lives of toil. But in the present day, they attributed it to individual moral failure, associated, for example, with not following an appropriate diet or taking regular exercise. Moreover, this was extended to encompass a failure of public duty, inducing strong feelings of self-blame when appropriate health guidelines were not followed – due, for example, to the demanding roles of mother and paid worker.

Findings like these have led some to ask whether we now live in a 'healthist' society (Cheek 2007). The term 'healthism' was coined by Robert Crawford some thirty or so years ago to refer to a new health consciousness. Writing in the 1980s, he argued that capitalist ideologies are refracted through health beliefs and the promotion of new medical-related procedures, such as ultrasound in pregnancy, cosmetic breast implants, new diet plans and exercise programmes (Crawford 1980, 1984). He proposed that when 'the macro-economic conditions that affect health appear out of control, self-control over the considerable range of personal behaviours that also affect health is an only remaining option' (Crawford 1984: 74). Writing some years later, he argued that health has become a logic of survival. In times of economic austerity, 'by making the body a task', by being health conscious – 'slim and fit', rather than 'fat and slothful', for example – individuals 'demonstrate' to self and others that they have the qualities 'that make them more equipped than their competitors for surviving the new economic realities' (Crawford 2006: 413). A contemporary example is provided by Sanchez-Taylor's (2012) study of young English women who chose to have expensive cosmetic breast augmentation surgery. They wanted their breasts to look 'fake' in order to demonstrate to others the investment they had made and the personal economic and social aspirations that this expressed.

Thus the traditional boundaries around what health is and how it is enacted have expanded, making it possible to incorporate ever more aspects of life into the domain of illness or potential illness and thereby to construct and morally police the proliferating divides between the healthy/sick, and the fit/unfit. If health has become the 'new morality', this raises the question: what happens to those who fall on the wrong side of healthy? We can look at this through the example of 'obesity'.

Obesity
Much has been written – some in extraordinarily dramatic words – over the last ten years or so, about an 'obesity epidemic'. Presumably intending to 'shock' the populace into action, the US Surgeon General characterized obesity as 'the terror within', contending that 'unless we do something about it, the magnitude of the dilemma will dwarf 9–11 or any other terrorist attempt' (quoted in Saguy and Almeling 2008: 53). In more muted terms, but conveying no less anxiety, a policy document from the Department of Health for England opined that rising 'overweight and obesity represent probably the most widespread threat to health and wellbeing in this country' (Department of Health 2011c: 5). The document presents 'excess weight' as a burden on the NHS, costing an estimated £4.2 billion in 2007 and expected to rise to £9.7 billion by the year 2050 (Department of Health 2011c). Yet the notion of an 'epidemic' has been much contested. As Jutel (2006) discusses, fatness is

not new; what is new is how we relate to it. Hence the label or diagnosis of obesity is not the result of a change in biological function – rather, it has arisen from new ways of seeing and classifying with biomedical science. Crucial to this, Jutel explains, is the increased emphasis that Western society places on normative appearance and on measurability, in particular, the Body Mass Index (BMI). BMI is calculated as weight in kilograms divided by the square of height in metres. The resulting figure is checked against a chart split into ranges of 'underweight', 'normal weight', 'overweight' and 'obese'. Critics have argued that not only is this an arbitrary measure, it does not even measure body fat but rather body mass, including muscle. In response to such concerns, Jutel concludes that 'overweight is not a disease any more than slenderness is an indicator of health. Like baldness, it is a description of physical appearance' (2006: 2276).

In chapter 2, we considered Shildrick's argument (made in relation to disability) that modern Western societies construct 'an inviolable self/body that is secure, distinct, closed, and autonomous' (2002: 51). In similar terms, Lupton writes that, both literally and figuratively, the overweight/obese/fat are seen as having 'let themselves go': 'fat flesh challenges notions of propriety because of its fluidity and excessiveness. It is wobbly and jiggly, it hangs loosely, it oozes over into people's spaces, confronts them with its monstrous dimensions' (2013: 3, 57). This stands in a 'binary opposition of symbolic meaning against the civilised thin body' (2013: 56). This helps to explain the strong stigma attached to overweight and obesity in much of the West. The Western media has been awash with stories of obesity for some years now. Saguy and Almeling (2008) found that, although the news media take their cues from scientific articles, they 'throw fat on the fire' – that is, they are more likely to use evocative language like an obesity 'epidemic' or a 'war' on obesity to apportion blame to the individual, and to moralize, such as blaming women's pursuit of a career for 'obese children'. Portrayals such as these filter easily through the public domain, carrying with them the potential to heighten the stigma attached to obesity and contribute to what Goffman (1963) called 'spoiled identities'.

Thus far then, we have seen that present-day Western societies place a strong emphasis on the self-responsibility of individuals to keep themselves well, and for getting sick when they do not. We turn now to consider the implications of this for living with chronic illness.

Chronic illness

Health policies across many countries emphasize the self-responsibility of the individual for the management of illness. Illustrations of this are the 'chronic disease self-management programme' pioneered at Stanford University in the US and the British Expert Patients Programme, referred to in chapter 7. However, sociological studies have been documenting the active steps that people take in managing chronic illness for well over thirty years now. A central strand of this research has been the social and biographical disruption that occurs when dealing with chronic, long-term, illness, especially when it is serious and debilitating. In the discussion of health earlier in the chapter, it was remarked that one of the reasons that health is unknowable to us is that there is a taken-for-grantedness of our experience when we feel healthy. In contrast, illness is often 'an abrupt, violent way of revealing the intimately bodily nature of our being' (Carel 2008: 27), making it difficult *not* to attend to the body.

Mind and body in chronic illness
Since the experience of chronic illness is extremely varied and experienced by people in divergent social circumstances, we need to be wary of over-generalizing. But when illness occurs, be this suddenly or in an insidious onset, the body tends to confront us as an alien presence, throwing embodiment, and especially the mind–body relationship, into sharp relief (Williams 1996). Numerous personal illness narratives illustrate this point. Here we will take one example. In Bloom's (1992) account, 'Sandy', an American woman then in her late forties, narrates her experience of kidney disease and cancer. Sandy's story of illness begins in high school, during a period of her life which she describes as extremely pressured by the need to succeed, both academically and in her other pursuits such as music. These pressures help to explain why, paradoxical though it may seem, Sandy was personally relieved to be diagnosed with kidney disease. In her own words, 'it was just the first time that I had really gotten in touch with myself, my reflective self' (1992: 322). The pressure to achieve in school was taken off and she was glad of a period of time in hospital when no one bothered her. Here, then, the self used the body to gain incapacity. Later, when Sandy underwent a kidney transplant at the age of 32, her body is objectified in perhaps one of the most forceful ways imaginable. She recounts the experience of coming around after surgery aware that her physicians and nurses were talking of the kidney's rejection by her body. At that point, as she puts it herself, 'everything in my mind went into the effort to make my body accept that kidney. And the only words I can put on it are just, it was sort of like, you know, "welcome" to this new kidney. You know; "'welcome' kidney, this is your body. This is your home"' (1992: 323). Her mind, then, kept her kidney in the body, something which Sandy herself believed in intensely as 'mind control'.

Bloom's (1992) analysis draws attention to a relationship between mind and body which has moved from a state of opposition (the body as constraint on the self) towards a new re-alignment via transcendence of the dualism. Between this, there lies a transitional stage in which the body and self are still distinct and distant from the unity of the healthy state, but not in opposition. The self masters the body and enables it to 'cultivate new abilities' which will ultimately result in a 'heightened harmony between body and self' (1992: 318). Arising from this is the final stage during which the body at last begins to emerge as a being in its own right – it becomes what Bloom (drawing on Gadow (1982)) refers to as the 'subject body'. As a subject, the body makes clear its own needs which are respected, in this case in the experience of skin cancer, even though, as I read it, this is far from effortless (a hallmark of the embodied state of health) since Sandy refers to the effort of making her mind and body work together in a 'finely-tuned harmony' to help her to resist cancer. Perhaps, as Williams (1996) relates, any 'negotiated settlement' is precarious, fragile and in need of constant repair work, reminding us of a point made earlier: that our relationships to our bodies, be this in health or in illness, are unlikely ever to be totally stable.

Recovery: all in the mind?

Accounts of illness often convey a privileging of mind over body or 'mind over matter'. This is evident, for example, in Pollock's (1995) interview-based study of families in the Nottingham area of England who either had no serious illness, or had a member suffering from multiple sclerosis or schizophrenia. While all of those interviewed felt that there was a reciprocal relationship between mind and body, they placed considerably more emphasis on the 'power of the mind to influence bodily processes and determine the individual's state of health than the converse' (1995: 51). Indeed, 87 per cent of respondents referred to the power of 'mind' over 'matter', a belief which for 25 per cent of these individuals was held very strongly (interestingly, half of the latter were multiple sclerosis sufferers or their spouses). Generally, the mind was felt to be the most vital aspect of the person, while the 'body as, "mere matter", was relegated to a position of secondary significance' (Pollock 1995: 52). While attitude of mind was felt to have no real role in the prevention of serious illness, it could be important for more minor conditions. As one respondent said, 'you can make yourself healthy or you can make yourself unhealthy. You can work for or against health. It's in the mind.' Mind over matter was crucial, however, in all recoveries, even from serious illness: 'I imagine it's up to the person . . . I mean, if you let yourself sort of . . . suffer, I suppose you'll suffer more than if you say "Oh, I'm not having this, I'm going to shake it off." Some people are stronger-minded than others' (respondents quoted in Pollock 1995: 53–4).

In an age of responsibilization, one is expected to 'be positive' and fight illness, not to 'give in' to it. Such beliefs may provide determination and cultivate hope. But, as Barbara Ehrenreich (2010) conveys in her evocatively titled book, *Smile or Die*, when attitude becomes a route to cure, many problems follow. Relating her own experience of breast cancer, Ehrenreich opines that, although the upbeat pink ribbon culture intends to inspire a positive outlook, it is replete with 'sticky sentiment' and infantilizes women (2010: 17). As Sulik (2012) discusses, this nurturing, empathetic and relational orientation of culture can be contrasted to the more prevalent masculine ethos of fight and struggle which finds expression, for example, in LIVESTRONG, cyclist Lance Armstrong's cancer charity. Recalling issues of masculinity and health discussed in chapter 5, Sulik opines that, while Armstrong challenges the masculine stereotype of illness denial, he also 'obscures its reality beneath heroism and an almost inhuman capacity' (2012: 83).

But whether they are targeted towards men, women or people in general, contemporary discourses of cancer survivorship are premised on a neoliberal logic of privatized risk management, whereby the 'good' subject/citizen is expected to take responsibility to manage their risks of cancer recurrence to alleviate the burden on health systems and those around them (Bell 2012). Any unhappiness needs to be apologized for and feelings of anger and fear get 'buried under a cosmetic layer of cheer'; if things do not work out, 'you did not try hard enough' (Ehrenreich 2010: 41). Drawing on his own experience, sociologist Arthur Frank conveys this simply but powerfully when he remarks, 'I have never heard an ill person praised for how well she expressed fear or grief or was openly sad. On the contrary, ill persons feel a need to apologise if they show any emotions other than laughter' (2002: 65).

Cancer support programmes encourage people to 'take charge' as individuals, by dietary change and managing their emotions, for example. Yet such lifestyle vigilance invariably leads to a sense of guilt when survivors lapse in will power or fail to live up to what counts as a 'healthy lifestyle' (Bell 2012). Also writing of her experience of cancer, American writer and civil rights activist Audre Lorde argued that the potential to link affliction to 'lifestyle choices' such as diet and cigarette smoking not only lays the ground open to fictions of unsurpassed personal responsibility, it draws attention away from environmental and other causes:

> Last week I read a letter from a doctor in a medical magazine which said that no truly happy person ever gets cancer. Despite my knowing better, and despite my having dealt with this blame-the-victim thinking for years, for a moment this letter hit my guilt button. Had I really been guilty of the crime of not being happy in this best of all possible infernos? ... The happiest person in this country cannot help breathing in smokers' cigarette fumes, auto exhaust, and airborne chemical dust.
>
> (Lorde 1980: 66–7)

Illness narratives and positive transformation

It is apparent, then, that mind over matter and its auxiliary, personal responsibility in recovery from illness, have the potential to disempower as well as to empower. They can lead to the denial of physical pain and emotional suffering and to the failure to validate what can be a wretched experience. But this does not take away from the wider need to make sense of illness and to craft a new life *with* illness.

As already remarked upon, in illness our once taken-for-granted place in society gets called into question: we are no longer who we were, we have changed from a 'well person' to a 'sick person'. Thus, recounting her own experience of sporadic LAM (lymphangioleiomyomatosis), a rare fatal lung disease, Carel explains: 'All the rules that governed my life until now have been radically broken and nothing, nothing, remained the same. I had to overhaul all my plans, expectations, goals, projects and horizons. Most importantly, I had to rethink my idea of a good life' (Carel 2008: 61). As these words suggest, coping with chronic illness commonly involves rethinking the self and re-finding one's place in society. Sociologists have identified illness narratives as a critical dimension of this process (Bury 2001; Frank 1995; Williams 1984). Bury (2001) employs the term 'moral narratives' to capture the personal evaluations that individuals use to account for altered relations between body, self and society in chronic illness. This can be observed in Gareth Williams' (1984, 1995) classic study of rheumatoid arthritis sufferers, which presents a series of contrasting narratives, including that of a 62-year-old woman whose narration emphasizes the desire not to be a burden on others. Bound up with this is her need to show that she is a responsible rather than a careless person, able, for example, to pay her debts, such as utility bills. She also wishes to make clear that, while she is aware that others may attribute any failings that they see to moral weakness rather than to 'the illness', she can work to avert this. For example, others may imply that she is 'letting herself go' or not keeping a clean and tidy house, but she can plan ahead and get things such as housework done 'now rather than later', mindful that she can never be sure when her illness will flare up. Williams concludes that this pursuit of moral virtue reveals her view of society and her place within it.

Arthur Frank, whose work has become a central point of reference on illness narratives, insists that stories do not just *describe* the experience of illness: stories *are* repair work, creating a new self out of the wreckage that illness inflicts on a life story (see, e.g., Frank 1993, 1995, 2007). He identifies three narrative types: restitution, chaos and quest (Frank 1995). Restitution narratives, the account preferred by modern medicine with its expectation that for every suffering there is a remedy, have the plot of: 'I was healthy, I am sick, I will be healthy again.' For the story-teller, there is an effort to fix what was wrong and return to the beginning 'as good as new'. Problems arise when the narrative of survival becomes unsustainable. This is painfully evident, for example, in David Rieff's account of his mother Susan Sontag's final illness. He relates that, suffering from a lethal form of blood cancer and unreconciled to mortality, his mother wanted to survive on any terms and sought out cures whose very slim odds of success she would not acknowledge, since 'she subscribed with her whole being' to the assumption 'that cures will eventually be found for most if not all diseases', including her own (Rieff 2008: 13, 62–3). Chaos narratives, by contrast, imagine a life that will never get better. They are an anti-narrative; the life of illness cannot be told, only lived. Words fail the body in an experience of 'time without sequence, telling without mediation and speaking about oneself without being fully able to reflect on oneself' (Frank 1995: 98). Finally, Frank points to quest stories of self-transformation and the offering of help to others through illness.

Through the telling of his own illness story of a heart attack and then cancer, Frank (2002) cultivates the quest story in order to foster the acceptance of illness as part of living and encourage people to talk about suffering as a route to personal and social renewal. Following Ricoeur (1991: 26), who stresses that 'the significance of a narrative stems from the intersection of the world of the text and the world of the reader' – or, we might add, listener – Frank argues that the moral genius of storytelling is as much for another as it is for oneself, as teller and listener both enter into the space of the story *for* the other. There is, then, an ethic of solidarity and commitment and of inspiration in many stories, especially where they are told in the public arena – for example, in the swelling number of published autobiographies.

Although conscious not to romanticize suffering, Frank positions the 'wounded storyteller' as a moral witness whose illness stories provide a glimpse of perfection, 're-enchanting a disenchanted world' (Frank 1995: 185). Earlier in the chapter, we considered Carel's (2008) use of the concept 'health within illness', which intends to convey the positive, *creative* experiences of personal growth, adaptation and rediscovery that occur in serious illness, such as her own. She counsels 'living in the present' or 'privileging the present' as a form of liberty, since worries of the future can be put aside. However, as these authors are aware, significant questions remain about the extent to which a culture which values health, control and personal responsibility can accommodate to such quests. As Clarke and colleagues point out, the turning of health into a social and moral obligation and 'a matter of ongoing moral self-transformation' is part of the increasing medicalization of life (2010b: 63).

Medicalization

Medicalization has moved from being a concept of marginal intellectual interest in the 1970s to a focal concern in the twenty-first century (Conrad 2013). Numerous definitions have been put forward over the years, but it in its simplest form it means 'to make medical' via the extension of medical meanings and medical control into more and more areas of daily living (Conrad 2013: 196). Although the precise origins of medicalization as a concept are hard to establish, two related intellectual developments are usually pointed to. First, during the 1970s, scholars drew attention to the turning of phenomena once seen as social deviance – such as irrational behaviour, high alcohol consumption, and disruptive behaviour in children – into medical problems, or what we now think of as mental illness, alcoholism and hyperactivity/ADHD (Conrad 1975; Foucault 1965; Szasz 1971). Second, there was marked criticism of the extension of medical control into ever more domains of social life and the related tendency to seek solutions for social problems by technical means (such as pharmacologies) at the individual level (Zola 1972) to the neglect of the socio-political causes of illness. Although, initially, deliberations on medicalization were 'gender neutral' (Riska 2003), they occurred around the same time that feminists were criticizing male medical control over women's bodies, especially in the domains of mental health, gynaecology and childbirth (e.g. Arms 1975; Ehrenreich and English 1978; see also chapter 3). Argument over the problematic consequences of medicalization also drew on the critiques of medical professional dominance, discussed in chapter 8, that also were prevalent at the time. Indeed, as Rose (2007b) points out, medicalization critiques can be seen as part of the deprofessionalization of medicine.

In the ensuing years, interest in medicalization has grown exponentially (Conrad 2007) and attention has shifted away from the medical profession and the expansion of medical social control as key drivers, to focus on the roles of biotechnology (particularly the pharmaceutical industry and genetics) and consumers (Bell and Figert 2012; Conrad 2004, 2013). Clarke and colleagues assess that, by around the mid-1980s, biotechnology was of sufficient importance to necessitate the replacement of medicalization with the new concept of *biomedicalization* (Clarke and Shim 2011; Clarke et al. 2010a). They argue that, while medicalization processes typically emphasize *control over* medical phenomena, such as diseases, injuries and bodily malfunctions, biomedicalization processes emphasize *transformations of* bodies and lives. This occurs through technoscientific interventions targeted not only at treatment but also at the detection of 'at-risk' groups and individuals and bodily enhancement of the healthy. This reminds us of issues discussed in chapter 1, namely, the 'new ontology of life' taking place at the molecular level of the body (Rose 2007a) and the 'yield of vitality produced by the biotechnical reformulation of living processes' (Waldby 2002: 310). The argument of Clarke and colleagues then is that we need to give more attention than hitherto has been the case to the biopolitical economy and to enhancements/optimization (Clarke et al. 2010a). The second way in which discussions of medicalization have shifted away from medical control is in the role now accorded to the consumer. The activity of individuals or social groups in seeking out medical diagnoses, treatments and bodily enhancements can be conceptualized as 'medicalization from below' (Conrad 2013; Furedi 2006). This has been nurtured by the explosion of direct-to-consumer (DTC) (i.e. bypassing the physician) advertising of drugs such as Viagra (for erectile problems) and Paxil (for anxiety and 'social phobia') on television, at various venues (such as sports events) and on public transport (in the US and New Zealand), and in the emergence of online pharmacies (Miah and Rich 2008). The significance of such developments has prompted some commentators to employ the relatively new concept 'pharmaceuticalization' as a subset of, or existing alongside, medicalization (see, e.g., Abraham 2010; Bell and Figert 2012; Conrad 2013).

The complexity of medicalization

Medicalization can have positive consequences, such as the lessening of stigma by the bestowing of more morally neutral medical labels upon socially shameful symptoms – for example, 'mental illness' rather than 'madness'. But, since medicalization tends also to bring about the disempowerment of the individual (though they may not see it this way themselves) and the depoliticization of social problems of living (Nye 2003), it is mainly construed as negative. To take two examples, when weight is medicalized via BMI (and the label of obesity), attention is upon the individual who needs to be 'fixed' by, for example, weight loss programmes or gastric bypass surgery, rather than on the fast-food industry. The diagnostic category of 'body-dysmorphic disorder' or BDD has re-emerged recently as an official psychiatric disorder amongst those defined as 'surgery addicts', most often women. This attributes the decision to undergo cosmetic surgery to psychic pain and legitimates surgery as a means to ameliorate suffering (Pitts-Taylor 2007), overlooking idealization of certain kinds of bodies and the normalizing power of medical treatments.

Medicalization is often depicted as a product of modernity, an 'inexorable juggernaut' (Davis 2010: 231) moving in one direction towards increasing medical control. Yet, phenomena which once were medicalized have also been *de*-medicalized, the most often-cited example being homosexuality which was declassified as an illness by the American Psychiatric Association in the 1970s. Medicalization and de-medicalization may also co-exist, as in the arena of childbirth. Rates of elective surgical Caesarean births have soared in a number of countries around the world over the last decade or so – to reach 26 per cent of all births across OECD countries and 47 per cent in Brazil (OECD 2011) – due to a combination of women's fear of perineal damage (affecting urinary and sexual functioning) and the influence of celebrities deemed 'too posh to push', and obstetricians' defensive practices for fear of being sued for failing to perform a Caesarean should something 'go wrong' during labour (Minkoff 2012). Yet, equally, many women resist medical birth, seeking out natural birth experiences that are as far as possible freed from medical intervention, and others navigate the difficult terrain *between* 'medical' and 'natural' birth (Annandale 2009).

Hence, medicalization is a more complex process than might appear at first glance, being elastic, multidirectional, both accepted and resisted, and, as Conrad (2103) has put it, in itself not normative – either good or bad – but morally neutral. This complexity can be further highlighted with two examples: biomedical enhancement of the body (taking the example of children's bodies) and the pharmaceuticalization of sexuality. Chapter 2 drew attention to the surgical shaping of women's feet so that they fit and look good in expensive designer shoes (Frank 2004). It was pointed out that such actions can be seen as part of new emerging 'relations between capital and work, bodies and the state, citizenship and social and medical inclusion (and exclusion)' (Scheper-Hughes 2001a: 43). Although it is some distance from the shaping of feet to fit shoes, Frank relates that the same basic equation applies to the surgical shaping of children: 'if the body does not fit, reshape it' (2004: 23). He deliberates on the example of limb-lengthening surgery for congenital achondroplasia (a form of short-limb dwarfism) which involves breaking the bones of the arms and/or legs and inserting a pin to increase bone length by pulling the two parts apart to prevent healing and promote the growth of new bone. This is part of what Rose (2007a) refers to as 'optimisation': seeking to secure the best possible personal future by the use of biomedical transformations of various kinds (surgical, pharmacological, genetic) designed to improve human form or functioning beyond what is necessary to sustain or restore health (Conrad 2007). Also exploring stature, Conrad (2007) considers the off-label administration of synthetic human growth hormone (hGH) to children with idiopathic short stature in the US. As he explains, virtually all human populations contain a range of heights, but because height is imbued with social meanings, not all heights are considered equal, with taller people seen as more attractive and commanding higher salaries in many societies. Under such circumstances, it is perhaps not surprising that parents see 'normal shortness' as a disadvantage that might be medically ameliorated by hGH. The question of how we should interpret limb-lengthening and the administration of hGH highlights the complexity of medicalization referred to above. As Frank contemplates, is it democratic humanism – 'the best chance for people who have been allocated low physical capital to get back onto as level a playing field as possible'? Or is it a more problematic normalization, 'fitting the body to the demands of society rather than calling on society to create accommodations for different bodies'? (2004: 23).

Sildenafil citrate, commonly known as Viagra, was developed initially for the treatment of erectile problems associated with conditions such as diabetes and some cancers. But it was soon marketed much more widely, promoting 'erectile problems' to the public as a new medical category. For example, by inviting viewers to 'ask your doctor if Viagra is right for you', Pfizer's DTC television advertisement in the US encouraged every man to consider himself as having an erectile or sexual problem that could be solved by a drug (Conrad 2007). Sexologist Leonore Tiefer (2006) argues that Viagra illustrates both the medicalization and the demedicalization of sexuality. On the one hand, it helps to define sexuality as a medical problem. On the other, as part of evolving consumerist and Internet technologies of sexual recreation and self-determination for privileged men and women of the *Sex and the City* (after the US television series) and baby-boom 'you can have it all' and 'positive ageing' generations, it has contributed to the demedicalization and 'recreationalization' of sexuality. The medicalization of reproductive processes has mainly affected women. But the wider re-conceptualization of masculinity as vulnerable and a risk to health and well-being (discussed in chapter 5) facilitates the marketing of Viagra as 'masculinity in a pill' (Loe 2006), and the 'Viagracization' of men's health highlights endeavours to restore what is conceived as the natural sexual capacity of the male body by medical means (Riska 2003).

Situating medicalization globally

Pointing to the role of the Internet, the global pharmaceutical industry's search for new markets, and the diffusion of Western biomedicine, Conrad remarks that 'medicalisation is going global' (2013: 210). However, since the conceptualizations of bio/medicalization that presently frame debate emerged out of a particular Western geopolitical context, they are not easily translatable. Clarke (2010) advises that none of the three patterns of the rise of *biomedicine, medicalization* (medical control over phenomena) and *biomedicalization* (transformations of bodies and lives) may be relevant beyond the West (or even outside the US where they primarily have been developed). Since practices of public health are increasingly reliant on high-tech biomedicine, concepts such as the 'biomedicalisation of public health' (Clarke 2010) or the 'pharmaceuticalisation of public health' (Bell and Figert 2012) may prove more useful in the global South. Bell and Figert exemplify this by drawing on Biehl's (2006) analysis of Brazil's AIDS Programme which combines free antiretroviral therapies alongside safe-sex prevention and harm reduction programmes. While this programme has been very successful in reducing mortality and improving quality of life, the right to health has become coterminous with the right to treatment with pharmaceuticals. Thus, by forefronting AIDS as the national problem, Brazil 'created a captive market for the pharmaceutical industry' now and into the future (Bell and Figert 2012: 781). Recalling the above discussion of the complexity and multidirectionality of medicalization, this highlights how pharmaceuticalization of public health is both a strategy of health improvement for individuals and an exercise of power by global interests in resource-poor nations (Bell and Figert 2012). This also draws our attention to the contradictory and unpredictable effects of globalization raised in chapter 2. Thus Clarke conveys that 'the localization of biomedical innovation is everywhere tempered and complicated by medical pluralisms, partialisms [the partial and contingent availability of various medicines], and multiple forms and loci of stratification' (2010: 389). Hence, medicalization is, as she puts it, often highly stratified, as assorted medical goods and procedures are targeted at different categories of persons, groups and populations in various parts of the world.

The sociology of diagnosis and contested illnesses

Some years ago, Brown (1990) coined the term 'the sociology of diagnosis', primarily with reference to the field of psychiatry and the faith in *DSM* (the *Diagnostic and Statistical Manual of Mental Disorders* (the fifth edition of which is due to be published as this book goes to press)). He points out that diagnosis is often an arena of struggle, the location where professionals and lay people 'fight over the roles of functions of illness' (1990: 402). Although there is no designated sociology of diagnosis, diagnosis is central to the sociology of health and medicine, playing a part, for example, in research on doctor–patient interaction and on illness experience. Since it establishes the authoritative position of medicine in society in affixing diagnostic labels, it also underpins discussions of medicalization (Jutel 2011; Jutel and Nettleton 2011).

Given that diagnostic categories help us interpret what we are experiencing, the absence of a diagnosis – or the medically unexplained – can be a problem. Contested illnesses, those 'dismissed as illegitimate – framed as "difficult", psychosomatic, or even non-existent – by researchers, health practitioners, and policy makers operating within conventional paradigms of knowledge' (Moss and

Teghtsoonian 2008: 7), bear an interesting relationship to medicalization. As Conrad and Stults (2008) put it, most scholarly concern has
been focused on *over*medicalization. Contestation can fall into this
category – for example, in resistance of diagnostic categories, such
as homosexuality as a disease; in advocating non-medical definitions of disability; and in challenging narrowly medical definitions
of conditions such as anorexia and mental illness. However, much of
the concern around contested illness exhibits a desire for *more* rather
than less medicalization (Conrad and Stults 2008). Examples of this
are legion, stretch back in time, and include, for example, Chronic
Fatigue Syndrome, Fibromyalgia, Repetitive Strain Injury and Gulf
War Syndrome.

In a discussion of Chronic Fatigue Syndrome and Multiple Chemical
Sensitivity, Dumit refers to these and other contested syndromes as
'illnesses you have to fight to get' (2006: 578) because they have no
known pathological basis, but debilitating symptoms. Focusing on
how illnesses are experienced in the US – where, as we saw in chapter
7, unless paying directly out of their pocket, most patients have needed
to obtain private insurance paid for either by their employers or by
themselves to cover their care – Dumit (2006: 578) allocates five characteristics to contested illnesses:

- They are chronic conditions which, like other chronic illnesses,
  pose problems for determining the costs of care.
- They are 'biomental'. Whether they are primarily mental, psychiatric, or biological in origin is contested.
- They are therapeutically diverse, which means that they are open
  to a wider range of therapeutic options, including complementary
  and alternative medicine.
- They have 'fuzzy boundaries', being 'crosslinked to other emergent
  illnesses as subsets, mistaken diagnosis, and comorbid conditions'.
- They are often caught up in legal and court battles, making them
  'legally explosive'.

Because the American biomedical system 'demands disease categories before [financial] compensation, and diagnosis before treatment',
individuals are denied care because they cannot legitimately enter
the sick role (see chapter 1) (Dumit 2006: 579). Of course, this point
applies beyond the US. For example, Lippel explores the medico-legal
controversies surrounding worker compensation for musculoskeletal
disorders, Fibromyalgia and Multiple Chemical Sensitivity in Quebec.
The worker's body becomes a 'nexus of contestation' for lawyers,
compensation boards and medical examiners (Lippel 2006: 48). Since
individuals are rarely granted the permission to be ill in the absence of
medically classified disease (Nettleton 2006), legitimacy strikes to the

core of contested illness. Nettleton (2006) has analysed what this means for individuals experiencing medically unexplained neurological symptoms. As she explains, since contested illnesses are, by definition, difficult to diagnose, patients often undergo extensive tests in order to try to ascertain the cause of their symptoms. A very uncomfortable uncertainty characterizes their experience, which is overlain with an enduring concern with legitimacy. Thus her respondents (outpatients at an English hospital) were not only highly concerned about being seen by others as a 'fake', 'fraud' or 'hypochondriac', but also began to ask themselves if they were 'just imagining it'.

Contested illnesses of the kind referred to so far often gain legitimate diagnostic labels through collective action of sufferers who meet face-to-face or online. Brown and colleagues characterize social movements which mobilize the collective experience of illness and provide a 'source of solidarity, motivation, and urgency' as 'embodied health movements' (Brown et al. 2012a: 16). As Beck (1992) initially argued, a questioning 'risk society' throws up numerous issue-based political and social alliances and coalitions, and health social movements are a part of this. They typically combine an emphasis on the emotional, lived-experience of illness with an appeal to medical science, which may also involve citizen–science alliances (Brown et al. 2012a). Some of the most visible embodied health movements have been around contested environmental illnesses, particularly those caused by pollutants such as those used in the petrochemical industries. Brown and colleagues explore Gulf War-related illness, which they dub a contested illness *par excellence*. In 2008, after protracted petitioning for over fifteen years, a US government Research Advisory Committee Report concluded, from scientific evidence, that Gulf War illness is a real condition, with 'real causes and serious consequences for affected veterans' (quoted in Brown et al. 2012b: 79). Symptoms reported by sufferers include nausea, loss of concentration, fatigue, irritable bowels and lack of muscle control, none of which they experienced prior to military service in the Gulf, during 1990 and 1991. Brown and co-authors detail the struggle that individuals faced in the absence of a diagnosis, such as denial of service-related disability compensation. Angered by their treatment, veterans began to speak out and join together, which led to some success in the award of benefits. Growing claims in the 1990s led the Department of Defense and Department of Health and Human Services to investigate the possible cause of the illness in various chemical compounds such as sarin gas, pesticides and anthrax vaccines. But much research was also directed at stress and psychological conditions, rather than markers for multisymptom illness, and environmental exposure was denied. Only when, after a long-drawn-out process, veterans were finally found to have been exposed to a range of chemicals, was the syndrome legitimized.

Patients-in waiting: genetic testing and screening for disease

Recent deliberations on screening and genetic testing bring together two of the overarching themes we have considered so far in the chapter, namely, biomedicalization and the responsibilization of life. It will be recalled that responsibilization refers to personalized risk-surveillance of the body to maintain health and avoid illness. Furedi (2002, 2005), whose argument we touched upon in chapter 2, maintains that illness has become normalized; we are all now seen as being *potentially* ill, that is the default state we live in today. He detects this in the notion of wellness, particularly in the need to work to keep well, the underlying message being that if you fail to do this you will revert to being ill. In this context, population-based medical screening (such as cervical screening) to uncover illness or individual genetic screening to detect susceptibility to illness (such as the 'breast cancer genes' BRCA1/2) ostensibly provide the information that the individual should *want* to know.

Armstrong (2012) explains that when screening programmes first appeared they were directed towards diseases which threatened others, such as tuberculosis and venereal disease. Population screening involves doctors and scientists searching out unknown or hidden disease in the population. Newborn phenylketonuria (PKU) screening is an example of this. As chronic illnesses became the major concern in the West, screening became more opportunistic, with health professionals undertaking periodic health-checks (such as weight, blood pressure) when patients visit their clinics. As Armstrong (2012) points out, this enables the recruitment of patients into their own risk-factor management. Rose conveys the significance of this in relation to genetic testing:

> The 'responsible citizen' has the obligation to know and to manage his or her life of susceptibilities – a kind of permanent management of genomic uncertainties . . . What is significant is the emergence of the very idea that the diagnosis of a condition – by means of genomic screening or other tests – that has not yet revealed itself in the actual life of the patient leads to a demand, perhaps even an obligation, for some kind of preventative intervention in relation to it.
>
> Rose (2007c: 147. 149)

Screening and testing involve the creation of new subjectivities, such as the 'at-risk' person or the 'patient-in-waiting'. A range of research shows that 'preventative' technologies, epitomized in health screening – for example, mammography for breast cancer, blood tests for prostate cancer, amniocentesis for foetal chromosomal abnormalities, and genetic screening for a range of diseases – are as likely to provoke as they are to close off risk. Tests which, on the face of it, provide the 'gift of knowing' (Kenen 1996), and the hope of a cure for a disease that might be detected, bring predicaments of their own, such as the liminal state into which potential patients are put as they await their test results (Lupton 2012).

While knowing the outcome of a test can be a relief from uncertainty, when there is little hope in the way of therapy knowing can foster guilt and a sense of hopelessness. It is important to be aware that, while genetic tests can confirm the diagnosis or detect some conditions, such as cystic fibrosis or Huntington's Disease, for others, such as breast cancer, colon cancer, they are only ever probabilistic. In addition, it is crucial to appreciate that genetic tests are just that: tests, not treatments. Thus, for example, while Huntington's Disease can be detected, there is no cure for it. For some other conditions such as genetic breast cancers, treatments are available but there are difficult choices to be made in relation to them. Further still, although PKU screening of newborn babies detects rare genetic symptoms before they develop, it may be unclear not only whether a disease may develop, but what the condition actually is (Timmermans and Buchbinder 2010, 2012, 2013). In other words, while genetic testing and screening generally raise common issues such as responsibilization, the dilemmas that arise for individuals and families vary considerably according to the condition concerned. In what follows, we will look at the example of genetic breast and ovarian cancer testing.

The mutation of the BRCA1/2 genes (breast cancer susceptibility genes 1 and 2), which are known as tumour suppressors, has been linked to hereditary breast cancer and ovarian cancer. They were discovered in the mid-1990s. Although rarer, breast cancer affects men as well as women and there is some evidence that they may struggle with a diagnosis of what is commonly viewed as a 'woman's disease' (Williams et al. 2003). There is an increased lifetime risk of developing breast and/or ovarian cancer in families with multiple cases and in women with an Ashkenazi (Central European and East European) Jewish background, though it should be noted that most breast cancers are *not* genetic. The presence of the BRCA1/2 genes is detected by a blood test. Not every person who has the BRCA1/2 mutation will develop breast or ovarian cancer, though the risk of doing so is higher than for those who do not have the mutation. So what, for example, should a young woman found to be at 'high risk' do? While, on the one hand, we might consider that she now has the knowledge to prevent an untimely death, she will never really know in any absolute sense that that is her fate. She could decide to 'wait and watch' and try to reduce the publicized risk factors (by, for example, lowering her dietary fat and alcohol intake). She could opt for chemoprevention by taking the drug generically known as tamoxifen, if she has access to it. She could opt for prophylactic mastectomy and perhaps also oophorectomy (removal of the ovaries) with all of the longer-term implications for reproductive capacity. The overall point is that she is impelled to decide: the option of not being tested at all carries the sanction of lack of personal responsibility (and maybe also of fortitude). For, after all, don't we 'want to know'? Returning briefly to pharmaceuticalization, several authors have pointed out that tamoxifen is marketed not to treat breast cancer, but to treat breast cancer *risk*. It is argued that this draws attention away from risk-reduction activities such as the elimination of cancer-causing agents (Fosket 2010; Klawiter 2008).

Researchers have pointed to the potential 'geneticization' or genetic prism (Lippman 1992) through which family and kinship relations have been viewed following the explosion of medical genetic testing since the 1980s. As Horstman and Kinkler (2011) sum up, the effects of testing for genetic diseases that run in families are complex and variable; if family members are constructed as a risk factor for diseases, it may cause conflict and tensions, but equally it may strengthen and reunite families. A number of researchers have explored the potential for genetic testing to medicalize families as kinship relations are, as Finkler and colleagues put it, 'given a new dimension that stresses faulty genes, rather than social status, position or even poverty' in the transmission of health risk (Finkler et al. 2003). As they cogently put it, while a person might sever their ties with what Giddens (1991) refers to as 'toxic parents', 'one cannot declare independence from one's genetic parents' (Finkler et al. 2003: 406). When the family is medicalized, the family as a whole, rather than just the individual, have the potential to become the patient, which brings ethical challenges in its wake. Returning to our prior example, if an individual wishes to know her genetic risk of breast cancer, at least one female relative will need to have been or be willing to be tested. If one family member gains knowledge of their risk, do others have a right to know, a right *not* to know? As Finkler and colleagues point out, in this context the 'autonomous individual recedes into the background' (2003: 411).

An issue inciting some concern in recent years is preimplantation genetic diagnosis (PGD). Returning to breast cancer, in 2006 the UK Human Fertilization and Embryology Authority (HFEA) ruled that women carrying the BRCA1/2 genes could use PGD to avoid giving birth to a baby carrying the genes. As, amongst others, Lock and Nguyen (2010) relate, this has raised concerns about the production of so-called 'designer babies'. Prenatal genetic screening has been available for some time now. In chapter 2, for example, we looked at Katz Rothman's (1988) concerns about the 'tentative pregnancy' created by amniocentesis for the diagnosis of Down's Syndrome. But Lock and Nguyen (2010) suggest that the HFEA change adds a whole new dimension, as PGD permits physicians and their patients to select out 'good' embryos for implantation, and leave 'bad' ones in storage or donate them for research. The potential role of epigenetics – changes in gene expression as the body interacts with its environment – is overlooked as attention is directed only to the individual, or potential individual. Ettorre draws attention to 'broken bodies' as new strategies of control are practised on pregnant women, whose bodies are regulated to behave in biomedically approved ways. She argues that reproductive genetics is a disciplinary process which focuses on the replication of 'bodies which must exemplify completeness (i.e. organs, limbs, torsos, crania filled with brains etc.), health, and well-being, individual potential and future welfare' (2002: 3).

Who gets treated and why?

In their depictions of biomedicalization, Clarke and colleagues (2010c) highlight doctor–patient interactions as often fraught and complicated by regulations and limitations of financial coverage for care. Moreover, as the preceding discussion of PGD signals, increasingly bioethical and moral concerns are also to the fore of clinical practice. At the start of the chapter we reflected on George Bernard Shaw's play *The Doctor's Dilemma* (Shaw 1980 [1911]). As we saw, the eponymous doctor's dilemma is a moral one of whom to treat when resources – in this case, a tuberculosis vaccine – are short. Shaw's play also vividly highlights the moral decisions that underlie medical practice, despite its claim to be an 'objective science'. Sensitive to the pleadings of a pretty young wife for her 23-year-old artist husband, Shaw's doctors put him on the list in preference to another, believing that he is a 'worthy case'. The twist in the tale comes, however, when they find out that the artist not only is a bigamist, but also has swindled each of the doctors out of a sum of money. Realizing not only this, but also that one of their own, an impoverished GP who has been devoted to the care of his patients, the London poor, for many years, also needs 'the cure', they pass the artist on to another doctor who kills him in the course of treatment. The mismatch between demand for care and resources means that the question of 'whom to treat' is still very much with us today, worldwide. And, as much as we might like to believe that the kind of care that people receive is based solely on clinical need, there is ample evidence that social and personal characteristics continue to play a role, in spite of attempts to avoid this.

In his fable of future healthcare regulation in America, Annas (1995) accentuates many of the controversies that surround the rationing of care. In this future time, if people want to buy an artificial heart they need a permit from the 'US National Health Agency' which picks people at random from a computer-generated list. In his tale, this scheme is challenged by a thoracic surgeon and two of her patients – one of whom is in need but does not qualify, being only 15 years old, and the other qualifies, but has not yet been picked. The fictional plaintiffs argue through the courts that the allocation mechanism is not rational since it is not related to need and because it violates the Fifth Amendment right to equal protection. A review of data collected during 2018 reveals that 50 per cent of applicants were rejected by the Agency. Fully 90 per cent of these were rejected on the basis of being incapable of ten additional years of life or because of chronic alcoholism or drug addiction. Additionally, 98 per cent of people whose IQ was less than 80 were rejected, as were: 80 per cent of those who had a history of mental illness, 75 per cent with a criminal record, 80 per cent of indigents, and 70 per cent of the unemployed.

In Britain, the NHS was set up in 1948 to be a comprehensive service which, according to the Beveridge Report which preceded it, 'would ensure that for every citizen there is available whatever medical treatment he [*sic*] requires in whatever form he requires it' (Beveridge 1942). As we saw in chapter 7, although it is possible to argue that healthcare is underfunded, there are reasons to believe that resources will never match demand, not only because of an ageing population, more chronic long-term illnesses, and advances in medical science, but also because of rising expectations of health and what medical care can deliver (Newdick 2005). Although healthcare rationing has always happened, it has only in recent years become a subject of more open discussion amongst policy makers and the public in a number of countries. To take the UK as an example, in 1999 the government set up the National Institute of Clinical Excellence, or NICE (recently retitled the National Institute for Health and Care Excellence). Amongst its objectives are to assess the evidence for particular medicines and medical procedures and through this to support 'evidence based medicine' (EBM) and evidence based practice, and to assess the effectiveness of certain kinds of care and procedures to rule them in or out for NHS care. The document *Social Value Judgements: Principles for the Development of NICE Guidelines* (NICE 2008: 23) outlines the judgements that NICE and its advisory bodies are expected to apply when making decisions about the effectiveness and cost-effectiveness of interventions. It details that equality legislation requires that patients should not be denied access to care because of factors such as their race, age, disability, sex/gender, sexual orientation, religion, beliefs, socio-economic status or lifestyle. Yet it also contains a proviso: 'if the behaviour is likely to continue and can make a treatment less clinically effective or cost effective then it may be appropriate to take this into account' (NICE 2008: 25).

This signals that the allocation of healthcare may not be based solely on clinical need. Neither, as a number of authors, such as Nurok and Henckes, have shown, is the way that medical decisions are made always based on objective clinical assessment. Rather, it is 'a socially complex process implicating a variety of actors in varying time frames within specific social and cultural contexts' (Nurok and Henckes 2009: 504). Thus, implicit rationing occurs in the social judgements about patients that physicians, nurses and other healthcare providers make every day in the course of their work. We can return again to obesity to explore how so-called 'lifestyle' factors can come into play. As we have seen elsewhere in the book, obesity is estimated to cost health systems in several countries, such as the UK and US, billions of pounds and dollars. The media in the UK have been replete with dialogue over the costs of 'heavy-duty ambulances' to transport the 'obese', and on issues such as whether the 'obese' should be offered gastric bypass surgery, hip and knee replacements on the NHS, in recent years. More often than not, in both the popular and medical press, discourse over 'lifestyle-related illnesses' assumes that they are simply the fault of the individual. But, although high calorific intake and lack of exercise are contributory factors, genetic background, maternal weight and socio-economic status are also important. The association with class raises the question of whether rationing by 'lifestyle' is also hidden rationing by class (Feiring 2008) and presumed social value.

While it is possible to discern associations at the population level, it is far harder to detect any connections between social valuation and decisions about care at the level of the care of individual patients. In their analysis of talk in eighteen cardiac catheterization conferences (covering 130 patients) in one large British teaching hospital during 1989–90, Hughes and Griffiths (1996) studied how cardiologists present cases to the cardiac surgeon who will make the judgement of whether to take the patient on for surgery or angioplasty. Of particular interest was the tension that could arise when physicians moved between a more technical discourse related to the coronary anatomy and feasibility of surgery and a social discourse which refers to age, lifestyle and other social structural factors. It is through this dialogue that physicians engage with a wider rationing debate that draws on notions of deservingness. Physicians in Hughes and Griffith's study stressed that technical suitability was their main concern, and, indeed, the authors found that this was to the fore when patient histories were presented. Thus, as angiograms were reviewed, attention was on the extent of narrowing of the coronary arteries, the state of the heart muscle supplied by the diseased artery, and whether the artery was suitable for grafting. But technical feasibility did not mean that the surgery would necessarily take place since longer-term risks and prognosis also came into play, and this was where correlates of risk such as age could be drawn upon, even if implicitly. There was evidence, for example, that the surgeon prioritized younger patients, since the average age for those designated 'urgent' on the waiting list was 48.2, while for those who were designated 'routine', it was 59.7 years, and for those 'on hold', 61.5 years.

As we saw in chapter 5, patient gender has long been associated with the kind of care received (Riska 2012; Welch et al. 2012). An area of sustained attention in recent years has been treatment for heart disease, and especially the question of whether gender expectations on the part of practitioners negatively impact on quality of care for women. Using the innovative method of video-vignettes, Arber and colleagues (2006) asked a sample of physicians in the US and UK to view scripted consultations where professional actors played the part of patients presenting with standard symptoms of CHD. They presented to the watching doctor seven signs and symptoms strongly suggestive of CHD, including chest pressure, elevated blood pressure, and pain through the back between the shoulder blades. The videos were identical apart from the characteristics of the actor-patient. After they had watched the video of the patient explaining their symptoms, the doctors were asked a number of questions, such as: Would you ask any additional questions? Would you conduct a physical examination? What are the possible diagnoses? What diagnostic tests would you do? What prescriptions would you advise? What advice would you give to the patient? Would you make any specialist referral? Would you want to see patient again (Arber et al. 2006: 107)? From the research they found that there was no influence of the social class or 'race' of the patient on the doctors' decision and no evidence of ageism. However, women 'patients' were asked fewer questions, received fewer examinations, fewer diagnostic tests and were prescribed the least medication appropriate for CHD. There was also evidence of 'gendered ageism' in that mid-life women were asked fewest questions and prescribed the least medication.

It has been known for some time now that moral evaluations of patients can impact on quality of patient care. Reflecting back on his research in the 1950s, Howard Becker (1993) relates that he found that US physicians in training disliked patients with nebulous complaints who took up their time, otherwise known as 'crocks'. The large body of research on doctor–patient interaction has demonstrated that personal judgements by physicians (and to a lesser extent other practitioners) impact significantly upon their decision-making. Issues of gender (moral evaluations of appropriate femininity, for example), social class, 'race', and age all influence clinical decision-making (see Clark et al. 1991). Some years after Becker's work, in the late 1970s, Roger Jeffery looked at characterizations of 'good' and 'bad' patients by staff working in three English Accident and Emergency (A&E) Departments (Casualty). A&E is unusual in terms of tertiary care, because patients are free to access the service on their own initiative (rather than relying on a gatekeeper). The result is a wider range of presenting patients and presenting conditions. The following dialogue between doctors and medical students gives a flavour of who 'bad patients' were:

> 'If there's anything interesting we'll stop, but there's a lot of rubbish this morning'
> 'We have the usual rubbish, but also a subdural haemorrhage'
> 'On nights [night shifts] you get some drunken dross in, but also some good cases'
>
> (Jeffery 1979: 92)

'Bad patients' were sub-classified as 'trivia', such as someone who has had a pain for three weeks, but gets the doctor out of bed in A&E at three o'clock in the morning; drunks; overdoses (often seen as attention seekers and typically women); and 'tramps' seen as just looking for a bed for the night. While social judgements such as these helped to define 'bad patients', 'good patients' were described almost entirely in terms of their medical characteristics, such as their symptoms or cause of their injury. More specifically, good patients were so designated because they allowed the junior doctors who populate A&E to practise the skills needed to pass their exams; to practise the skills of their chosen specialism, such as surgery; and because they generally stretched and challenged them. 'Bad patients' could suffer from poor-quality care, such as being kept waiting, being shut off in separate rooms, and generally from lack of sympathy and occasional verbal hostility. Since Jeffery's study was conducted some years ago now, questions might reasonably be asked about whether these attitudes are a relic of the past? The research by Nurok and Henckes (2009) on social value judgements of patients by paramedics in Paris and New York, referred to in chapter 1 (in the discussion of 'scientific neutrality'), suggests not. It will be recalled that the paramedics are called to a patient living in a New York housing project known to have many patients with HIV/AIDs. First, the paramedics make a judgement of low social value and show little interest in the patient. However, when they arrive on the scene, they see that the patient is in a severely ill state and they can do something to treat her. Yet when she has been treated, they again fail to show sympathy as they turn again to her characteristic as a drug overdose, which devalues her.

Conclusions

The theme that has run through this chapter has been the emphasis that is now placed upon individual choices about health, such as what treatment to opt for, and the moral responsibility actually to make those choices, and the consequences that follow. In the course of the discussion, we have observed the compulsion to make sense of illness in terms of one's own place in the world that places a premium on personal control and responsibility. This ethos can cultivate a sense of empowerment. But, conversely, subjugation can result from the inability actually to do anything to alter one's circumstances. Thus the drive to present oneself as healthy in the face of sometimes quite severe illness can be disempowering for the individual. Far from cultivating a sense of agency, the result can be despair. In the healthcare context, there is an impulsion to seek information and to make choices. Yet the ability of the patient to do this is very much circumscribed by the highly politicized nature of the healthcare milieu. Of course, the degree to which these tensions are felt by any one individual will vary enormously according to the illness concerned and the personal circumstances involved. The concerns discussed are not new to this age, but they are now arguably more tenacious and wounding. For this reason, the tension between reflexivity and the imperative of choice in illness might be viewed as a trope for the contemporary social condition.

Notes

1 Enduring theoretical legacies

1 Preamble to the Constitution of the World Health Organisation as adopted by the International Health Conference, New York, 19–22 June 1946; signed on 22 July 1946 by the representatives of 61 States (Official Records of the World Health Organisation, no. 2, p. 100) and entered into force on 7 April 1948, www.who.int/about/definition/en/print.html (accessed 9 January 2014).

3 Feminism, gender theories and health

1 There is no authoritative text of Sojourner Truth's 1851 speech, but similar versions can be found on various websites such as www.sojournertruth.org/ (accessed 15 January 2014).

4 Socio-economic inequalities in health

1 Age-standardization makes allowance for the differences in the age structure of a population.
2 The G-20 is the group of twenty Finance Ministers and Central Bank governors established in 1999 in the wake of the financial crisis of the late 1990s.
3 Prozac (fluoxitine hydrochloride) is a widely prescribed antidepressant drug.

5 Gender inequalities in health

1 The poverty groups were 'formed by ranking local authority districts according to poverty and grouping them into 10ths of equal population size on the basis of this ranking" (Shaw et al. 2005: 1019).

References

Abbott, Andrew (1988) *The System of Professions*. Chicago, University of Chicago Press.

Abraham, John (2010) Pharmaceuticalization of society in context: theoretical, empirical and health dimensions. *Sociology* **44** (4), 603–22.

Acheson Report (1998) *Independent Inquiry into Inequalities in Health*. London, Stationery Office.

Acker, Joan (2006) *Class Questions: Feminist Answers*. Oxford, Rowman and Littlefield.

Adelson, Naomi (1998) Health beliefs and the politics of Cree well-being. *Health* **2** (1), 5–22.

Ahmad, Waqar (1993) Making black people sick: 'race' and health in health research. In: Ahmad Waqar (ed.) *'Race' and Health in Contemporary Britain*. Buckingham, Open University Press, pp. 11–33.

Ahmad, Waqar (1996) The trouble with culture. In: David Kelleher and Sheila Hillier (eds.) *Researching Cultural Differences in Health*. London, Routledge, pp. 190–219.

Ahmad, Waqar and Bradby, Hannah (2007) Locating ethnicity and health: exploring concepts and contexts. *Sociology of Health and Illness* **29** (6), 795–810.

AIHW (Australian Institute of Health and Welfare) (2006) *Australia's Health 2006*. Canberra, AIHW.

AIHW (Australian Institute of Health and Welfare) (2008) *Australia's Health 2008*. Canberra, AIHW.

AIHW (Australian Institute of Health and Welfare) (2010) *Australia's Health 2010*. Canberra, AIHW.

Alcock, Pete (2006) *Understanding Poverty*, 3rd edn. Basingstoke, Palgrave.

Allen, Davina (2001) *The Changing Shape of Nursing Practice*. London, Routledge.

Allen, Pauline, Bartlett, Will, Perotin, Virginie, Zamora, Bernarda and Turner, Simon (2011) New forms of provider in the English National Health Service. *Annals of Public and Cooperative Economics* **82** (1), 77–95.

Allett, John (2001) Bernard Shaw, The Doctor's Dilemma: scarcity, socialism and the sanctity of life. *The Journal of Value Enquiry* **35**(2), 227–45.

Allsop, Judith (2006) Medical dominance in a changing world: the UK case. *Health Sociology Review* **15** (5), 444–57.

Altman, Stuart and Shactman, David (2011) *Power, Politics, and Universal Health Care*. New York, Prometheus Books.

American Society for Aesthetic Plastic Surgery (2012) *15th Annual Cosmetic Surgery National Data Bank Statistics*. www.surgery.org/sites/default/files/ASAPS-2011-Stats.pdf (accessed 30 January 2014).

Andrews, Ahmed and Jewson, Nick (1993) Ethnicity and infant deaths: the implications of recent statistical evidence for materialist explanations. *Sociology of Health & Illness* **15**(2), 137–56.

Annals of Internal Medicine (2002) Medical professionalism in the new millennium: a physician charter. *Annals of Internal Medicine* **136** (3), 243–6.

Annandale, Ellen (2007) Assembling Harriet Martineau's gender and health jigsaw. *Women's Studies International Forum* **30** (4), 355–66.

Annandale, Ellen (2009) *Women's Health and Social Change*. London, Routledge.

Annandale, Ellen and Hammarström, Anne (2011) Constructing the 'gender-specific body': a critical discourse analysis of publications in the field of gender-specific medicine. *Health* **15** (6), 577–93.

Annandale, Ellen and Kuhlmann, Ellen (2012) Gender and health-care: the future. In: Ellen Kuhlmann and Ellen Annandale (eds.) *The Palgrave Handbook of Gender and Healthcare*. London, Palgrave, pp. 505–20.

Annandale, Ellen, Clark, Judith and Allen, Elizabeth (1999) Interprofessional working: an ethnographic case study of emergency health care. *Journal of Interprofessional Care* **13** (2), 139–50.

Annas, George (1995) Minerva v. National Health Agency. In: Chris Hables Gray with Heidi J. Figueroa-Sarriera and Steven Mentor (eds.) *The Cyborg Handbook*. London, Routledge, pp. 169–81.

Appleby, John (2012) Rises in healthcare spending: where will it end? *British Medical Journal* **345**, e7127.

Arber, Sara, McKinlay, John, Adams, Ann, Marceau, Lisa, Link, Carol and O'Donnell, Amy (2006) Patient characteristics and inequalities in doctors' diagnosis and management strategies relating to CHD. *Social Science & Medicine* **62** (1), 103–15.

Ariès, Philippe (1981) *The Hour of Our Death*. London, Allen Lane.

Arms, Suzanne (1975) *Immaculate Deception*. New York, Simon and Schuster.

Armstrong, David (1983) *The Political Anatomy of the Body*. Cambridge, Cambridge University Press.

Armstrong, David (2012) Screening: mapping medicine's temporal spaces. In: N. Armstrong and H. Eborall (eds.) *The Sociology of Medical Screening*. Chichester, Wiley-Blackwell, pp. 17–32.

Arney, William Ray and Bergen, Bernard J. (1984) *Medicine and the Management of Living*. London, University of Chicago Press.

Aschenbrand, Periel (2006) *The Only Bush I Trust Is My Own*. London, Corgi Books.

Askham, Janet and Chisholm, Alison (2006) *Patient-centred Medical Professionalism: Towards an Agenda for Research and Action*. Oxford, Picker Institute Europe.

Atkinson, Michael (2008) Exploring male femininity in the 'crisis': men and cosmetic surgery. *Body and Society* **14** (1), 67–87.

Babb, Penny, Butcher, Hayley, Church, Jenny and Zealey, Linda (2006) *Social Trends 36*. Basingstoke, Palgrave.

Backhans, Mona C., Lundberg, Michael and Månsdotter, Anna (2007) Does increased gender equality lead to a convergence of health outcomes for men and women? A study of Swedish municipalities. *Social Science & Medicine* **64**, 1892–903.

Bajekal, Madhavi, Osborne, Velda, Yar, Mohammad and Meltzer, Howard (2006) *Focus on Health*. Basingstoke, Palgrave.

Balin, Miriam (1994) *The Sickroom in Victorian Fiction*. Cambridge, Cambridge University Press.

Barker, D. J. P. (1998) *Mothers and Babies in Later Life*, 2nd edn. Edinburgh, Churchill Livingstone.

Barrett, Michele and Phillips, Anne (1992) Words and things: materialism and method in contemporary feminist analysis. In: M. Barrett and A. Phillips (eds.) *Destabilising Theory*. Cambridge, Polity Press, pp. 201–19.

Bartley, Mel (2004) *Health Inequality: An Introduction to Theories, Concepts and Methods*. Cambridge, Polity Press.

Bastien, Joseph (1985) Qollahuaya-Andean body concepts: a topographical-hydraulic model of physiology. *American Anthropologist* **87**(3), 595–611.

Batty, G. David, Der, Geoff, Macintyre, Sally and Deary, Ian J. (2006) Does IQ explain socioeconomic inequalities in health? Evidence from a population based cohort study in the west of Scotland. *British Medical Journal* **332**, 580–84.

Baudrillard, Jean (2007 [1977]) *Forget Foucault*. Los Angeles, Semiotext(e).

Baudrillard, Jean (2009) *Why Hasn't Everything Already Disappeared?* (trans. Chris Turner). London, Seagull Books.

Bauman, Zygmunt (1993) The sweet scent of decomposition. In: C. Rojek and B. Turner (eds.) *Forget Baudrillard?* London, Routledge, pp. 22–46.

Bauman, Zygmunt (1998) *Globalization: The Human Consequences.* Cambridge, Polity Press.

Bauman, Zygmunt (2000) *Liquid Modernity.* Oxford, Polity Press.

Bauman, Zygmunt (2001) *The Individualized Society.* Oxford, Polity Press.

Bauman, Zygmunt (2002) Individually together. In: Ulrich Beck and Elisabeth Beck-Gernsheim (eds.) *Individualization.* London, Sage, pp. xiv–xix.

Bauman, Zygmunt (2005) *Liquid Life.* Cambridge, Polity Press.

Bauman, Zygmunt (2007) *Liquid Times.* Cambridge, Polity Press.

Baumgardner, Jennifer and Richards, Amy (2000) *Young Women, Feminism, and the Future.* New York, Farrar, Straus and Giroux.

Baunach, Dawn Michelle (2003) Gender, mortality, and corporeal inequality. *Sociological Spectrum* **23**(3), 331–58.

Beck, Ulrich (1992) *Risk Society.* London, Sage.

Beck, Ulrich (1999) *World Risk Society.* Cambridge, Polity Press.

Beck, Ulrich (2000) *What is Globalization?* Cambridge, PolityPress.

Beck, Ulrich (2002) Zombie categories: interview with Ulrich Beck. In: Ulrich Beck and Elisabeth Beck-Gernsheim (eds.) *Individualization.* London, Sage, pp. 202–13.

Beck, Ulrich and Beck-Gernsheim, Elisabeth (2002) *Individualization.* London, Sage.

Becker, Carl (1999) Money talks, money kills – the economics of transplantation in Japan and China. *Bioethics* **13** (3/4), 236–44.

Becker, Ernest (1973) *The Denial of Death.* New York, Free Press.

Becker, Howard (1993) How I learned what a crock was. *Journal of Contemporary Ethnography* **22**(1), 28–35.

Bell, Kirsten (2012) Remaking the self: trauma, teachable moments, and the biopolitics of cancer survivorship. *Culture, Medicine and Psychiatry* **36**(4), 584–600.

Bell, Susan and Figert, Anne (2012) Medicalization and pharmaceuticalization at the intersections: looking backward, sideways and forward. *Social Science & Medicine* **75** (5), 775–83.

Berridge, Virginia (ed.) (2003) Witness seminar. The Black Report and The Health Divide. In: Virginia Berridge and Stuart Blume (eds.) *Poor Health: Social Inequality Before and After the Black Report.* London, Frank Cass Publishers, pp. 131–71.

Berridge, Virginia and Blume, Stuart (eds.) (2003) *Poor Health: Social Inequality Before and After the Black Report.* London, Frank Cass Publishers.

Best, Steven and Kellner, Douglas (1991) *Postmodern Theory.* London, Macmillan.

Bevan, Nye (1952) *In Place of Fear.* London, William Heinemann Ltd.

Bevan Commission (2011) *NHS Wales: Forging a Better Future. A report by the Bevan Commission 2008–2011.* Cardiff, National Assembly for Wales.

Beveridge, William (1942) *Social Insurance and Allied Services* (The Beveridge Report). London, Stationery Office, Cmd 6404.

Bhopal, Raj (1988) Spectre of racism in health and health care: lessons from history and the United States. *British Medical Journal* **27** (316), 1970–3.

Biehl, João (2006) Pharmaceutical governance. In: Adriana Petryna, Andrew Lakoff and Arthur Kleinman (eds.) *Global Pharmaceuticals*. Durham, Duke University Press, pp. 206–39.

Bird, Chloe and Rieker, Patricia (2008) *Gender and Health: The Effects of Constrained Choices and Social Policies*. New York, Cambridge University Press.

Birke, Lynda (2003) Feminism and the idea of 'the biological'. In: Simon Williams, Lynda Birke and Gillian Bendelow (eds.) *Debating Biology*. London, Routledge, pp. 39–52.

Blair, Tony (1998) *The Third Way*. Fabian Pamphlet 558. London, Fabian Society.

Blanden, Jo and Gibbons, Steve (2006) *The Persistence of Poverty across Generations: A View from Two British Cohorts*. Bristol, Policy Press.

Blane, David (2006) The life course approach, the social gradient and health. In: Michael Marmot and Richard Wilkinson (eds.) *Social Determinants of Health*, 2nd edition. Oxford, Oxford University Press, pp. 54–77.

Blank, Robert (2012) Transformation of the US healthcare system: why is change so difficult? *Current Sociology* **60** (4), 415–26.

Blaxter, Mildred (1990) *Health and Lifestyles*. London, Tavistock/Routledge.

Blaxter, Mildred (2002) *Mildred Blaxter (Life History Interview)* by Paul Thompson. www.esds.ac.uk/qualidata/online/data/blaxter/interview.aspred (accessed 30 January 2014).

Blaxter, Mildred (2003) Biology, social class and inequalities in health: their synthesis in 'health capital'. In: Simon J. Williams, Lynda Birke and Gillian A. Bendelow (eds.) *Debating Biology*. London, Routledge, pp. 69–83.

Blaxter, Mildred (2010) *Health*, 2nd edn. Cambridge, Polity Press.

Blaxter, Mildred and Poland, Fiona (2002) Moving beyond the survey in explaining social capital. In: Catherine de Swaan and Antony Morgan (eds.) *Social Capital for Health*. London, Health Development Agency, pp. 85–107.

Bloom, Leslie Rebecca (1992) How can we know the dancer from the dance? Discourses of the self-body. *Human Studies* **15**, 313–34.

Bloom, Samuel (2002) *The Word as Scalpel: A History of Medical Sociology*. Oxford, Oxford University Press.

Blumer, Herbert (1969) *Symbolic Interactionism: Perspective and Method*. Englewood Cliffs, NJ, Prentice-Hall.

Boero, Natalie (2010) Bypassing blame: bariatric surgery and the case of biomedical failure. In: Adele Clarke, Laura Mamo, Jennifer Fosket, Jennifer Fishman and Janet Sim (eds.) *Biomedicalization: Technoscience, Health, and Illness in the U.S.* London, Duke University Press, pp. 307–30.

Bordo, Susan (1993) *Unbearable Weight: Feminism, Western Culture and the Body.* London, University of California Press.

Boston Women's Health Book Collective (1978) *Our Bodies, Ourselves.* London, Penguin Books.

Boston Women's Health Book Collective (2011) *Our Bodies, Ourselves,* 9th edn. New York, Simon and Schuster.

Bourdieu, Pierre (1984) *Distinction.* London, Routledge, Kegan and Paul.

Bradby, Hannah (2012) Race, ethnicity and health: the costs and benefits of conceptualising racism and health. *Social Science & Medicine* **75** (6), 955–8.

Bradby, Hannah and Nazroo, James (2010) Health, ethnicity and race. In: William Cockerham (ed.) *The New Blackwell Companion to Medical Sociology.* Oxford, Blackwell, pp. 113–29.

Braziel, Jana Evans (2008) *Diaspora: An Introduction.* Oxford, Blackwell.

Brint, Steven (2006) Saving the 'soul' of professionalism: Freidson's institutional ethics and the defence of professional autonomy. *Knowledge, Work and Society* **4** (2),101–29.

British Heart Foundation (2005) *Coronary Heart Disease Statistics 2005.* London, British Heart Foundation.

British Medical Journal (2013) Francis interview: what doctors must learn from my report. *British Medical Journal* **346**, f878.

Broom, Alex and Tovey, Philip (eds.) (2009) *Men's Health: Body, Identity and Social Context.* Oxford, Wiley-Blackwell.

Brondolo, Elizabeth., Gallo, Linda and Myers, Hector (2009) Race, racism and health: disparities, mechanisms and interventions. *Journal of Behavioral Medicine* **21**, 1–8.

Brown, Nik, Machin, Laura and McLeod, Danae (2011) Immunitary bioeconomy: the economisation of life in the international cord blood market. *Social Science & Medicine* **72** (7), 1115–22.

Brown, Phil (1990) The name game: toward a sociology of diagnosis. *Journal of Mind and Behavior* **11** (3–4), 385–406.

Brown, Phil, Morello-Frosch, Rachel, Zavestoski, Stephen, et al. (2011) Health social movements: advancing traditional medical sociology concepts. In: Bernice Pescosolido, Jack Martin, Jane McLeod and Anne Rogers (eds.) *Handbook of the Sociology of Health, Illness and Healing.* London, Springer, pp. 136–77.

Brown, Phil, Morello-Frosch, Rachel, Zavestoski, Stephen and the Contested Illness Research Group (2012a) *Contested Illnesses: Citizens, Science and Social Movements.* London, University of California Press.

Brown, Phil, Zavestoski, Stephen, Cordner, Alissa, et al. (2012b) A narrowing gulf of difference? Disputes and discoveries in the study of Gulf-War-related illnesses. In: Phil Brown, Rachel Morello-Frosch, Stephen Zavestoski and the Contested Illness Research Group. *Contested Illnesses: Citizens, Science and Social Movements*. London, University of California Press, pp. 79–107.

Brown, Tim (2011) Vulnerability is universal: considering the place of 'security' and 'vulnerability' within contemporary global health discourse. *Social Science & Medicine* **72** (3), 319–26.

Brundtland, Gro Harlem (2001) Addressing the challenges of unequal distribution. World Economic Forum, Plenary Seminar, www.who.int/director-general/speeches/2001/english/20010129_davosunequal distr.en.html (accessed 30 January 2014).

Bryan, Beverly, Dadzie, Stella and Scafe, Suzanne (1985) *The Heart of the Race*. London, Virago.

Burawoy, Michael (2005) For public sociology. *American Sociological Review* **70** (4), 4–28.

Burkitt, Ian (1999) *Bodies of Thought*. London, Sage.

Burns, Tom (1992) *Erving Goffman*. London, Routledge.

Bury, Mike (2001) Illness narratives: fact or fiction? *Sociology of Health & Illness* **23** (3), 263–85.

Bury, Mike (2008) New dimensions of health care organisation. In: D. Wainwright (ed.) *A Sociology of Health*. London, Sage, pp. 151–72.

Bush, Judith, Moffat, Suzanne and Dunn, Christine (2001) 'Even the birds around here cough': stigma, air pollution and health in Teeside. *Health & Place* **7**(1), 47–56.

Butler, Judith (1990) *Gender Trouble*. London, Routledge.

Butler, Judith (2010) *Frames of War: When is Life Grievable?* London, Verso.

Buzinde, Christine and Yarnal, Careen (2012) Therapeutic landscapes and postcolonial theory: a theoretical approach to medical tourism. *Social Science & Medicine* **74**, 783–7.

Calnan, M. and Sanford, E. (2004) Public trust in health care: the system or the doctor? *Quality and Safety in Health Care* **13**(2), 92–7.

Calnan, Michael and Rowe, Rosemary (2006) Researching trust relations in health care: conceptual and methodological challenges. *Journal of Health Organisation and Management* **20** (5), 348–58.

Cancer Research UK (2011) *Skin Cancer – UK Incidence Statistics*, http://info.cancerresearchuk.org/cancerstats/types/skin/incidence/ (accessed 28 June 2012).

Carel, Havi (2008) *Illness*. Durham, Acumen.

Carlisle, Sandra (2001) Inequalities in health: contested explanations, shifting discourses and ambiguous policies. *Critical Public Health* **11** (3), 267–81.

Casalino, Lawrence (2004) Unfamiliar tasks, contested jurisdictions: the changing organisation field of medical practice in the United States. *Journal of Health and Social Behaviour* **45** (extra issue), 59–75.

Castells, Manuel (2010) *The Rise of the Network Society*, 2nd edn. Oxford, Wiley-Blackwell.

Centeno, Miguel and Cohen, Joseph (2012) The arc of neoliberalism. *Annual Review of Sociology* **38**, 317–40.

Chandola, Tarani, Ferrie, Jane, Sacker, Amanda and Marmot, Michael (2007) Social inequalities in self reported health in early old age: follow-up of prospective cohort study. *British Medical Journal* **334**, 990–3.

Charles, Nickie and Walters, Vivienne (2008) 'Men are leavers alone and women are worriers': gender differences in discourses of health. *Health, Risk & Society* **10** (2), 117–32.

Charmaz, Kathy (2008) A future for symbolic interactionism. In: N. K. Denzin, J. Salvo and M. Washington (eds.) *Studies in Symbolic Interaction*, vol. XXXII. Bingley, Emerald, pp. 51–9.

Charmaz, Kathy (2010) Studying the experience of chronic illness through grounded theory. In: Graham Scambler and Sasha Scambler (eds.) *New Directions in the Sociology of Chronic Illness and Disabling Conditions*. London, Palgrave, pp. 6–36.

Charmaz, Kathy and Rosenfeld, Dana (2006) Reflections of the body, images of self: visibility and invisibility in chronic illness and disability. In: Dennis Waskul and Philip Vannini (eds.) *Body/embodiment*. Aldershot, Ashgate, pp. 36–49.

Cheek, Julianne (2007) Healthism: a new conservatism? *Qualitative Health Research* **18** (7), 974–82.

Chen, Ying-Yeh, Subramanian, S.V., Acevedo-Garcia, Doloros and Kawachi, Ichiro (2005) Women's status and depressive symptoms: a multilevel analysis. *Social Science & Medicine* **60** (1), 49–60.

Civitas (2010) *The Impact of the NHS Market*. London, Civitas.

Clark, Jack, Potter, Deborah and McKinlay, John (1991) Bringing social structure back into clinical decision making. *Social Science & Medicine* **32**, 853–66.

Clarke, Adele (2010) Epilogue: thoughts on biomedicalization in its transnational travels. In: Adele Clarke, Laura Mamo, Jennifer Fosket, Jennifer Fishman and Janet Sim (eds.) *Biomedicalization: Technoscience, Health, and Illness in the U.S.* London, Duke University Press, pp. 380–405.

Clarke, Adele and Shim, Janet (2011) Medicalization and biomedicalization revisited: technoscience and transformations of health, illness and American medicine. In: Bernice Pescosolido, Jack Martin, Jane McLeod and Anne Rogers (eds.) *Handbook of the Sociology of Health, Illness and Healing*. London, Springer, pp. 173–99.

Clarke, Adele, Shim, Janet, Mamo, Janet, Fosket, Jennifer R. and Fishman, Jennifer (2010a) Biomedicalization: a theoretical and substantive introduction. In: Adele Clarke, Laura Mamo, Jennifer Fosket, Jennifer Fishman and Janet Sim (eds.) *Biomedicalization: Technoscience, Health, and Illness in the U.S.* London, Duke University Press, pp. 1–44.

Clarke, Adele, Shim, Janet, Mamo, Janet, Fosket, Jennifer R. and Fishman, Jennifer (2010b) Biomedicalization: technoscientific transformations of health, illness, and U.S. biomedicine. In: Adele Clarke, Laura Mamo, Jennifer Fosket, Jennifer Fishman and Janet Sim (eds.) *Biomedicalization: Technoscience, Health, and Illness in the U.S.* London, Duke University Press, pp. 47–87.

Clarke, Adele, Fosket, Jennifer, Mamo, Laura, Fishman, Jennifer and Shim, Janet (2010c) Charting (bio)medicine and (bio)medicalization in the United States, 1890–present. In: Adele Clarke, Laura Mamo, Jennifer Fosket, Jennifer Fishman and Janet Sim (eds.) *Biomedicalization: Technoscience, Health, and Illness in the U.S.* London, Duke University Press, pp. 88–103.

Clarke, Simon (2006) *From Enlightenment to Risk*. London, Palgrave.

Clinton, Hillary (2003) *Living History*. London, Headline Book Publishing.

Coburn, David (2000) Income inequality, social cohesion and the health status of populations: the role of neo-liberalism. *Social Science & Medicine* 51, 135–46.

Coburn, David (2004) Beyond the income inequality hypothesis: class, neo-liberalism, and health inequalities. *Social Science & Medicine* 58, 41–56.

Coburn, David (2006) Medical dominance then and now: critical reflections. *Health Sociology Review* 15 (5), 432–43.

Cockerham, William C. (2000) Health lifestyles in Russia. *Social Science & Medicine* 51, 1313–24.

Cockerham, William and Cockerham, Geoffrey (2010) *Health and Globalization*. Cambridge, Polity Press.

Cockerham, William and Scambler, Graham (2010) Medical sociology and sociological theory. In: William Cockerham (ed.) *The New Blackwell Companion to Medical Sociology*. Oxford, Blackwell, pp. 3–26.

Coleman, D. A and Salt, John (1996) The ethnic group question in the 1991 Census: a new landmark in British social statistics. In D. A. Coleman and John Salt (eds.) *Ethnicity in the 1991 Census*, vol. I. London, HMSO, pp. 1–32.

Comaroff, Jean and Comaroff, John L. (2001) Millennial capitalism: first thoughts on a second coming. In: Jean Comaroff and John L. Comaroff (eds.) *Millennial Capitalism and the Culture of Neoliberalism*. London, Duke University Press, pp. 1–56.

Commonwealth of Australia (2007) *Tackling Wicked Problems: A Public Policy Perspective*. Barton Act, Attorney General's Department.

Connell, John (2006) Medical tourism: sea, sun, sand and . . . surgery. *Tourism Management* 27, 1093–100.

Connell, R. W. and Messerschmidt, James W. (2005) Hegemonic masculinity: rethinking the concept. *Gender and Society* 19 (6), 829–59.

Connell, R. W. and Wood, Julian (2005) Globalization and business masculinities. *Men and Masculinities* **7** (4), 347–64.

Connell, Raewyn (2007) *Southern Theory*. Cambridge, Polity Press.

Connell, Raewyn (2009) *Gender*, 2nd edn. Cambridge, Polity Press.

Connell, Raewyn (2010) Understanding neoliberalism. In: Susan Braedley and Meg Luxton (eds.) *Neoliberalism and Everyday Life*. London, McGill-Queen's University Press, pp. 22–36.

Conrad, Peter (1975) The discovery of hyperkinesis: notes on the medicalization of deviant behavior. *Social Problems* **32**, 12–21.

Conrad, Peter (2004) The shifting engines of medicalization. *Journal of Health and Social Behavior* **46** (March), 3–14.

Conrad, Peter (2007) *The Medicalization of Society*. Baltimore, The Johns Hopkins University Press.

Conrad, Peter (2013) Medicalization: changing contours, characteristics, and contexts. In: W Cockerham (ed.) *Medical Sociology on the Move*. London, Springer, pp. 195–214.

Conrad, Peter and Stults, Cheryl (2008) Contestation and medicalization. In: Pamela Moss and Katherine Teghtsoonian (eds.) *Contesting Illness*. Toronto, Toronto University Press, pp. 323–36.

Cooley, Charles (1902) *Human Nature and Social Order*. New York, C. Scribner's Sons.

Cooper, Melinda (2008) *Life as Surplus: Biotechnology and Capitalism in the Neoliberal Era*. London, University of Washington Press.

Cornwell, Jocelyn (1984) *Hard Earned Lives*. London, Tavistock.

Council of Europe (2005) *Recent Demographic Developments in Europe 2004*. Strasburg: Council of Europe.

Courtenay, Will (2011) *Dying to be Men*. London, Routledge.

Coward, Rosalind (1999) *Sacred Cows*. London, Harper Collins.

Craig, Gillian (2007) 'Nation', 'migration' and tuberculosis. *Social Theory and Health* **5**, 267–84.

Crawford, Robert (1980) Healthism and the medicalization of everyday life. *International Journal of Health Services* **10** (3), 365–88.

Crawford, Robert (1984) A cultural account of 'health': control, release, and the social body. In: J. McKinlay (ed.) *Issues in the Political Economy of Health Care*. London, Tavistock, pp. 60–103.

Crawford, Robert (2006) Health as meaningful social practice. *Health* **10** (4), 401–20.

Crenshaw, Kimberlé (1989) Demarginalizing the intersection of race and sex: a black feminist critique of antidiscrimination doctrine, feminist theory and antiracist politics. *University of Chicago Legal Forum* 139–67.

Crossley, Nick (1996) Body-subject/body-power: agency, inscription and control in Foucault and Merleau-Ponty. *Body and Society* **2**(2), 99–116.

Crossley, Nick (2006a) *Reflexive Embodiment in Contemporary Society*. Buckingham, Open University Press.

Crossley, Nick (2006b) The networked body and the question of reflexivity. In: Dennis Waskul and Phillip Vannini (eds.) *Body/embodiment*. Aldershot, Ashgate, pp. 21–34.

CSDH (Commission on the Social Determinants of Health) (2008) *Closing the Gap in a Generation: Health Equity through Action on the Social Determinants of Health. Final Report of the Commission on Social Determinants of Health*. Geneva, World Health Organisation.

Currie, Graeme and Brown, Andrew (2003) A narratological approach to understanding processes of organizing in a UK hospital. *Human Relations* **56** (5), 563–86.

Curtis, Sarah (2004) *Health and Inequality. Geographical Perspectives*. London, Sage.

Curtis, Sarah and Rees Jones, Ian (1998) Is there a place for geography in health inequality? *Sociology of Health & Illness* **20** (5), 645–672.

da Silva, Filipe Carreira (2007) *G. H. Mead*. Cambridge, Polity Press.

Dahlgren, Göran and Whitehead, Margaret (2006) *Levelling up (Part 2): A Discussion Paper on European Strategies for Tackling Inequalities in Health*. Copenhagen, WHO.

Daly, Mary (1984) *Pure Lust: Elemental Feminist Philosophy*. London, Women's Press.

Daly, Mary (1990) *Gyn/ecology: The Metaethics of Radical Feminism*. Boston, Beacon Press.

Darwin, Charles (1859) *On the Origin of Species by Means of Natural Selection*. London, John Murray.

Davies, Celia (2000) Care and the transformation of professionalism. In: Celia Davies, Linda Finlay and Anne Bullman (eds.) *Changing Practice in Health and Social Care*. London, Open University / Sage, pp. 343–54.

Davis, Joseph (2010) Medicalization, social control and the relief of suffering. In: William Cockerham (ed.) *The New Blackwell Companion to Medical Sociology*. Oxford, Wiley-Blackwell, pp. 211–41.

Davis, Kathy (1995) *Reshaping the Female Body*. New York, Routledge.

Davis, Kathy (1997) 'My body is my art': cosmetic surgery as feminist utopia. In: Kathy Davis (ed.) *Embodied Practices*. London, Sage, pp. 168–81.

Davis, Kathy (2002) Feminist body/politics as world traveller: translating *Our Bodies, Our Selves*. *European Journal of Women's Studies* **9** (3), 223–47.

Davis, Kathy (2008) Intersectionality as buzzword. *Feminist Theory* **9** (1), 67–85.

Day, Katy, Gough, Brendan and McFadden, Majella (2004) 'Warning! Alcohol can seriously damage your health'. A discourse analysis of recent British newspaper coverage of women and drinking. *Feminist Media Studies* **4** (2), 166–183.

Day, Robert A. and Day, JoAnne, V. (1977) Negotiated order theory: an appreciation and a critique. *Sociological Quarterly* **18**, 126–42.

UNIVERSITY OF WINCHESTER
LIBRARY

de Tocqueville, Alexis (1967 [1835, 1840]). *Democracy in America*. New York, Harper and Row.

de Vogli, Roberto (2011) Neoliberal globalisation and health in a time of economic crisis. *Social Theory and Health* **9**, 311–25.

DeNavas-Walt, Carmen, Proctor, Bernadette and Smith, Jessica (2011) *Income, Poverty and Health Insurance Cover in the United States: 2010*. Current Population Reports pp. 60–239. Washington, DC, US Government Printing Office.

Dent, Mike (2006a) Patient choice and medicine in health care. *Public Management Review* **8** (3), 449–62.

Dent, Mike (2006b) Disciplining the medical profession? Implications of patient choice for medical dominance. *Health Sociology Review* **15** (5), 458–68.

Dent, M., Fallon, C., Wendt C., et al. (2011) Medicine and user involvement within European healthcare: a typology for European comparative research. *International Journal of Clinical Practice* **65** (12), 1218–120.

Department of Health (1989) *Working for Patients*. London: Stationery Office, Cm 555.

Department of Health (1991) *The Patient's Charter*. London, Stationery Office.

Department of Health (1997) *The New NHS: Modern, Dependable*. London, Stationery Office, Cm 3807.

Department of Health (2000a) *The NHS Plan*. London, Stationery Office, Cm 4818-I.

Department of Health (2000b) *A Health Service for All the Talents*. London, Department of Health.

Department of Health (2001) *The Expert Patient: A New Approach to Chronic Disease Management for the 21st Century*. London, Department of Health.

Department of Health (2002a) *Delivering the NHS Plan: Next Steps on Investment. Next Steps on Reform*. London, Stationery Office.

Department of Health (2002b) *Learning from Bristol*. London, HMSO, Cm 5363.

Department of Health (2006) *Turning the Corner: Improving Diabetes Care*. London, Department of Health.

Department of Health (2007a) *Tackling Health Inequalities: 2004–06 Data and Policy Update for the 2010 National Target*. London, Department of Health.

Department of Health (2007b) *Trust, Assurance and Safety*. London, HMSO.

Department of Health (2008) *Health Profile of England 2008*. London, Department of Health.

Department of Health (2010a) *Healthy Lives, Healthy People: A Strategy for Public Health in England*. London: Stationery Office, Cm 7985.

Department of Health (2010b) *Equity and Excellence: Liberating the NHS*. London, Stationery Office, Cm 7881.

Department of Health (2011a) *Healthy Lives, Healthy People*. London, Department of Health, Cm 8134.

Department of Health (2011b) *NHS Future Forum: Summary Report on Proposed Changes to the NHS*. London, Department of Health.

Department of Health (2011c) *Healthy Lives, Healthy People: A Call to Action on Obesity*. London, HMSO.

Department of Health (2012a) *Poly Implant Prothèse (PIP) Breast Implants: Final Report of the Expert Group*. London, Department of Health.

Department of Health (2012b) *The New Public Health Role of Local Authorities*. London, Department of Health.

Department of Health (2012c) *Caring for Our Future*. London, Stationery Office, Cm 8378.

Department of Health (2013a) *The NHS Constitution for England*. London, Department of Health.

Department of Health (2013b) *Report of the Mid Staffordshire NHS Foundation Trust Public Inquiry: Executive Summary*. London, Stationery Office.

Derrida, Jacques (1982) *Margins of Philosophy*. Chicago, University of Chicago Press.

Descartes, René (2008 [1637]) *A Discourse on Method* (trans. John Veitch). New York, Cosimo Inc.

Dex, Shirley, Joshi, Heather, Smith, Kate, Ward, Kelly and Plewis, Ian (2005) Introduction. In: Shirley Dex and Heather Joshi (eds.) *Children of the 21st Century*. Bristol, Policy Press, pp. 1–23.

DHSS (Department of Health and Social Security) (1983) *NHS Management Enquiry Report (Griffiths Report)*. London, DHSS.

Dickens, Peter (2000) *Social Darwinism*. Buckingham, Open University Press.

Dickenson, Donna (2008) *Body Shopping: Converting Body Parts into Profit*. Oxford, One World Press.

Dickinson, Helen and Miller, Robin (2011) GP commissioning: implications for the third sector. *Voluntary Sector Review* **2** (2), 265–73.

Dingwall, Robert (2008) *Essays on Professions*. Aldershot, Ashgate.

Dixon-Woods, Mary, Yeung, Karen and Bosk, Charles (2011) Why is UK medicine no longer a self-regulating profession? The role of scandals involving 'bad apple' doctors. *Social Science & Medicine* **73**, 1452–9.

Dmitrieva, Elena (2001) The Russian health care experiment: transition of the health care system and rethinking the sociology of medicine. In: W. Cockerham (ed.) *The Blackwell Companion to Medical Sociology*. Oxford, Blackwell, pp. 320–33.

Dopson, Sue, Locock, Louise, Gabbay, John, Ferlie, Ewan and Fitzgerald, Louise (2003) Evidence-based medicine and the implementation gap. *Health* **7** (3), 311–30.

Dorling, Danny. (2010) *Injustice*. Bristol, Policy Press.

Dorling, Danny (2013) *Unequal Health*. Bristol, Policy Press.

Doyal, Lesley (2005) Understanding gender, health, and globalisation: opportunities and challenges. In: Ilona Kickbush, Kari Hartwig and Justin List (eds.) *Globalization, Women and Health in the Twenty-first Century*. London, Palgrave, pp. 9–27.

Dubos, René (1960) *Mirage of Health*. London, George Allen and Unwin.

Duménil, Gérard and Lévy, Dominique (2011) *The Crisis of Neoliberalism*. Cambridge, MA, Harvard University Press.

Dumit, Joseph (2006) Illnesses you have to fight to get: facts as forces in uncertain, emergent illnesses. *Social Science & Medicine* **62**, 577–90.

Durkheim, Émile (1895) *The Rules of Sociological Method*. New York, Free Press.

Durkheim, Émile (1970 [1897]) *Suicide*. London, Routledge.

Dworkin, Sahri (2005) Who is epidemiologically fathomable in the HIV/AIDS epidemic? Gender, sexuality, and intersectionality in public health. *Culture, Health and Sexuality* **7** (6), 615–23.

Edwards, Jane (2012) The health needs of gay and lesbian women. In: E. Kuhlmann and E. Annandale (eds.) *The Palgrave Handbook of Gender and Healthcare*. London, Palgrave, pp. 290–305.

Ehrenreich, Barbara (2010) *Smile or Die*. London, Granta.

Ehrenreich, Barbara and English, Deidre (1978) *For Her Own Good: Two Centuries of the Experts' Advice to Women*. New York, Anchor Press.

Ehrenreich, Barbara and English, Deidre (2005) *For Her Own Good: Two Centuries of the Experts' Advice to Women*, 2nd edn. London, Anchor Books.

Eisenstein, Zillah (1988) *The Female Body and the Law*. London, University of California Press.

Elbe, Stefan (2005) AIDS, security, biopolitics. *International Relations* **19**(4), 403–419.

Elbe, Stefan (2010) *Security and Global Health*. Cambridge, Polity Press.

Elias, Norbert (1985) *The Loneliness of the Dying*. Oxford, Blackwell.

Ellaway, Anne, Benezeval, Michaela, Green, Michael, Leyland, Alastair and Macintyre, Sally (2012) 'Getting sicker quicker': does living in a more deprived neighbourhood mean your health deteriorates faster? *Health and Place* **18**, 132–7.

Elston, Mary Ann (2009) *Women in Medicine: The Future*. London, Royal College of Physicians.

Engels, Friedrich (1993 [1845]) *The Condition of the Working Class in England in 1844*. Oxford, Oxford University Press.

Enthoven, Alain (1993) The history and principles of managed competition. *Health Affairs*, Supplement, pp. 25–48.

Epstein, Steven (2007) *Inclusion: The Politics of Difference in Medical Research*. Chicago, University of Chicago Press.

Erikson, Robert and Goldthorpe, John H. (1992). *The Constant Flux: A Study of Class Mobility in Industrial Societies*. Oxford, Clarendon Press.

Ettorre, Elizabeth (2002) *Reproductive Genetics, Gender and the Body.* London, Routledge.

Evetts, Julia (2006) Short note: the sociology of professional groups. *Current Sociology* **54** (1), 133–43.

Farquhar, Dion (1996) *The Other Machine: Discourse and Reproductive Technologies.* London, Routledge.

Farrimond, Hannah (2012) Beyond the caveman: Rethinking masculinity in relation to men's help-seeking. *Health* **16** (2), 208–25.

Fausto-Sterling, Anne (2003) The problem with sex/gender and nature/nurture. In: Simon Williams, Lynda Birke and Gillian Bendelow (eds.) *Debating Biology.* London, Routledge, pp. 123–32.

Fausto-Sterling, Anne (2005) The bare bones of sex: part 1 – sex and gender. *Signs* **30** (5), 1491–526.

Feiring, E. (2008) Lifestyle, responsibility and justice. *Journal of Medical Ethics* **34**, 33–6.

Ferlie, Ewan, Ashburner, Lynn and Pettigrew, Andrew (1996) *The New Public Management in Action.* Oxford, Oxford University Press.

Figlio, Karl (1987) The lost subject of medical sociology. In: Graham Scambler (ed.) *Sociological Theory and Medical Sociology.* London, Tavistock, pp. 77–109.

Fine, Garry Alan (1993) The sad demise, mysterious disappearance, and glorious triumph of symbolic interactionism. *Annual Review of Sociology* **19**, 61–87.

Finkler, Kaja., Skrzynia, Cécile and Evans, James (2003) The new genetics and its consequences for family, kinship, medicine and medical genetics. *Social Science & Medicine* **57**, 403–12.

Fisher, Jill (2007) Coming soon to a physician near you: medical neoliberalism and pharmaceutical clinical trials. *Harvard Health Policy Review* **8** (1), 61–70.

Fitzpatrick, Ray and Chandola, Tarani (2000) Health. In: A. H. Halsey and Josephine Webb (eds.) *Twentieth-century British Social Trends.* Basingstoke, Palgrave, pp. 94–127.

Flax, Jane (1990) *Thinking Fragments: Psychoanalysis, Feminism, and Postmodernism in the Contemporary West.* Oxford, University of California Press.

Foley, Ellen (2008) Neoliberal reform and health dilemmas. *Medical Anthropology Quarterly* **22** (3), 157–272.

Ford, Chandra and Airhihenbuwa, Collins (2010) The public health critical race methodology: praxis for antiracism research. *Social Science & Medicine* **71** (8), 1390–8.

Fosket, Ruth (2010) Breast cancer risk as disease. In: Adele Clarke, Laura Mamo, Jennifer Fosket, Jennifer Fishman and Janet Sim (eds.) *Biomedicalization: Technoscience, Health, and Illness in the U.S.* London, Duke University Press, pp. 331–52.

Foucault, Michel (1965) *Madness and Civilisation*. New York, Bantam Books.

Foucault, Michel (1977) *Language, Counter-Memory, Practice*. Ithaca, Cornell University Press.

Foucault, Michel (1979) *Discipline and Punish*. New York, Vintage Books.

Foucault. Michel (1980) *Michel Foucault: Power/Knowledge* (ed. C. Gordon). Brighton, Harvester.

Foucault, Michel (1982) The subject of power. *Critical Enquiry* **8**, 777–95.

Foucault, Michel (1985) *The Use of Pleasure*. Harmondsworth, Penguin.

Foucault, Michel (1986) *The Care of the Self*. Harmondsworth, Penguin.

Foucault, Michel (1988) Technologies of the self. In: M. Luther, M. Martin, H. Gutman and P. H. Hutton (eds.) *Technologies of the Self*. Amherst, University of Massachusetts Press, pp. 16–49.

Foucault, Michel (1989 [1963]) *The Birth of the Clinic*. London, Routledge.

Fowler, Lori (2009) *Implants for Graduation?* Saarbrüken, VDM Verlag Dr Müller Aktiengesellschaft and Co.

Fox, Nick (1992) Foucault, Foucauldians and sociology. *British Journal of Sociology* **49** (3), 415–33.

Fox, Nick (1999) *Beyond Health: Postmodernism and Embodiment*. London, Free Association Books.

Frank, Arthur (1992) Twin nightmares of the medical simulacrum: Jean Baudrillard and David Cronenberg. In: William Stearns and William Chaloupka (eds.) *Jean Baudrillard: The Disappearance of Art and Politics*. London, Macmillan, pp. 82–97.

Frank, Arthur (1993) The rhetoric of self-change: illness experience as narrative. *The Sociological Quarterly* **34**, 39–52.

Frank, Arthur (1995) *The Wounded Storyteller: Body, Illness, and Ethics*. London, University of Chicago Press.

Frank, Arthur (2002) *At the Will of the Body. Reflections on Illness*. New York, Mariner Books.

Frank, Arthur (2004) Emily's scars: surgical shapings, technoluxe, and bioethics. *Hastings Center Report* March–April, 18–29.

Frank, Arthur (2007) Five dramas of illness. *Perspectives in Biology and Medicine* **50** (3), 379–94.

Frankenberg, Ruth (1993) *White Women, Race Matters: The Social Construction of Whiteness*. London, Routledge.

Franklin, Sarah (2011) Transbiology: a feminist account of being after IVF. *The Scholar and Feminist Online* **9.1–9.2**, (video) http://barnard.edu/sfonline/reprotech/franklin_01.htm (accessed 30 January 2014).

Freidson, Eliot (1988 [1970]) *Profession of Medicine*. London, University of Chicago Press.

Freidson, Eliot (1989) *Medical Work in America*. London, Yale University Press.

Freidson, Eliot (1994) *Professionalism Reborn*. Cambridge, Polity Press.

Freidson, Eliot (2001) *Professionalism: The Third Logic*. Cambridge, Polity Press.

Freund, Peter (1990) The expressive body: a common ground for the sociology of emotions and health and illness. *Sociology of Health & Illness* **12**(4), 451–477.

Freund, Peter (2011) Embodying psychosocial health inequalities: bringing back materiality and bioagency. *Social Theory and Health* **9**, 59–70.

Friedan, Betty (1963) *The Feminine Mystique*. New York, Dell.

Friedan, Betty (1981) *The Second Stage*. New York, Summit Books.

Frohlich, Katherine L., Corin, Ellen and Potvin, Louise (2001) A theoretical proposal for the relationship between context and disease. *Sociology of Health & Illness* **23** (6), 776–97.

Fuchs Epstein, Cynthia (1988) *Deceptive Distinctions: Sex, Gender and the Social Order*. London, Yale University Press.

Fuller, Steve (2006) *The New Sociological Imagination*. London, Sage.

Furedi, Frank (2002) *Culture of Fear*. London, Continuum.

Furedi, Frank (2005) Our unhealthy obsession with sickness, www.spiked-online.com/Articles/0000000CA958.htm (accessed 30 January 2014).

Furedi, Frank (2006) The end of medical dominance. *Society* **43** (6), 140–8.

Fuss, Diana (1989) *Essentially Speaking*. London, Routledge.

Gadamer, Hans Georg (1996) *The Enigma of Health*. Cambridge, Polity Press.

Gadow, Sally (1982) Body and self: a dialectic. In: V. Kestenbaum (ed.) *The Humanity of the Ill: Phenomenological Perspectives*. Knoxville, University of Tennessee Press, pp. 86–100.

Galdas, Paul (2009) Men, masculinity and help-seeking behaviour. In: Alex Broom and Philip Tovey (eds.) *Men's Health: Body, Identity and Social Context*. Oxford, Wiley-Blackwell, pp. 63–82.

Galobardes, Bruna., Lynch, John W. and Davey Smith, George (2004) Childhood socioeconomic circumstances and cause-specific mortality in adulthood: systematic review and interpretation. *Epidemiologic Reviews* **26**, 7–21.

Gatens, Moira (1983) A critique of the sex/gender distinction. In: Judith Allen and Paul Patton (eds.), *Beyond Marxism*. Leichhardt, Intervention Publishing, pp. 143–160.

Gatens, Moira (1992) Power, bodies and difference. In: Michèle Barrett and Anne Phillips (eds.) *Destabilising Theory*. Cambridge, Polity Press, pp. 120–37.

Giardina, Michael (2003) 'Bending it like Beckham' in the popular media. *Journal of Sport and Social Issues* **27** (1), 65–82.

Gibel Azoulay, Katya (2008) Reflections on race and the biologization of difference. In: Sander Gilman (ed.) *Race in Contemporary Medicine*. London, Routledge, pp. 50–76.

Gibson, Andy, Britten, N. and Lynch, James (2012) Theoretical directions for an emancipatory concept of patient and public involvement. *Health* **16** (5), 531–47.

Giddens, Anthony (1991) *Modernity and Self Identity*. Cambridge, Polity Press.

Giddens, Anthony (2000) *The Third Way and its Critics*. Cambridge, Polity Press.

Giddens, Anthony (2002) *Runaway World*, 2nd edn. London, Profile Books.

Gilbert, Leah and Selikow, Terry-Ann (2012) HIV / AIDS and gender. In: Ellen Kuhlmann and Ellen Annandale (eds.) *The Palgrave Handbook of Gender and Healthcare*. London, Palgrave, pp. 209–23.

Gilman, Charlotte Perkins (1915) *Herland* (unabridged). Mineola, NY, Dover Publications.

Gilman, Charlotte Perkins (1963 [1935]). *The Living of Charlotte Perkins Gilman*. Madison, WI, University of Wisconsin Press.

Gilman, Charlotte Perkins (1973 [1892]) *The Yellow Wallpaper*. New York, The Feminist Press.

Gilman, Charlotte Perkins (1996 [1898]) *Women and Economics* (ed. Carl N. Degler). London, Harper Torchbooks.

Gilman, Sander (1991) *The Jew's Body*. London, Routledge.

Gilroy, Paul (1990) One nation under a groove: the cultural politics of 'race' and racism in Britain. In: David Goldberg (ed.) *Anatomy of Racism*. Minneapolis, University of Minnesota Press, pp. 263–82.

Gilson, Lucy (2003) Trust and the development of health care as a social institution. *Social Science & Medicine* **56**, 1453–68.

Gjonça, Arjan, Tomassini, Cecilia, Toson, Barbara and Smallwood, Steve (2005) Sex differences in mortality, a comparison of the United Kingdom and other developed countries. *Health Statistics Quarterly* **26**, 6–16.

Glaser, Barney (1965) The constant comparative method of qualitative analysis. *Social Problems* **12**, 436–45.

Glaser, Barney and Strauss, Anselm (1965) *Awareness of Dying*. Chicago, Aldine.

Glaser, Barney and Strauss, Anselm (1999 [1967]) *The Discovery of Grounded Theory*. London, Aldine Transaction.

Gleeson, Denis and Knights, David (2006) Challenging dualism: public professionalism in 'troubled' times. *Sociology* **40** (2), 277–95.

Global Fund (2012) www.theglobalfund.org/en/about/donors/ (accessed 16 November 2012).

GMC (General Medical Council) (2011) *The State of Medical Education and Practice in the UK in 2011*. London, General Medical Council.

Goffman, Erving (1961) *Asylums*. Harmondsworth, Penguin.

Goffman, Erving (1963) *Stigma*. London, Penguin.

Gold, Margaret (1977) A crisis of identity: the case of medical sociology. *Journal of Health and Social Behavior* **18** (June), 160–8.

Goldberg, David (1990) The social formation of racist discourse. In: David Goldberg (ed.) *Anatomy of Racism*. Minneapolis, University of Minnesota Press, pp. 295–318.

Goldberg, David (2009) *The Threat of Race: Reflections on Racial Neoliberalism*. Oxford, Wiley-Blackwell.

Gomes, Barbara and Higginson, Irene (2008) Factors influencing death at home in terminally ill patients with cancer: systematic review. *British Medical Journal* **332**, 515–21.

Gorman, Bridget K. and Ghazal Read, Jen'nan (2006) Gender disparities in adult health: an examination of three measures of morbidity. *Journal of Health and Social Behaviour* **47** (June), 95–100.

Gorsky, M. (2008) The British NHS 1948–2008: a review of the historiography. *Social History of Medicine* **21** (3), 437–60.

Gouldner, Alvin (1970) *The Coming Crisis of Western Sociology*. New York, Equinox Books.

Graham, Hilary (2002) Building an inter-disciplinary science of health inequalities: the example of lifecourse research. *Social Science & Medicine* **55**, 2005–16.

Graham, Hilary (2012) Ensuring the health of future populations. *British Medical Journal* **345**, e7573.

Graves, Joseph and Rose, Michael (2007) Against racist medicine. In: Sander Gilman (ed.) *Race in Contemporary Medicine*. London, Routledge, pp. 175–87.

Gray, John (2002) *False Dawn – The Delusions of Global Capitalism*. London, Granta Publications.

Grimsley, M. and Bhat, Ashok (1988) Health. In: Ashok Bhat, Roy Carr-Hill and Sushel Ohri (eds.) *Britain's Black Population: A New Perspective*, 2nd edn. Aldershot, Gower, pp. 177–207.

Groopman, Jerome (2007) *How Doctors Think*. New York, Houghton Mifflin Company.

Grosz, Elizabeth (1990) Contemporary theories of power and subjectivity. In: Senja Gunew (ed.) *Feminist Knowledge: Critique and Construct*. London, Routledge, pp. 59–120.

Grosz, Elizabeth (1995) *Space, Time, and Perversion*. London, Routledge.

Gruenewald, Tara, Karlamangla, Arun, Hu, Perry, et al. (2011) History of socioeconomic disadvantage and allostatic load in later life. *Social Science & Medicine* **74** (1), 75–83.

Gupta, Jyotsna Agnihotri (2006) Towards transnational feminisms: some reflections and concerns in relation to the globalisation of reproductive technologies. *European Journal of Women's Studies* **13** (1), 23–38.

Habermas, Jürgen (1984) *The Theory of Communicative Action*, vol. I, *Reason and the Rationalization of Society*. London, Heinemann.

Hacking, John, Muller, Sara and Buchan, Iain (2011) Trends in mortality from 1965 to 2008 across the English north–south divide: comparative observational study. *British Medical Journal* **342**, 508, www.bmj.com/ highwire/filestream/374611/field_highwire_article_pdf/0.pdf (accessed 30 January 2014).

Hafferty, Fredrick (2003) Finding soul in a 'medical profession of one'. *Journal of Health Politics, Policy and Law* **18** (1), 133–58.

Hafferty, Frederick (2006) Measuring professionalism: a commentary. In: D. T. Stern (ed.) *Measuring Medical Professionalism*. Oxford, Oxford University Press, pp. 281–306.

Hafferty, Fredrick and McKinlay, John (1993) Cross cultural perspectives on the dynamics of medicine as a profession. In: Fredrick Hafferty and John McKinlay (eds.) *The Changing Medical Profession: An International Perspective*. Oxford, Oxford University Press, pp. 210–26.

Halkowski, Timothy and Gill, Virginia Teas (2010) Conversation analysis and ethnomethodology: the centrality of interaction. In: Ivy Bourgeault, Robert Dingwall and Raymond De Vries (eds.) *The SAGE Handbook of Qualitative Methods in Health Research*. London, Sage, pp. 212–28.

Hall, Mark (2006) Researching medical trust in the United States. *Journal of Health Organization and Management* **20** (5), 456–67.

Hall, Mark, Dugan, Elizabeth, Zheng, Beiyao and Mishra, Aneil (2001) Trust in physicians and medical institutions: what is it, can it be measured, and does it matter? *Milbank Quarterly* **79** (4), 613–39.

Hall, Stuart (1992) 'New ethnicities'. In: James Donald and Ali Rattansi (eds.) *'Race', Culture and Difference*. London, Sage, pp. 252–9.

Hallam, Julie (2000) *Nursing the Image*. London, Routledge.

Ham, Christopher (2009) *Health Policy in Britain*, 6th edn. London, Palgrave.

Ham, Christopher (2012) What will the Health and Social Care Bill mean for the NHS in England? *British Medical Journal* **344**, e2159.

Ham, Chris, Dixon, Anna and Brooke, Beatrice (2012) *Transforming the Delivery of Health and Social Care: The Case for Fundamental Change*. London, Kings Fund.

Handley, Geoff, Higgins, Kate, Sharma, Bhavna with Bird, Kate and Cammack, Diana (2009) *Poverty and Poverty Reduction in Sub-Saharan Africa: An Overview of the Issues*. London, Overseas Development Institute (ODI).

Hanisch, Carol (2006 [1970]) The personal is political, www. carolhanisch.org/CHwritings/PIP.html (accessed 1 August 2011).

Haraway, Donna (1991) *Simians, Cyborgs, and Women: The Reinvention of Nature*. London, Free Association Books.

Harden, Jeni (2001) 'Mother Russia' at work: gender divisions in the medical profession. *European Journal of Women's Studies* **8** (2), 181–99.

Harman, Chris (2009) *Zombie Capitalism: Global Crisis and the Relevance of Marx*. London, Bookmarks Publications.

Harper Bulman, Kate and McCourt, Christine (2002) Somali refugee women's experiences of maternity care in west London: a case study. *Critical Public Health* **12** (4), 365–80.

Harrison, Steve, Hunter, David, Marnoch, Gordon and Pollitt, Christopher (1992) *Just Managing: Power and Culture in the National Health Service*. London, Macmillan.

Hart, Nicky (1982) Is capitalism bad for your health? *British Journal of Sociology* **33**, 435–43.

Harvey, David (1989) *The Condition of Postmodernity*. Oxford, Basil Blackwell.

Harvey, David (2010) *The Enigma of Capital*. London, Profile Books.

Harvey, Janet, Annandale, Ellen, Loan-Clarke, John, Suhomlinova, Olga and Teasdale, Nina (2014) *Mobilising Identities: The Shape and Realities of Middle and Junior Managers' Working Lives*. Final Report to NIHR Service Delivery and Organisation Programme, www.journalslibrary.nihr.ac.uk/hsdr (accessed 6 February 2014).

Hausmann, Ricardo, Tyson, Laura D., and Zahidi, Saadia (2009) *The Global Gender Gap Report 2009*. Geneva, World Economic Forum.

Heidegger, Martin (1962 [1927]) *Being and Time*. Oxford, Blackwell.

Herzlich, Claudine (1973) *Health and Illness: A Social Psychological Analysis*. London, Academic Press.

Hill, Mary A. (1980) *Charlotte Perkins Gilman: The Making of a Radical Feminist 1860–1896*. Philadelphia, PA, Temple University Press.

Hinote, Brian P., Cockerham, William C. and Abbott, Pamela (2009) The specter of post-communism: women and alcohol in eight post-Soviet states. *Social Science & Medicine* **68** (7), 1254–62.

HM Treasury (2010) *Spending Review 2010*. London, Stationery Office, Cm7942.

Holtzman, N. A. (2002) Genetics and social class. *Journal of Epidemiology and Community Health* **56**, 529–35.

hooks, bell (1984) *Feminist Theory: From Margin to Centre*. Boston, South End Press.

Hor, Su-yin, Godbold, Natalya, Collier, Aileen and Iedema, Rick (2013) Finding the patient in patient safety. *Health,* published online 23 January, http://hea.sagepub.com/content/early/2013/01/30/1363 459312472082 (accessed 30 January 2014).

Horobin, Gordon (1985) Medical sociology in Britain: true confessions of an empiricist. *Sociology of Health & Illness* **7**, 94–107.

Horstman, Klasien and Finkler, Kaja (2011) Genetics, health care, family and kinship in a global perspective: situated processes of co-construction. *Social Science and Medicine* **72**, 1739–42.

Horton, Richard (2005) Medicine: the prosperity of virtue. *The Lancet* **366**, 1985–7.

Howarth, Glennys (2007) *Death and Dying: A Sociological Introduction*. Cambridge: Polity Press.

Howarth, Glennys (2009) The demography of dying. In: Allan Kellehear (ed.) *The Study of Dying*. Cambridge, Cambridge University Press, pp. 99–122.

Hughes, David and Griffiths, Lesley (1996) 'But if you look at the coronary anatomy . . . ': risk and rationing in cardiac surgery. *Sociology of Health & Illness* **18**, 172–97.

Human Rights Watch (2003) *Policy Paralysis: A Call for Action on HIV/AIDS and Human Rights Abuse against Women and Girls in Africa*. New York, Human Rights Watch, www.hrw.org/en/reports/2003/12/01/policy-paralysis (accessed 30 January 2014).

Hunt, Kate and Batty, David (2009) Gender and socio-economic inequalities in mortality and health behaviours: an overview. In: Hilary Graham (ed.) *Understanding Health Inequalities*, 2nd edn. Maidenhead, Open University Press, pp. 141–61.

Hunt, Kate, Adamson, Joy and Galdas, Paul (2012) Gender and help-seeking: towards gender-comparative studies. In: E. Kuhlmann and E. Annandale (eds.) *The Palgrave Handbook of Gender and Healthcare*. London, Palgrave, pp. 207–21.

Hunter, David (2008) *The Health Debate*. Bristol, Policy Press.

Hunter, David (2009) Leading for health and wellbeing: the need for a new paradigm. *Journal of Public Health* **31** (2), 202–4.

Hunter, David (2011) Change of government: one more big bang health care reform in England's National Health Service. *International Journal of Health Services* **41**, 159–74.

Hyde, Paula, Granter, Edward, McCann, Leo and Hassard, John (2012) The lost health service tribe: in search of middle managers. In: Helen Dickinson and Russell Mannion (eds.) *The Reform of Health Care*. London, Palgrave, pp. 7–20.

Idler, E. and Benyamani, Y. (1997) Self-rated health and mortality: a review of twenty-seven community studies. *Journal of Health and Social Behaviour* **38**, 21–37.

Illingworth, Patricia (2005) *Trusting Medicine: The Moral Costs of Managed Care*. London, Routledge.

Inhorn, Marcia (2003) Global infertility and the globalization of new reproductive technologies: illustrations from Egypt. *Social Science & Medicine* **56** (9), 1837–51.

Inhorn, Marcia and Whittle, Lisa (2001) Feminism meets the 'new' epidemiologies: toward an appraisal of antifeminist biases in epidemiological research on women's health. *Social Science & Medicine* **53** (5), 553–67.

IPSOS MORI (2013) www.ipsos-mori.com/Assets/Docs/Polls/Feb 2013_Trust_Topline.PDF (accessed 30 January 2014).

Irvine, Donald (2006) Book review of *Measuring Medical Professionalism* by D. Stern and *Understanding Doctors' Performance* by J. Cox et al. *British Medical Journal* **333**, 49.

Jackson, Carolyn and Tinkler, Penny (2007) 'Ladettes' and 'modern girls': troublesome young femininities. *Sociological Review* **55** (2), 251–72.

Jacobson, Ruth, Jacobs, Susie and Marchbank, Jen (2000) Introduction: states of conflict. In: Susie Jacobs, Ruth Jacobson and Jennifer Marchbank (eds.) *States of Conflict: Gender, Violence and Resistance.* London, Zed Books, pp. 1–23.

Jeffery, Roger (1979) Normal rubbish: deviant patients in the casualty department. *Sociology of Health & Illness* **1**, 90–108.

Jewson, Nick (1976) The disappearance of the sick-man from medical cosmology: 1770–1870. *Sociology* **10**, 225–44.

Johansson, Sheila Ryan (1977) Sex and death in Victorian England. In: Martha Vicinus (ed.) *A Widening Sphere: Changing Roles of Victorian Women.* London, Indiana University Press, pp. 163–71.

Johnson, Malcolm (1975) Medical sociology and sociological theory. *Social Science & Medicine* **9**, 227–32.

Jones, Colin and Porter, Roy (1998) Introduction. In: Colin Jones and Roy Porter (eds.) *Reassessing Foucault: Power, Medicine and the Body.* Florence, KY, Routledge, pp. 1–16.

Jutel, Annemarie (2006) The emergence of overweight as a disease entity: measuring up to normality. *Social Science & Medicine* **63**, 2268–76.

Jutel, Annemarie (2011) *Putting a Name to It: Diagnosis in Contemporary Society.* Baltimore, MD, Johns Hopkins University Press.

Jutel, Annmarie and Nettleton, Sarah (2011) Towards a sociology of diagnosis: reflections and opportunities. *Social Science & Medicine* **73**, 793–800.

Jylha, Marja (2009) What is self-rated health and why does it predict mortality? Towards a unified conceptual model. *Social Science & Medicine* **69** (3), 307–16.

Kaiser Foundation (2010) Summary of the New Health Reform Law. www.kff.org/healthreform/8061.cfm (accessed 15 August 2012).

Kandrack, Mary-Anne, Grant, Karen R. and Segall, Alexander (1991) Gender differences in health related behaviour. *Social Science & Medicine* **32** (5), 579–90.

Karlsen, Saffron (2004) 'Black like Beckham?' Moving beyond definitions of ethnicity based on skin colour and ancestry. *Ethnicity and Health* **9** (2), 107–37.

Karlsen, Saffron, Nazroo, James, McKenzie, Kwame, Bhui, Kamaldeep and Weich, Scott (2005) Racism, psychosis and common mental disorder among ethnic minority groups in England. *Psychological Medicine* **35**, 1795–803.

Katz Rothman, Barbara (1988) *The Tentative Pregnancy.* London, Pandora.

Kawachi, Ichiro and Kennedy, Bruce K. (1997) Socioeconomic

determinants of health: health and social cohesion: why care about income inequality? *British Medical Journal* **314**, 1037–144.

Kay, Rebecca (2006) *Men in Contemporary Russia: The Fallen Heroes of Post-Soviet Change?* Aldershot, Ashgate.

Kellehear, Allan (2009) What the social and behaviour studies say about dying. In: Allan Kellehear (ed.) *The Study of Dying*. Cambridge, Cambridge University Press, pp. 1–26.

Kelly, Michael (1992) Self, identity and radical surgery. *Sociology of Health & Illness* **14**, 390–415.

Kenen, Regina (1996) The at-risk health status and technology: a diagnostic invitation and the 'gift' of knowing. *Social Science & Medicine* **42**, 1545–53.

Kennedy, Ian (2001) *Report of the Public Inquiry into Children's Heart Surgery at the Bristol Royal Infirmary 1984–1995: Learning from Bristol*. London, Stationery Office, Cmd 5207.

Kernick, David (ed.) (2004) *Complexity and Healthcare Organization*. Oxford, Radcliffe Medical Press.

Kertzer, David and Arel, Dominique (2002) Censuses, identity formation and the struggle for political power. In: David Kertzer and Dominique Arel (eds.) *Census and Identity: The Politics of Race, Ethnicity, and Language in National Census*. Cambridge, Cambridge University Press, pp. 1–42.

Kimmel, Michael (2008) *Guyland: The Perilous World Where Boys Become Men*. New York, HarperCollins.

Kimmel, Michael (2009) Has a Man's World Become a Woman's Nation? In: Heather Boushey and Ann O'Leary (eds.) *The Shriver Report: A Woman's Nation Changes Everything*. Center for American Progress, pp. 323–57, www.americanprogress.org/issues/2009/10/pdf/awn/a_womans_nation.pdf (accessed 30 January 2014).

Kings Fund (2011) *The Future of Leadership and Management in the NHS*. London, Kings Fund.

Kings Fund (2012) *Medical Engagement*. London, Kings Fund.

Klawiter, Maren (2008) *The Biopolitics of Breast Cancer*. London, University of Minneapolis Press.

Klein, Naomi (2007) *The Shock Doctrine: The Rise of Disaster Capitalism*. London, Penguin Books.

Klein, Renate (2008) From test-tube women to bodies without women. *Women's Studies International Forum* **31**, 157–75.

Klein, Rudolph (2010) *The New Politics of the NHS*, 6th edn. Oxford, Radcliffe Publishing.

Kleinman, Arthur (1988) *The Illness Narratives*. New York, Basic Books.

Kleinman, Arthur (2006) *What Really Matters*. Oxford, Oxford University Press.

Klumb, Petra L. and Lampert, Thomas (2004) Women, work, and well-being 1950–2004: a review and methodological critique. *Social Science & Medicine* **58**, 1007–24.

Klunklin, Areewan and Greenwood, Jennifer (2006) Symbolic interactionism in grounded theory studies: women surviving with HIV/AIDS in rural Northern Thailand. *Journal of the Association of Nurses in AIDS Care* **17** (5), 32–41.

Kohn, Linda, Corrigan, Janet and Donaldson, Molla (2000) *To Err is Human: Building a Safer Health System.* Washington, DC, National Academy Press.

Kraemer, Sebastian (2000) The fragile male. *British Medical Journal* **321**, 1609–12.

Krieger, Nancy (1987) Shades of difference: theoretical underpinnings of the medical controversy on black/white differences in the United States, 1830–1870. *International Journal of Health Services* **17**, 259–78.

Krieger, Nancy (2001) Theories for social epidemiology in the 21st-century: an ecosocial perspective. *International Journal of Epidemiology* **30** (4), 668–77.

Krieger, Nancy (2003) Does racism harm health? Did child abuse exist before 1962? On explicit questions, critical science, and current controversies. *American Journal of Public Health* **93** (2), 194–9.

Krieger, Nancy (2008) Proximal, distal, and the politics of causation: what's level got to do with it? *American Journal of Public Health* **98** (2), 221–30.

Krieger, Nancy (2009). Ladders, pyramids and champagne: the iconography of health inequalities. *Journal of Epidemiology and Community Health* **62**, 1098–104.

Krieger, Nancy and Davey Smith, George (2004) 'Bodies count', and body counts: social epidemiology and embodying inequalities. *Epidemiologic Reviews* **26**, 92–103.

Kuh, Diana and Ben-Shlomo, Yoav (1997) *A Lifecourse Approach to Chronic Disease Epidemiology.* Oxford, Oxford University Press.

Kuh, Diana, Hardy, Rebecca, Langenberg, Claudia, Richards, Marcus and Wadsworth, Michael (2002) Mortality in adults aged 26–54 years related to socioeconomic conditions in childhood and adulthood. *British Medical Journal* **325**, 1076–80.

Kuhlmann, Ellen (2006) *Modernising Health Care.* Bristol, Policy Press.

Kuhlmann, Ellen and Burau, Viola (2008) The 'healthcare' state in transition. *European Societies* **10** (4), 619–33.

Labonté, Ronald (2008) Global health policy: finding the right frame? *Critical Public Health* **18** (4), 467–82.

Lamb, Julie, Levy, Marcy and Reich, Michael (2004) *Wounds of War.* Cambridge, MA, President and Fellows of Harvard College.

Landry, Donna and MacLean, Gerald (1993) *Materialist Feminisms.* Oxford, Blackwell.

Langford, Ann and Johnson, Brian (2009) Social inequalities in adult mortality by the National Statistics Socio-economic Classification, England and Wales, 2001–03. *Health Statistics Quarterly* **42** (Summer), 6–21.

Lauderdale, Diane (2006) Birth outcomes for Arabic-named women in California before and after September 11. *Demography* **43** (1), 185–201.

Lawler, Stephanie (2005) Introduction: class, culture and identity. *Sociology* **39** (5), 797–806.

Lawton, Julia (2003) Lay concepts of health and illness: past research and future agendas. *Sociology of Health and Illness* **25**, 23–40.

Leder, Drew (1998) A tale of two bodies: the Cartesian corpse and the lived body. In: Don Welton (ed.) *Body and Flesh*. Oxford, Blackwell, pp. 35–50.

Lee, Ellie and Frayn, Elizabeth (2008) The 'feminization' of health. In: David Wainwright (ed.) *A Sociology of Health*. London, Sage, pp. 115–33.

Lee, Kelley (2005) Global social change and health. In: Kelley Lee and Jeff Collin (eds.) *Global Change and Health*. Maidenhead, Open University Press, pp. 13–27.

Legato, Marianne (2002) *Eve's Rib*. New York, Harmony Books

Legato, Marianne (2003) Beyond women's health: the new discipline of gender-specific medicine. *Medical Clinics of North America* **87**, 917–37.

Legato, Marianne (2006) Foreword. *Gender Medicine*, Supplement 1, *The 1st World Congress on Gender-specific Medicine*, p. S16.

Lemke, Thomas (2011) *Bio-politics: An Advanced Introduction*. London, New York University Press.

Leon, David (2011) Trends in European life expectancy: a salutary view. *International Journal of Epidemiology* **40** (2), 271–7.

Levy, Ariel (2005) *Female Chauvinist Pigs*. New York, The Free Press.

Leys, Colin and Player, Stewart (2011) *The Plot against the NHS*. Pontypool, Merlin Press.

Light, Donald (1995) Countervailing powers: a framework for professions in transition. In: Terry Johnson, Gerry Larkin and Mike Saks (eds.) *Health Professions and the State in Europe*. London, Routledge, pp. 25–41.

Light, Donald (2000) The medical profession and organisational change: from professional dominance to countervailing power. In: Chloe Bird, Peter Conrad and Allen Fremont (eds.) *Handbook of Medical Sociology*, 5th edn. New York, Prentice Hall, pp. 201–16.

Light, Donald (2010) Historical and comparative reflections on the US national health insurance reforms. *Social Science & Medicine* **72**, 129–32.

Lindesmith, Alfred and Strauss, Anselm. L. (1969) *Readings in Social Psychology*. London, Holt, Rinehart and Winston.

Lippel, Katherine (2006) Workers' compensation and controversial illnesses. In: Pamela Moss and Katherine Teghtsoonian (eds.) *Contesting Illness*. Toronto, Toronto University Press, pp. 47–68.

Lippman, Abby (1992) Led (astray) by genetic maps: the cartography of the human genome and health care. *Social Science & Medicine* **35**, 1469–76.

Lochner, Kimberly A., Kawachi, Ichiro, Brennan, Robert T. and Buka, Stephen L. (2003) Social capital and neighbourhood mortality rates in Chicago. *Social Science & Medicine* **56**, 1797–805.

Lock, Margaret and Nguyen, Vinh-Kim (2010) *An Anthropology of Biomedicine*. Oxford, Wiley-Blackwell.

Loe, Meika (2006) The Viagra blues: embracing or resisting the Viagra body. In: Dana Rosenfeld and Christopher Faircloth (eds.) *Medicalized Masculinities*. Philadelphia, Temple University Press, pp. 21–44.

Lohan, Maria (2009) Developing a critical men's health debate in academic scholarship. In: Brendan Gough and Steve Robertson (eds.) *Men, Masculinities and Health*. London, Palgrave, pp. 11–29.

Lorde, Audrey (1980) *The Cancer Journals*. London, Sheba Feminist Publishers.

Lorde, Audrey (1984) *Sister Outsider*. New York, Crossing Press.

Lupton, Deborah (2012) *Medicine as Culture*. 3rd edn. London, Sage.

Lupton, Deborah (2013) *Fat*. London, Routledge.

Lury, Celia (2000) The united colours of diversity. In: Sarah Franklin, Celia Lury and Jackie Stacy (eds.) *Global Nature, Global Culture*. London, Sage, pp. 146–87.

Lynch, John W., Davey Smith, George, Kaplan, George A. and House, James S. (2000) Income inequality and mortality: importance to health of individual income, psychosocial environment, or material conditions. *British Medical Journal* **320**, 1200–4.

Lyndon Shanley, Mary (1993) Surrogate mothering and women's freedom. *Signs* **18** (3), 618–639.

Lyons, Antonia C. and Willott, Sara A. (2008) Alcohol consumption, gender identities and women's changing social positions. *Sex Roles* **59**, 694–71.

Lyotard, Jean-François (1984) *The Postmodern Condition*. Manchester, Manchester University Press.

McCullough, Michael E. and Laurenceau, Jean-Philippe (2004) Gender and the natural history of self-rated-health: a 59-year longitudinal study. *Health Psychology* **23** (6), 651–5.

McDonald, Ruth (2012) Restratification revisited: the changing landscape of primary care in England and California. *Current Sociology* **60** (4), 441–55.

McKeown, Thomas (1976) *The Role of Medicine*. Oxford, Blackwell.

McKinlay, John (1977) The business of good doctoring or doctoring as good business: reflections on Freidson's view of the medical game. *International Journal of Health Services* **7**, 459–83.

McKinlay, John and Arches, Joan (1985) Toward the proletarianisation of physicians. *International Journal of Health Services* **15**, 161–95.

McKinlay, John and Marceau, Lisa (2002) The end of the golden age of doctoring. *International Journal of Health Services* **32** (2), 379–416.

McKinlay, John and Marceau, Lisa (2008) When there is no doctor: reasons for the disappearance of primary care physicians in the US during the early 21st century. *Social Science & Medicine* **67**, 1481–91.

McManus, Sally, Meltzer, Howard, Brugha, Traolach, Bebbington, Paul and Jenkins, Rachel (2009) *Adult Psychiatric Morbidity in England, 2007*. London, The NHS Information Centre.

McNay, Lois (1992) *Foucault and Feminism*. Cambridge: Polity Press.

McPhedran, Samara and Baker, Jeanine (2008) Recent Australian suicide trends for males and females at the national level: has the rate of decline differed? *Health Policy* **87**, 350–8.

Mackenbach, Johan (2005) Genetics and health inequalities: hypotheses and controversies. *Journal of Epidemiology and Community Health* **59**, 268–73.

Mackenbach, Johan (2006) Socio-economic inequalities in health in Western Europe. In: Johannes Siegrist and Michael Marmot (eds.) *Social Inequalities in Health*. Oxford, Oxford University Press, pp. 223–50.

Mackenbach, Johan (2008) Social justice in the land of Cockaigne. *Journal of Epidemiology and Community Health* **62**, 2.

Mackenbach, Johan (2010) Can we reduce health inequalities? An analysis of the English strategy (1970–2010). *Journal of Epidemiology and Community Health* **65**: 568–75.

Mackenbach, Johan, Bos, Vivian, Anderson, Otto, et al. (2003) Widening socioeconomic inequalities in mortality in six Western European countries. *International Journal of Epidemiology* **32**, 830–7.

Macintyre, Sally (2001) Inequalities in health: is research gender blind? In: D. A. Leon and G. Walt (eds.) *Poverty, Inequality, and Health*. Oxford, Oxford University Press, pp. 283–93.

Macintyre, Sally (2003) Before and after the Black Report: four fallacies. In: Virginia Berridge and Stuart Blume (eds.) *Poor Health: Social Inequality Before and After the Black Report*. London, Frank Cass Publishers, pp. 198–219.

Macintyre, Sally, Hunt, Kate and Sweeting, Helen (1996) Gender differences in health: are things as simple as they seem? *Social Science & Medicine* **42** (4), 617–24.

Macintyre, Sally, Ellaway, Anne and Cummins, Steven (2002) Place effects on health: how can we conceptualise, operationalise and measure them? *Social Science & Medicine* **55**, 125–39.

Makdisi, Saree, Casarino, Cesare and Karl, Rebecca (1996) Preface and introduction: Marxism, communism and history: a reintroduction. In: Saree Makdisi, Cesare Casarino and Rebecca Karl (eds.) *Marxism Beyond Marxism*. London, Routledge, pp. ix–x and 1–13.

Månsdotter, Anna, Lindholm, Lars, Lundberg, Michael, Winkvist,

Anna and Öhman, Ann (2006) Parental share in public and domestic spheres: a population study on gender equality, death, and sickness. *Journal of Epidemiology and Public Health* **60**, 616–20.

Markens, Susan (2007) *Surrogate Motherhood*. London, University of California Press.

Marmor, Ted and Oberlander, Jonathan (2011) The patchwork: health reform, American style. *Social Science & Medicine* **72**, 125–8.

Marmot, Michael (2005) *Status Syndrome*. London, Bloomsbury.

Marmot, Michael and Wilkinson, Richard (2001) Psychosocial and material pathways in relation between income and health: a response to Lynch et al. *British Medical Journal* **322**, 1233–6.

Marmot Review (2010) *Fair Society, Healthy Lives: Strategic Review of Health Inequalities in England Post 2010*, www.marmotreview.org (accessed 30 January 2014).

Martin, Emily (1999) The woman in the flexible body. In: Adele Clarke and Virginia Olesen (eds.) *Revisioning Women, Health, and Healing*. London, Routledge, pp. 97–115.

Martin, Graham and Learmonth, Mark (2012) A critical account of the rise and spread of 'leadership': the case of UK healthcare. *Social Science & Medicine* **74**, 281–8.

Martineau, Harriet (1861) *Health, Husbandry, and Handicraft*. London, Bradbury and Evans.

Martineau, Harriet (2003 [1844]) *Life in the Sick-Room* (ed. M. Frawley). Ormskirk, Broadview Press.

Marx, Karl (1974 [1894]) *Capital: A Critique of Political Economy*, vol. III, Book 3, *The Process of Capitalist Production as a Whole* (ed. F. Engels). London, Lawrence and Wishart.

Mead, George Herbert (1972 [1934]) *Mind, Self, and Society* (ed. C.W. Morris). London, University of Chicago Press.

Mechanic, David (2001) The managed care backlash: perceptions and rhetoric in health care policy and potential for healthcare reform. *Milbank Quarterly* **79** (1), 35–54.

Mechanic, David (2004a) The rise and fall of managed care. *Journal of Health and Social Behavior* **45** (extra issue), 76–96.

Mechanic, David (2004b) In my chosen doctor I trust. *British Medical Journal* **329**, 1418–19.

Merleau-Ponty, Maurice (1962) *Phenomenology of Perception*. London, RKP.

Miah, Andy and Rich, Emma (2008) *The Medicalization of Cyberspace*. London, Routledge.

Miles, Robert (1994) *Racism After 'Race Relations'*. London, Routledge.

Miles, Robert and Brown, Malcolm (2003) *Racism*, 2nd edn. London, Routledge.

Miles, Steven (2002) On a charter to defend medical professionalism: whose profession is it anyway? *Hastings Center Report* **46** (3), 46–8.

Milewa, Timothy (2009) Health care, consumerism and the politics of identity. In: Jonathan Gabe and Michael Calnan (eds.) *The New Sociology of the Health Service*. London, Routledge, pp. 161–76.

Minkoff, Howard (2012) Fear of litigation and caesarean section rates. *Seminars in Perinatology* **36** (5), 390–4.

Mishler, Eliot (1989) Critical perspectives on the biomedical model. In: Phil Brown (ed.) *Perspectives in Medical Sociology*. Belmont, CA, Wadsworth, pp. 153–66.

Mohan, John (2009) Visions of privatisation. In: Jonathan Gabe and Michael Calnan (eds.) *The New Sociology of the Health Service*. London, Routledge, pp. 79–98.

Mohan, John, Barnard, Steve, Jones, Kelvyn and Twigg, Liz (2004) *Social Capital, Place and Health: Creating, Validating and Applying Small-area Indicators in the Modelling of Health Outcomes*. London, Health Development Agency.

Mol, Annemarie (2007) *The Body Multiple: Ontology in Medical Practice*. Durham, NC, Duke University Press.

Mol, Annemarie (2008) *The Logic of Care*. London, Routledge.

Monaghan, Lee, Hollands, Robert and Pritchard, Gary (2010) Obesity epidemic entrepreneurs: types, practices and interests. *Body and Society* **16** (2), 37–71.

Montgomery, Catherine, Hosegood, Victoria, Busza, Joanna and Timæus, Ian (2006) Men's involvement in the South African family: engendering change in the AIDS era. *Social Science & Medicine* **10**, 2411–19.

Moody, Kim (2011) Capitalist care: will the Coalition government's 'reforms' move the NHS further towards a US-style healthcare market? *Capital and Class* **35** (3), 415–34.

Moon, Graham, Quarendon, Gemma, Barnard, Steve, Twigg, Liz and Blyth, Bill (2007) Fat nation: deciphering the distinctive geographies of obesity in England. *Social Science & Medicine* **65** (1), 20–31.

Moore, Sarah (2010) Is the healthy body gendered? Toward a feminist critique of the new paradigm of health. *Body and Society* **16** (2), 95–118.

Morello-Frosch, Rachel, Zavestoski, Steve, Brown, Phil, Gasior Altman, Rebecca, McCormick, Sabrina and Mayer, Brian (2006) Embodied health movements. In: Scott Frickel and Kelly Moore (eds.) *The New Political Sociology of Science*. Madison, University of Wisconsin Press, pp. 244–71.

Morgan, Joan (2000) *When Chickenheads Come Home to Roost: My Life as a Hip-Hop Feminist*. New York, Touchstone.

Morgan, Robin (1996) Light bulbs, radishes and the politics of the 21st century. In: Diane Bell and Renate Klein (eds.) *Radically Speaking: Feminism Reclaimed*. London, Zed Books, pp. 5–8.

Morgan, Oliver and Baker, Allan (2006) Measuring deprivation in

England and Wales using 2001 Carstairs scores. *Health Statistics Quarterly* **21** (Autumn), 28–33.

Moser, Kath, Shkolnikov, Vladimir and Leon, David A. (2005) World mortality 1950–2000: divergence replaces convergence from the late 1980s. *Bulletin of the World Health Organisation* **83**, 202–9.

Moss, Nancy (2002) Gender equity and socioeconomic inequality: a framework for the patterning of women's health. *Social Science & Medicine* **54** (5), 649–61.

Moss, Pamela and Teghtsoonian, Katherine (2008) Power and illness: authority, power and context. In: Pamela Moss and Katherine Teghtsoonian (eds.) *Contesting Illness*. Toronto, Toronto University Press, pp. 3–27.

Mukta, Parita (2012) Who or what do we care about in the 21st century? *International Sociology* **27** (4), 446–63.

Muntaner, Charles and Lynch, John (2002) Income inequality, social cohesion, and class relations: a critique of Wilkinson's neo-Durkheimian research programme. In: Vicente Navarro (ed.) *The Political Economy of Social Inequalities*. Amityville, NY, Baywood, pp. 325–45.

Murcott, Anne (1977) Blind alleys and blinkers: the scope of medical sociology. *Scottish Journal of Sociology* **1** (2), 155–71.

Mutizwa-Mangiza, Dorothy (1999) *Doctors and the State: The Struggle for Professional Control in Zimbabwe*. Aldershot, Ashgate.

Mythen, Gabe (2008) Reappraising the risk society thesis. *Contemporary Sociology* **55** (6), 793–813.

Narayan, Deepa. (2000) *Voices of the Poor: Can Anyone Hear Us?* Oxford, Oxford University Press.

Nathanson, Constance (1975) Illness and the feminine role: a theoretical review. *Social Science & Medicine* **9** (2), 57–62.

Nathanson, Constance (1977) Sex, illness and medical care: a review of data, theory and method. *Social Science & Medicine* **11**, 13–25.

National Center for Health Statistics (NCHS) (2010) *Health, United States, 2009*. Hyattsville, MD, National Center for Health Statistics, www.cdc.gov/nchs/hus/updatedtables.htm (accessed 30 January 2014).

National Center for Health Statistics (NCHS) (2012) *Health, United States, 2011*. Hyatsville, MD, NCHS.

National Institute for Clinical Excellence (NICE) (2008) *Social Value Judgements: Principles for the Development of NICE Guidelines*, 2nd edn, http://www.nice.org.uk/media/C18/30/SVJ2PUBLICATION 2008.pdf (accessed 30 January 2014).

Navarro, Vicente (1989) Race *or* class, or race *and* class. *International Journal of Health Services* **19**, 311–14.

Navarro, Vicente (2002) Health and equity in the world in the era of 'globalization'. In: Vicente Navarro (ed.) *The Political Economy of Social Inequalities*. Amityville, NY, Baywood, pp. 109–20.

Navarro, Vicente (2004) Commentary: is *capital* the solution or the problem? *International Journal of Epidemiology* **33**, 672–4.

Nayak, Anoop (2006) Displaced masculinities: chavs, youth and class in the post-industrial city. *Sociology* **40** (5), 813–31.

Nazroo, James (2010) Health and health care. In: Alice Bloch and John Solomos (eds.) *Race and Ethnicity in the 21st Century*. London, Palgrave, pp. 112–37.

NCSR (National Centre for Social Research) (2007) *Smoking, Drinking and Drug Use among Young People in England in 2006*. London: National Centre for Social Research.

Nettleton, Sarah (1992) *Power, Pain and Dentistry*. Buckingham, Open University Press.

Nettleton, Sarah (2006) 'I just want permission to be ill': towards a sociology of medically unexplained symptoms. *Social Science & Medicine* **62**, 1167–78.

Newdick, Christopher (2005) *Who Should We Treat? Rights, Rationing, and Resources in the NHS*, 2nd edn. Oxford, Oxford University Press.

Newman, Janet and Kuhlmann, Ellen (2009) Consumers enter the political stage? The modernisation of health care in Britain and Germany. *Journal of European Social Policy* **17** (2), 99–111.

NHS Information Centre (2004) *Health Survey for England, 2004: The Health of Minority Ethnic Groups*, vol. I. London: The Information Centre (NHS).

Nugus, Peter, Greenfield, David, Travaglia, Joanne, Westbrooke, Johanne and Braithwaite, Jeffery (2010) How and where clinicians exercise power: interprofessional relations in health care. *Social Science & Medicine* **71**, 898–909.

Numerato, Dino, Salvatore. Dominico and Fattore, Giovani (2012) The impact of management on medical professionalism: a review. *Sociology of Health and Illness* **34** (4), 626–44.

Nuñes, Everardo Duarte (2001) Social science and health in Brazil. In: W. Cockerham (ed.) *The Blackwell Companion to Medical Sociology*. Oxford, Blackwell, pp. 233–44.

Nurok, Michael and Henckes, Nicholas (2009) Between professional values and the social valuation of patients: the fluctuating economy of pre-hospital emergency work. *Social Science & Medicine* **68**, 504–10.

Nye, Robert (2003) The evolution of the concept of medicalization in the late twentieth century. *Journal of the History of the Behavioral Sciences* **39** (2), 115–29.

O'Brien, Rosaleen, Hunt, Kate and Hart, Graham (2005) 'It's cavemen stuff, but that is to a certain extent how men operate': men's accounts of masculinity and help seeking. *Social Science & Medicine* **61** (3), 503–16.

O'Connor, James (1973) *The Fiscal Crisis of the State*. New York, St Martin's Press.

Oakley, Ann (1972) *Sex, Gender and Society*. London, Temple Smith.

Oakley, Ann (1974) *The Sociology of Housework*. Oxford, Blackwell.

OECD (2011) *Health at a Glance: Europe 2011*. OECD Publishing, www.oecd-ilibrary.org/social-issues-migration-health/health-at-a-glance-2011_health_glance-2011-en (accessed 30 January 2014).

OECD (2012) *Health at a Glance: Europe 2012*. OECD Publishing, www.oecd-ilibrary.org/social-issues-migration-health/health-at-a-glance-europe-2012_9789264183896-en (accessed 30 January 2014).

Office of Health Economics (2011) NHS funding and expenditure. Standard Note SN/SG/724 (14 September 2011).

Office of Health Economics (2012) NHS funding and expenditure. Standard Note SN/SG/724 (3 April 2012).

Olesen, Virginia (2002) Resisting 'fatal unclutteredness': conceptualising the sociology of health and illness into the millennium. In: Gillain Bendelow, Mick Carpenter, Caroline Vautier and Simon Williams (eds.) *Gender, Health and Healing*. London, Routledge, pp. 254–66.

ONS (2009a) *Social Trends 39*. London, Palgrave Macmillan.

ONS (2009b) *General Household Survey 2007*. London, ONS.

ONS (2010) *Suicides: UK Suicides Increase in 2008*. www.statistics.gov.uk/cci/nugget.asp?id=1092 (accessed 30 January 2010).

ONS (2011) *Social Trends 41*. London, ONS.

ONS (2012) *Ethnicity and National Identity in England and Wales 2011*. London, ONS.

ONS (2013) *The General Lifestyle Survey 2011*, www.ons.gov.uk/ons/dcp171776_302351.pdf (accessed 30 January 2014).

OPCS (1992) *1841–1990 Mortality Statistics, Serial Tables: England and Wales*. Series DH1 25. London, HMSO.

Orlan (2014) Official website, www.orlan.net/ (accessed 15 January 2014).

Ostrowska, Antonia (2001) In and out of communism: the macrosocial context of health in Poland. In: William Cockerham (ed.) *The Blackwell Companion to Medical Sociology*. Oxford, Blackwell, pp. 334–46.

Oxfam (2009) *Your Money or Your Life*. Rome, Oxfam International.

Pampel, Fred (2008) Tobacco use in sub-Saharan Africa: estimates from the Demographic Health Surveys. *Social Science & Medicine* **66**, 1772–83.

Pantazis, Christina, Gordon, David and Townsend, Peter (2006) *Poverty and Social Exclusion in Britain: The Millennium Survey*. Bristol, Policy Press.

Parckar, G. (2008) *Disability and Poverty in the UK*. London, Leonard Cheshire Disability.

Parekh, Anushree, MacInnes, Tom and Kenway, Peter (2010) *Monitoring Poverty and Social Exclusion 2010*. York, The Joseph Rowntree Foundation.

Parsons, Talcot (1951) *The Social System*. New York, Free Press.

Parsons, Talcot (1975) The sick role and the role of the physician reconsidered. *Milbank Memorial Fund Quarterly* (Summer), 257–78.

Parsons, Talcot (1978) *Action Theory and the Human Condition*. New York, Free Press.

Patsopoulos, Nikolaos A., Tatsioni, Athina and Ioannidis, John P. A. (2007) Claims of sex differences: an empirical assessment in genetic associations. *Journal of the American Medical Association* **298** (8), 880–93.

Payne, Sarah (1991) *Women, Health and Poverty: An Introduction*. London, Harvester Wheatsheaf.

Payne, Sarah (2006) *The Health of Men and Women*. Cambridge, Polity Press.

Pelling, M. and Webster, C. (1979) Medical practitioners. In: C. Webster (ed.) *Health, Medicine and Mortality in the Sixteenth Century*. Cambridge: Cambridge University Press, pp. 167–235.

Pennsylvania Department of Health (2011) Office of Men's Health Bill in the 109th Congress, www.portal.state.pa.us/portal/server.pt/community/healthy_men/14171/office_of_men's_health_bill_in_the_109th_congress/557735 (accessed 10 August 2011).

Pepperell, Robert (2003) *The Posthuman Condition*. Bristol, Intellect Ltd.

Perenboom, R, van Herten, L., Boshuizen, H. and van den Bos, G. (2005) Life expectancy without chronic morbidity: trends in gender and socioeconomic disparities. *Public Health Reports* **120** (1), 46–54.

Pfeiffer, James and Chapman, Rachel (2010) Anthropological perspectives on structural adjustment and public health. *Annual Review of Anthropology* **39**, 149–65.

Phillips, Susan (2007) Measuring the health effects of gender. *Journal of Epidemiology and Community Health* **62**, 368–71.

Pickett, Kate and Pearl, Michelle (2001) Multilevel analysis of neighbourhood socioeconomic context and health outcomes: a critical review. *Journal of Epidemiology and Community Health* **55**, 111–22.

Pierce, Mary and Armstrong, David (1996) Afro-Caribbean lay beliefs about diabetes: an exploratory study. In David Kelleher and Sheila Hillier (eds.) *Researching Cultural Differences in Health*. London, Routledge, pp. 91–102.

Pietilä, Ilkka and Rytkönen, Marja (2008) 'Health is not a man's domain': lay accounts of gender difference in life-expectancy in Russia. *Sociology of Health & Illness* **30** (7), 1070–83.

Pilnick, Alison (2002) *Genetics and Society: An Introduction*. Buckingham, Open University Press.

Pilnick, Alison, Hindmarsh, Jon, and Gill, Virginia Teas (2009) Beyond 'doctor and patient': developments in the study of healthcare interactions. *Sociology of Health & Illness* **31** (6), 787–802.

Pitts-Taylor, Victoria (2007) *Surgery Junkies*. London, Rutgers University Press.

Plsek, Paul and Greenhalgh, Trisha (2001) The challenge of complexity in health care. *British Medical Journal* 323, 625–8.

Pollock, Allyson (2004) *NHS PLC*. London, Verso.

Pollock, Allyson and Price, David (2011) The final frontier: the UK's new coalition government turns the English National Health Service over to the global health care market. *Health Sociology Review* 20 (3), 294–305.

Pollock, Allyson, Price, David, Roderick, Peter, Treuherz, Tim, McCoy, David, McKee, Martin and Reynolds, Lucy (2012) How the Health and Social Care Bill 2011 would end entitlement to comprehensive health care in England. *The Lancet*, 379, 387–9.

Pollock, Anne (2010) Reading Friedan: toward a feminist articulation of heart disease. *Body and Society* 16 (4), 77–97.

Pollock, Kirsten (1995) Attitude of mind as a means of resisting illness. In: Alan Radley (ed.) *Worlds of Illness*. London, Routledge, pp. 49–70.

Popay, Jennie, Thomas, Carol, Williams, Gareth, Bennett, Anthony, Gatrell, Anthony and Bostock, Lisa (2003a) A proper place to live: health inequalities, agency and the normative dimensions of space. *Social Science & Medicine* 57, 55–69.

Popay, Jennie, Bennett, Sharon, Thomas, Carol, Gatrell, Anthony and Bostock, Lisa (2003b) Beyond 'beer, fags, egg and chips'? Exploring lay understandings of social inequalities in health. *Sociology of Health & Illness* 25 (1), 1–23.

Pope, Harrison, Phillips, Katherine and Olivardia, Roberto (2000) *The Adonis Complex*. New York, The Free Press.

Porter, Roy (1997) *The Greatest Benefit to Mankind*. London, HarperCollins.

Pourroy, Janine (1996) *Behind the Scenes at ER*. London, Ebury Press.

Power, Chris and Kuh, Diana (2006) Lifecourse development of unequal health. In: Johannes Siegrist and Michael Marmot (eds.) *Social Inequalities in Health*. Oxford, Oxford University Press, pp. 27–54.

Power, Chris, Atherton, Kate, Strachen, David P. et al. (2007) Life-course influences on health in British adults: effects of socio-economic position in childhood and adulthood. *International Journal of Epidemiology* 36 (3), 522–31.

Prah Ruger, Jennifer (2005) The changing role of the World Bank in global health. *American Journal of Public Health* 95 (1), 60–70.

Pugh, Helena and Moser, Kath (1990) Measuring women's mortality differences. In: Helen Roberts (ed.) *Women's Health Counts*. London, Routledge, pp. 93–112.

Putnam, Robert D. (2000) *Bowling Alone*. London, Simon and Schuster.

Quadango, Jill (2010) Institutions, interest groups, and ideology: an agenda for the sociology of health care reform. *Journal of Health and Social Behavior* 51 (2), 125–36.

Rasulo, Domenica, Bajekal, Madhavi and Yar, Mohammed (2007) Inequalities in health expectancies in England and Wales – small area analysis from the 2001 Census. *Health Statistics Quarterly* **34** (Summer), 35–44.

Ratcliffe, Peter (2004) *'Race', Ethnicity and Difference: Imagining the Inclusive Society*. Buckingham, Open University Press.

Raymond, Janice (2007) *Women as Wombs*. Melbourne, Spinifex Press.

RCP (Royal College of Physicians) (2005) *Doctors in Society: Medical Professionalism in a Changing World*. London, RCP.

Redfern, Michael (2001) *The Royal Liverpool Children's Inquiry Report* (*The Redfern Report*). London, The Stationery Office.

Reed, Kate (2003) *Worlds of Health*. Connecticut, Praeger.

Relman, Arnold (2010) *A Second Opinion: Rescuing America's Health Care*. New York, Public Affairs.

Ricoeur, Paul (1991) Life in quest of narrative. In: David Wood (ed.) *On Paul Ricoeur: Narrative and Interpretation*. London, Routledge, pp. 20–33.

Rieff, David (2008) *Swimming in a Sea of Death: A Son's Memoir*. London, Granta.

Rieker, Patricia and Bird, Chloe (2000) Sociological explanations of gender differences in mental and physical health. In: Chloe Bird, Peter Conrad and Allen Fremont (eds.) *Handbook of Medical Sociology*, 5th edn. New Jersey, Prentice-Hall, pp. 98–109.

Riska, Elianne (2003) Gendering the medicalization thesis. *Gender Perspectives on Health and Medicine* **7**, 59–87.

Riska, Elianne (2008) The feminization thesis: discourses on gender and medicine. *NORA* **16** (1), 3–18.

Riska, Elianne (2010) Health professions and occupations. In: William Cockerham (ed.) *The New Blackwell Companion to Medical Sociology*. Oxford, Wiley-Blackwell, pp. 337–54.

Riska, Elianne (2012) Coronary heart disease: gendered public health discourses. In: Ellen Kuhlmann and Ellen Annandale (eds.) *The Palgrave Handbook of Gender and Healthcare*. London, Palgrave, pp. 178–208.

Riska, Elianne and Novelskaite, Aurelija (2008) Gendered careers in post-Soviet society: views on professional qualities in surgery and paediatrics. *Gender Issues* **25** (4), 229–45.

Riska, Elianne and Novelskaite, Aurelija (2011) Professionalism and medical work in a post-Soviet society: between four logics. *Anthropology of East Europe Review* **29** (1), 82–93.

Ritchie, Jean (2000). *An Inquiry into Quality and Practice within the NHS Arising from the Actions of Rodney Ledward*. London, Stationery Office

Rittel, Horst and Webber, Melvin (1973) Dilemmas in a general theory of planning. *Policy Sciences* **4**, 155–69.

Robinson, Sally (2000) *Marked Men: White Masculinity in Crisis*. New York, Columbia University Press.

Rogers, Anne and Pilgrim, David (2010) *A Sociology of Mental Health and Illness*, 4th edn. Maidenhead, McGraw Hill / Open University Press.

Rose, David and Pevalin, David J. (with O'Reilly, Karen) (2005) *The National Statistics Socio-economic Classification: Origins, Development and Use*. London, ONS/Palgrave.

Rose, Nikolas (2007a) *The Politics of Life Itself*. Oxford, Princeton University Press.

Rose, Nikolas (2007b) Beyond medicalization. *Lancet* **369**, 700–1.

Rose, Nikolas (2007c) Genomic susceptibility as an emergent form of life? Genetic testing, identity and the remit of medicine. In: Regula Valérie Burri and Joseph Dumit (eds.) *Biomedicine as Culture*. London, Routledge, pp. 141–50.

Roth, Julius (1963) *Timetables*. New York, Bobbs-Merrill.

Rousseau, Jean-Jacques (1966 [1762]) *Émile* (trans. B. Foxley). London, Dent.

Rowden, Rick (2009) *The Deadly Ideas of Neoliberalism*. London, Zed Books.

Rowe, Rosemary and Calnan, Michael (2006) Trust relations in health care – the new agenda. *European Journal of Public Health* **16** (1), 4–6.

Rowland, Robyn and Klein, Renata (1996) Radical feminism: history, politics, action. In: Diane Bell and Renate Klein (eds.) *Radically Speaking: Feminism Reclaimed*. London, Zed Books, pp. 9–36, 37–44.

Rutz, Wolfgang (2004) Men's health on the European WHO Agenda. *Journal of Men's Health and Gender* **1**, 22–5.

Sabo, Donald and David, Gordon (1995) Rethinking men's health and illness. In: Donald Sabo and David Gordon (eds.) *Men's Health and Illness: Gender, Power and the Body*. London, Sage, pp. 1–21.

Saguy, Abigail and Almeling, Rene (2008) Fat in the fire? Science, the news media, and the 'obesity epidemic'. *Sociological Forum* **23** (1), 53–83.

Saks, Mike (2003) *Orthodox and Alternative Medicine*. London, Sage.

Salant, Talya and Santry, Heena (2006) Internet marketing of bariatric surgery: contemporary trends in the medicalization of obesity. *Social Science & Medicine* **62**, 2445–57.

Saltonstall, Robin (1993) Healthy bodies, social bodies: men's and women's concepts and practices of everyday health. *Social Science & Medicine* **36** (1), 7–14.

Sanchez-Taylor, Jacqueline (2011) 'When cosmetic surgery is a marker of ambition'. *The Guardian*, www.guardian.co.uk/commentisfree/2011/feb/14/cosmetic-surgery-travel-risks (accessed 7 July 2011).

Sanchez-Taylor, Jacqueline (2012) Fake breasts and power: gender, class and cosmetic surgery. *Women's Studies International Forum* **35**, 458–66.

Saurel-Cubizolles, M-J., Chastang, J.-F., Menvielle, G., Leclerc, A., Luce, D., for the EDISC group (2009) Social inequalities in mortality by causes among men and women in France. *Journal of Epidemiology and Community Health* **63**, 197–202.

Savage, Mike (2000) *Class Analysis and Social Transformation.* Buckingham, Open University Press.

Savage, Mike, Devine, Fiona, Cunningham, Niall, et al. (2013) A new model of social class? Findings from the Great British Class Survey Experiment. *Sociology* **47**, 219–50.

Scambler, Graham (2002) *Health and Social Change.* Buckingham, Open University Press.

Scambler, Graham (2009) Capitalists, workers and health: illness as a 'side-effect' of profit-making. *Social Theory and Health* **7** (2), 117–28.

Scambler, Graham and Scambler, Sasha (2010) Introduction: the sociology of chronic and disabling conditions: assaults on the lifeworld. In: Graham Scambler and Sasha Scambler (eds.) *New Directions in the Sociology of Chronic and Disabling Conditions.* London, Palgrave, pp. 1–7.

Scarborough, Peter, Wickramasinghe, Kremlin, Bhatnager, Prachi and Rayner, Mike (2011) *Trends in Coronary Heart Disease, 1961–2011.* London, British Heart Foundation.

Scheff, Thomas (2006) *Goffman Unbound!* London, Paradigm Publishers.

Scheper-Hughes, Nancy (2001a) Commodity fetishism in organ trafficking. In: Nancy Scheper-Hughes and Loïc Wacquant (eds.) *Commodifying Bodies.* London, Sage, pp. 31–62.

Scheper-Hughes, Nancy (2001b) Bodies for sale – whole or in parts. In: Nancy Scheper-Hughes and Loïc Wacquant (eds.) *Commodifying Bodies.* London, Sage, pp. 1–8.

Scheper-Hughes, Nancy and Lock, Margaret (1987) The mindful body: a prolegomenon to future work in medical anthropology. *Medical Anthropology Quarterly* **1** (1), 6–41.

Schlosser, Eric (2002) *Fast Food Nation.* London, Penguin.

Schofield, Toni (2012) Men's health and well-being. In: Ellen Kuhlmann and Ellen Annandale (eds.) *The Palgrave Handbook of Gender and Healthcare*, 2nd edn. London, Palgrave, pp. 273–89.

Schoon, Ingrid (2006) *Risk and Resilience: Adaptation in Changing Times.* Cambridge, Cambridge University Press.

Schoon, Ingrid, Sacker, Amanda and Bartley, Mel (2003) Socio-economic adversity and psychosocial adjustment: a developmental–contextual perspective. *Social Science & Medicine* **57** (6), 1011–15.

Schrecker, Ted, Labonté, Ronald and De Vogli, Roberto (2008) Globalisation and health: the need for a global vision. *The Lancet* **372**, 1670–2.

Sen, Amartya (1992) Missing women: social inequality outweighs women's survival advantage in Asia and North Africa. *British Medical Journal* **304** (7 March), 587–8.

Sen, Amartya (2003) Missing women – revisited. *British Medical Journal* **327** (6 December), 1297–8.

Sen, Gita and Östlin, Piroska (2010) Gender as a social determinant of health: evidence, policies and innovations. In: Gita Sen and Piroska

Östlin (eds.) *Gender Equity in Health: The Shifting Frontiers of Evidence and Action*. London, Routledge, pp. 1–46.

Sen, Gita, Ostlin, Piroska and George, Asha (2007) *Unequal, Unfair, Ineffective and Inefficient. Gender Inequality in Health: Why it Exists and How We Can Change It*. Stockholm, Karolinska Institutet.

Seale, Clive (1998) *Constructing Death*. Cambridge: Cambridge University Press.

Sennett, Richard (2000) Street and office: two sources of identity. In: Will Hutton and Anthony Giddens (eds.) *On The Edge: Living with Global Capitalism*. London, Jonathan Cape, pp. 175–90.

Sennett, Richard (2008) *The Craftsman*. London, Penguin.

Shaw, George Bernard (1980 [1911]) *The Doctor's Dilemma: A Tragedy*. New York, Penguin.

Shaw, Mary, Dorling, Daniel, Gordon, David and Davey Smith, George (1999) *The Widening Gap: Health Inequalities and Policy in Britain*. Bristol, Policy Press.

Shaw, Mary, Davey Smith, George and Dorling, Danny (2005) Health inequalities and New Labour: how the promises compare with real progress. *British Medical Journal* **330** (30 April), 1016–21.

Shaw Hughner, Renee and Schultz Kleine, Susan (2004) Views of health in the lay sector: a compilation and review of how individuals think about health. *Health* **8** (4), 395–422.

Shildrick, Margrit (1997) *Leaky Bodies and Boundaries*. London, Routledge.

Shildrick, Margrit (2002) *Embodying the Monster: Encounters with the Vulnerable Self*. London, Sage.

Shildrick, Margrit (2009) *Dangerous Discourses of Disability, Subjectivity and Sexuality*. London, Palgrave.

Shilling, Chris (2002) Culture, the 'sick role' and the consumption of health. *British Journal of Sociology* **53** (4), 621–38.

Shilling, Chris (2005) *The Body in Culture, Technology and Society*. London, Sage.

Shipman Inquiry Fifth Report (2004) *Independent Public Inquiry into the Issues Arising from the Case of Harold Frederick Shipman*. London, HMSO, Cm 6394.

Shorter, Edward (1982) *A History of Women's Bodies*. London, Allen Lane.

Singh, Gopal K. and Siahpush, Mohammad (2006) Widening socio-economic inequalities in US life expectancy, 1980–2000. *International Journal of Epidemiology* **35**, 969–79.

Skellington, Richard (1996) *'Race' in Britain Today*, 2nd edn. London, Open University Press / Sage.

Skolbekken, John-Arne, Österlie, Wenche and Formso, Siri (2008) Brittle bones, pain and fractures – lay constructions of osteoporosis among Norwegian women attending the Nord-Trøndelag Health Study (HUNT). *Social Science & Medicine* **66**, 2562–72.

Smaje, Chris (1996) The ethnic patterning of health: new directions for theory and research. *Sociology of Health and Illness* **18**, 139–71.

Smedley, Brian, Smith, Adrienne and Nelson, Alan (2003) *Unequal Treatment: Confronting Racial and Ethnic Disparities in Health Care.* Washington, DC, National Academies Press.

Snow, Rachel (2010) The social body: gender and the burden of disease. In: Gita Sen and Piroska Östlin (eds.) *Gender Equity in Health: The Shifting Frontiers of Evidence and Action,* London, Routledge, pp. 47–69.

Solar, O. and Irwin, A. (2007) A conceptual framework for action on the social determinants of health. Discussion paper for the Commission on Social Determinants of Health. Paper 2 (Policy and Practice). Geneva, World Health Organisation.

Solomos, John and Back, Les (1994) Conceptualizing racisms: social theory, politics and research. *Sociology* **28**, 143–61.

Stacey, Jackie (2000) The global within: consuming nature, embodying health. In: Sarah Franklin, Celia Lury and Jackie Stacey (eds.) *Global Nature, Global Culture.* London, Sage, pp. 97–145.

Stacey, Meg (1981) The division of labour revisited or overcoming the two Adams. In: P. Abrams, R. Deem, J. Finch and P. Rock (eds.) *Practice and Progress: British Sociology 1950–1980.* London, Allen and Unwin, pp. 172–90.

Stacey, Meg (1992) *Regulating British Medicine.* Chichester, John Wiley and Sons.

Stacey, Meg (2002) Concluding comments. In: Gillian Bendelow, Mick Carpenter, Caroline Vautier and Simon Williams (eds.) *Gender, Health and Healing.* London, Routledge, pp. 267–83.

Stanistreet, D., Bambra, C. and Scott-Samuel, A. (2005) Is patriarchy the source of men's higher mortality? *Journal of Epidemiology and Community Health* **59**, 873–6.

Starr, Paul (1982) *The Social Transformation of American Medicine.* New York, Basic Books.

Statistics Canada (2001) Death – shifting trends. *Health Reports* **12** (3), 41–6.

Steptoe, Andrew (2006) Psychobiological processes linking socio-economic position with health. In: Johannes Siegrist and Michael Marmot (eds.) *Social Inequalities in Health.* Oxford, Oxford University Press, pp. 101–126.

Stevens, Fred (2010) The convergence and divergence of modern health systems. In: William Cockerham (ed.) *The New Blackwell Companion to Medical Sociology.* Oxford, Wiley-Blackwell, pp. 434–54.

Straus, Robert (1957) The nature and status of medical sociology. *American Sociological Review* **22**, 200–4.

Strauss, A., Schatzman, L., Ehrlich, D., Bucher, R. and Sabshin, M. (1963) The hospital and its negotiated order. In: Eliot Freidson (ed.) *The Hospital in Modern Society.* London, The Free Press, pp. 147–69.

Strauss, Anselm (1978) *Negotiations*. San Francisco, Jossey-Bass.

Strauss, Anselm (1993) *Continual Permutations of Action*. New York, Aldine de Gruyter.

Strauss, Anselm and Glaser, Barney (1975) *Chronic Illness and the Quality of Life*. St Louis, Mosby.

Strauss, Anselm, Fagerhaugh, Shizuko, Suczeck, Barbara and Weiner, Carolyn (1985) *The Social Organisation of Medical Work*. Chicago, University of Chicago Press.

Strong, P. M. (1979) Sociological imperialism and the profession of medicine. *Social Science & Medicine* **13a**, 199–215.

Strong, P. M. (2001 [1979]) *The Ceremonial Order of the Clinic: Parents, Doctors and Medical Bureaucracies*, 2nd edn. Aldershot: Ashgate.

Strong, Philip and Robinson, Jane (1990) *The NHS Under New Management*. Buckingham, Open University Press.

Stuckler, David, King, Lawrence and McKee, Martin (2009) Mass privatisation and the post-communist mortality crisis: a cross-national analysis. *The Lancet* **373**, 399–407.

Sulik, Gayle (2012) *Pink Ribbon Blues: How Breast Cancer Culture Undermines Women's Health*. Oxford, Oxford University Press.

Sunder Rajan, Kaushik (2006) *Biocapital: The Constitution of Postgenomic Life*. London, Duke University Press.

Sweeny, Kieran and Griffiths, Frances (eds.) (2002) *Complexity and Healthcare*. Abingdon, Radcliffe Medical Press.

Szasz, Thomas (1971) *The Manufacture of Madness*. London, Routledge & Kegan Paul.

Tallis, Raymond (2004) *Hippocratic Oaths, Medicine and its Discontents*. London, Atlantic Books.

Tarlov, Alvin R. (1996) Social determinants of health: the socio-biological translation. In: David Blane, Eric Brunner and Richard Wilkinson (eds.) *Health and Social Organisation*. London, Routledge, pp. 71–93.

Taylor, James Stacey (2005) *Stakes and Kidneys: Why Markets in Human Body Parts are Morally Imperative*. Aldershot, Ashgate.

Ten Have, Paul (1995) Medical ethnomethodology: an overview. *Human Studies* **18**, 245–61.

Thomas, Carol (2010) Medical sociology and disability theory. In: Graham Scambler and Sasha Scambler (eds.) *New Directions in the Sociology of Chronic Illness and Disabling Conditions*. London, Palgrave, pp. 37–56.

Thun, Michael, Carter, Brian, Feskanich, Diane, Freedman, Neal, Prentice, Ross, Lopez, Alan, Hartge, Patricia and Gapstur, Susan (2013) 50-year trends in smoking-related mortality in the United States. *New England Journal of Medicine* **368** (4), 351–64.

Tiefer, Leonore (2006) The Viagra phenomenon. *Sexualities* **9**, 273–94.

Timmermans, Stefan (2008) Oh look, there is a doctor after all: about the resilience of professional medicine. A commentary on McKinlay and Marceau. *Social Science & Medicine* **67**, 1492–6.

Timmermans, Stefan and Buchbinder, Mara (2010) Patients-in-waiting: living between sickness and health in the genomics era. *Journal of Health and Social Behavior* **51** (4), 408–23.

Timmermans, Stefan and Buchbinder, Mara (2012) Expanded newborn screening: articulating an ontology of diseases with bridging work in the clinic. In: Natalie Armstrong and Helen Eborall (eds.) *The Sociology of Medical Screening*. Chichester, Wiley-Blackwell, pp. 47–59.

Timmermans, Stefan and Buchbinder, Mara (2013) *Saving Babies? The Consequences of Newborn Genetic Screening*. London, University of Chicago Press.

Toffoletti, Kim (2007) *Cyborgs and Barbie Dolls*. London, I. B. Tauris and Co Ltd.

Toh, Chee-Keong (2009) The changing epidemiology of lung cancer. In: M. Verma (ed.) *Cancer Epidemiology*, vol. II, *Modifiable Factors*. New York, Humana Press, pp. 397–411.

Torsheim, Torbjørn, Ravens-Sieberer, Ulrike, Hetland, Jorn, Välimmaa, Raili, Danielson, Mia. and Overpeck, Mary (2006) Cross-national variation of gender differences in adolescent subjective health in Europe and North America. *Social Science & Medicine* **62**, 815–27.

Tousijn, Willem (2006) Beyond decline: consumerism, managerialism and the need for a new medical professionalism. *Health Sociology Review* **15** (5), 469–80.

Townsend, Peter and Davidson, Nick (1982) *Inequalities in Health (the Black Report)*. London, Penguin.

Tritter, Jonathan, Koivusalo, Meri, Ollila, Eeva and Dorfman, Pail (2010) *Globalisation, Markets and Healthcare Policy*. London, Routledge

Tudor Hart, Julian (2010) *The Political Economy of Health Care*, 2nd edn. Bristol, Policy Press.

Tunstall, H. V. Z., Shaw, Mary and Dorling, Danny (2004) Places and health. *Journal of Epidemiology and Public Health* **58**, 6–10.

Turner, Bryan (1997) From governmentality to risk: some reflections on Foucault's contribution to medical sociology. In: Alan Petersen and Robin Bunton (eds.) *Foucault, Health and Medicine*, London, Routledge, pp. ix-xxi.

Turner, Bryan (2004) *The New Medical Sociology*. London, W. W. Norton Company.

Turner, Jonathan (2009) The sociology of emotions: basic theoretical arguments. *Emotion Review* **1** (4), 340–54.

Turner, Jonathan and Stets, Jan (2005) *The Sociology of Emotions*. Cambridge, Cambridge University Press.

Turner, Leigh (2010) 'Medical tourism' and the global marketplace in health services: U.S patients, international hospitals, and the search for affordable healthcare. *International Journal of Health Services* **40** (3), 443–67.

UN (2009) *Human Development Report 2009*. New York: United Nations Human Development Program.

UN (2013) *Human Development Report 2013*. New York, United Nations Human Development Program.

UN Human Rights Council (2009) *Report of the Special Rapporteur on the Adverse Effects of the Movement and Dumping of Toxic and Dangerous Products and Wastes on the Enjoyments of Human Rights*. United Nations. A/HRC/12/26, http://daccess-dds-ny.un.org/doc/UN DOC/GEN/G09/145/75/PDF/G0914575.pdf?OpenElement (accessed 30 January2014).

UNAIDS (2010) *Agenda for Accelerated Country Level Action for Women, Girls, Gender Equity and HIV*. Geneva, UNAIDS.

UNICEF (2005). *Child Poverty in Rich Countries*. UNICEF Innocenti Report Card 6. Florence, UNICEF Innocenti Research Center.

UNICEF (2011) *The State of the World's Children 2011*. New York, UNICEF.

Urry, John (2000) *Sociology Beyond Societies*. London, Routledge.

Urry, John, (2007) *Mobilities*. Cambridge, Polity Press.

Ussher, Jane (2011) Gender matters: differences in depression between women and men. In: David Pilgrim, Anne Rogers and Bernice Pescosolido (eds.) *The Sage Handbook of Mental Health and Illness*. London, Sage, pp. 103–26.

Vallgårda, Signild (2010) Tackling social inequalities in health in the Nordic countries: targeting a residuum or the whole population? *Journal of Epidemiology and Community Health* **64**, 495–6.

Van de Velde, Sarah, Bracke, Piet and Levecque, Katia (2010) Gender differences in depression in 23 European countries: cross-national variation in the gender gap in depression. *Social Science & Medicine* **71** (2), 305–13.

Van de Velde, Sarah, Huijts, Tim, Bracke, Piet and Bambra, Clare (2013) Macro-level equality and depression in men and women in Europe. *Sociology of Health & Illness* **35** (5), 682–98.

Vannini, Phillip (2008) The geography of disciplinary amnesia: eleven scholars reflect on the international state of symbolic interactionism. In: N. K. Denzin, J. Salvo and M. Washington (eds.) *Studies in Symbolic Interaction*, vol. XXXII. Bingley, Emerald, pp. 5–18.

Verbrugge, Lois (1985) Gender and health: an update on hypotheses and evidence. *Journal of Health and Social Behavior* **24** (March), 6–30.

Verbrugge, Lois (1988) Unveiling higher morbidity for men. In: M. White Riley (ed.) *Social Structures and Human Lives*. London, Sage, pp. 138–60.

Vincent, Charles (2010) *Patient Safety*, 2nd edn. Oxford, Wiley-Blackwell.

Wacquant, Loïc (2002) Scrutinizing the street: poverty, morality, and the pitfalls of urban ethnography. *American Journal of Sociology* **107** (6), 1468–532.

Wadham, Ben (2002) Global men's health and the crises of western masculinity. In: Bob Pease and Keith Pringle (eds.) *A Man's World: Changing Men's Practices in a Globalised World*. London, Zed Books, pp. 69–84.

Wadman, Cecilia, Boström, Gunnel, and Karlsson, Ann-Sofie (2008) *Health on Equal Terms? Results from the 2006 Swedish National Public Health Survey*. Ostersund, Swedish National Public Health.

Waitzkin, Howard (2000) *The Second Sickness*, revised and updated edn. Oxford: Rowan and Littlefield.

Waitzkin, Howard (2001) *At the Frontlines of Medicine: How the Health Care System Alienates Doctors and Mistreats Patients*. Lanham, MD, Rowman and Littlefield.

Waitzkin, Howard (2011) *Medicine and Public Health at the End of Empire*. London, Paradigm Publishers.

Wajcman, Judy (2004) *Technofeminism*. Cambridge, Polity Press.

Walby, Sylvia (2007) *Gender (In)equality and the Future of Work*. London, Equal Opportunities Commission.

Walby, Sylvia (2009) *Globalization and Inequalities: Complexity and Contested Modernities*. London, Sage.

Walby, Sylvia (2011) *The Future of Feminism*. Cambridge, Polity Press.

Wald, Priscilla (2008) *Contagious: Cultures, Carriers and the Outbreak Narrative*. Durham, NC, Duke University Press.

Waldby, Catherine (1996) *AIDS and the Body Politic*. London, Routledge.

Waldby, Catherine (2000) *The Visible Human Project: Informatic Bodies and Posthuman Medicine*. London, Routledge.

Waldby, Catherine (2002) Stem cells, tissue cultures and the production of biovalue. *Health* **6** (3), 305–23.

Waldby, Catherine and Mitchell, Robert (2006) *Tissue Economies: Blood, Organs, and Cell Lines in Late Capitalism*. Durham, NC, Duke University Press.

Walter, Tony (1994) *The Revival of Death*. London, Routledge.

Walter, Tony (2009) Jade's body: the ultimate reality show. *Sociological Research Online* **14** (5), www.socresearchonline.org.uk/14/5/1.html (accessed 30 January 2014).

Warin, Megan (2011) Foucault's progeny: Jamie Oliver and the art of governing obesity. *Social Theory and Health* **9**, 24–40.

Waring, Justin and Bishop, Simon (2012) Going private: clinicians' experiences of working in UK independent treatment centers. *Health Policy* **104**, 172–8.

Waring, Justin and Bishop, Simon (2013) McDonaldization or commercial re-stratification: the corporatization and the multimodal organisation of English doctors. *Social Science & Medicine* **82**, 147–55.

Waskul, Denis D. and Vannini, Phillip (2006) Introduction: the body in symbolic interactionism. In: Denis D. Waskul and Phillip Vannini (eds.) *Body/embodiment: Symbolic Interactionism and the Sociology of the Body*. Aldershot, Ashgate, pp. 1–18.

Welch, Lisa, Lutfey, Karen, Gerstenberger, Eric and Grace, Matthew (2012) Gendered uncertainty and variation in physicians' decisions for coronary heart disease: the double-edged sword of 'atypical symptoms'. *Journal of Health and Social Behavior* **53** (3), 313–28.

Wells, Claudia and Gordon, Emma (2008) Geographical variations in premature mortality in England and Wales, 1981–2006. *Health Statistics Quarterly* **38** (Summer), 6–18.

Wenchao, Jin, Joyce, Robert, Phillips, David and Sibieta, Luke (2011) *Poverty and Inequality in the UK: 2011*. London, Institute for Fiscal Studies, www.ifs.org.uk/comms/comm118.pdf (accessed 30 Janaury 2014).

West, Patrick and Sweeting, Helen (2003) Fifteen, female and stressed: changing patterns of psychological distress over time. *Journal of Psychology and Psychiatry* **44** (3), 399–411.

Wheen, Francis (1999) *Karl Marx*. London, Fourth Estate.

White, Alan and Cash, Keith (2004) The state of men's health in Europe. *Journal of Men's Health and Gender* **1** (1), 60–6.

White, Chris, van Glen, Folkert and Chow, Yuan Huang (2003) Trends in social class differences in mortality by cause, 1986 to 2000. *Health Statistics Quarterly* **20** (Winter), 25–37.

White, Chris, Glickman, Myer, Johnson, Brian and Corbin, Tania (2007) Social inequalities in adult male mortality by the National Statistics Socio-economic Classification, England and Wales, 2001–03. *Health Statistics Quarterly* **36** (Winter), 6–18.

WHO (2002) *Current Practices and Controversies in Assisted Reproduction*. Geneva, WHO.

WHO (2003) *Atlas of Health in Europe*. Copenhagen, Regional Office for Europe.

WHO (2004a) *Global Strategy on Diet, Physical Activity and Health*. Geneva, WHO.

WHO (2004b) *Gender and Health Research: Mental Health*. Geneva, WHO.

WHO (2007) *A Safer Future: Global Public Health Security in the 21st Century*. Geneva, WHO.

WHO (2009) *World Health Statistics 2009*, www.who.int/whosis/whostat/2009/en/index.html (accessed 30 January 2014).

WHO (2010) *World Health Statistics 2010*, www.who.int/whosis/whostat/EN_WHS10_Full.pdf (accessed 30 January 2014).

WHO (2011a) *World Health Statistics 2011*, www.who.int/whosis/whostat/EN_WHS2011_Full.pdf (accessed 30 January 2014).

WHO (2011b) *WHO Report on the Global Tobacco Epidemic, 2011*. Geneva, WHO.

WHO (2011c) *Governance for Health in the 21st Century: A Study Conducted for the WHO Regional Office for Europe*. Copenhagen, WHO Regional Office for Europe.

WHO (2012) *World Health Statistics 2012*, http://apps.who.int/iris/bitstream/10665/44844/1/9789241564441_eng.pdf?ua=1 (accessed 30 Janaury 2014).

WHO (2013) *World Health Statistics 2013*, www.who.int/gho/publications/world_health_statistics/EN_WHS2013_Full.pdf (accessed 30 January 2014).

Wilkinson, Iain (2010) *Risk, Vulnerability and Everyday Life*. London, Routledge.

Wilkinson, Richard (2000) Deeper than 'neo-liberalism': a reply to David Coburn. *Social Science & Medicine* **51** (7), 997–1000.

Wilkinson, Richard (2005) *The Impact of Inequality*. London, Routledge.

Wilkinson, Richard (2007) The challenge of prevention: a response to Starfield's commentary: pathways of influence on equity in health. *Social Science & Medicine* **64**, 1367–70.

Wilkinson, Richard and Pickett, Kate (2009) *The Spirit Level: Why Do More Equal Societies Almost Always Do Better?* London, Allen Lane.

Williams, B. G., Iredale, R., Brain, K., Barrett-Lee, P. and Gray, J. (2003) Experiences of men with breast cancer: an exploratory focus group study. *British Journal of Cancer* **89**, 1834–6.

Williams, David R. (2012) Miles to go before we sleep: racial inequalities in health. *Journal of Health and Social Behavior* **53** (3), 279–95.

Williams, Gareth (1984) The genesis of chronic illness: narrative reconstruction. *Sociology of Health and Illness* **6**, 175–200.

Williams, Gareth (1995) Chronic illness and the pursuit of virtue in everyday life. In: Alan Radley (ed.) *Worlds of Illness*. London: Routledge, pp. 92–108.

Williams, Gareth (2003) The determinants of health: structure, context and agency. *Sociology of Health & Illness* **25**, 131–54.

Williams, Gareth (2007) Health inequalities in their place. In: Steve Cropper, Alison Porter, Gareth Williams et al. (eds.) *Community Health and Wellbeing*. Bristol, Policy Press, pp. 1–22.

Williams, Simon (1996) The vicissitudes of embodiment across the chronic illness trajectory. *Body and Society* **2**, 23–47.

Williams, Simon (2004) Bioattack or panic attack? Critical reflections on the ill-logic of bioterrorism and biowarfare in late/postmodernity. *Social Theory and Health* **2**, 67–93.

Williams, Simon (2006) Medical sociology and the biological body: where are we now and where do we go from here? *Health* **10** (1), 5–30.

Williams, Simon, Birke, Lynda and Bendelow, Gillian (2003) Introduction: debating biology. In: Simon Williams, Lynda Birke and Gillian Bendelow (eds.) *Debating Biology*. London, Routledge, pp. 1–11.

Willis, Evan (1983) *Medical Dominance*. Sydney, Allen and Unwin.

Willis, Evan (2006) Taking stock of medical dominance. *Health Sociology Review* **15** (5), 421–31.

Wizemann, Theresa M. and Pardue, Mary-Lou (2001) *Exploring the Biological Contributions to Human Health: Does Sex Matter?* Washington, DC, National Academy Press.

Wolf, Naomi (1994) *Fire with Fire*. London, Vintage Books.

Wollstonecraft, Mary (1992 [1792]) *A Vindication of the Rights of Woman*. London, Penguin Books.

Wrede, Sirpa (2012) Nursing: globalisation of a female-gendered profession. In: Ellen Kuhlmann and Ellen Annandale (eds.) *The Palgrave Handbook of Gender and Healthcare*, 2nd edn. London, Palgrave, pp. 471–87.

Zalewski, Marysia (2009) *Feminism After Postmodernism*. London, Routledge.

Zalewski, Marysia (2010) 'I don't even know what gender is': a discussion of the connections between gender, gender mainstreaming and feminist theory. *Review of International Studies* **36**, 3–27.

Zaninotto, Paola, Wardle, Heather, Stamatakis, Emmanuel, Mindell, Jennifer and Head, Jenny (2006) *Forecasting Obesity to 2010*. London, National Centre for Social Research.

Zheng, Hui (2009) Rising U.S. income inequality, gender and individual self-rated health. *Social Science & Medicine* **69** (9), 1333–42.

Zola, Irving (1972) Medicine as an institution of social control. *Sociological Review* **20**, 487–504.

Zuckerman, Diana (2010) Reasonably safe? Breast implants and informed consent. *Reproductive Health Matters* **18** (35), 94–102.

Index

Page numbers in *italics* denote a figure/table

UNIVERSITY OF WINCHESTER
LIBRARY